T0207491

Lecture Notes in Computer Science 13866

Founding Editors

Gerhard Goos
Juris Hartmanis

The series Lecture Notes in Computer Science (LNCS), including its subseries Lecture Notes in Artificial Intelligence (LNAI) and Lecture Notes in Bioinformatics (LNBI), has established itself as a medium for the publication of new developments in computer science and information technology research, teaching, and education.

LNCS enjoys close cooperation with the computer science R & D community, the series counts many renowned academics among its volume editors and paper authors, and collaborates with prestigious societies. Its mission is to serve this international community by providing an invaluable service, mainly focused on the publication of conference and workshop proceedings and postproceedings. LNCS commenced publication in 1973.

Jan Mazal · Adriano Fagiolini · Petr Vašík ·
Agostino Bruzzone · Stefan Pickl ·
Vlastimil Neumann · Petr Stodola ·
Stefano Lo Storto
Editors

Modelling and Simulation for Autonomous Systems

9th International Conference, MESAS 2022
Prague, Czech Republic, October 20–21, 2022
Revised Selected Papers

Springer

Editors
Jan Mazal 🆔
NATO M&S COE
Rome, Italy

Adriano Fagiolini 🆔
University of Palermo
Palermo, Italy

Petr Vašík 🆔
Brno University of Technology
Brno, Czech Republic

Agostino Bruzzone 🆔
University of Genoa
Genova, Italy

Stefan Pickl 🆔
Bundeswehr University Munich
Munich, Germany

Vlastimil Neumann 🆔
University of Defence
Brno, Czech Republic

Petr Stodola 🆔
University of Defence
Brno, Czech Republic

Stefano Lo Storto
NATO M&S COE
Rome, Italy

ISSN 0302-9743   ISSN 1611-3349 (electronic)
Lecture Notes in Computer Science
ISBN 978-3-031-31267-0   ISBN 978-3-031-31268-7 (eBook)
https://doi.org/10.1007/978-3-031-31268-7

This Springer imprint is published by the registered company Springer Nature Switzerland AG
The registered company address is: Gewerbestrasse 11, 6330 Cham, Switzerland

Preface

This volume contains selected papers presented at the Modelling and Simulation for Autonomous Systems (MESAS) Conference, held during on October 20–21, 2022 in Prague, Czech Republic.

The initial idea to launch the MESAS project was introduced by the NATO Modelling and Simulation Centre of Excellence in 2013, with the intent to bring together the Modelling and Simulation and the Autonomous Systems/Robotics communities and to collect new ideas for concept development and experimentation in this domain. From that time, the event has gathered (in regular, poster, and way ahead sessions) fully recognized experts from different technical communities in the military, academia, and industry.

The main topical parts of the 2022 edition of MESAS were "Future Challenges of Advanced M&S Technology", "M&S of Intelligent Systems", and "AxS in Context of Future Warfare and Security Environment". The community of interest submitted 37 papers for consideration. Just 24 submissions underwent a review by three Technical Committee members or selected independent reviewers. The committee, in the context of the review process outcome, decided to accept 22 papers to be presented and 21 of these papers were accepted to be included in the conference proceedings.

December 2022

Jan Mazal
Adriano Fagiolini
Petr Vasik
Stefano Lo Storto
Agostino Bruzzone
Stefan Pickl
Vlastimil Neumann
Petr Stodola

MESAS 2022 Organizer

NATO Modelling and Simulation Centre of Excellence
(NATO M&S COE)

The NATO M&S COE is a recognized international military organization activated by the North Atlantic Council in 2012 and does not fall under the NATO Command Structure. Partnering nations provide funding and personnel for the centre through a memorandum of understanding. The Czech Republic, Italy, the USA, and Germany are the contributing nations, as of this publication. The NATO M&S COE supports NATO transformation by improving the networking of NATO and nationally owned M&S systems, promoting cooperation between nations and organizations through the sharing of M&S information, and serving as an international source of expertise. The NATO M&S COE seeks to be a leading world-class organization, providing the best military expertise in modelling and simulation technology, methodologies, and the development of M&S professionals. Its state-of-the-art facilities can support a wide range of M&S activities including, but not limited to, education and training of NATO M&S professionals on M&S concepts and technology with hands-on courses that expose students to the latest simulation software currently used across the alliance; concept development and experimentation using a wide array of software capability and network connections to test and evaluate military doctrinal concepts as well as new simulation interoperability verification; and the same network connectivity that enables the COE to become the focal point for NATO's future distributed simulation environment and services. Further details can be found at https://www.mscoe.org/.

Organization

Program Committee Chairs

Bruzzone, Agostino	Genoa University, Italy
Mazal, Jan	University of Defence, Czech Republic
Novotny, Jiri	NATO M&S COE, Italy
Stodola, Petr	University of Defence, Czech Republic
Vasik, Petr	Brno University of Technology, Czech Republic

Program Committee Members

Azayev, Teymur	Czech Technical University In Prague, Czech Republic
Balogh, Richard	Slovak University of Technology in Bratislava, Slovakia
Bergeon, Yves	Écoles de Saint-Cyr Coëtquidan, France
Cossentino, Massimo	Istituto di Calcolo e Reti ad Alte Prestazioni, Italy
David, Walter	Ronin Institute, USA
Derevianko, Anna	Brno University of Technology, Czech Republic
Eryganov, Ivan	Brno University of Technology, Czech Republic
Faigl, Jan	Czech Technical University in Prague, Czech Republic
Fucik, Jakub	Cyber and Information Warfare Command, Czech Armed Forces, Czech Republic
Holub, Jan	Czech Technical University in Prague, Czech Republic
Hrdina, Jaroslav	Brno University of Technology, Czech Republic
Jahnen, Sebastian	Bundeswehr University Munich, Germany
Katsaros, Panagiotis	Aristotle University of Thessaloniki, Greece
Kralicek, Jiri	University of Defence, Czech Republic
Kulich, Miroslav	Czech Technical University in Prague, Czech Republic
Lopez-Toledo, Israel	US Army Corps of Engineers, Engineer Research and Development Center, USA
Loucka, Pavel	Brno University of Technology, Czech Republic
Mansfield, Thomas	NATO STO Centre for Maritime Research and Experimentation, Italy
Mazal, Jan	University of Defence, Czech Republic

Monroe, John	U.S. Army Engineer Research and Development Center (ERDC), USA
Motsch, Jean	Écoles de Saint-Cyr Coëtquidan, France
Navrat, Ales	Brno University of Technology, Czech Republic
Nohel, Jan	University of Defence, Czech Republic
Novotny, Jiri	NATO M&S COE, Italy
Palasiewicz, Tibor	University of Defence, Czech Republic
Pasley, Dylan	US Army Corps of Engineers, Engineer Research and Development Center, USA
Prenosil, Vaclav	Masaryk University, Czech Republic
Proietti, Paolo	MIMOS, Italy
Rajchl, Matej	Brno University of Technology, Czech Republic
Skala, Vaclav	University of Western Bohemia, Czech Republic
Starý, Vadim	University of Defence, Czech Republic
Stodola, Petr	University of Defence, Czech Republic
Stütz, Peter	Bundeswehr University Munich, Germany
Tulach, Petr	LOGIO, Czech Republic
Vasik, Petr	Brno University of Technology, Czech Republic
Zahradka, David	Czech Technical University in Prague, Czech Republic
Zahradníček, Pavel	University of Defence, Czech Republic
Zamponi, Virginia	Old Dominion University, USA
Čubanová, Slavka	Czech Technical University in Prague, Czech Republic

Contents

M&S of Intelligent Systems – R&D and Application

Performance Comparison of Visual Teach and Repeat Systems for Mobile Robots

Maxim Simon[(✉)], George Broughton, Tomáš Rouček, Zdeněk Rozsypálek,
and Tomáš Krajník

Faculty of Electrical Engineering, Czech Technical University, Prague, Czechia
simonmax@fel.cvut.cz

Abstract. In practical work scenarios, it is often necessary to repeat specific tasks, which include navigating along a desired path. Visual teach and repeat systems are a type of autonomous navigation in which a robot repeats a previously taught path using a camera and dead reckoning. There have been many different teach and repeat methods proposed in the literature, but only a few are open-source. In this paper, we compare four recently published open-source methods and a Boston Dynamics proprietary solution embedded in a Spot robot. The intended use for each method is different, which has an impact on their strengths and weaknesses. When deciding which method to use, factors such as the environment and desired precision and speed should be taken into consideration. For example, in controlled artificial environments, which do not change significantly, navigation precision and speed are more important than robustness to environment variations. However, the appearance of unstructured natural environments varies over time, making robustness to changes a crucial property for outdoor navigation systems. This paper compares the speed, precision, reliability, robustness, and practicality of the available teach and repeat methods. We will outline their flaws and strengths, helping to choose the most suitable method for a particular utilization.

1 Introduction

The ability to navigate is a necessity for any autonomous mobile robot. Many navigation systems use precise metric maps to estimate the robot's location and plan a path to the target [33]. These systems are typically based on the simultaneous localisation and mapping principle (SLAM), where a robot localises itself in a map while building it as it moves through the environment [2, 18]. To achieve sufficient robustness, SLAM-based navigations often require specific hardware and significant computational power. This is not ideal if navigation is deployed on resource-constrained robots alongside a suite of software that performs other robotic tasks. Due to that, navigation needs to be as compact as possible, both

This research was funded by Czech Science Foundation research project number 20-27034J 'ToltaTempo'.

hardware-wise and computational power-wise. SLAM systems often use LiDAR to create a map of the environment [46]. It can be easier to retrieve more accurate data regarding the position of the robot's surroundings from a LiDAR than an equivalent grade camera. However, a LiDAR sensor is often too heavy for smaller robots, especially drones, and too expensive for projects with a lower budget. Additionally, when used, LiDAR can be detected from a long distance, while camera is a passive sensor. Some SLAM methods use stereo [39], depth [13] or a monocular cameras [11,35] to create a map of their surroundings. However, in [2] it is concluded that for many scenarios, full SLAM is not strictly necessary as a robot can move across a priori known paths without the need for a metric globally consistent map of its surroundings.

In particular, visual teach and repeat (VT&R) systems serve solely to repeat previously taught paths [6,14,25], but they are typically easier to operate and more robust. These systems do not require the use of globally consistent maps [14]. Rather, they rely on low-level perceptual information [6] processed either by classic, point-based features [25] or by neural networks [43]. Despite not using globally consistent maps and relying on visual servoing techniques [3], several works showed that their position error relative to the taught path can be bound [25,26].

In a typical VT&R scenario, a robot is taught a trajectory by a human via teleoperation. As it is taught the path, the robot saves both how it moved and camera images. Then, using the saved data, it can autonomously repeat that path. VT&R systems comfortably run using off-the-shelf cameras, which are generally much cheaper and lighter alternatives to LiDARs. Moreover, camera image preprocessing can be done by specialised and optimised hardware [8,45], so even small robotic platforms can utilise camera-based navigation [8]. Camera-based teach and repeat systems are the perfect choice for cheaper robotic systems because they typically only require odometry and a camera [25]. Following a path repeatedly while using cheap and light hardware together with computationally efficient software leaves the robot's resources free for other tasks.

A considerable challenge for visual-based systems is their relatively low robustness to changing the appearance of the environment over time [17,28, 29,31,48]. For example seasonal changes or the relocation of visual landmarks, such as structures or cars. There were several attempts to cope with the issue, e.g., the use of features trained specifically to be robust to environmental changes [21,49], photogrammetric methods to remove shadows [19,37], invariant representations [30], multiple-map management [1,7,27,34], map adaptation [12,16] and appearance prediction [22,36,40]. The advent of deep learning for image processing brought different approaches that allowed the use of generic pre-learned features [47], features trained on relevant datasets [4,43], or even methods that are learned on the fly during robot navigation [41]. Even though VT&R systems have achieved impressive autonomously-traversed distances and durations [15,44], an open-source, robust, computationally efficient, and reliable visual teach and repeat system capable of long-term operation is yet to come.

Several teach and repeat systems have been developed so far, some of which continue to be improved: so-called Bearnav, teach and repeat navigation based on the convergence theorem from Czech Technical University in Prague (CTU) [26], Fast and Robust Bio-inspired teach and repeat navigation (FRB) from Queensland University of Technology (QUT) [10], and visual teach and repeat for long-range rover autonomy from University of Toronto [14,38].

These teach and repeat systems differ in their strengths and weaknesses. The first version of Bearnav has been in development since 2008 [24]. It consists of optimised modules designed to achieve precise and robust navigation. However, it is primarily meant to test the performance of the individual components of the VT&R, and therefore, it lacks practicality and user-friendliness. The second version of Bearnav is meant primarily to be easier to deploy and use. Moreover, unlike Bearnav 1, which is written in C++, Bearnav 2 is implemented in Python. FRB is aimed at resource-constrained systems and can be deployed even on small robots. VTR 2.0, a long-range system from the University of Toronto and the Oxford Robotics Group, has undergone extensive tests showing its capability to traverse long paths [38].

Fig. 1. The Spot, a legged robot from Boston Dynamics, which was used to carry out all experiments.

1.1 Contribution

Each of the aforementioned teach and repeat systems focuses on solving a different issue and is meant for different environments and scenarios. There are different demands for systems used in factories and systems used for scouting terrain inaccessible to humans. In this paper, we perform an extensive experimental evaluation comparing several teach and repeat navigation methods. We deploy these methods on Spot, see Fig. 1, a Boston Dynamics legged robot, which is increasingly popular because of its terrain-handling capabilities. We test three variants of the Bearnav method [25], FRB [10] and Autowalk, which is a Spot-embedded method. The VTR(2.0 and 3.0) system, recently released by the University of Toronto, was not tested because the code was not publicly available when we planned the experiments for this study. Every system excels at something different, and getting familiar with each of them is time-consuming. The purpose of this paper is to present a fair evaluation of all four systems and provide insights into their strengths and weaknesses. This will assist potential users of visual teach and repeat in selecting a suitable method for their intended scenario and environment, as well as to point out weaknesses of teach and repeat methods for future research.

2   Teach and Repeat Methods Evaluated in This Work

This section provides an overview of each of the aforementioned teach and repeat systems used in our comparison.

2.1 Bearnav-Based Methods

Bearnav uses an approach where a map created during the mapping phase is divided into several conjoined segments. A similar method was already used in [5,6], where the ends of the segments are recognized with camera images and odometry. However, the works [25] presented a mathematical proof showing that even if the ends of the segments are determined solely by odometry, the position error converges to a finite value. Thus the robot can navigate simply by adjusting its heading based on the registration of the current image and an image perceived at the same position along the segment during the mapping phase. Bearnav presented an original approach in [25] where odometry alone is used to recognize the robot position along the segment and identify the segments' ends, while the camera images are used only to correct its heading. One would expect that the odometric drift would cause the system to fail over time. However, the mathematical analysis presented in [25] showed, that the heading correction can suppress the effects of the odometry noise if the trajectory is not just a simple line. In [25], mathematical and experimental proofs of this concept were presented for polygonal paths only. Later, in [26], Bearnav was proven to work for arbitrarily shaped smooth routes, not just polygonal paths. However, Bearnav was created to prove the mathematical properties of the VT&R navigation. Thus, it was not intended to be user-friendly or easy to deploy. Therefore, the current version of Bearnav 1, publicly available on [23], is quite challenging to use in practice. Moreover, its C++ implementation is rather monolithic, making its deployment on non-standard platforms difficult. However, the system was tested on a variety of wheeled and tracked robots [32], where it showed good navigation precision and robustness.

Bearnav 2. Implemented in Python [20], was created to make the navigation system more user-friendly while retaining the precision and robustness of its predecessor. It uses the same working principle as Bearnav 1 but has more additional features to improve its practical usability. The newer version of Bearnav also presents higher modularity and allows the rapid development of new image processing methods, including deep-learning neural networks. For example, to improve the robustness of image matching, a Siamese neural network was developed [43] and integrated into Bearnav 2.

2.2   Fast and Robust Bio-inspired Teach and Repeat

FRB [10] is a new open-source teach and repeat navigation system [9]. It uses image data to recognize segments' ends and to correct longitudinal localization inaccuracies caused by odometry errors, such as wheel slips (based on image matching, it adjusts how far along the path the robot thinks it is). To increase robustness to lighting changes between the teach and repeat phases and to reduce memory space required, it alters all images recorded during the mapping phase. Further, direct visual comparison techniques are used instead of feature matching, which should prove more robust to lighting changes, even for images with lower resolution. Overall, FRB aims to further improve the robustness and practical usability of teach and repeat navigation by deviating from the purposeful simplicity of Bearnav.

2.3   Autowalk

Autowalk is a commercial teach and repeat system pre-installed on the Spot robot from Boston Dynamics. Out of the methods tested here, it is the only navigation system that is not open-source, and its exact working principles are unknown. The Autowalk can be controlled using the Spot's tablet provided by Boston Dynamics, where the navigation interface is simply a mobile app. The weakness of the Autowalk lies in the necessity of placing a physical fiducial marker, printed on paper for example, at the beginning and the end of the planned route. However, it is the easiest to use compared to other tested methods and has features that make its use rather convenient. The presented experiments were performed with Autowalk version 3.1.0.

We performed a series of tests in various environments to evaluate how the methods performed at repeating a taught path. This comprised teaching each method a closed path, then displacing the robot 2.5 m to the side of the path to inject an artificial error and observe the method's capability to correct it. The methodology was adopted from [25, 26].

Due to difficulties with training all the methods at the same time, each method was separately taught the same path. The robot was then displaced and commanded to traverse the path three times with the convergence to the taught path observed. This whole process was repeated three times per method, meaning that for one method in one environment, the Spot was offset three times and underwent a total of nine laps of autonomous repeating of a path.

2.4   Hardware

All experiments were performed using Spot, an agile four-legged robot from Boston Dynamics, running software version 3.1.0. We did not perform any experiments on wheeled or tracked robots. In our experience, legged, wheeled and tracked robots generally perform similarly while using VT&R. The only camera used for all teach and repeat programs except Autowalk, which can by default be used only with the Spot's front stereo camera, was a USB Logitech HD Webcam C920, attached to the front of the Spot. The Spot has an embedded inward-angled stereo camera pair, which is far from ideal for monocular VT&R methods. Additionally, these cameras were not available on the market, so we opted for an off-the-shelf available camera.

The Spot has a payload which was developed for a subterranean DARPA challenge [42] mounted on top. From the payload, only an Intel NUC and Nvidia Jetson were used for our experiments. The Jetson is an Nvidia AGX Xavier with 32 GB RAM, 32 GB storage, and an 8-core Nvidia Carmel CPU. The GPU on the Jetson is Nvidia Volta architecture with 512 CUDA cores and 64 Tensor cores. The NUC is an Intel i7-10th gen with 32 GB RAM. The teach and repeat methods were run solely on the Jetson, whereas the NUC was running a teleoperation node, which allows the Spot to be controlled by a Logitech joypad. This Logitech Wireless Gamepad F710 remote control was used to teleoperate the Spot along a path during the teach phase. A tablet, which comes with the Spot, was used for teleoperation during the mapping phase for Autowalk.

To establish the robot's accurate ground truth position during both the teach and the repeat traversals, we used a Leica Total Station TS16 R500. A Total Station is a device set up on a tripod, as seen in Fig. 2, which follows a prism secured to the top of the Spot such that it is visible from all angles. A laser is reflected from the prism, from which the Total Station calculates the prism's 3D position with 5 mm accuracy. Note that the Total Station does not measure the orientation of the robot.

2.5   Software Setup and Configuration

Each open-source method was downloaded onto the Jetson from its GitHub page. Each method then differed in the changes and adjustments needed for the program to run correctly.

Fig. 2. The Spot robot (on the left) autonomously repeating a taught path. A Leica Total Station (on the right on a tripod) was used for measuring the Spot's ground truth position.

Commonly, when a teach and repeat method is deployed on a new robot, four ROS topics must be set: a camera topic, a topic to publish velocity commands during path traversal, a topic from which velocity commands are recorded during the mapping phase, and an odometry topic.

Bearnav 1 does not have all of these four necessary topics set up as parameters in the launch files. Therefore we had to set them directly in the code. Additionally, it has a specific setup of those topics. It does not record how the Spot is moving, which is what the other methods do. Bearnav 1 listens to the controller, saves all commands sent from it, and then sends them to the Spot. As it listens to the controller, it uses these inputs to control the robot and thus ensures that no non-repeatable map is recorded. For example, the Spot is typically controlled with a joystick and can rotate in place. However, during Bearnav 1 mapping, the program listens directly to the controller's arrow keys and uses these to drive the robot. Therefore the Spot is unable to turn in place as the method does not allow it, as the method requires some forward velocity to do turns. As a result, the method cannot reproduce turning in place. However, this feature is not specified anywhere on the GitHub page, which makes it difficult to configure Bearnav 1 correctly. It should also be mentioned that Bearnav 1 requires an obsolete version of OpenCV. We configured this version on the Spot and let Bearnav 2 and FRB use it.

Bearnav 2 has all four topics set as parameters in the launch files. The GitHub Readme contains a more detailed explanation of the correct setup, making it significantly easier to deploy on a robot. Another benefit of this framework is that it has implemented multiple backends for image processing and also provides a trained Siamese neural network as an alternative method to process the images. Therefore for Bearnav 2, we decided to evaluate the method for both traditional image features (SIFT), similar to Bearnav 1, and the Siamese neural network. The Siamese neural network consists of a pair of standard convolutional neural networks, where one looks at the map image, and one looks at the current image. These two networks are then joined and passed through a fully connected layer to output the final alignment value, as described in [43].

Fast and Robust Bio-Inspired Teach and Repeat (FRB) has all the necessary topics included in the launch file. It has many additional parameters, which can be tuned. Four launch files on the GitHub page were used during their testing of the teach and repeat method. We had to choose one and delete a few non-useful parameters specific to their robots and experiments. Most parameters regarding the teach and repeat program are described in the Readme on GitHub. However, deploying FRB on the Spot was still difficult because many parameters need to be tuned to a specific value; otherwise, the program will not work correctly, and there is no guide on how to tune them or which are essential. The parameteres were tuned extensively. For unknown reasons, the program stops, on average, once per 40 m during the repeat run and needs to be restarted. Despite that, the method repeats the path as it should and converges to the taught path if displaced. It should be noted that to work, the Spot is walking at a stable speed of 0.5 m/s during the FRB's repeat phase. The other tested systems copy the speeds at which the Spot moved during the mapping phase, which in our case was 2.0 m/s.

Autowalk needed no adjustments, apart from printing out the fiducial marker, as it is a pre-installed, ready-to-use feature on a Spot. It is also, by default, prepared on a Spot's tablet from Boston Dynamics. No command line is needed for use. Autowalk is launched and fully controlled, even teleoperated along a path, from an app on the tablet.

2.6   Testing Environments

The first set of experiments took place during the day in a structured courtyard in front of the CTU Charles Square campus in Prague, shown in Fig. 3. It should be the least difficult environment for teach and repeat systems as it is well-lit, with buildings, benches, sidewalk and a road providing a significant number of image features and sharp distinguishable edges, which are a necessity for all the methods of image matching, based on which the methods calculate their heading corrections. Additionally, the taught paths are mostly on a pavement, reducing slipping and tripping of the Spot's legs resulting in precise odometry.

The second set of experiments took place in the same courtyard again late at night, see Fig. 3. Even though the courtyard is lit by street lights, the lighting is significantly worse than during the day. Images taken by the camera are often too dark, or over-exposed in places, and the programs fail to match them with other images. However, there were no people in the courtyard at night and no cars were moving. This more stable environment can have a positive effect on the outcome.

Fig. 3. Spot's view of the path during its traversal. The methods were evaluated in several different out-door conditions, from left to right: structured courtyard with buildings, the same courtyard late at night, unstructured environment in a park, with fewer navigational features.

The third and last set of experiments was conducted during the day in a public urban park called Park Kinských. Almost no buildings could be seen from the taught path. The vast majority of the surroundings were trees and grass, with some benches and people. This can be seen in a third image of Fig. 3. Trees and bushes are difficult for image matching because leaves provide many similar edges that are hard to distinguish from each other. If there are only trees in the camera's field of view, image matching can often fail. Walking people also introduce a problem, as they cause a changing environment. If a program saves an image of a person walking, but then during the repeat phase, the person is already gone, the two compared images differ significantly, and the number of matches is again reduced. Non-stable environments in general are one of the hardest for teach and repeat methods to be deployed in.

2.7   Experimental Setup for Autowalk

Autowalk differs from the other teach and repeat methods. It is not open-source, but rather a pre-implemented application, and because we are doing our research using Spot, we had the opportunity to test and compare it. As it is an application developed for Spot and deployed on the robot during manufacturing, it has an unfair advantage against the other methods, which, despite our best efforts, will not have all parameters tuned perfectly for this robot. Additionally, a physical fiducial marker, similar to a QR code, needs to be placed both at the beginning and the end of a recorded path, otherwise, Autowalk will not record or replay a path. This fact makes it difficult to evaluate the Autowalk method against the others, because having a fiducial at the start and the end, of course, creates an unfair advantage. Spot can align itself very precisely, based solely on the fiducial, before even starting to attempt to repeat a path. However, we felt that Autowalk is still a promising take on a teach and repeat navigation system and that it should deserve a place in our testing. Therefore we introduced several different scenarios and observed how Autowalk behaved.

3 Results

3.1 Path Following

In this section we present the results of the experiments. We chose several different evaluations of the tests, to avoid bias.

Teach and repeat navigation systems should remain stable after they converge to the taught path [25]. This can be seen in Fig. 4, where Bearnav 1 achieved stability after its second lap. There are a few additional factors to take into account, how fast a method converges and how close to the taught path it stays after converging.

We attempted to avoid any evaluations which would concentrate solely on the speed of convergence because this value is greatly affected by the teach and repeat methodology and how the controllers are tuned. As we can never tune controllers for all the methods perfectly, the results would introduce bias and not reflect the accuracy of the methods, but rather the precision of the controllers' tunings.

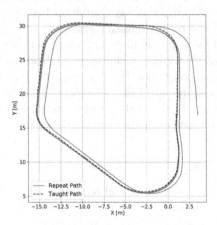

Fig. 4. Plot of three path traversals and the corresponding mapped path. The convergence towards the taught path is visible.

Precision. Here we evaluate the precision of the finishing point of the traversal's offset from the end of the mapped path. For each method in each environment, the Spot did 3 traversal sets, which each consisted of 3 autonomous repeats of a map. We measured the error of the Spot's position at the end of each traversal set. If a method is repeating a circular path, the closer to the taught beginning it is after a lap, the better position it has for starting the next repetition. This approach can clearly show how close to the taught path a method will stay after achieving stability.

We chose two ways to measure this precision. In the first, results from which can be seen in Table 1, we measure the distance between the Spot's position at the end of each traversal set and the endpoint of a map. This method results in greater errors, because longitudinal errors, displacement in the direction of travel, are taken into account along with the side offset. This occurrence can be seen in Fig. 5, where although the robot may be very close to the true path, it may be behind the position where it believes itself to be (visible at the top of the left-hand image).

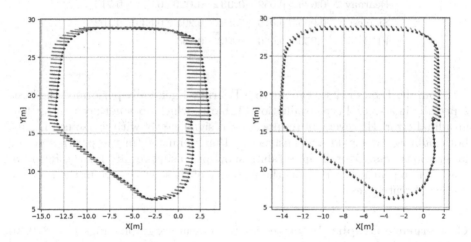

Fig. 5. The first two laps of a repeat phase. Arrows point from specific distances in the mapped path to where the Spot was after walking the same distances in the repeat phase.

Another way is to measure the distance from the Spot's positions at the end of each traversal set to the nearest point of the map. These results are shown in Table 2. This technique only measures the side offset relative to the taught path. We show these results, because in some scenarios the longitudinal offset is not an important factor, especially in closed paths, where the biggest concern is to not diverge from the taught trajectory.

From the measured values we calculated mean and standard deviation to show both accuracy and consistency of the methods. Note that an "x" means the method failed to finish a traversal set.

Table 1. Mean and standard deviation of the distance in meters between the Spot's positions at the end of each traversal set and **the endpoint** of a map.

	Day		Night		Park	
	μ	σ	μ	σ	μ	σ
Bearnav 1	**0.092**	0.051	0.382	0.033	**0.480**	**0.067**
Bearnav 2	0.112	0.071	**0.040**	0.025	1.695	1.034
Siamese	0.105	0.041	0.063	**0.022**	1.123	1.045
FRB	0.320	**0.038**	0.703	0.053	x	x

Table 2. Mean and standard deviation of the distance in meters between the Spot's positions at the end of each traversal set and **the nearest point** of a map.

	Day		Night		Park	
	μ	σ	μ	σ	μ	σ
Bearnav 1	**0.018**	**0.014**	0.109	0.003	**0.440**	**0.069**
Bearnav 2	0.095	0.059	**0.032**	**0.029**	0.751	0.713
Siamese	0.065	0.016	0.200	0.201	0.639	0.702
FRB	0.250	0.080	0.413	0.133	x	x

From the Tables 1, 2 we can see that Bearnav 1 generally performed the best, especially in a second type evaluation (Table 2), which does not account for longitudinal error. However, its results worsen significantly with worse conditions, both lighting (at night) and unstructured environment (in the park), showing lower robustness. Overall these tables show promising results for the future of teach and repeat navigations as the majority of these errors are in the range of dozens of centimeters.

Convergence Graphs. In this section we present six graphs, Figs. 6, 7, 8, 9, 10 and 11, which show the errors' evolution by distance. The distance is evaluated in two seperate ways.

In the first three graphs, Figs. 6, 7, 8, the error is calculated as the distance from where the robot was after walking a specific length during the mapping phase to where it is after walking the same length during the repeat phase. The convergence of the methods to the taught path is clearly visible. This evaluation takes into account longitudinal error. The point of this is that if a method has a longitudinal offset but no side offset, it calculates its position with an error. Usually, more forward than the robot is actually located, which results in future errors, such as turning before the mapped turn.

Graphs comparing the evolution of the error as a function of the distance travelled of all five methods. The error is calculated as a distance from where the robot was after walking a specific length during the mapping phase to where it is after walking the same length during the repeat phase.

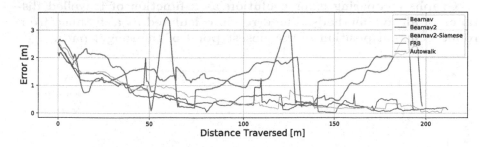

Fig. 6. Courtyard during the day

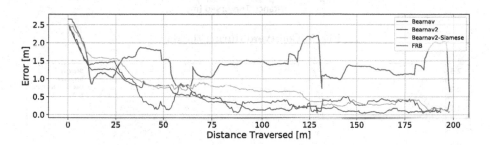

Fig. 7. Courtyard at night

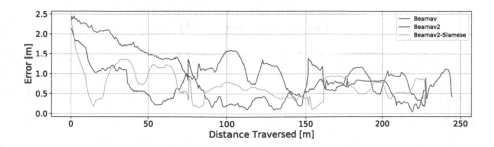

Fig. 8. Public park during the day

However, in closed loops, longitudinal errors can be corrected by teach and repeat navigation systems, even if they do not explicitly perform longitudinal corrections. If a taught path is a closed loop, the direction of the robot's lateral offset will rotate, and at the end of the path, it will have covered 360° and thus the system will have converged in every direction [25]. This is visualized in Fig. 5, where the offsets in two directions are represented by the rainbow area and the length of arrows. Only one of these, area or length, will significantly shrink after a turn, because it is actively performing only lateral corrections, which affect the offset only in one direction, were made on the preceding straight. Moreover, because the path is a closed loop, both the rainbow area and the arrows grew significantly smaller towards the end.

Graphs comparing error evolution as a function of travelled distance of all five methods. The error is calculated as a distance from robot's current position to the closest point of the taught path.

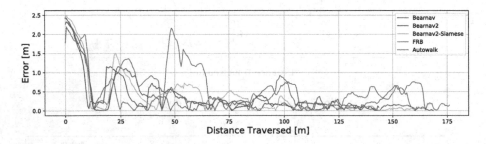

Fig. 9. Courtyard during the day

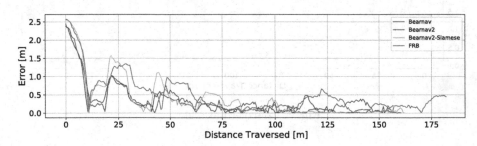

Fig. 10. Courtyard at night

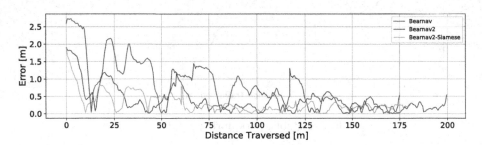

Fig. 11. Public park during the day

The bias of this evaluation is for systems that do perform explicit longitudinal corrections, such as FRB. FRB compares not only the current view to the estimated image in the map, but also to some ahead and behind the estimated position. If any match better, it will assume it is located at that position. Therefore FRB can lag behind to where it should be, but still calculate its position precisely, thus no error occurs. This phenomenon can be seen in Figs. 6, 7, 8. The error is growing even after the method has converged, and then it significantly drops at the end of a lap. This because the robot is behind the corresponding mapped positions, which is counted as an error. However, FRB knows its position and therefore reduces its offset towards the end of the path, as it arrives at the correct path end, without stopping short.

The second type of evaluation, presented in Figs. 9, 10, 11, again error over distance, calculates the error from the robot's current position to the closest point of the taught path. In this way, we do not evaluate the longitudinal error, but solely the lateral offset.

The weakness of this evaluation lies in crossing the path at turns. If a method is lagging behind, its error will be based solely on its lateral offset. However because it is behind, it will turn before reaching the real position of a taught turn, which will result in crossing the taught trajectory. The error will suddenly drop very low, even though the method did not get any closer to converging.

A few logistical notes should be made. FRB failed all traversal sets in the park, therefore its error is not plotted in the Public park graphs. Autowalk converged to a mapped path only under specific conditions, further discussed in Sect. 3.2. Even though these conditions were met in both the courtyard at night and in the public park environment, Autowalk did not show a clear convergence. The plotted traversal sets are chosen by us as the most precise for each method in each environment. Because our initial evaluation methods were independent for Autowalk, it underwent only one traversal set in the courtyard during the day, which is plotted.

In Figs. 6, 7, 8, 9, 10, 11, it can be seen how each of the methods performed significantly better in the second type of evaluation, which does not account for longitudinal error. They lagged behind the mapped positions. This trend is substantial for Bearnav 2, both with Siamese neural network and without. In the courtyard during the day and at night, both of these methods performed close to no error and even outperformed Bearnav 1. Bearnav 1, however, mostly outperformed these two methods in the evaluation shown in Tables 1, 2. This is due to two reasons.

Firstly, each method ends in a slightly different place at the end of the graphs. Some methods ended the path a few meters before the mapped end. This causes a high offset in Table 1 because it ended far away from a mapped endpoint. Additionally, in the first method of evaluation, which does account for longitudinal error, see graphs in Figs. 6, 7, 8, it can be seen that neither Bearnav 2 nor Siamese performed significantly better than Bearnav 1. These facts show that Bearnav 2 and Siamese are precise methods, and if some form of longitudinal error corrections would be added, they could become exceptional teach and repeat navigation systems. Secondly, it can be seen that some methods (Bearnav 1, Bearnav 2 in the park, and FRB in the courtyard at night) performed reasonably well during the traversal set, but in the end, the error spikes up. As the repeat phase is finished, the method does not have time to correct this offset. This to a certain point contradicts the values found in Tables 1, 2, which only measured the precision of these endpoints.

Robustness to different environments can be inferred from these graphs as well. For example, both Siamese and FRB have very similar curves through out the graphs, meaning their performance was less affected by worse lighting or unstructured environments.

A non-parametric Mann-Whitney-Wilcoxon test was performed on the results to evaluate if the differences between the values were statistically significant or not. The test was performed for each scenario, and across the errors on all laps and also only on the final lap. The tests allowed us to reject the null hypothesis of there being no difference between the methods with an alpha value of 0.05 in all scenarios.

3.2   Autowalk

For Autowalk, we could not just offset the Spot at the beginning of every fourth lap, as we did with the other methods, because Autowalk needs to see a fiducial marker before attempting to traverse a route. The Spot knows the dimensions of the fiducial printed on a sheet of paper, and because it is a distinguishable 2D square, the Spot can align both its rotation and distance solely on seeing a fiducial. Therefore we displaced both the fiducial and the Spot in several ways, and here we show how Autowalk reacted to each scenario. These results are shown in Fig. 12.

Because Autowalk did converge with an artificially injected error, we have compared the measurements from the first scenario with the other teach and repeat methods in the graphs in Fig. 6 and 9. It should be noted that Autowalk was not created to converge from an artificially introduced error. It is a program with many features developed to assist the user and it follows a path without difficulties if the circumstances stated in the manual are met i.e. the fiducial is not moved.

3.3   Computational Performance

A significant advantage of teach and repeat navigation systems is their low computational power consumption. As the navigation is often run together with other programs, we are interested in how much computational resources the methods consume. We ran each of the tested methods on the Spot and measured how much the RAM and CPU of the Jetson were occupied. Without any teach and repeat system running on the Jetson, there is 1.7 GB of RAM and 18% of each CPU's core in use. While Bearnav 1 is running and the Spot is repeating a previously taught path 1.9 GB of RAM is consumed. CPU has one core running on a 100% and others on 80%. Bearnav 2 takes up 2.1 GB of RAM and 25% of each core. Using the Siamese neural network, these values increase to 4.8 GB RAM and 100% of each core. Additionally, it is the only method using the GPU,

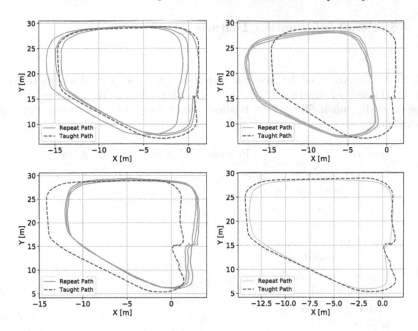

Fig. 12. Upper left: Both the Spot and the fiducial were displaced, then Autowalk was started and immedietly stopped. Afterward, we teleoperated the Spot back to a starting position, removed the fiducial, and restarted the Autowalk repeat. The Spot then traversed 3 laps autonomously. This is the only scenario we found in which Autowalk converged to a taught path. **Upper right:** Both the Spot and the fiducial were displaced, then Autowalk was launched and the Spot traversed 3 laps autonomously without converging. Autowalk moved the whole path consistently with the fiducials offset and then traversed this path with high precision. **Bottom left:** Both the Spot and the fiducial were displaced, then Autowalk was launched, same as the previous scenario, but after the Spot started to repeat the first lap, the fiducial was taken away. The Spot then traversed 3 laps autonomously. The only time it saw the fiducial was in the beginning. It can be seen how it diverged from the offset path without being able to correct based on a fiducial. **Bottom right:** We let the Spot repeat a path without any offset and with fiducial in place. This is a visualization of how Autowalk repeats a path. Note that the sudden sharp turn on the right side of every map is where the Spot turned 90° to face the fiducial and align itself.

with 65% utilisation on average. FRB consumes 2.0 GB of RAM and an average of 35% of each CPU core. The computational power of Autowalk could not be measured as it does not run on Jetson but on an internal hardware of a Spot, which, best to our knowledge, can not be accessed. The lowest RAM usage was achieved by Bearnav 1, followed by FRB and Bearnav 2. The lowest CPU usage was achieved by Bearnav 2, followed by FRB and Bearnav 1. The Siamese network was the most resource-intensive from both the computational and memory perspective.

3.4   Additional Information/Features

Table 3. A comparison of the advertised additional features available from the tested methods. The asterisk means that FRB allows naming a path, but it requires parameter change in both launch files. There is also a possibility to automatically timestamp recorded maps.

Feature	Bearnav 1	Bearnav 2	FRB	Autowalk
Can turn in place	×	✓	✓	✓
Can strafe within a map	×	✓	×	✓
Functions during Spot stair traversal	✓	✓	✓	✓
Allows to set speed of robot for repetition	✓	×	✓	✓
Repeats a path at the mapping speed of robot	✓	✓	×	✓
Performs longitudinal adjustments	×	×	✓	
Record miscellaneous topics into map	×	✓	✓	×
Compatible with ROS 2	×	✓	×	×
Possibility to name map	✓	✓	×*	✓
Save map directly from remote controller	✓	×	×	✓
Alter recorded path	×	×	×	✓
Option to take shortcuts during repeat	×	×	×	✓

Each of the tested systems differs in many additional characteristics and traits. Some are minor but convenient, such as the ability to name a map. Others, however, bare higher significance, because they determine what kind of paths will a method be able to traverse. If a method cannot turn in place without any forward velocity, its indoor deployment possibilities will be limited, as it will struggle to walk through hallways or turn into doorframes. In Table 3 we provide an overview showing each method's features.

3.5   Discussion

During the installation process and experiments conducted, we dealt with bugs in each code and saw each method deployed in practical environments. We recorded and replayed several dozen paths for each method. During this time we got a feeling for how the methods perform in different scenarios. In the following Table 4 we show our ranking of the compared methods based on empirical data, measurements, and experience. This data is obviously highly subjective, however, we believe that it provides clear information on each of the method's performance.

Table 4. Quantitative and qualitative ranking of the methods based on the experiments performed. The first rank means the best performance, e.g., least memory intensive or the most robust.

	Accuracy	Robustness	Deployment	CPU use	Memory	User experience
Bearnav 1	1st	1st	4th	3rd	1st	4th
Bearnav 2	3rd	2nd	1st	1st	3rd	2nd
Siamese	2nd	3rd	2nd	4th	4th	2nd
FRB	4th	5th	3rd	2nd	2nd	3rd
Autowalk	5th	4th	N/A	N/A	N/A	1st

4   Conclusion

We have presented the results of extensive short-term experiments that compared the performance of five different visual teach and repeat navigation systems, Bearnav 1, Bearnav 2, Bearnav 2 with Siamese neural network, Fast and Robust Bio-inspired teach and repeat, and Autowalk from Boston Dynamics. The experiments took place in three diverse environments to provide additional information that could assist in choosing or evaluating these navigation methods. These environments were a structured courtyard during the day, the same area at night, and an unstructured natural environment during the daytime.

It is important to note that these systems are best suited for environments that do not undergo significant changes while the navigation is in use. VT&R methods repeat a previously taught path, the path has to be known beforehand, and if changes occur after the teach phase, a new path may need to be recorded.

Our results demonstrate that to evaluate a teach and repeat method, one must consider the specific criteria that are the most important for the intended use. Each of the methods' performances varied across several areas of testing. A method may excel in one area, however, one missing feature makes it undeployable for certain tasks. Another system performs worse overall, but its extensive robustness to light conditions makes it a possible choice for further long-term development.

A general area that could be improved in teach and repeat navigation systems is the ease of deployment. Every method, except the pre-installed Autowalk, required several days or weeks of work, alterations, and research until it was repeating a taught path while correctly converging. An incomplete documentation of each method on how to compile, integrate and deploy it on a robotic platform revealed the difference between a developed program to confirm a hypothesis and a finished product, usable in practice. Visual teach and repeat navigation is generally easy to use, but the lack of documentation of current open-source methods is a danger to this fact.

However, the experiments showed high robustness to non-ideal visual conditions, such as low lighting or natural environments. Deployment of every program was successful in each of the three environments, with only one exception. Even though precision dropped in the unstructured environment, the trend of a stable convergence could still be seen.

References

1. Bürki, M., Dymczyk, M., Gilitschenski, I., Cadena, C., Siegwart, R., Nieto, J.: Map management for efficient long-term visual localization in outdoor environments. In: 2018 IEEE Intelligent Vehicles Symposium (IV), pp. 682–688. IEEE (2018)
2. Cadena, C., et al.: Past, present, and future of simultaneous localization and mapping: toward the robust-perception age. IEEE Trans. Rob. **32**(6), 1309–1332 (2016)
3. Chaumette, F., Hutchinson, S.: Visual servo control, part I: Basic approaches. IEEE Robot. Autom. Mag. **13**(4), 82–90 (2006). http://www.irisa.fr/lagadic/publi/publi/Chaumette07a-eng.html
4. Chen, Z., et al.: Deep learning features at scale for visual place recognition. In: 2017 IEEE International Conference on Robotics and Automation (ICRA) (2017)
5. Chen, Z., Birchfield, S.T.: Qualitative vision-based mobile robot navigation. In: Proceedings 2006 IEEE International Conference on Robotics and Automation, ICRA 2006, pp. 2686–2692. IEEE (2006)
6. Chen, Z., Birchfield, S.T.: Qualitative vision-based path following. IEEE Trans. Rob. **25**(3), 749–754 (2009)
7. Churchill, W.S., Newman, P.: Experience-based navigation for long-term localisation. IJRR (2013). https://doi.org/10.1177/0278364913499193
8. Čížek, P., Faigl, J.: Real-time FPGA-based detection of speeded-up robust features using separable convolution. IEEE Trans. Industr. Inf. **14**(3), 1155–1163 (2017)
9. Dall'Osto, D., Fischer, T.: FRB github. https://github.com/QVPR/teach-repeat/
10. Dall'Osto, D., Fischer, T., Milford, M.: Fast and robust bio-inspired teach and repeat navigation. In: 2021 IEEE/RSJ International Conference on Intelligent Robots and Systems (IROS), pp. 500–507 (2021). https://doi.org/10.1109/IROS51168.2021.9636334
11. Davison, A.J., Reid, I.D., Molton, N.D., Stasse, O.: MonoSLAM: real-time single camera slam. IEEE Trans. Pattern Anal. Mach. Intell. **29**(6), 1052–1067 (2007)
12. Dayoub, F., Duckett, T.: An adaptive appearance-based map for long-term topological localization of mobile robots. In: 2008 IEEE/RSJ International Conference on Intelligent Robots and Systems, pp. 3364–3369. IEEE (2008)
13. Engelhard, N., Endres, F., Hess, J., Sturm, J., Burgard, W.: Real-time 3D visual SLAM with a hand-held RGB-D camera. In: Proceedings of the RGB-D Workshop on 3D Perception in Robotics at the European Robotics Forum, Vasteras, Sweden, vol. 180, pp. 1–15 (2011)
14. Furgale, P., Barfoot, T.D.: Visual teach and repeat for long-range rover autonomy. J. Field Robot. **27**(5), 534–560 (2010)
15. Halodová, L., et al.: Adaptive image processing methods for outdoor autonomous vehicles. In: Mazal, J. (ed.) MESAS 2018. LNCS, vol. 11472, pp. 456–476. Springer, Cham (2019). https://doi.org/10.1007/978-3-030-14984-0_34
16. Halodová, L., et al.: Predictive and adaptive maps for long-term visual navigation in changing environments. In: 2019 IEEE/RSJ International Conference on Intelligent Robots and Systems (IROS), pp. 7033–7039. IEEE (2019)

17. Hawes, N., et al.: The strands project: long-term autonomy in everyday environments. IEEE Robot. Autom. Mag. **24**(3), 146–156 (2017)
18. Khairuddin, A.R., Talib, M.S., Haron, H.: Review on simultaneous localization and mapping (SLAM). In: 2015 IEEE International Conference on Control System, Computing and Engineering (ICCSCE), pp. 85–90. IEEE (2015)
19. Krajník, T., Blažíček, J., Santos, J.M.: Visual road following using intrinsic images. In: 2015 European Conference on Mobile Robots (ECMR), pp. 1–6. IEEE (2015)
20. Krajník, T., Broughton, G., Rouček, Tomáš Rozsypálek, Z.: BearNav2 github. https://github.com/broughtong/bearnav2
21. Krajník, T., Cristóforis, P., Kusumam, K., Neubert, P., Duckett, T.: Image features for visual teach-and-repeat navigation in changing environments. Robot. Auton. Syst. **88**, 127–141 (2016)
22. Krajnik, T., Fentanes, J.P., Cielniak, G., Dondrup, C., Duckett, T.: Spectral analysis for long-term robotic mapping. In: 2014 IEEE International Conference on Robotics and Automation (ICRA), pp. 3706–3711. IEEE (2014)
23. Krajník, T., Filip, M., Broughton, G., Rouček, Tomáš Rozsypálek, Z.: BearNav github. https://github.com/gestom/stroll_bearnav/tree/core
24. Krajník, T., Přeučil, L.: A simple visual navigation system with convergence property. In: Bruyninckx, H., Přeučil, L., Kulich, M. (eds.) European Robotics Symposium 2008. Springer Tracts in Advanced Robotics, vol. 44, pp. 283–292. Springer, Heidelberg (2008). https://doi.org/10.1007/978-3-540-78317-6_29
25. Krajník, T., Faigl, J., Vonásek, V., Košnar, K., Kulich, M., Přeučil, L.: Simple yet stable bearing-only navigation. J. Field Robot. **27**(5), 511–533 (2010). https://doi.org/10.1002/rob.20354, https://onlinelibrary.wiley.com/doi/abs/10.1002/rob.20354
26. Krajník, T., Majer, F., Halodová, L., Vintr, T.: Navigation without localisation: reliable teach and repeat based on the convergence theorem. In: 2018 IEEE/RSJ International Conference on Intelligent Robots and Systems (IROS), pp. 1657–1664 (2018). https://doi.org/10.1109/IROS.2018.8593803
27. Linegar, C., Churchill, W., Newman, P.: Work smart, not hard: recalling relevant experiences for vast-scale but time-constrained localisation. In: 2015 IEEE International Conference on Robotics and Automation (ICRA), pp. 90–97. IEEE (2015)
28. Lowry, S., Milford, M.J.: Supervised and unsupervised linear learning techniques for visual place recognition in changing environments. IEEE Trans. Rob. **32**(3), 600–613 (2016)
29. Lowry, S., et al.: Visual place recognition: a survey. IEEE Trans. Rob. **32**(1), 1–19 (2015)
30. Lowry, S., Wyeth, G., Milford, M.: Unsupervised online learning of condition-invariant images for place recognition. In: Proceedings of the Australasian Conference on Robotics and Automation. Citeseer (2014)
31. Macario Barros, A., Michel, M., Moline, Y., Corre, G., Carrel, F.: A comprehensive survey of visual slam algorithms. Robotics **11**(1), 24 (2022)
32. Majer, F., et al.: A versatile visual navigation system for autonomous vehicles. In: Mazal, J. (ed.) MESAS 2018. LNCS, vol. 11472, pp. 90–110. Springer, Cham (2019). https://doi.org/10.1007/978-3-030-14984-0_8
33. Matias, L.P., Santos, T.C., Wolf, D.F., Souza, J.R.: Path planning and autonomous navigation using AMCL and AD. In: 2015 12th Latin American Robotics Symposium and 2015 3rd Brazilian Symposium on Robotics (LARS-SBR), pp. 320–324. IEEE (2015)

34. Mühlfellner, P., Bürki, M., Bosse, M., Derendarz, W., Philippsen, R., Furgale, P.: Summary maps for lifelong visual localization. J. Field Robot. **33**(5), 561–590 (2016)
35. Mur-Artal, R., Montiel, J.M.M., Tardós, J.D.: Orb-SLAM: a versatile and accurate monocular slam system. IEEE Trans. Rob. **31**(5), 1147–1163 (2015). https://doi.org/10.1109/TRO.2015.2463671
36. Neubert, P., Sünderhauf, N., Protzel, P.: Superpixel-based appearance change prediction for long-term navigation across seasons. RAS **69**, 15–27 (2014). https://doi.org/10.1016/j.robot.2014.08.005
37. Paton, M., MacTavish, K., Ostafew, C., Barfoot, T.: It's not easy seeing green: lighting-resistant stereo visual teach-and-repeat using color-constant images. In: Proceedings of the IEEE International Conference on Robotics and Automation (ICRA) (2015)
38. Paton, M., MacTavish, K., Berczi, L.-P., van Es, S.K., Barfoot, T.D.: I can see for miles and miles: an extended field test of visual teach and repeat 2.0. In: Hutter, M., Siegwart, R. (eds.) Field and Service Robotics. SPAR, vol. 5, pp. 415–431. Springer, Cham (2018). https://doi.org/10.1007/978-3-319-67361-5_27
39. Paz, L.M., Piniés, P., Tardós, J.D., Neira, J.: Large-scale 6-DoF slam with stereo-in-hand. IEEE Trans. Rob. **24**(5), 946–957 (2008)
40. Rosen, D.M., Mason, J., Leonard, J.J.: Towards lifelong feature-based mapping in semi-static environments. In: ICRA, pp. 1063–1070. IEEE (2016)
41. Rouček, T., et al.: Self-supervised robust feature matching pipeline for teach and repeat navigation. Sensors **22**(8), 2836 (2022)
42. Rouček, T., et al.: DARPA subterranean challenge: multi-robotic exploration of underground environments. In: Mazal, J., Fagiolini, A., Vasik, P. (eds.) MESAS 2019. LNCS, vol. 11995, pp. 274–290. Springer, Cham (2020). https://doi.org/10.1007/978-3-030-43890-6_22
43. Rozsypálek, Z., et al.: Contrastive learning for image registration in visual teach and repeat navigation. Sensors **22**, 2975 (2022)
44. Rozsypálek, Z., Rouček, T., Vintr, T., Krajník, T.: Non-cartesian multidimensional particle filter for long-term visual teach and repeat in changing environments. IEEE Robot. Autom. Lett. (2023, to appear)
45. Sledevič, T., Serackis, A.: Surf algorithm implementation on FPGA. In: 2012 13th Biennial Baltic Electronics Conference, pp. 291–294. IEEE (2012)
46. Sun, L., Yan, Z., Zaganidis, A., Zhao, C., Duckett, T.: Recurrent-OctoMap: learning state-based map refinement for long-term semantic mapping with 3-D-lidar data. IEEE Robot. Autom. Lett. **3**(4), 3749–3756 (2018)
47. Sünderhauf, N., Shirazi, S., Dayoub, F., Upcroft, B., Milford, M.: On the performance of convnet features for place recognition. In: 2015 IEEE/RSJ International Conference on Intelligent Robots and Systems (IROS), pp. 4297–4304. IEEE (2015)
48. Valgren, C., Lilienthal, A.J.: SIFT, SURF & seasons: appearance-based long-term localization in outdoor environments. Robot. Auton. Syst. **58**(2), 149–156 (2010)
49. Zhang, N., Warren, M., Barfoot, T.D.: Learning place-and-time-dependent binary descriptors for long-term visual localization. In: 2018 IEEE International Conference on Robotics and Automation (ICRA), pp. 828–835. IEEE (2018)

Hellinger Metrics for Validating High Fidelity Simulators Using Target Tracking

Kjetil Vasstein(✉) ⓘ, Øystein Kaarstad Helgesen ⓘ,
and Edmund Førland Brekke ⓘ

Department of Engineering Cybernetics, Norwegian University of Science
and Technology (NTNU), O. S. Bragstads plass 2D, 7032 Trondheim, Norway
{kjetil.vasstein,oystein.k.helgesen,edmund.brekke}@ntnu.no

Abstract. To achieve autonomy at sea, it is believed simulations will be essential in testing, analysing and verifying autonomous systems due to the scarcity and high cost of obtaining real data for all relevant scenarios. This reliance on simulation raises the question on how much synthetic data can be trusted, especially from sensor data such as lidars, radars and cameras. Methods for validating specific sensor models exists, however these are often focusing on perceptional differences without considering the sensors impact on the autonomy's situational awareness. In this paper we make an attempt to analyse this using a JIPDA target tracker, by comparing its performance on real and synthetic lidar data with various Hellinger metrics for Bernoulli and multi-Bernoulli multi-target densities. Our work showcases a method that quantifies sensor fidelity of synthetic data based on tracker performance, a step towards building trust to simulators targeted at validating autonomy systems.

Keywords: Simulation validation · Multi-target tracking ·
Multi-Bernoulli · Hellinger distance · Finite set statistics · Csiszár
information functional · Maritime autonomy · Situational awareness

J. Mazal et al. (Eds.): MESAS 2022, LNCS 13866, pp. 25–43, 2023.
https://doi.org/10.1007/978-3-031-31268-7_2

1 Introduction

High fidelity sensor simulations is playing an ever increasing role in the development of autonomous vehicles. Especially in the machine learning community the use of simulation as a substitution for real world testing and training gives the developers a source for variable, accurate and unlimited data. This has the potential to give better generalisations and bigger test scopes which is required to guarantee safe and reliable autonomous operations. Having high fidelity is of benefit here as it is thought to help transition the artificial intelligence (AI) algorithms from simulations to real world applications.

However, the simulations' execution time is dependent on the level of fidelity, meaning there must be a balance between data quantity and quality. Unfortunately, judging fidelity of simulators targeting autonomy such as Carla [7], Gemini [14] and AirSim [12] is often done by intuition on what "looks" more real. This is despite the driver, captain or pilot in autonomy cases being a machine. This can lead us astray when improving simulation models and give us false hope for the final deployment as what looks more real for us humans does not necessarily imply the same for the AI [6, p. 3171]. To get an optimal relation between simulation and autonomy, we need to answer how fidelity affects the AI's performance. This will be the goal of any simulation framework that promises to deliver on high data quantity at the right quality. Having adequate metrics that measures fidelity relative to its impact on autonomy systems will help to establish validation techniques that can benchmark the simulation performance, moreover help ensuring the simulation development goes in the right direction.

Transferring autonomy systems developed in simulation to reality is a particular case of domain adaptation [6, p. 3]. Here the simulation the autonomous agent is trained and tested in is defined as the source domain, and its real world deployment defined as the target domain. There are several known methods that helps to improve this transition. Domain randomisation is a technique where the simulator uses procedural generation to vary textures, content and situations to increase the chance for the AI to perceive the real world as yet another variation [13]. Augmenting the source domain to better reassemble the target domain from generative adversarial networks (GAN) [11] is yet another technique. However most, of these methods rely on machine learning concepts to make autonomy deployable in target domains. Since machine learning uses a black box modelling concept that is unexplainable and unpredictable, it is questionable if these techniques can be considered safe and viable for validation. As an example, the use of CycleGAN [19] to improve the quality of synthetic images showed no performance increase for the autonomy despite the images looking more realistic [6]. If this problem applies in general to machine learning is speculative, as reasoning about black box systems is far from trivial. This gives motivation for a validation approach that relies less on black box systems to be more explainable.

Instead of focusing on what the AI perceives, one could instead focus on what the AI understands of the situation, i.e., to study the Situational Awareness (SITAW) of the AI. The approaches we have discussed so far and which is fairly popular is end-to-end learning. Here SITAW is incorporated into a black box system often created through machine learning using artificial neural networks. The input to these systems are raw sensor data while the output may be signals to actuators, meaning that SITAW may actually not exist in any meaningful sense. Without any internal insight of the black box system, validation of these systems are hard to do without testing the whole system. A more validation friendly approach is to modularize the system as much as possible, so that the pipeline can be divided into components using machine learning and explainable model-based techniques. Here SITAW plays a role in the higher modularisation scheme in addition to containing modules of its own.

Core tasks in a SITAW system are detection and tracking, which can be solved by means of Bayesian filters. The role of detectors is to give information about potential surrounding entities, i.e., detections. The tracker on the other hand, consists (among others) of filters with the purpose of ensembling the present detections with previous beliefs about the targets to establish tracks on them. When assuming that the targets' measurements, processes and initialisations follow Gaussian models, the Kalman filter or its extended version can be used as a closed form solution of the general Bayesian filter. Here target states are estimated based on noisy measurements originating from either targets or from false alarms. This requires the tracker to also associate measurements to targets which can be done in several ways. In the Probabilistic Data Association (PDA) [3] family of tracking methods, individual measurements are used to update target states based on the likelihood of it originating from the target or from clutter. The Joint Integrated PDA (JIPDA) [10] is a multi-target extension of the Integrated PDA [9] which extends PDA with estimates of target existence probability.

A concept similar to domain adaptation for trackers is filter tuning. Here various metrics help guide the developer to tune the tracker towards the final deployment. For single-target/single-sensor analysis, metrics could either be measuring a point-point distance, or probability distribution distance between what is estimated by a tracker and what is considered to be the *ground truth*. The current state of the art in the tracking field is however in multi-target tracking, where *Finite-Set Statistics* (FISST) have been responsible for several innovations. Among these are the creation of metrics better suited for evaluating multi-target trackers, where the *Csiszár's Information Functionals* is an example of a mathematical framework responsible for several of them [18]. Albeit this was originally intended for developing performance, efficiency and robustness metrics to evaluate tracker to tracker, the Csiszár information functional more generally compares probability distributions. This have found use cases in fields outside the tracking community, where the functional have among others been used in domain adaptations for GAN [2].

Other attempts of measuring autonomy performance have also been conducted in recent years, among which the robotic platform RoboThor have targeted how well robots can adapt to real world situations when being trained in synthetically recreated environments [6]. Here the agents performance is judged by its navigational performance using *Success Rate* and *Success weighted by Path*

Length for each completed task. Results shows that even with almost pixel perfect reconstructed camera data used for navigation, there can be a significant difference in the agent's performance between simulation and reality. However, since the metrics mainly measures the navigational performance, moreover relies on end-to-end testings for obtaining results, this makes it hard to tell where in the autonomy pipeline the simulation and real world performance diverges.

A similar attempt of comparing simulation to reality with the use of synthetic reproduction have also been done for SITAW [15]. Here an autonomous ferry [4] including a digital twin representation [14] was used to gather datasets running through a detection and JIPDA tracking pipeline on both synthetic and real sensor data, comparing the trackers Gaussian posteriors using a Hellinger distance as a performance metric (Fig. 1). One of the benefits of this was the ability to analyse arbitrary sensor data that could individually and collectively be studied for its impact on the tracker. In addition, the metric measures a particular portion of the autonomy pipeline rather the full end-to-end performance, making it both fast and specific of what it is measuring in the autonomy. However, the proposed Hellinger metric only considered single target kinematics with no attention to the trackers existence probability moreover track associations between synthetic and real data. The full output of a JIPDA have in contrary been shown to be a *multi-Bernoulli multi-object density function* (MBMDF) [16], which have also been confirmed by recent studies of the *Visual Interacting Multiple Model* JIPDA (VIMMJIPDA) extension [5].

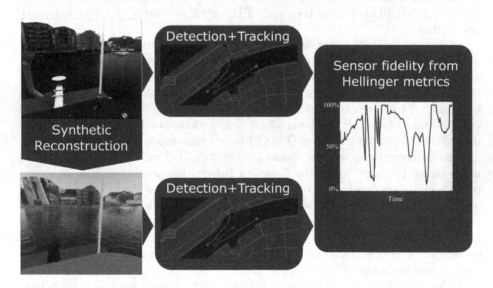

Fig. 1. Pipeline description

In this paper we will extend the attempt of comparing tracker performance on synthetic and real data using the same dataset as [15] focusing on its lidar data.

We will include Bernoulli and multi-Bernoulli existence models by using Csiszár information functionals to facilitate for both single and multi-target cases. The new metrics will generalise and be compared to the previous Hellinger attempts in [15] by evaluating simulation performance with respect to reality, the effects of existence probabilities, and the metrics ability to measure tracker performance. This analysis can be used to obtain perspectives on 1) the simulations validity such as sensor fidelity, 2) scenario reproduction, and 3) the tracker's indifference or sensitiveness to simulated data with respect to reality.

We begin with outlining core concepts and definitions from FISST in Sect. 2 before detailing each step in the pipeline description (Fig. 1) in the subsequent sections. Here we begin defining and deriving Hellinger metrics, before venturing into the JIPDA tracker in Sect. 4 where data is being processed to estimates, covariances and existence probabilities of target entities in the datasets. This is followed by describing the synthetic and real dataset in Sect. 5. In Sect. 6 we go through some of the findings when comparing the datasets with the various performance metrics before we have a discussion in Sect. 7. Finally, we do a summary and conclude the paper with suggestions of future work in Sect. 8.

2   Finite-Set Statistics (FISST) for Metric Constructions

In order for target trackers to be considered viable, filter tuning is a necessary step in any research and design process. This relies on performance metrics, often based on statistical properties and assumptions of the filter. For the JIPDA tracker, targets are assumed to be represented as multivariate Gaussian distributions:

$$\mathcal{N}(\boldsymbol{x}; \boldsymbol{\mu}, \mathbf{P}) := \frac{1}{(2\pi)^{\frac{n}{2}} |\mathbf{P}|^{\frac{1}{2}}} \exp\left(-\frac{1}{2}(\boldsymbol{x} - \boldsymbol{\mu})^T \mathbf{P}^{-1}(\boldsymbol{x} - \boldsymbol{\mu})\right) \qquad (1)$$

for a vector $\boldsymbol{x}$ with n-dimensions subjected to the expectation value $\boldsymbol{\mu}$ and covariance matrix $\mathbf{P}$. Relying on the Gaussian distribution allows us to check statistical metrics that must be in place for the filter to be considered viable. Among these are the *Normalised Estimation Error Squared* (NEES):

$$NEES(\boldsymbol{x}, \boldsymbol{\mu}, \mathbf{P}) := (\boldsymbol{x} - \boldsymbol{\mu})^T \mathbf{P}^{-1}(\boldsymbol{x} - \boldsymbol{\mu}). \qquad (2)$$

This measures the distance between a point $\boldsymbol{x}$ with a distribution consisting of an estimate $\boldsymbol{\mu}$ and covariance $\mathbf{P}$. In filter tuning for single target tracking, $\boldsymbol{x}$ is thought to be the ground truth giving us NEES values we interpret as *filter confidence*. The name *ground truth* refers to high accuracy measurements of target states that will be compared to the less perfect filter estimates. This becomes a comparison between two datasets we will note as A and B.

However, when the datasets are both distributions as is the case when comparing tracker outputs, a different approach is needed to handle additional information such as having two sets of covariance matrices instead of just one as in (2). In addition, distributions coming from the tracker is often accompanied by existence probabilities, which requires special treatment for single and multi-target cases.

In this section we will introduce mathematics from FISST that can be used to handle these concerns. We begin with defining random finite sets before we continue with *multi-object density functions* (MDF) for cases of Bernoulli and *multi-Bernoulli* (MB) distributions for existence probabilities. This is followed by defining Csiszár's information functionals from which special cases of Hellinger metrics is further derived and analysed in Sect. 3.

2.1   Random Finite Sets

We define X to be the set of potential objects at each time instance k: $X = \{\boldsymbol{x}_1, ..., \boldsymbol{x}_\xi\}$, with each vector containing states of the object $\boldsymbol{x} = [x_1, ..., x_n]^T$. ξ is the cardinality of the set which represents the number of object realizations: $|X| = \xi$.

2.2   Multi-object Density Functions (MDF)

A MDF is written as $f_\Xi(X)$ where the subscript Ξ notes the space containing the RFS X.

Set Integral. For an MDF the set integral is defined to be [8, p. 62]:

$$\int f_\Xi(X)\delta X := \sum_{\xi \geq 0} \frac{1}{\xi!} \int_{-\infty}^{\infty} f_\Xi(\{(\boldsymbol{x}_1), ..., (\boldsymbol{x}_\xi)\})d\boldsymbol{x}_1...d\boldsymbol{x}_\xi \qquad (3)$$

Bernoulli. The simplest MDF to choose for a tracker is the Bernoulli distribution [8, p. 100]:

$$f_\Xi(X) := \begin{cases} 1 - q_\Xi & \text{when } X = \{\emptyset\} \\ q_\Xi p_\Xi(\boldsymbol{x}) & \text{when } X = \{\boldsymbol{x}\} \\ 0 & \text{when } |X| \geq 2 \end{cases} \qquad , \qquad (4)$$

where q denotes the existence probability of a target and $p_\Xi(\boldsymbol{x})$ the kinematic probability density function.

Multi-Bernoulli (MB). For handling multiple targets, the Bernoulli distribution is generalised to the MB distribution. Where Bernoulli can handle a maximum of one target, MB can handle multiple targets in a total of s Bernoulli components each with a unique existence probability. The MBMDF can be written as follows [8, p. 101]:

$$f_\Xi(X) := \sum_{\sigma \subseteq 1:s} \prod_{i=1}^{s} a_\Xi^i \prod_{i=1}^{\xi} b_\Xi^{\sigma(i)},$$

$$a_\Xi^i := \left(1 - q_\Xi^i\right), \tag{5}$$

$$b_\Xi^{\sigma(i)} := \frac{q_\Xi^{\sigma(i)} p_\Xi^{\sigma(i)}(\boldsymbol{x}_i)}{1 - q_\Xi^{\sigma(i)}},$$

where a_Ξ^i and $b_\Xi^{\sigma(i)}$ are used for simplifying notations later in Sect. 3.3. The Bernoulli components of active targets are selected by a mapping σ from $\{1, \ldots \xi\}$ to $\{1, \ldots s\}$ where the total quantity of active targets becomes $|\sigma| = \xi$.

Special Case of Bernoulli and MB. If there is only a single Bernoulli component, then the Bernoulli distribution $f_\mathcal{B}(X)$ is a special case of the MB distribution $f_{\mathcal{MB}}(X)$:

$$f_\mathcal{B}(X) = f_{\mathcal{MB}}(X) \qquad \text{when } s = 1. \tag{6}$$

2.3 Csiszár Information Functionals

Csiszár information functionals are defined as [8, p. 154]:

$$\mathcal{I}_\mathcal{C}(f_A; f_B) := \int \mathcal{C}\left(\frac{f_A(X)}{f_B(X)}\right) f_B(X) \delta X, \tag{7}$$

where f_A and f_B are MDF posteriors for multi-object trackers. If $\mathcal{C}$ is a *convex kernel* then $\mathcal{I}_\mathcal{C}(f_A; f_B) \geq 0$ where equality occurs only if $f_A = f_B$ almost everywhere.

3 Hellinger Performance Metrics

A special case of Csiszár's information functionals can be derived by choosing the kernel $\mathcal{C}(x) = \frac{1}{2}(\sqrt{x} - 1)^2$, giving us a normalised Hellinger information functional that can be used to derive various Hellinger metrics [8, p. 155]:

$$\mathcal{I}_\mathcal{H}(f_A; f_B) = 1 - \int \sqrt{f_A(X) f_B(X)} \delta X. \tag{8}$$

We will begin by using this to derive the conventional Hellinger metric. This will then be generalised to consider the case of single-target existence, before we end the section with our most generic metric that handles the case for multi-target tracking.

3.1   Hellinger Distance for Gaussian Distributions

For Hellinger distances of single valued functions, the Hellinger functional becomes a normal Hellinger distance:

$$\mathcal{I}_\mathcal{H}(f_A;f_B) = \mathcal{I}_\mathcal{H}(p_A;p_B) = 1 - \int \sqrt{p_A(\boldsymbol{x})p_B(\boldsymbol{x})}dy. \tag{9}$$

where p_A and p_B are kinematic probability density functions for each respective dataset. If the distributions are in additional Gaussian, the term takes the special form [1, p. 6]:

$$\mathcal{I}_\mathcal{H}(\mathcal{N}_A;\mathcal{N}_B) = \sqrt{1 - d \times \exp\left\{-\frac{1}{8}NEES(\boldsymbol{x}_A,\boldsymbol{x}_B,\mathbf{D})\right\}},$$

$$d := \sqrt{\frac{\sqrt{|\mathbf{P}_A||\mathbf{P}_B|}}{|\mathbf{D}|}}, \tag{10}$$

$$\mathbf{D} := \frac{\mathbf{P}_A + \mathbf{P}_B}{2},$$

where d gives information about the co-variance difference and the exponential term of the bias, both between the value 0 and 1. The united covariance between the distributions is noted as $\mathbf{D}$. Note we use $NEES$ here to reuse notation, not to draw parallels to its other known properties in the tracking community.

3.2   Bernoulli Hellinger Distance for Gaussian Distributions

It can be shown that the Bernoulli case of the Hellinger functional can be expressed as:

$$\mathcal{I}_{B,\mathcal{H}}(f_A;f_B) = 1 - \int \sqrt{f_A(X)f_B(X)}dx$$
$$= 1 - \sqrt{q_A q_B} - \sqrt{(1-q_A)(1-q_B)} + \sqrt{q_A q_B}\mathcal{I}_\mathcal{H}. \tag{11}$$

where q_A and q_B are existence probabilities for the target existing in each respective datasets. If we set the existence probabilities to 1, most terms cancels out and we are left with the conventional Hellinger distance, i.e., Bernoulli Hellinger is a generalisation of Hellinger.

If the distributions are Gaussian, (10) can be used for an explicit solution for $\mathcal{I}_\mathcal{H}$. Otherwise, (9) must be handled either analytically or numerically for $\mathcal{I}_\mathcal{H}$

3.3   MB-Hellinger Distance for Gaussian Distributions

$$\mathcal{I}_{MB,\mathcal{H}}(f_A;f_B) = 1 - \int \sqrt{f_A(X)f_B(X)}\delta X.$$

In the MB case the MDF's are MB (5), where (3) expresses the integral form. The product of the two MDF's can be written as:

$$f_A(X)f_B(X) = \sum_{\sigma_A \subseteq 1:s_A} \prod_{i=1}^{s_A} a_A^i \prod_{i=1}^{\xi} b_A^{\sigma_A(i)} \sum_{\sigma_B \subseteq 1:s_B} \prod_{i=1}^{s_B} a_B^i \prod_{i=1}^{\xi} b_B^{\sigma_B(i)}$$

$$= \sum_{\sigma_A \subseteq 1:s_A} \sum_{\sigma_B \subseteq 1:s_B} \prod_{i=1}^{s_A} a_A^i \prod_{i=1}^{s_B} a_B^i \prod_{i=1}^{\xi} b_A^{\sigma_A(i)} b_B^{\sigma_B(i)},$$

Since a single MB is non zero only if the cardinality is less than or equal the amount of track instances, when combining two MB we get the following criteria: $|\sigma_A| - |\sigma_B| = \xi$, i.e we only need to sum the minimum number of track instances found in one of the datasets since rest will be zero. Given that the probability density functions are Gaussian, the last product can be written as follows:

$$b_A^{\sigma_A(i)} b_B^{\sigma_B(i)} = g_{A,B}\mathcal{N}(\boldsymbol{x}; \mu_A^{\sigma_A(i)}, \mathbf{P}_A^{\sigma_A(i)})\mathcal{N}(\boldsymbol{x}; \mu_B^{\sigma_B(i)}, \mathbf{P}_B^{\sigma_B(i)})$$

$$= g_{A,B}\mathcal{N}(\mu_A^{\sigma_A(i)}; \mu_B^{\sigma_B(i)}, \mathbf{P}_A^{\sigma_A(i)} + \mathbf{P}_B^{\sigma_B(i)})\mathcal{N}(\boldsymbol{x}; \boldsymbol{v}^i, \mathbf{C}^i),$$

where the terms are defined as:

$$g_{A,B} := \frac{q_A^{\sigma_A(i)} q_B^{\sigma_B(i)}}{\left(1 - q_A^{\sigma_A(i)}\right)\left(1 - q_B^{\sigma_B(i)}\right)},$$

$$\boldsymbol{v}^i := \mathbf{C}^i\left((\mathbf{P}_A^{\sigma_A(i)})^{-1}\mu_A^{\sigma_A(i)} + (\mathbf{P}_B^{\sigma_B(i)})^{-1}\mu_B^{\sigma_B(i)}\right)^{-1},$$

$$\mathbf{C}^i := \left((\mathbf{P}_A^{\sigma_A(i)})^{-1} + (\mathbf{P}_B^{\sigma_B(i)})^{-1}\right)^{-1}.$$

Finally, the products of the Gaussian densities can be concatenated as follows:

$$\prod_{i=1}^{\xi} \mathcal{N}(\boldsymbol{x}; \boldsymbol{v}^i, \mathbf{C}^i) = k_\xi \mathcal{N}(\boldsymbol{x}; \boldsymbol{u}, \mathbf{O}),$$

$$\boldsymbol{u} := \begin{bmatrix} \boldsymbol{v}^1 \\ \vdots \\ \boldsymbol{v}^\xi \end{bmatrix}, \mathbf{O} := \begin{bmatrix} \mathbf{C}^1 & & \\ & \ddots & \\ & & \mathbf{C}^\xi \end{bmatrix}, k_\xi := \frac{|\mathbf{O}|^{\frac{1}{2}}}{\prod_{i=1}^{\xi} |\mathbf{C}^i|^{\frac{1}{2}}}.$$

Importance Sampling. In comparison to Hellinger and the Bernoulli Hellinger metrics, the integral term in MB-Hellinger is not trivial to solve explicitly due to the square root of sums. Because of this we use importance sampling to approximate the integral. We choose our importance density to be the normalised version of the Gaussian mixture $f_A(X)f_B(X)$, with its co-variances inflated by more than 2 to compensate for the square root (we have used a value of 3.6). This gives us enough coverage of the sampling area to estimate the integral.

4   JIPDA Tracker

In this section we give a brief introduction to the JIPDA tracker used in this work as well as the sensor pipeline used to process lidar data.

4.1   Lidar Detection Pipeline

Sensor data from the lidar is natively supplied as a point cloud and requires multiple processing steps before it can be utilized by the tracker.

Land Filtering. Active sensors such as lidar will, if in range, yield positive returns from non-target entities such as land and buildings. If these detections are used directly in the tracker without processing they might induce a large amount of false tracks. To combat this, map based filtering is employed to remove unwanted lidar returns. Based on data from the Norwegian Mapping Authority, a binary occupancy grid is generated for the operating area. The lidar point cloud is then projected onto this map and any point falling within a land cell is removed.

Clustering. Another issue with lidar sensor data is that the sensor resolution is high enough to yield multiple returns from a single target. This violates the assumption that only one measurement originates from each target that JIPDA makes in the data association process. To mitigate this issue a single-link hierarchical clustering method [17] is employed which merges any point within a specified distance threshold into a single cluster. The center of this cluster is then assumed to be the true detection.

4.2   Tracker Outline

The tracker used in this work is a special case of the VIMMJIPDA [5] using only a single constant velocity (CV) model. In continuous-time this model is described by

$$\dot{x} := \mathbf{A}x + \mathbf{G}n \tag{12}$$

with x as the current target state given by $x = \begin{bmatrix} x_1 & x_2 & x_3 & x_4 \end{bmatrix}^{\mathrm{T}}$ where x_1 and x_2 denote the north and east position while x_3 and x_4 are the corresponding velocities. The process noise n models target acceleration and is assumed to be white with diagonal covariance. The matrices $\mathbf{A}$ and $\mathbf{G}$ are defined as

$$\mathbf{A} := \begin{bmatrix} 0 & 0 & 1 & 0 \\ 0 & 0 & 0 & 1 \\ 0 & 0 & 0 & 0 \\ 0 & 0 & 0 & 0 \end{bmatrix} \qquad \mathbf{G} := \begin{bmatrix} 0 & 0 \\ 0 & 0 \\ 1 & 0 \\ 0 & 1 \end{bmatrix} \tag{13}$$

which in discrete form result in the model

$$x_k := \mathbf{F}x_{k-1} + v_k \qquad v_k \sim \mathcal{N}(\mathbf{0}, \mathbf{Q}_k) \tag{14}$$

where $\mathbf{F}$ is the discrete state transition matrix and v_k the discretized process noise.

For each return the lidar measures the range of the object using time-of-flight as well as the direction of the return signal. By discarding height information this results in a sensor model using polar coordinates given by

$$f_z(\boldsymbol{x}_k) := \begin{bmatrix} \sqrt{x_1^2 + x_2^2} \\ \arctan(x_2/x_1) \end{bmatrix} + w_k \qquad w_k \sim \mathcal{N}(\mathbf{0}, \mathbf{R}) \qquad (15)$$

where f_z is the measurement function and w_k the sensor noise described by the covariance matrix $\mathbf{R}$. Due to non-linearities in the measurement function, this would usually require an extended Kalman filter (EKF). However, by projecting the measurements into Cartesian coordinates [17] we can use the linear measurement model

$$f_z(\boldsymbol{x}_k) = \begin{bmatrix} x_1 \\ x_2 \end{bmatrix} + w_k \qquad w_k \sim \mathcal{N}(\mathbf{0}, \mathbf{JRJ}^{\mathrm{T}}) \qquad (16)$$

where $\mathbf{J}$ is the Jacobian of the polar to Cartesian conversion and $\mathbf{R}$ the measurement noise in polar coordinates.

5 Datasets

The datasets used in this paper comes from experiments done in [15] where an autonomous ferry named milliAmpere was used as a research platform to record sensor data [4]. From this a synthetically reconstructed dataset was also made using the Gemini platform [14]. In this section we go through a brief description of the datasets from this study.

5.1 Setup

MilliAmpere was setup as *ownship* consisting of multiple exteroceptive sensors such as electro optical and infrared cameras as well as radar and lidar. In addition, the ferry used a highly accurate navigation system based on Real-Time Kinematic GPS with sub-metre level position accuracy. To generate scenarios of multi-target interest, multiple targets equipped with GPS sensors for ground truth recording were used. Target 1, Havfruen, was used as a medium sized leisure craft capable of high speeds and rapid maneuvers. Target 2, Finn, functioned as a small leisure craft slower and less maneuverable than Havfruen. Target boats and ownship can be seen in Fig. 3b.

Fig. 2. Images from the visual analysis of the synthetic reconstruction done in [15]. Geometric and positional reconstruction of targets is intact, but discrepancies of the city model can be seen from e.g the missing red building. (Color figure online)

5.2   Ground Truth Recording

Positional data of target vessels and ownship were recorded using different receivers as described in Table 1. Each vessel had 2 receivers in order to validate position, increase ground truth accuracy, and give a heading estimate later used by Gemini to generate correct ship orientations.

Table 1. GNSS recievers.

Ship	GNSS Receiver	Accuracy
milliAmpere	Hemisphere Vector VS330	1–10 cm
Havfruen	ZED-F9P	1 cm
Finn	Garmin eTrex 10	1 m

5.3   Scenarios

In the original study, a total of 9 scenario recordings was created. We chose to focus on scenario 8 with the target vessels following each other (Fig. 3a). A drone footage of the scenario can be seen in Fig. 3b that was recorded at Ravnkloa in the city of Trondheim.

5.4   Lidar

The experiment used a Velodyne VLP-16 puck that was later reconstructed synthetically using Gemini's lidar sensor [14] with improved beam modelling using among others a spherical projection filter [15, p. 40]. To get suitable reconstruction of the real lidar data, 3D models of Trondheim city and participating target boats where used in conjunction with recorded ground truth data. The original data contained both camera and lidar data, while our analysis choose to use lidar only for simplicity. Instead the camera data was used as a visual confirmation to see the synthetic reconstruction besides real images from the ownship perspective (Fig. 2).

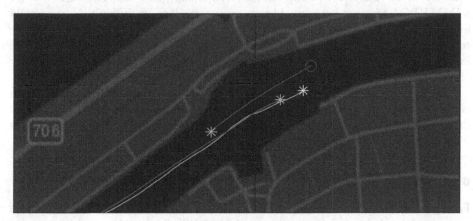

(a) Paths of the attending boats starting from locations marked with a circle and ending with stars. Illustration is taken from [15]

(b) Scenario setup in the operating environment with the image facing south. Photo: Mikael Sætereid / Fosen innovasjon

Fig. 3. Illustrations of scenario 8. The attending boats Havfruen, Finn and milliAmpere (ownship) are coloured as red, green and blue respectively in each illustration. (Color figure online)

6   Evaluation

Our intention is to study effects that contribute to the Hellinger metrics derived in Sect. 3, and what relations they have to each other.

Previous analysis of the dataset showed the ground truth for the ownship velocity to be noisy [15, p. 92]. Moreover, getting good velocity estimates for VIMMJIPDA trackers have in addition proven itself to be difficult [5], especially for targets with large extensions. The synthetic data also have discrepancies due to incomplete 3D models as seen earlier in Fig. 2. To lessen the influence of these known effects, we choose to run the Hellinger metrics on tracks in near proximity of the target vessels and disregard the velocity estimates from the tracker.

We have chosen to study the remaining effects by comparing the metrics in context of how tracks overlap in position when generated by real and synthetic data (Fig. 4). Each track are here represented as a covariance ellipse based of a 95% confidence interval from the Gaussian distribution it represents (1).

6.1   Track Association

For Hellinger and Bernoulli Hellinger a validation gate with radius 5m centered at ground truth is used for track association (Fig. 4). Tracks outside the gate are discriminated, while if more than one track from a dataset is present in the gate, the closest estimate to ground truth is chosen. For the MB-Hellinger, no association method is required since each track is compared to each other weighted by their existence probability. As a result, from Table 2 we have a low MB-Hellinger distance in the first case while for Hellinger and Bernoulli Hellinger the distances are high at the same time instances since there's no pair of tracks inside their gates. Furthermore, the MB-Hellinger is always defined since it does not need validation gates that risks being empty as happens with Finn in two cases.

6.2   False Tracks

False tracks from the datasets can be seen in Fig. 4 as ellipses without a real or synthetic counterpart. Due to their high existence probabilities we get a large MB-Hellinger distance. By manually downweighting the existence probabilities of these tracks, we see in Fig. 4c a large effect when comparing the normal and weighted MB-Hellinger.

6.3   Bernoulli Hellinger a Special Case of MB-Hellinger

In (11) we showed that the Hellinger is a special case of the Bernoulli Hellinger. We also stated in Sect. 2.2 to the Bernoulli Hellinger being a special case of MB-Hellinger. In Fig. 4c we have a situation with Havfruen where we can see tendencies of this relationship. Also the succeeding dip for Finn in the same figure can be seen in the MB-Hellinger metric as well. It is worth noting that in these occasions the MB-Hellinger is always bigger than Bernoulli, which can be explained by MB evaluating all tracks instead of specific tracks as with the other metrics. This shows how difficult it is for MB-Hellinger to be equal to Bernoulli Hellinger in comparison to Hellinger being equal to Bernoulli Hellinger as seen in the metric plots for either Havfruen or Finn in Fig. 4.

Table 2. Metric results for normal (N) and weighted (W) MB-Hellinger, Bernoulli-Hellinger (B-H) and Hellinger (H) from cases shown in Fig. 4

Case	MB-Hellinger		Havfruen		Finn	
	N	W	H	B-H	H	B-H
a	0.11	0.11	1.00	1.00	N/A	N/A
b	0.92	0.92	1.00	1.00	N/A	N/A
c	1.00	0.10	0.44	0.44	1.00	1.00

7 Discussion

In this paper we have been focusing on analysing results from a real and synthetic lidar sensor. It is, however, worth pointing out that because of how the Bayesian filter works, the method presented here can be used for all sensor types given there is a detection model (e.g. as in Sect. 4.1), and models on how to handle the detections in the filter (e.g. as in Sect. 4.2). This have been previously demonstrated in [15] where the impact of individual sensors (such as lidars and cameras) on the tracker could be quantified using the metric.

A big difference between single versus multi distribution metrics is the way track association between the datasets are handled. From Fig. 4a we can see that increasing the validation gates slightly would have allowed Hellinger and Bernoulli-Hellinger to give a measure on Havfruen. This measure would likely have been closer to that of MB-Hellinger rather than 1. Similarly, the gates also causes trouble in several cases for Finn, where the metric becomes undefined when the gates are empty (Table 2). A solution could be to say empty gates gives a metric value of 0, but given that there might be tracks just outside the gate as we see in Fig. 4b, moreover that a low metric value would bias the results to seem better from the lack of track data, the proper way of handling an empty gate becomes questionable. In comparison to dealing with gates, this is a task easier handled by MB's checking and weighting each tracks permutation. However, if downgrading of existence probabilities for false tracks is necessary, one would need to argue why this tuning is needed for comparing datasets. One reason could be if the tracker is overconfident on false tracks stemming from differences such as water reflections. This would be both computationally demanding to simulate and to properly reconstruct, while likely being a non crucial difference between synthetic and real data for autonomy purposes.

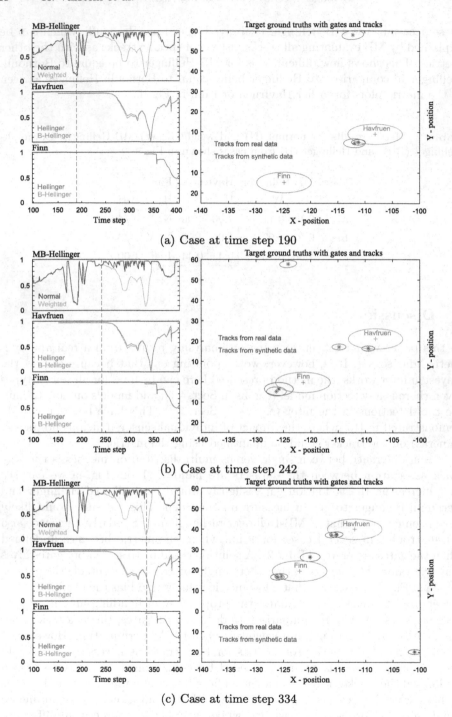

Fig. 4. Cases of interest. Left: Distances for single and multi-target Hellinger metrics. Right: covariance plot for tracks with ground truth and validation gates. (Color figure online)

The close similarity of Bernoulli-Hellinger and Hellinger for both Finn and Havfruen in Fig. 4 and the fact that this only happens when the existence probabilities in both datasets are close to 1 (Sect. 3.2), shows that the JIPDA is overconfident on tracks close to the targets. Furthermore, the false tracks in Fig. 4c contribute 0.9 to the metric when looking at the difference between the normal and weighted MB-Hellinger in Table 2. This shows how much false tracks impacts the MB-Hellinger metric when dealing with an overconfident JIPDA. If we argue that the situation depicted in Fig. 4c should have resulted in a lower metric value, the Hellinger metric might be to strict in comparison to other metric candidates suited for the Csiszár Information Functional.

False tracks is not the only discrepancy we have between the datasets. Even after removing these and the presumed sub-optimal velocity estimates, there is still fairly high metric values with huge spread in range over time. These differences could range from transformation errors due to sensor mountings to environmental reproduction discrepancies as seen in Fig. 2 that have a substantial enough effect on the tracker. More elaborate visualisation techniques are needed to see metrics, sensor data and the situational awareness picture layered on top of each other or being interchanged to make further analysis on this.

What might be of benefit in this regard is the ability to do single target analysis such as Hellinger and Bernoulli Hellinger in contrary to the MB-Hellinger. For judging sensor fidelity where a complete environment reconstruction is not possible, studying single targets with proper ground truth and 3D models might be easier to do and quantify. MB-Hellinger on the other hand takes a more global approach of measuring everything found in a specified area, potentially including unfortunate discrepancies as seen in the missing building in Fig. 2. The land filtering done as a preprocessing step in the JIPDA pipeline can accommodate for portions of this, but in uncontrolled environments where autonomy operates, even a bird which have not been accommodated for could show up as a false track not seen in the simulated dataset. If the tracker is over confident on these tracks, the result will be high MB-Hellinger distances which is the tendency seen in Fig. 4. On the other hand, if the goal of the metric is to measure the complete reprodusability of an experiment including that of false tracks, this may still be of benefit. Otherwise for purposes concerning sensor modeling, MB-Hellinger would need a better method for discriminating the unintended tracks in the environment.

8   Conclusion

In this paper we have shown the use of single-target and multi-target Hellinger metrics for quantifying the performance difference of a multi-target tracker when subjected to real and synthetically reconstructed data. We have demonstrated how the Hellinger distance can be used in various ways to judge single target as well as multi-target comparisons, their relationship to each other in addition to their various pros and cons in analysis work. From this the paper have contributed with a method of evaluating the MB-Hellinger by means of importance sampling. In addition we have presented results from a use case where the metric is used for comparing real and simulated data created with respect to validating SITAW systems. Further work includes more sophisticated visualisation tools to be able to explain and analyse the remaining Hellinger distance obtained in the results. Due to the close dependency on a tracker for establishing the metrics in the first place, an interesting study would also be to see how well the metrics would perform as an alternative to existing validation metrics such as COSPA and OSPA. In this work exploring other distances such as the Kullback-Leibler in Csiszár's information functionals and doing a sensitivity analysis of existence would be in place.

Acknowledgment. This work was supported in part by the Research Council of Norway through Projects 223254, 331921 and 309230, and by NTNU through the Autoferry project.

References

1. Abou-Moustafa, K.T., Torre, F.D.L., Ferrie, F.P.: Designing a metric for the difference between Gaussian densities. In: Angeles, J., Boulet, B., Clark, J.J., Kövecses, J., Siddiqi, K. (eds.) Brain, Body and Machine. AINSC, vol. 83, pp. 57–70. Springer, Cham (2010). https://doi.org/10.1007/978-3-642-16259-6_5
2. Acuna, D., Zhang, G., Law, M.T., Fidler, S.: f-domain adversarial learning: theory and algorithms. In: Proceedings of the 38th International Conference on Machine Learning. PMLR, vol. 139, pp. 66–75 (2021). https://doi.org/10.48550/arXiv.2106.11344
3. Bar-Shalom, Y., Tse, E.: Tracking in a cluttered environment with probabilistic data association. Automatica **11**(5) (1975). https://doi.org/10.1016/0005-1098(75)90021-7
4. Brekke, E.F., Eide, E., Eriksen, B.O.H., et al.: milliAmpere: an Autonomous Ferry Prototype. J. Phys.: Conf. Ser. **2311**(1) (2022). https://doi.org/10.1088/1742-6596/2311/1/012029
5. Brekke, E.F., Hem, A.G., Tokle, L.C.N.: Multitarget tracking with multiple models and visibility: derivation and verification on maritime radar data. IEEE J. Oceanic Eng. **46**(4) (2021). https://doi.org/10.1109/JOE.2021.3081174
6. Deitke, M., Han, W., Herrasti, A., et al.: RoboTHOR: an open simulation-to-real embodied AI platform. In: Proceedings of the IEEE/CVF Conference on Computer Vision and Pattern Recognition, pp. 3161–3171 (2020). https://doi.org/10.1109/CVPR42600.2020.00323
7. Dosovitskiy, A., Ros, G., Codevilla, F., Lopez, A., et al.: CARLA: an open urban driving simulator. In: Proceedings of the 1st Annual Conference on Robot Learning. PMLR, vol. 78, pp. 1–16 (2017). https://doi.org/10.48550/arXiv.1711.03938
8. Mahler, R.P.S.: Advances in Statistical Multisource-Multitarget Information Fusion. Artech House (2014)
9. Musicki, D., Evans, R., Stankovic, S.: Integrated Probabilistic Data Association (IPDA). In: The 31st IEEE Conference on Decision and Control. vol. 4, pp. 3796–3798 (1992). https://doi.org/10.1109/CDC.1992.370951
10. Musicki, D., Evans, R.: Joint integrated probabilistic data association: JIPDA. IEEE Trans. Aerosp. Electron. Syst. **40**(3) (2004). https://doi.org/10.1109/TAES.2004.1337482

11. Richter, S.R., AlHaija, H.A., Koltun, V.: Enhancing Photorealism Enhancement. arXiv (2021). https://doi.org/10.48550/ARXIV.2105.04619. Preprint
12. Shah, S., Dey, D., Lovett, C., et al.: AirSim: high-fidelity visual and physical simulation for autonomous vehicles. In: Field and Service Robotics. SPAR, vol. 1, pp. 621–635 (2018). https://doi.org/10.1007/978-3-319-67361-5_40
13. Tobin, J., Fong, R., Ray, A., et al.: Domain Randomization for Transferring Deep Neural Networks from Simulation to the Real World. In: IEEE/RSJ International Conference on Intelligent Robots and Systems, pp. 23–30 (2017). https://doi.org/10.1109/IROS.2017.8202133
14. Vasstein, K., Brekke, E.F., Mester, R., et al.: Autoferry Gemini: a real-time simulation platform for electromagnetic radiation sensors on autonomous ships. In: IOP Conference Series: Materials Science and Engineering, vol. 929 (2020). https://doi.org/10.1088/1757-899x/929/1/012032
15. Vasstein, K.: A high fidelity digital twin framework for testing exteroceptive perception of autonomous vessels. Master's thesis, NTNU (2021). https://hdl.handle.net/11250/2781031
16. Williams, J.: Marginal multi-Bernoulli filters: RFS derivation of MHT, JIPDA, and association-based MeMBer. IEEE Trans. Aerosp. Electron. Syst. 51(3) (2015). https://doi.org/10.1109/TAES.2015.130550
17. Wilthil, E.F., Flåten, A.L., Brekke, E.F.: A target tracking system for ASV collision avoidance based on the PDAF. In: Fossen, T.I., Pettersen, K.Y., Nijmeijer, H. (eds.) Sensing and Control for Autonomous Vehicles. LNCIS, vol. 474, pp. 269–288. Springer, Cham (2017). https://doi.org/10.1007/978-3-319-55372-6_13
18. Zajic, T., Mahler, R.P.S.: Practical information-based data fusion performance evaluation. In: Proceedings of Signal Processing, Sensor Fusion, and Target Recognition VIII, vol. 3720, pp. 92–103 (1999). https://doi.org/10.1117/12.357148
19. Zhu, J.Y., Park, T., Isola, P., et al.: Unpaired image-to-image translation using cycle-consistent adversarial networks. In: IEEE International Conference on Computer Vision, pp. 2242–2251 (2017). https://doi.org/10.1109/ICCV.2017.244

A Metaheuristic Approach for Inspection and Reconnaissance of Organized Areas

David Zahradka[1,2]([envelope]) [ORCID], Jan Mikula[1,2] [ORCID], and Miroslav Kulich[2] [ORCID]

[1] Department of Cybernetics, Czech Technical University in Prague,
Prague, Czech Republic
{david.zahradka,jan.mikula}@cvut.cz
[2] Czech Institute of Informatics, Robotics and Cybernetics,
Czech Technical University in Prague, Prague, Czech Republic
kulich@cvut.cz

Abstract. In this paper, we present a metaheuristic approach for path planning for area surveillance and inspection using unmanned aerial vehicles. The focus is on organized areas, such as city streets or storage zones. We exploit the row-like spatial organization of these scenarios and formulate the problem as a Distance-Constrained Rural Postman Problem. We represent the area of interest as a graph, where edges correspond to surveillance targets, such as city streets or rows of field storage areas, and vertices to their entry and exit points. The subtour length constraints represent the limited flight time of unmanned aerial vehicles. The goal is then to traverse every target edge exactly once, resulting in paths inspecting the area of interest entirely. We propose a Greedy Randomized Adaptive Search Procedure metaheuristic as a solution to this problem. Furthermore, we show that the same problem formulation and metaheuristic can be used for deep inspection of specific locations identified for further inspection in the previous step.

Keywords: optimization · surveillance · inspection · routing

1 Introduction

Consider a situation where it is necessary to conduct reconnaissance of an area to detect potential dangers in, e.g., a city or a field storage. In other words, perform a scan of the whole area to find locations with anomalous readings.

Unmanned Aerial Vehicles (UAVs) are well suited for such tasks and have been utilized for such purposes [19]. Battery-powered UAVs are especially good candidates due to their portability and cost. However, they have very limited flight time, and efficient planning is therefore required to minimize the required length of such mission.

Due to the limited battery capacity, it is often not possible to perform a thorough scan of every location of interest, especially in large areas. Therefore, the reconnaissance task can be split into:

J. Mazal et al. (Eds.): MESAS 2022, LNCS 13866, pp. 44–63, 2023.
https://doi.org/10.1007/978-3-031-31268-7_3

- brief **surveillance scanning** to identify locations exhibiting anomalous readings, and second,
- **inspection**, in which deeper scans are performed, but only for a subset of all locations identified as anomalous during surveillance.

Some areas, such as cities or storage zones, are often organized in grid-like structures, with distinct line segments corresponding to rows of building blocks or storage units, separated by intersecting avenues or pathways. An intuitive way to plan the surveillance mission for UAVs in these organized areas is to plan a path in a zig-zag manner. The UAV would fly over one whole segment and then continue with the closest unvisited one, with occasional trips to the recharging depot to recharge batteries. During the surveillance mission, quicker sensory scans are performed to search for anomalous locations, such as locations with high readings on a thermal camera. Since the mission can cover a large area, the UAV should not stop at each target to avoid the risk of significantly prolonging the mission. These scans then have to be brief, since the UAV is moving. The locations with anomalous readings are then stored in memory, and after finishing surveillance, an inspection mission is planned so that every discovered anomalous location is thoroughly inspected.

This optimization problem can be formulated in many ways as the multi-goal path planning problem. An example of that is the widely studied Vehicle Routing Problem (VRP) [20] and its many flavors, such as the Electric VRP [11] and the Capacitated VRP [18]. The Orienteering Problem (OP) family can also be used to some extent. However, as the OP allows solutions that do not contain all locations of interest, it might not be best suited for the task. Another way of formulating the task is to use the Generalized Traveling Salesman Problem (GTSP) [10], in which the goal is to visit all sets of vertices. This translates to visiting exactly one vertex from each set. The closest problem formulation is the Arc Routing Problem (ARP) [5], where all edges of a graph need to be visited, and its generalization, the Rural Postman Problem (RPP) [7], where the goal is to visit a specific subset of edges. However, none of the mentioned problem formulations accurately describe the problem at hand.

Therefore, we utilize the grid-like geometric organization of the areas to propose the Distance-Constrained Rural Postman Problem (RPP-DC) problem formulation for the surveillance and inspection task with a single UAV. We create a graph over the area of interest, where vertices are the endpoints of the line segments of interest, e.g., ends of the building blocks or intersections at the ends of a street, and edges between these vertices are the line segments themselves. These edges must be included in every feasible solution. On top of these mandatory edges, additional edges are added so that the graph is fully connected. The vehicle can use these for traversal, but they are optional.

This allows exploiting the geometric row-like layout of the organized areas to obtain good quality solutions faster. Furthermore, the same problem formulation can be used both for surveillance and inspection. The only difference is that in surveillance, the segments generally have a nonzero length, while in inspection, their two endpoints overlap. Figure 1 shows an example of the usage of RPP-DC

for both surveillance and inspection. Note that for both surveillance, shown in
Fig. 1b and inspection in Fig. 1c, the same problem formulation is used.

Furthermore, we present a set of heuristic and metaheuristic solvers able to
solve the RPP-DC, compare them and present an analysis of the effect of their
internal variables on their performance.

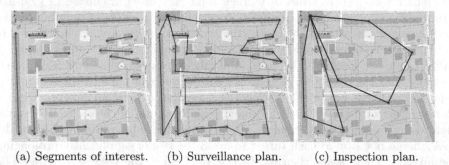

(a) Segments of interest.   (b) Surveillance plan.   (c) Inspection plan.

Fig. 1. City surveillance and inspection planning example. Blue lines represent segments of interest, blue dots represent segment endpoints, red and orange cycles are two
subtours. Recharging depot on the top left. Map from Open Street Map [16] (Color
figure online).

2   Related Works

From the TSP family of problem formulations, the Multiple Traveling Salesman Problem (MTSP) can be used for path planning for UAVs with multiple
subtours, which can be used to model the limited battery capacity. However,
in general, the number of subtours is specified as an input parameter and not
decided ad-hoc. The requirement to traverse a whole segment at once can be
modeled using GTSP [10], also known as the Set TSP. In the GTSP, each vertex belongs to some set, and it is necessary to visit only one vertex from each
set. By representing the segments of interest as a set of two vertices, each for
one direction of traversal, and by assigning the vertices to one set, it is possible to eliminate dual surveillance of the same segment. A combination of the
aforementioned, the Multi-Tour Set TSP, presented in [14], is used to solve the
problem of Power Transmission Line inspection, which is closely related to the
presented surveillance and inspection problem. The proposed problem formulation even models limited battery capacity for the determination of the number
of subtours. In [14], a solution is also presented using the Greedy Randomized
Adaptive Search Procedure (GRASP).

The reward-collecting OP family is also widely used for UAV planning due
to its ability to model the limited flight time or distance of UAVs. An example
could be the Dubins OP [17], which has been successfully used for UAV path
planning. While the OP is for single tours, multiple tours can be planned using
the Team OP [3]. However, since the goal is to maximize reward collected by

visiting locations of interest within some flight time or distance constraint, it is possible to obtain solutions that do not visit every location of interest.

The VRP family is a generalization of the TSP. In its basic definition, VRP is equal to the MTSP. Its generalization, the Capacitated VRP (CVRP), introduces a capacity limit for the subtours, which limits the maximum number of vertices visited before returning to the starting depot. The CVRP has been solved using many heuristics, such as Variable Neighborhood Search [1] and a variation of GRASP [12]. The capacity can also be used as a distance constraint by assigning some cost to the edges of the graph instead of the vertices. Another generalization of the VRP, called the Electric VRP (EVRP), introduces a distance constraint by limiting the distance the electric vehicle is able to drive before stopping to recharge its batteries in one of multiple recharging stations. The EVRP is solved, for example, using GRASP [21].

Another problem family which is related to planning for reconnaissance is coverage planning, where the goal is to find a path visiting every point in an area of interest. A survey on coverage planning for UAVs is conducted in [2]. A related problem to coverage planning is the Watchman Routing Problem (WRP) [15], in which, given a line-of-sight function, the goal is to find a path such that the whole area is observed. However, while these techniques can be used for surveillance planning, full coverage is not necessary for surveillance of organized areas, as we can have previous knowledge of what is to be the object of surveillance, e.g., building blocks, while parking lots might not be interesting and are, therefore, left out to reduce complexity.

The final and perhaps the closest problem formulation to the studied problem is the ARP [5]. In the ARP, the goal is to find such a path in a graph that it visits all arcs (edges) of a graph, in contrast to visiting vertices in TSP. If only a subset of the graph's edges needs to be visited, the problem is known as the RPP [7]. As we are interested in reconnaissance for areas with row-like features, this problem formulation is applicable to the problem at hand by representing the row-like objects of interest as edges in a graph. However, RPP does not consider tour length limits, representing the battery capacity limit and an extension is, therefore, necessary.

Extending the RPP with tour length limits, and, therefore, considering multiple tours, results in a very similar problem formulation as the Multi-Tour Set TSP [14]. The main difference is that in Multi-Tour Set TSP, the act of surveying or inspecting a segment of interest is encoded by visiting a vertex representing a pylon. This can be directly translated to traversing an edge representing the segment of interest itself (the power transmission line), and vice versa. Therefore, both these problem formulations are applicable and interchangeable. However, if the segments of interest are represented as edges, it is a more straightforward and direct representation of the problem at hand. Consider an edge belonging to two vertices: instead of grouping the vertices together into a set, and visiting one of the vertices then represents traversing the edge, simply requiring the edge to be traversed more closely represents the act of surveillance and inspection of the segment. For this reason, we consider the RPP with tour length limits as a better representation of the problem. Additionally, in the Set TSP problem family, the goal in general is to visit a subset of vertices while visiting all sets, whereas in the problem of surveillance and inspection, the goal is to visit all locations of interest. Therefore, the RPP with tour length limits, where the goal is to traverse all selected edges, is a better classification of the problem.

3   RPP-DC Problem Formulation

The organized environment can be represented as a tuple (G_s, d_s, E_c, v_0, C), where $G_s = (V_s, E_s)$ is a connected undirected *spatial* graph with vertices $V = \{0, 1, \ldots, n-1\}$, $d_s : E \to \mathbb{R}$ represents the costs of edges E_s, e.g., corresponding to Euclidean distance. Then, $E_c \subset E_s$ is a set of target edges that need to be visited. These directly correspond to the so-called line segments of interest in the surveyed area, such as building blocks. Vertex $v_0 \in V_s$ is the recharging depot, and $C \in \mathbb{R}$ is the capacity of the vehicle. Since the vertex labeling is arbitrary, we can set $v_0 = 0$ without a loss of generality.

Since G_s is not necessarily complete, we create an undirected *abstract* graph $G_a = (V_a, E_a)$ where $V_a \subset V_s$ are the endpoints of each $e \in E_c$ and v_0, $E_c \subset E_a$ and $e \in E_a \setminus E_c$ are generated so that G_a is complete. The new edges correspond to the shortest paths between V_a in G_s. The edge costs $d_a : E \to \mathbb{R}$ are obtained by solving All Pairs Shortest Paths while $d_a^e = d_s^e; \forall e \in E_c$. Thus we obtain an RPP-DC representation of the organized environment as a tuple (G_a, d_a, E_c, v_0, C). Note that under some circumstances, G_a can be equal to G_s.

As all edges $e \in E_a$ are paths in the original connected G_s, all solutions obtained on G_a can be translated back. By constructing the complete graph G_a, we are able to represent even areas with, for example, streets or corridors with dead ends or areas with no-fly zones, where an edge between two vertices in G_s might not exist but a path does. The edges $e \in E_a \setminus E_c$, therefore, represent means of travel over the area. In contrast to E_c, traversing these edges is optional.

Each $e \in E_a$ can be entered from either of its endpoints, and the UAV must leave through the other one. The recharging depot v_0 represents the location where the UAV can safely land to recharge its battery or have it replaced with a new one by an operator. Only one v_0 exists. The capacity C represents the maximum distance the UAV can travel with a fully charged battery before the battery is depleted and recharging or battery swapping is required. This can only be done at the recharging depot v_0.

The RPP-DC solution consists of a set of subtours (Fig. 2). Each subtour is an ordered sequence of $e \in E_a$: $\langle e_0, e_1, \ldots, e_0 \rangle$, where e_0 represents the recharging station, and each pair of consecutive edges in the subtour $\{e_{j-1}, e_j\}$ must have a common vertex. The goal is then to find the shortest set of subtours, each of length $d_a^i < C$ where d_a^i is the length of subtour i, that includes every E_c exactly once and each subtour starts and ends at v_0. For consistency, visiting the recharging depot v_0 means traversing a virtual zero-length edge e_0 that starts and ends at the location of v_0.

The criterion to minimize is the total cost L:

$$L = \sum_i^n \sum_j^{m_i} d_a^{i,j} \tag{1}$$

where n is the number of subtours, m_i is the number of edges in subtour i and $d_a^{i,j}$ is the cost of edge of G_a at position j in subtour i. As we consider a single UAV executing all subtours sequentially, interactions between different subtours are not necessary to resolve.

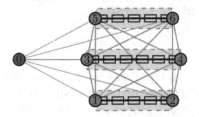 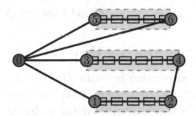

(a) An example RPP-DC graph G_a.   (b) An example RPP-DC solution on G_a.

Fig. 2. RPP-DC illustrations. Green is the recharging depot v_0, blue are the endpoints of edges E_c. In the example graph G_a (left), red are the edges E_c and yellow are all other edges of the fully connected graph. In the example solution (right), red is the resulting path that traverses every E_c. (Color figure online)

3.1 Surveillance

In the context of the RPP-DC, surveillance means traversing through all segments of interest in the designated area. This means traversing all edges E_c of the graph. In contrast to a coverage problem, we want to visit only specific interesting parts of the area, such as all blocks in a city district. During surveillance, a brief scan of these locations is conducted during the traversal in search of anomalous readings, such as high heat signatures. Specific locations with anomalous readings are then marked and thoroughly investigated during the inspection phase.

3.2 Inspection

The problem of inspection in RPP-DC is to visit all locations marked for inspection during surveillance to perform a more thorough scan. These can be, for example, vehicles or specific buildings in the city streets that were identified during surveillance, such as buildings featuring an unusually high heat signature. As these are specific locations, they do not require the UAV to move through them but to hover around to collect data. Inspection can be easily formulated as the RPP-DC by representing the locations as virtual edges with two equal endpoints and with cost representing the time needed to collect the necessary data.

4   Proposed Solvers

In this Section, the proposed solvers are presented and explained. First, it is necessary to generate an initial solution. In Sect. 4.1, we propose two different approaches: a greedy and a geometric constructive procedure. Then, if the solution is good enough, it can be kept as-is or further optimized using optimization heuristics. A combination of multiple heuristics is then known as a metaheuristic. In Sect. 4.2, we present two optimization strategies to improve the initial solution provided by constructive heuristics. The presented metaheuristics are the Variable Neighborhood Descent (VND) [13] and GRASP [8].

4.1   Constructive Heuristics

The constructive heuristics take an instance as an input and produce a feasible solution. We implement variations on the Greedy Constructive Procedure (GCP) and a constructive procedure utilizing the geometric properties of the problem.

Greedy Constructive Procedure. The GCP is a standard heuristic that iterates through all unassigned edges and adds the one resulting in the lowest cost increase into the solution, ensuring that there is always enough battery capacity to return back to the depot.

This is done in the following manner: The procedure starts with an infeasible solution containing only the virtual depot edge e_0. Then, it iterates over all edges not yet included in the solution and forms a list of closest neighbors for each one of them. The proximity is evaluated simply as Euclidean distance. The closest unvisited neighbor is selected and added to the solution. If no edge can be added without violating the capacity constraint, e_0 is added, and the process begins again. The procedure ends when the solution is feasible, meaning that all edges from E_c are included and at no point is the capacity constraint violated. We also use a stochastic variant, called the Randomized GCP, where instead of always selecting the closest neighbor, we form a candidate list of closest neighboring edges and select a random one among them.

Geometric Constructive Procedure. An intuitive solution to the RPP-DC in a grid-like organized area is to plan a path row-by-row. Such planning is called Boustrophedon planning, and it has been used for path planning for surveillance [4]. The geometric heuristic utilizes the same approach to generate a feasible solution. Note that this approach is only viable if G_s and G_a are equal or at least very similar. If there are many edges in G_a that represent longer paths in G_s due to, e.g., no-fly zones, this procedure can not take this into account and the quality of its solutions will decrease. An example can be two rows, which are very close together, but they are separated by a no-fly zone, for example because of the presence of a power transmission line. In such case, the procedure would try to add both rows into a single subtour, since they are close, even though there might be a long detour necessary to travel between them.

First, we find the average orientation of the rows and use it to define the x-axis. Then, we order the row segments using $y_{max}^e = max(y_1^e, y_2^e)$, where $y_{1,2}^e$ are the y coordinates of the endpoints of segment e. Afterward, given a distance threshold d_t, the following is repeated: We obtain e_0 as the first unassigned segment from the ordered list and create a new group. For this group, we calculate the distance threshold on y axis as $y_{group} = y_{max}^{e_0} - d_t$. Then, we iterate through the ordered list of segments and add segment e_i into the group if $y_{max}^{e_i} \geq y_{group}$. If $y_{max}^{e_i} < y_{group}$, we create a new group and continue the process with $e_0 \leftarrow e_i$. This is repeated until all segments are assigned to a group.

In these groups, we order the segments similar to the previous step based on the x coordinates of their endpoints. Each odd group is ordered in reverse. Then, based on this ordering, we connect the segments in the group and connect groups between each other, forming a zig-zag pattern. This gives us a path through all edges in E_c. To find the solution for the RPP-DC, we first add the recharging depot v_0 and then connect to the path via the closest unvisited vertex. Feasibility is ensured by checking whether we can return to the depot from the next vertex in the path within capacity limit C. If not, a trip to the depot is inserted, and the process is repeated until all edges E_c are visited.

4.2 Optimization-Based Metaheuristics

The optimization heuristics take an initial, feasible solution as input and attempt to optimize the initial solution by performing small changes. We propose two optimization algorithms, VND and GRASP, for the RPP-DC.

Variable Neighborhood Descent. The VND is a local search method first proposed as a deterministic variant of the Variable Neighborhood Search, which differs by not producing random solutions from the current solution's neighborhoods, but rather improving solutions [6,13]. A VND pseudoalgorithm can be seen in Algorithm 1. It is defined by the so-called operators, which are methods that take a feasible solution as an input and a set of parameters and output a feasible solution. A neighborhood is then a set of solutions that can be generated by all possible applications of an operator. The operators are heuristics for local search, which try to improve the solution using a specific modification strategy, e.g., reversing a part of the solution or exchanging two segments in the existing solution. If an operator finds an improving solution, the solution is accepted, and the search begins again from the first operator.

The criteria for accepting a solution may differ. In the First Accept approach, the first improving solution that is found is accepted, ending the search of the neighborhood and restarting the procedure. With Best Accept, the whole neighborhood is explored, and the best-found improving solution is accepted. Each strategy is better in different circumstances [9]. For the purposes of this paper, we use Best Accept.

If the operator fails to find any improving solution, the search is repeated with the next operator on the list. If no operator was able to find an improving

---

Algorithm 1. VND

    Input: Feasible RPP-DC solution
    Output: Best found RPP-DC solution

1: **while** Improvement **do**
2:     Pick first neighborhood operator
3:     Improvement = false
4:     **while** Unexplored solutions in neighborhood **do**
5:         Apply operator to obtain new solution
6:         **if** Found an improving solution **then**
7:             Improvement = true
8:             Remember solution
9:         **end if**
10:     **end while**
11:     **if** Improvement **then**
12:         Remember best found solution
13:         Restart neighborhood exploration
14:     **else**
15:         Move to next neighborhood
16:     **end if**
17: **end while**
18: **return** Best found solution

---

solution, the procedure ends, outputting the current (best found) solution. The selection and ordering of operators is of extreme importance for the VND. Since the procedure begins with the first operator every time an improving solution is found, it is the most frequently called one. It is beneficial, then, to order the operators in such a way that the first operator on the list is the most efficient among them. We implement eight different operators:

1. SwapDirection(i) - Reverse the direction of traversal of edge i
2. 2opt(i,j) - Reverse the ordering of edges between positions i and j in the route and reverse the direction of traversal
3. InsertEdge(i,j) - Remove an edge from position i and insert it in front of position j
4. SwapEdges(i,j) - Exchange edges on positions i and j
5. Edges3point(i,j) - Exchange two edges directly in front and after position i with an edge on position j
6. EdgesOrOpt2(i,j) - Remove two edges directly in front and after position i and insert them in front of position j
7. EdgesOrOpt3(i,j) - Remove three edges directly in front and after position i and insert them in front of position j
8. EdgesOrOpt4(i,j) - Remove four edges directly in front and after position i and insert them in front of position j

The operators 3–8 can be represented by a single, more complex operator called *2string(i,j,x,y)*, which removes x edges directly in front and after a position i and y edges directly in front and after position j and exchanges them. This gives us the final set of operators: *SwapDirection*, *2opt* and *2string*. Using the *2string* operator results in slightly different behavior than calling the original five operators in a sequence. For example, if operator 3 would find an improving solution, it is accepted, and the search restarts. The neighborhoods generated by operators 4–8 would not be explored in that iteration. With *2string*, all their neighborhoods are explored simultaneously, and the best solution among them is accepted.

A variation of the VND, the Randomized VND (RVND), is a stochastic method where the order of operators is shuffled before starting each search. While this eliminates the option to manually tune the operator ordering, if it is unknown which operator is the best-performing one for the specific problem being solved, it can help eliminate a computation overhead created by bad operator order.

Greedy Randomized Adaptive Search Procedure. GRASP is a multi-start metaheuristic, where first, an initial solution is created. This initial solution is then optimized using a local search heuristic, such as VND, to find a locally optimal solution. After reaching the local optimum in regards to the optimized criterion (distance in our case), the solution is remembered, and the process is repeated until a terminating condition is satisfied, such as the maximum number of starts, or in our case, maximum runtime. The best found solution from all runs of the procedure is kept and outputted as the resulting solution.

In order for GRASP to obtain different solutions for each start, the initial solution must be randomized. Therefore, it uses the Randomized GCP. For local search, we use the VND described in Sect. 4.2. The GRASP metaheuristic is described in Algorithm 2.

Algorithm 2. GRASP

Input: Problem instance
Output: Best found RPP-DC solution

1: **while** Not max runtime **do**
2:     Solution = new feasible initial solution
3:     Improve Solution by local optimization (R/VND)
4:     Cost = Solution.cost
5:     **if** Cost < Best cost **then**
6:         Best cost = Cost
7:         Best solution = Solution
8:     **end if**
9: **end while**
10: **return** Best solution

---

5   Experimental Analysis

In this Section, we present the testing instances and the results of our experiments. The testing instances are described in Sect. 5.1. We analyze the effects of internal parameters of different solvers in Sect. 5.2, and in Sect. 5.3 we present the comparison of different solvers. To leverage the randomized nature of some of the heuristics, we perform 10 runs with different random number generator seeds equal to the number of the run and select the best results. The used seeds are therefore $seed = [0, \ldots, 9]$. The capacity C for the experiments is set to 20000 for surveillance and 5000 for inspection to model the longer time it takes to perform a thorough scan of a location.

As the metric, we use the relative cost, defined as $\frac{c_i - c_{best}}{c_{best}}$, where c_i is the cost of the compared solution and c_{best} is the best-found solution for the instance during the experiment. Therefore, there will be at least one $c_i = c_{best}$ for each instance and its resulting relative cost will be 0.

5.1   Instances

For the purposes of experimental evaluation, we generated 28 surveillance instances with varying complexity. These are formed by sampled parallel lines, forming the "streets", occasionally cut by empty diagonal lines and optionally with few empty areas. From the surveillance instances, the instances for inspection were obtained by randomly sampling the segments forming the rows and obtaining a set of distinct locations for deeper inspection. For simplification, all of the instances have the exact same *spatial* and *abstract* representations, and edge costs correspond to the Euclidean distance between their endpoints. Example surveillance instances can be seen in Fig. 3 and corresponding example inspection instances in Fig. 4.

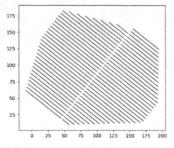

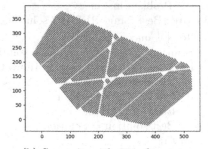

(a) Scenario with 70 elements.   (b) Scenario with 371 elements.

Fig. 3. Example surveillance scenarios.

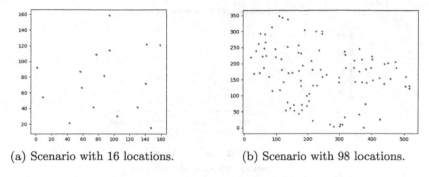

(a) Scenario with 16 locations.   (b) Scenario with 98 locations.

Fig. 4. Example inspection scenarios.

5.2   Internal Parameters

In this Section, we present our analysis of the effect of the meta-parameters of the algorithms. The first parameter is the Randomized Candidate List Size (RCL), which is relevant only to the randomized solvers. The second internal parameter is the maximum runtime. This parameter influences only the GRASP meta-heuristic.

Randomized Candidate List Length. The candidate list length for the Randomized GCP is the number of closest neighbors from which we select the random edge to be added. Note that for $RCL = 1$, the Randomized GCP becomes GCP. Therefore, Randomized GCP should have $RCL \geq 2$ and $RCL = 1$ is included only for comparison to standard GCP.

In Fig. 5, it can be seen that the performance of the Randomized GCP decreases with the amount of randomization. This is due to the fact that with a larger candidate list, the chance of selecting a worse candidate edge to add to the solution is noticeably higher. The effect is significantly more noticeable in the inspection scenarios, where the resulting solution cost can be more than two times the solution cost obtained using the standard GCP ($RCL = 1$).

Randomized Candidate List Length in GRASP. As mentioned, multi-start heuristics like GRASP require randomization in initial solution generation. This is why the Randomized GCP is used, as it can generate various starting points for the optimization procedure. Since GRASP benefits from diversity in the initial solution generation and is able to optimize the solutions afterward, the effect of the RCL parameter cannot be inferred only from the performance of the constructive heuristic but also has to be investigated.

The effect of the RCL parameter on the solution quality of GRASP can be seen in Fig. 6. The results for surveillance scenarios can be seen in Fig. 6a. In contrast to the results with only the Randomized GCP, the RCL parameter does not have an obvious correlation with the solution quality. It can be seen that $RCL \geq 2$ performs better than $RCL = 1$ on smaller instances. In the largest

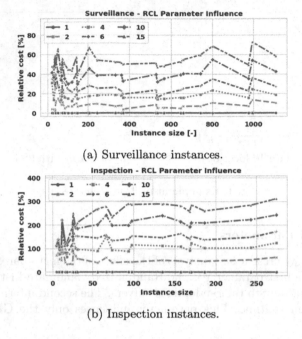

(a) Surveillance instances.

(b) Inspection instances.

Fig. 5. Effect of RCL parameter on the Randomized GCP.

instances, however, $RCL = 1$ performs the best out of all values. Overall, however, $RCL = 4$ is the best performing, as it does not exhibit poorer performance in small instances like $RCL = 2$, and there are only a couple of instances where it performed worse.

In inspection instances, as seen in Fig. 6b, $RCL = 1$ never achieves better results than higher values do. This can be attributed to the smaller size of the instances. Even here, $RCL = 4$ performs consistently well. Therefore, we select 4 as the value of RCL for the experiments.

Overall, in the experiments, GRASP with Randomized GCP consistently outperforms GRASP with standard GCP ($RCL = 1$). This shows the benefit of including a stochastic factor in initial solution generation for GRASP. This is due to the fact that it is a multi-start heuristic and as such, it benefits from having different input solutions into each of its optimization phases. Additionally, in contrast to experiments with only the standard and Randomized GCP, $RCL = 4$ in GRASP performs better than $RCL = 2$. This can be explained by the additional local search that is performed on the generated initial solutions, where more diversity obtained with $RCL = 4$ makes for better starting points for optimization.

Maximum Runtime. The maximum runtime is an important factor influencing the quality of solutions GRASP produces. The other optimization-based solvers also have a maximum runtime limit. However, they finish even when

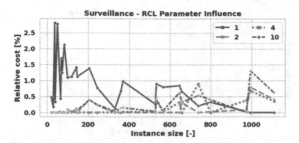

(a) Surveillance instances. Runtime 100 s.

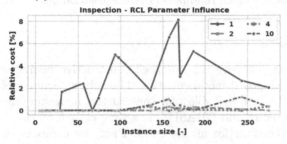

(b) Inspection instances. Runtime 100 s.

Fig. 6. Effect of RCL parameter on the Greedy Randomized Adaptive Search Procedure.

they reach a local optimum, which happens earlier than the maximum runtime elapses. Therefore, we report only the average time to find a solution and analyze the influence of this parameter only on GRASP.

In Table 1, we show the average time needed to find the local optimum where applicable. For GRASP, we compared the relative cost found by GRASP with varying maximum runtime in Fig. 7. From the results, we can see that with larger maximum runtime, the cost of the solution tends to be better. The improvement starts to be less pronounced from $t_{max} = 50$ s upwards, and the difference between $t_{max} = 100$ s and $t_{max} - 500$ s is within 1% at maximum. Therefore, we select $t_{max} = 100$ s as the best compromise between runtime and solution quality. Since the inspection scenarios are smaller and therefore require significantly less computation time, we do not consider them when setting the maximum runtime.

Table 1. Average runtime to reach the local optimum [ms].

Constructor	Greedy	RandGreedy	Geom
Standalone	0.07	0.11	0.05
+VND	2821.26	4652.49	4400.57
+RVND	6889.10	16245.66	18449.66

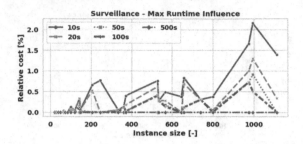

Fig. 7. Effects of maximum runtime on GRASP solution quality with $RCL = 4$.

5.3   Performance

In this Section, we compare the proposed constructive heuristics and the performance of the proposed metaheuristics. The solver parameters used in these experiments can be seen in Table 2 for constructive heuristics and in Table 3 for optimization heuristics and GRASP. They were chosen as the best-performing on average and the same for all instances. First, we compare the performance of different constructive heuristics and then a selection of the best-performing solvers.

Table 2. Parameters for constructive heuristics used in experiments.

Solver	t_{max} [s]	RCL [-]	Runs [-]
Greedy	100	N/A	1
RandGreedy	100	2	10
Geom	100	N/A	1

Table 3. Parameters for optimization heuristics and metaheuristics used in experiments. Note that the number of runs of optimization heuristics takes priority over the number of runs for constructive heuristics.

Solver	t_{max} [s]	Runs [-]
VND	100	1
RVND	100	10
GRASP	100	1

Performance of Constructive Heuristics. We compare the greedy, the randomized greedy, and the geometric constructors in Fig. 8. The Randomized GCP used the best-performing parameter $RCL = 2$.

It can be seen that the standard GCP provided the best results. In surveillance scenarios, the Randomized GCP often provided solutions within 10% of the standard GCP. The geometric heuristic was outperformed in both surveillance and inspection scenarios, with a dramatic increase in relative cost in the inspection scenarios. This can be explained by the lack of geometric structure the geometric heuristic is designed to exploit.

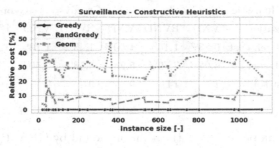

(a) Surveillance instances.

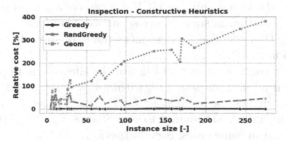

(b) Inspection instances.

Fig. 8. Relative cost of the proposed constructive heuristics.

Comparison of Solvers. First, we compare the solvers consisting only of a combination of a constructive and a local search heuristic. The results for the surveillance scenarios can be seen in Table 4 and for inspection in Table 5. The only solver capable of consistently finding solutions within 1% of the relative cost in both surveillance and inspection scenarios is the GCP coupled with VND. Interestingly, there is a higher overlap in solvers that found the best solution for the instance in inspection than surveillance. This could be explained by the smaller size of inspection instances.

Table 4. Performance of combinations of constructive heuristics and local search methods in surveillance instances.

Cons. Heuristic	Greedy		RandGreedy		Geom	
Optimization	VND	RVND	VND	RVND	VND	RVND
Average rel. cost	0.51%	0.36%	0.72%	0.56%	0.73%	0.90%
Max rel. cost	2.25%	2.63%	2.26%	2.04%	2.23%	3.06%
No. best sol.	3	12	3	5	6	4

Table 5. Performance of combinations of constructive heuristics and local search methods in inspection instances.

Cons. Heuristic	Greedy		RandGreedy		Geom	
Optimization	VND	RVND	VND	RVND	VND	RVND
Average rel. cost	0.83%	1.15%	1.49%	1.43%	1.73%	1.71%
Max rel. cost	6.08%	7.79%	5.24%	5.58%	5.50%	6.03%
No. best sol.	15	14	9	9	9	10

In Fig. 9a, it can be seen that the solutions found by GRASP in surveillance instances are better than the solutions found by using only the GCP, even when combined with VND. Using only the GCP, we can obtain solutions within 10% of the best found solution in surveillance scenarios. Combining the greedy constructive with VND is effective, as it reduces the maximum deviation from the best found solution to 3%.

In inspection scenarios, as seen in Fig. 9b, the effect is more pronounced, as greedy on its own often finds solutions within 40% relative cost, with a peak of over 60%. This makes the standalone GCP a bad choice for reconnaissance planning. Coupling with VND, similar to surveillance, significantly improves the solution quality and in some cases, even outperforms GRASP.

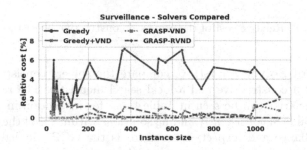

(a) Surveillance instances.

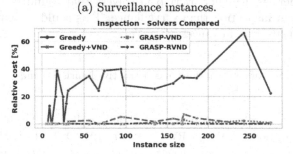

(b) Inspection instances.

Fig. 9. Comparison of best-performing solvers and GCP.

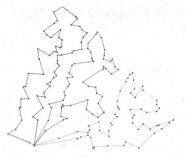

(a) Surveillance with 646 goals.   (b) Inspection of 168 goals.

Fig. 10. Example solutions obtained using GRASP+RVND. Each color is one subtour. (Color figure online)

GRASP with both VND and RVND produces high-quality solutions, even when the tuning process was done only for GRASP-VND. In inspection, GRASP-RVND even finds better solutions than GRASP-VND. On large instances, however, GRASP is often outperformed by greedy with VND. Example solutions can be seen in Fig. 10.

6   Conclusion

In this paper, we presented a metaheuristic approach for path planning for area surveillance and inspection for UAVs. We focus on organized areas with distinct geometrical features, such as rows of building blocks and streets. We presented an RPP-DC problem formulation capable of representing both problems. In the problem formulation, the goal is to visit a user-defined subset of edges of interest, representing line segments subject to surveillance and inspection, on a fully connected graph. The solution consists of multiple subtours, each starting and ending in a specific recharging depot, and is limited in length by the capacity constraint.

We designed a set of testing instances for the problem, consisting of 28 surveillance scenarios and corresponding inspection scenarios. Finally, we present a set of heuristic and metaheuristic solvers, such as variants of the greedy constructive heuristic, a geometric constructive procedure, VND with its stochastic counterpart RVND as local search methods, and GRASP metaheuristic. The internal parameters of the solvers are experimentally analyzed and tuned, and the solvers' performance is evaluated and compared. GRASP produces solutions with the lowest cost, both when using VND and RVND. On large instances, however, it can be outperformed by a greedy heuristic coupled with VND.

Acknowledgement. The work has been supported by the Grant Agency of the Czech Technical University in Prague, grant No. SGS21/185/OHK3/3T/37. Computational resources were supplied by the project "e-Infrastruktura CZ" (e-INFRA CZ

LM2018140) supported by the Ministry of Education, Youth and Sports of the Czech Republic.

References

1. Amous, M., Toumi, S., Jarboui, B., Eddaly, M.: A variable neighborhood search algorithm for the capacitated vehicle routing problem. Electron. Notes Discret. Math. **58**, 231–238 (2017)
2. Cabreira, T.M., Brisolara, L.B., Paulo R, F.J.: Survey on coverage path planning with unmanned aerial vehicles. Drones **3**(1), 4 (2019)
3. Chao, I.M., Golden, B.L., Wasil, E.A.: The team orienteering problem. Eur. J. Oper. Res. **88**(3), 464–474 (1996)
4. Coombes, M., Chen, W.H., Liu, C.: Boustrophedon coverage path planning for UAV aerial surveys in wind. In: 2017 International Conference on Unmanned Aircraft Systems (ICUAS), pp. 1563–1571. IEEE (2017)
5. Corberán, Á., Laporte, G.: Arc Routing: Problems, Methods, and Applications. SIAM (2015)
6. Duarte, A., Sánchez-Oro, J., Mladenović, N., Todosijević, R.: Variable neighborhood descent. In: Martí, R., Pardalos, P.M., Resende, M.G.C. (eds.) Handbook of Heuristics, pp. 341–367. Springer, Cham (2018). https://doi.org/10.1007/978-3-319-07124-4_9
7. Eiselt, H.A., Gendreau, M., Laporte, G.: Arc routing problems, part ii: the rural postman problem. Oper. Res. **43**(3), 399–414 (1995)
8. Feo, T.A., Resende, M.G.: Greedy randomized adaptive search procedures. J. Global Optim. **6**(2), 109–133 (1995)
9. Hansen, P., Mladenović, N.: First vs. best improvement: an empirical study. Discret. Appl. Math. **154**(5), 802–817 (2006)
10. Laporte, G., Nobert, Y.: Generalized travelling salesman problem through n sets of nodes: an integer programming approach. INFOR: Inf. Syst. Oper. Res. **21**(1), 61–75 (1983)
11. Lin, J., Zhou, W., Wolfson, O.: Electric vehicle routing problem. Transp. Res. Procedia **12**, 508–521 (2016)
12. Marinakis, Y.: Multiple phase neighborhood search-grasp for the capacitated vehicle routing problem. Expert Syst. Appl. **39**(8), 6807–6815 (2012)
13. Mladenović, N., Hansen, P.: Variable neighborhood search. Comput. Oper. Res. **24**(11), 1097–1100 (1997)
14. Nekovář, F., Faigl, J., Saska, M.: Multi-tour set traveling salesman problem in planning power transmission line inspection. IEEE Robot. Autom. Lett. **6**(4), 6196–6203 (2021)
15. Ntafos, S.: Watchman routes under limited visibility. Comput. Geom. **1**(3), 149–170 (1992)
16. OpenStreetMap contributors: Planet dump retrieved from https://planet.osm.org. https://www.openstreetmap.org (2017)
17. Pěnička, R., Faigl, J., Váňa, P., Saska, M.: Dubins orienteering problem. IEEE Robot. Autom. Lett. **2**(2), 1210–1217 (2017)
18. Ralphs, T.K., Kopman, L., Pulleyblank, W.R., Trotter, L.E.: On the capacitated vehicle routing problem. Math. Program. **94**(2), 343–359 (2003)

19. Stodola, P., Kozůbek, J., Drozd, J.: Using unmanned aerial systems in military operations for autonomous reconnaissance. In: Mazal, J. (ed.) MESAS 2018. LNCS, vol. 11472, pp. 514–529. Springer, Cham (2019). https://doi.org/10.1007/978-3-030-14984-0_38
20. Toth, P., Vigo, D.: The Vehicle Routing Problem. SIAM (2002)
21. Woller, D., Kozák, V., Kulich, M.: The GRASP metaheuristic for the electric vehicle routing problem. In: Mazal, J., Fagiolini, A., Vasik, P., Turi, M. (eds.) MESAS 2020. LNCS, vol. 12619, pp. 189–205. Springer, Cham (2021). https://doi.org/10.1007/978-3-030-70740-8_12

Simulation of Autonomous Robotic System for Intelligence and Reconnaissance Operations

Milos Cihlar[1] (iD), Petr Raichl[1] (iD), Petr Gabrlik[1] (iD), Jiri Janousek[1] (iD),
Petr Marcon[1(✉)] (iD), Ludek Zalud[1] (iD), Tomas Lazna[1] (iD), Karel Michenka[2] (iD),
Jan Nohel[2] (iD), and Alexandr Stefek[2] (iD)

[1] Faculty of Electrical Engineering and Communictaion, Brno University of Technology,
Technicka 12, 616 00 Brno, Czech Republic
marcon@vut.cz
[2] University of Defence, Brno, Czech Republic

Abstract. This paper examines the possibilities of realistic simulations of robotic systems employed for intelligence and reconnaissance operations in the outdoor environment. Including simulation into the development process accelerates and facilitates testing, verification, and evaluation of algorithms, and prevents potential damage of expensive hardware. To achieve fast and flexible development, we utilize a widely used Robotic Operating System (ROS) framework, which, together with Gazebo simulator, enables to deploy robots and test algorithms in both real-world and simulation. Gazebo supports a wide range of customization options, including the creation of own worlds, robots, and sensors. Moreover, the solution allows to deploy a multiple heterogenous robots within one simulation instance to test cooperative missions. To demonstrate the potential of this simulation concept for intelligence operations, we introduce a scenario involving several flying and terrestrial robots during a Chemical, Biological, Radiological, Nuclear, and Explosive (CBRNE) mission comprising a radiation source search. For this purpose, we deployed realistic robotic platforms into the aerial photogrammetry-based 3D world, and, above all, we improved the standard radiation plugin to collect credible data. The results indicate that the concept fulfills requirements for intelligence and reconnaissance robotic operation simulation.

Keywords: Simulation · mobile robots · Unmanned Aircraft System · Unmanned Ground Vehicle · swarm · ROS · Gazebo

1 Introduction

In the last twenty years, robotics, especially mobile robotics, has been on the rise. Modern robotic systems are equipped with a variety of sensors, actuators, computers, and other equipment, that aim to accomplish a desired mission, a task that can be performed by a human, or an activity that a human does not want or cannot perform. A robot competent in performing these tasks must be capable of basic movement, orientation, perception, and decision-making. Therefore, robots are complex hardware devices with complicated software. Sensors are expensive, hardware is difficult to work with, and the risk of accidents is high. These reasons make the development extremely expensive. There is pressure and a tendency to move the development, testing, and debugging of algorithms to simulators, which greatly speed up, simplify and cheapen robot development and research [1–4].

The 2020 survey showed that approximately 72% of robotics organizations use simulators for their activities [5]. Types of commonly used robotic simulators are described and compared in the literature [6]. With correctly modeled robots and simulation environments, the software used in the simulation can be directly used in the real world [7]. Therefore, this article deals with the possibilities of simulating mobile robots in real-world inspired environments for fast and effective detection of CBRN threats. Obtaining information through CBRN reconnaissance will contribute to the protection of military units and ensure awareness within the fulfillment of Intelligence analyses of a battlefield to identify and specify CBRN threats. Moreover, the cooperation of the swarm of flying robots (Unmanned Aircraft Systems, UASs) with terrestrial robots (Unmanned Ground Vehicles, UGVs) takes advantage of fast aerial mapping and ground reconnaissance with high sensitivity.

2 Materials and Methods

2.1 Gazebo

Gazebo is an open-source 3D robotics simulator developed by Open Source Robotics Foundation used for indoor and outdoor missions [2]. Nowadays, simulation plays an important role in robotics research, and it is used for design, development, verification, validation, testing, and proving entire robotics systems. Today's robots represent complex hardware devices including numerous sensors, and they may be deployed to fulfill different tasks in various environments. Therefore, well-designed robotic simulators accelerate the development time. The Gazebo has become the most popular robotic simulator because it provides many options to simulate indoor and outdoor 3D environments, numerous robots, objects, and sensors that are protected before the damage, unlike real-world experiments. Moreover, Gazebo enables easy integration into the Robotic Operating System (ROS) [8], a widely used robotic framework. The application itself consists of two main parts: first, *gzserver*, which executes the physics update-loop and sensor data generation; second, *gzclient*, which runs a graphical user interface. Both components are independent of each other [1].

2.1.1 World

The Gazebo world represents a simulated environment where the robots operate and perform desired tasks, and typically it embodies a simplified representation of a portion of a real-world environment to achieve authentic conditions. The world, 3D model, may be assembled in two major ways: manually utilizing a software tool for 3D modeling, or by using a technique for environment scanning such as laser scanning or photogrammetry. The latter approach is advantageous especially outdoors since it enables to obtain a 3D representation of a large-scale area with minimal effort and with a reasonable level of detail. Within this paper, we use UAS photogrammetry-based model of a real-world in

COLLADA format, which is compatible with the Gazebo. The world has an approximate area of 2 ha, and since it involves flat areas, numerous buildings, vegetation, and other non-traversable zones, it represents a suitable world for simulating the operation of a heterogeneous robotic system (Fig. 1).

Fig. 1. The Gazebo world generated from the UAS photogrammetry-based 3D model.

2.1.2 Unmanned Ground Vehicle

The simulation scenario presented within this paper involves the deployment of simulated a UGV (Fig. 2), namely a four-wheel skid steering mobile robot based on a real UGV Orpheus. This custom-built platform was designed for reconnaissance purposes, and it stands out for its mechanical robustness and maneuverability in an outdoor environment. The robot integrates ROS-based software to enable motion control and reading sensor data in both the real-world and simulation. Within the proposed scenario, the UGV has equipped with a $2'' \times 2''$ NaI (Tl) radiation detector (see *Gazebo Radiation Plugin* section).

Gazebo loads models and worlds from the self-descriptive System Description Format (SDF) file. This approach is unsuitable for editing by hand and dynamic robot configuration because SDF is not scriptable. Therefore, the SDF file contains similar duplicate link descriptions. The solution for the swollen code is a parser for the Unified Robot Description Format (URDF) that provides macro for XML language (XACRO). URDF is XML robot model representation. The format consists of an exclusive robot tag, its links, and nested visual and collision tags. The independent definition of visual and collision properties enables collision simplification with the simultaneous preservation of the robot's looks. This simplification saves computation time and resources. Joints combine links together.

Inertial tags are required in each link for proper parsing to SDF format. This tag defines the mass of links and their moment of inertia. Hence, the main physical properties are determined. The gazebo tag is optional and defines other simulation properties such as damping, friction, contacts, and repulsion force. It also includes plugins for specifying a link's behavior [1].

Fig. 2. Orpheus model in Gazebo simulator.

XACRO provides a math constant, simple math, and parametric macros for a significant reduction of a line of code. XACRO makes code more clear and adjustable. Making a robot with macros allows adjusting (by loading a YAML file) the robot's settings, especially its sensors, without managing multiple similar files with robot descriptions.

2.1.3 Unmanned Aircraft System

The software architecture for the UASs is based on several components, namely, on the PX4 flight stack, the MRS UAV control and estimating system [3], and custom-made high-level algorithms for mission control (Fig. 3). Except the PX4, which is designed for flight controllers (such as Pixhawk, for example), the components are ROS-based, and run on the on-board computer while using real robots. However, all the software may run on a PC together with the Gazebo simulator to evaluate algorithms before real experiments.

In general, the models of UASs for Gazebo are created similarly to the UGV model described above, and the MRS UAV system already includes several simulated platforms inspired by real vehicles. For our simulation, we employed Tarot t650 UAS (Fig. 4), and integrated the radiation plugin (see *Gazebo Radiation Plugin* section) into the system. The solution enables the deployment of multiple robots simultaneously and performs various tasks from waypoint following to complex algorithms such as autonomous landing, for example [9].

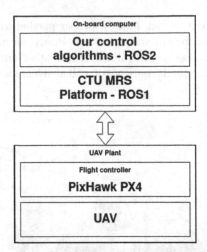

Fig. 3. System architecture of Unmanned Aircraft System.

Fig. 4. Simulation of UASs in Gazebo world.

2.1.4 Gazebo Radiation Plugin

Radioactivity simulation is done with the help of two plugins attached to the detector and radiation source model in the Gazebo simulator. The source is modeled as a point radioactivity source with constant activity. The physics of the radiation measurement consists of two principles: first, it depends on the number of particles that go through the simulated detector, which is strongly correlated with distance; second, the attenuation due to obstacles between sources and sensor is taken into account. The plugins are based on the *gazebo_radiation_plugin* ROS package, which also consider the situation when the radiation source is close to the detector, and intensity goes to infinity according to the inverse square law. The implementation captures half of the released particles when the distance goes to zero, which reflects reality satisfyingly [4].

We reimplemented the plugin for ROS2, and improved it to respect the effects of the radiation background, and sensor's dead time, a phenomenon causing the detector cannot to count particles due to the previous particle pass. Therefore, the package was adjusted to behave similarly to a real NaI(Tl) detector. The difference between ideal sensors and sensors with dead time illustrates Fig. 5.

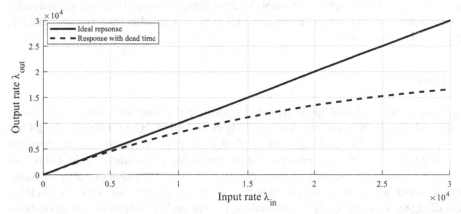

Fig. 5. The response comparison of an ideal sensor and the sensor with dead time.

The property of dead sensor time τ is modeled as a function that transforms input ideal rate λ_{in} to output real rate λ_{out}.

$$\lambda_{out} = \lambda_{in} e^{-\lambda_{in} \tau} \tag{1}$$

2.2 Simulation Scenario

To demonstrate Gazebo's capabilities for simulating multi-robot CBRN missions, we built a real-world scenario involving a squad conducting a CBRN reconnaissance using robotic assets in an urban area with potential radiation contamination.

The contamination is characterized by a single-point radiation source, namely, a Co-60 isotope exhibiting the activity of 170 MBq, positioned in the container in the vicinity of the middle building. However, in terms of the simulated robotic reconnaissance, these parameters were not available.

The robotic mission consists of two main phases. The former rests in the automatic aerial radiation data collection employing three identical UASs equipped with compact $1.5 \times 1.5''$ NaI(Tl) detectors. To obtain rough, equally distributed data in the minimum amount of time, the area of interest is divided into three portions and mapped by the individual UASs in parallel. The goal is to operate at a minimal, obstacle-free altitude, and fly in parallel lines with spacing equal to half of the above-ground level (AGL) altitude.

The latter phase involves terrestrial reconnaissance by using the UGV fitted with a 2 × 2″ NaI(Tl) detector. The UGV operation is intended to be manual, i.e. remotely controlled, or semi-automatic constituting an operation mode comprising waypoint-following. In general, the waypoints may be created utilizing the photogrammetry-based map manually or automatically. The latter approach is feasible, for example, by using Maneuver Control System CZ software developed at the University of Defense, which calculates the shortest and safest route of movement based on a combination of the effects of surface character, elevation, weather, enemy deployment and own troops [10, 11]. In any case, the goal is to visit the potential radiation hotspot found in the interpolated aerial radiation map, and collect more accurate radiation data suitable for a spectral analysis and source identification.

3   Results

The UAS operation lasted approximately 5:08 min in the simulation time and 5:50 min in the real time at PC with Intel(R) Core(TM) i5-10210U CPU 1.60 GHz, 8 GB DDR4 RAM. Across the 2.1 km long flight at 20 m AGL (Fig. 6), more than 10 thousand radiation measurements were performed with a minimum and maximum values of 67 and 245 CPS (Counts Per Second), respectively (Fig. 7). After the radiation data processing and interpolation, a single hotspot may be clearly recognized just above the location containing the source (Fig. 8). Based on the approximate hotspot position, waypoints for the ground reconnaissance were manually selected, and UGV followed the coordinates automatically. This part of the mission lasted 3.5 min in the real time, and about 200 radiation measurements were accomplished within 180 m long ride. Thanks to the higher sensitivity of the onboard detection system and smaller distance from the source, the data exhibit minimum and maximum value of 169 and 3688 CPS, respectively (Fig. 9).

Fig. 6. The flight trajectories of the individual UASs.

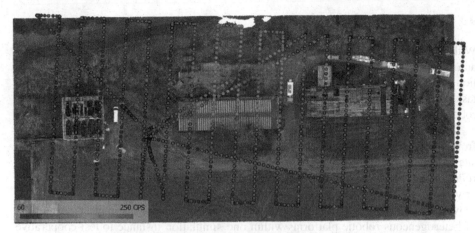

Fig. 7. Aerial radiation data collected by all the UASs.

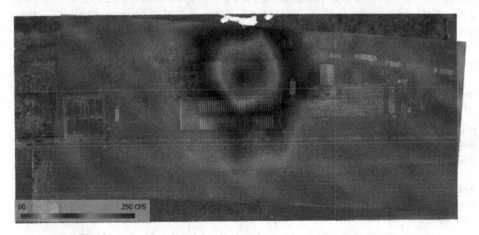

Fig. 8. Interpolated aerial radiation data collected by all the UASs.

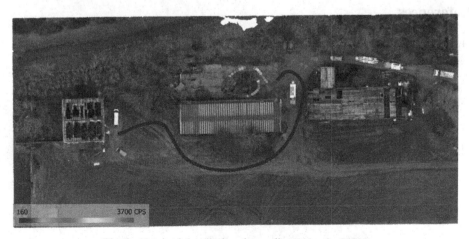

Fig. 9. Terrestrial radiation data collected by the UGV.

4 Discussion and Conclusion

Within this paper, we presented basic possibilities of highly realistic simulations for autonomous robotic operations during reconnaissance missions. The employed simulation software, Gazebo, integrates a physics engine with sufficient accuracy for desired tasks and enables setting up the simulation realistically in terms of the environment, robotic platforms, and sensors.

We demonstrated that the simulation environment, or world, may be easily assembled from the aerial photogrammetry or laser scanning-based 3D models of real-world study sites allowing us to test various scenarios in natural conditions. The models of the robotic platforms were created concerning their actual physical parameters, including the drive type, which is essential to achieve reliable behavior while traversing the terrain or moving in the environment, in general. Gazebo enables the deployment of a large number of heterogeneous robotic platforms within one simulation instance to test cooperative missions involving robot interactions; the main limitation rests in the availability of computational resources. To demonstrate the capability of utilizing various sensors, we used customized gamma radiation sensors to detect radiation sources. Similarly, other sensors can be incorporated into the simulation as well. Currently, the following sensors are available: RGB camera, depth camera, laser rangefinder, LiDAR, GPS, IMU, and others.

The goal of the presented simulated mission including the operation of four robots (two different platforms), and radiation hotspot localization was not to demonstrate advanced navigation and localization algorithms, but rather to introduce an overall concept. We plan to utilize this approach to test high-level algorithms for mission control during scenarios comprising a swarm of UASs fulfilling reconnaissance goals, and thus prevent potential failures and damages of real robots.

Acknowledgments. The research was funded from the Ministry of the Interior of the Czech Republic (MVCR) grant no. VJ02010036 (An Artificial Intelligence-Controlled Robotic System for Intelligence and Reconnaissance Operations).

References

1. Cihlar, M.: Simulation of robotic search of lost radiation sources. Master thesis. Brno (2022)
2. Koenig, N., Howard, A.: Design and use paradigms for Gazebo, an open-source multi-robot simulator. In: 2004 IEEE/RSJ International Conference on Intelligent Robots and Systems (IROS), vol. 3, pp. 2149–2154 (2004)
3. Baca, T., et al.: The MRS UAV system: pushing the frontiers of reproducible research, real-world deployment, and education with autonomous unmanned aerial vehicles. J. Intell. Robot. Syst. **102**, 26 (2021)
4. Wright, T., West, A., Licata, M., Hawes, N., Lennox, B.: Simulating ionising radiation in gazebo for robotic nuclear inspection challenges. Robotics **10**, 86 (2021)
5. Afzal, A., Katz, D.S., Goues, C.L., Timperley, C.S.: A study on the challenges of using robotics simulators for testing (2020)
6. Collins, J., Chand, S., Vanderkop, A., Howard, D.: A review of physics simulators for robotic applications. IEEE Access **9**, 51416–51431 (2021)

7. Takaya, K., Asai, T., Kroumov, V., Smarandache, F.: Simulation environment for mobile robots testing using ROS and Gazebo. In: 2016 20th International Conference on System Theory, Control and Computing (ICSTCC), pp. 96–101 (2016)
8. Quigley, M., et al.: ROS: an open-source Robot Operating System. Presented at the ICRA Workshop on Open Source Software, Kobe, Japan, p. 5 (2009)
9. Marcon, P., Janousek, J., Kadlec, R.: Vision-based and differential global positioning system to ensure precise autonomous landing of UAVs. In: 2018 Progress in Electromagnetics Research Symposium, Toyama, pp. 542–546 (2018)
10. Nohel, J., Flasar, Z.: Maneuver control system CZ. In: Mazal, J., Fagiolini, A., Vasik, P. (eds.) MESAS 2019. LNCS, vol. 11995, pp. 379–388. Springer, Heidelberg (2019). https://doi.org/10.1007/978-3-030-43890-6_31
11. Nohel, J., Zahradnicek, P., Flasar, Z., Stodola, P.: Modelling the manoeuvres of ground reconnaissance elements in urban areas. In: 2021 Communication and Information Technologies (KIT), pp. 1–6 (2021)

Autonomous Navigation for the Movement of the Robot in the Tube

Stepan Konecky[1]($\boxtimes$) and Lukas Machalek[2]

[1] University of Defence, Brno, Czech Republic
stepan.konecky@unob.cz
[2] Brno University of Technology, Brno, Czech Republic

Abstract. The paper deals with the issue of autonomous navigation for the movement of a robot in a tube. The solution is to determine the center of a given conic section using three operations in the Geometric Algebra for Conic Sections (GAC). The article describes an engine that renders given conic sections through basic operations in the GAC. At the end of the work, an algorithm is described that calculates the axis of the tube based on the points that are located in the space from the image, where we place the center of the ellipse obtained by the image filter and fitting algorithm.

Keywords: Geometric Algebra · Geometric Algebra for Conics · Computer Graphics · Projective Geometry · Image Filters · Autonomous Navigation · Csharp · Unity Engine

1 Introduction

Autonomous navigation is a very up to date topic. There are a lot of sensors that provide specific data, that can be used to analyze environment and use it for trajectory planning. One of the most used sensors are cameras, which capture the environment as an image from camera's perspective. Sophisticated algorithms then make an estimation about the environment in front of that camera. But extraction of details for orientation from a single picture is very difficult without any information about the environment. Before the software can be developed, simulations are necessary. First step can be simple example of that environment, which can be clearly recognizable by the algorithms, because it has direct signs. Autonomous navigation of a robot with camera in a tube can be initialized with simulation, which is described by this paper. Easy case to solve is just a straight tube. The robot with a camera and light source can simply be navigated to the direction of the darkest point in an image, given by the camera. In a case of a curved tube, the same approach can lead to a collision with the tube surface. Safe path would follow the tube axis.

Geometric algebra (GA) is a powerful tool for applications in various research areas, such as mechanics and image processing. Due to geometric interpretation of GA elements, it is possible to check the algorithm correctness immediately in a software. Thus, the application in geometric oriented tasks is quite appropriate.

J. Mazal et al. (Eds.): MESAS 2022, LNCS 13866, pp. 74–86, 2023.
https://doi.org/10.1007/978-3-031-31268-7_5

2   Problem Statement

Goal of this paper is to find a conic that follows elliptic contour, that can be seen in a curved tube (Fig. 2) and make path using the center of the conic. We create a testing tube and develop an algorithm, the first part of which generates such conic. The second part extracts point in space as the center of that conic.

3   Approach to the Solution

Suppose a camera, lying somewhere on the tube axis, with a point light source illuminating some neighborhoods. Let the camera be rotated, so that it is oriented to same direction as a tangent of the axis. Then the camera can capture 2 types of images (Fig. 1: Camera view in a straight tube Fig. 2: Camera view in a curved tube).

Fig. 1. Camera view in a straight tube   **Fig. 2.** Camera view in a curved tube

If we use certain image filters, we can extract a set of points (pixels of the image) highlighting a character of the tube in certain distance in front of the camera. These points (pixels) are using conic fitting algorithm to get conic (in this case our aim is to always get an ellipse) in IPNS representation (vector in $\mathcal{R}^{5,3} \subset \mathcal{G}_{5,3}$).

From the ellipse properties we can further estimate a navigation trajectory through the tube. Note that in this Section we will use three kind of points; point of image (pixel with coordinates i, j) is denoted by $I_{i,j}$, point projected onto rectangle (2D subspace of Euclidean space $\mathcal{R}^3$) is denoted by $\bar{u}_{\mathrm{proj}}$ (and its scaled variation u_{proj}), and point from Euclidean space $\mathcal{R}^3$ is denoted by u.

In the first part we briefly introduce principle of creating 3D object in graphical software. Then we analyze the camera view in the dark tube (illuminated by a point source of light in the camera's position) and define a highlight matrix carrying points for the conic fitting algorithm. By means of projective geometry in computer graphics, we analyze and try to restore the tube axis using gained ellipses from conic fitting algorithm from different points in the tube. In this Section we commonly use term point, by what we mean vector that goes from origin to that point.

In the tube a plane intersection with the tube results in a circle with and from our camera position can be viewed as a circle or an ellipse. In Figs. 3, 4 we can see discussed situation, where green plane is set by point of the axis and by its tangent in that point. We can already see the connection between the curved tube and ellipse observed from camera position.

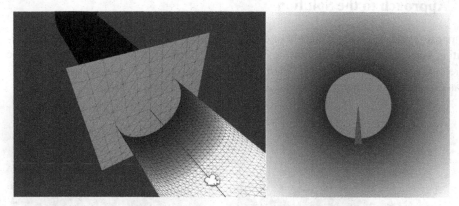

Fig. 3. Plane intersection example in a straight tube.

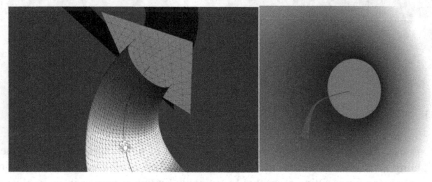

Fig. 4. Plane intersection example in a curved tube

3.1 Tube Generation

In this Subsection we briefly introduce computer graphic software (Unity) on tube generation. Tube assumed in this paper can be an object that consist of 2 types of segments; cylinder and torus. Tube can have only constant diameter and its surface has to be continuous and transition between the cylinder and the torus has to be smooth. Then the tube axis is either a line or part of a circle, which follow each other smoothly. The Fig. 5 shows the principle of creating the tube mesh. Note that vectors p, t_c are normalized.

Object in 3D computer graphics consist of triangles, see [14]. In Unity, first we have to create a set of points, which lie on the tube. After that we create a set which connects the points in particular way. As we can see on the right part of Fig. 5, the triangle is created by certain 3 points. Important is the order of points, because it carries also information about the normal of the triangle. For example, taking triangle indexed by $\{1, 0, m\}$, results in downward facing normal and triangle indexed by $\{0, 1, m\}$ result in upward facing normal (Fig. 6).

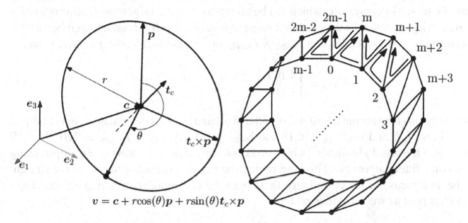

$$v = c + r\cos(\theta)p + r\sin(\theta)t_c \times p$$

Fig. 5. A way to create a tube mesh in the computer geometry

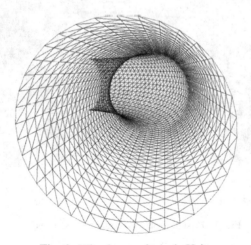

Fig. 6. Wire frame of tube in Unity

3.2 Pixels Selection

In this subsection we introduce two methods how to get a set of points, which we will fill the conic fitting algorithm. As we discussed in the introduction to this Section, suppose a camera that lies on the tube axis and in addition, it is pointed in the direction of a tangent to the axis. If the conic, produced by the fitting algorithm, is centered in the middle of the image, then the tube is straight in some neighborhood in front of the camera. If the center is not in the middle of the image, then the tube is curved in some distance. An example for the first case is Fig. 1 and for the second see Fig. 2. Question is how to find a set of points that can generate ellipses shown in Figs. 3, 4.

The first algorithm for finding such set is taking points with certain brightness (color value). Let I be considered as a cameras screen. Unity has function 2DTexture.GetPixel(i,j).grayscale, which can be understood as the brightness (converts a color value to a gray scale) of the pixel, because it converts ARGB format into number within zero and one. Now, let H_b be a I_{width} X I_{height} brightness highlighting matrix, where

$$H_{b i,j} = \begin{cases} 1 \text{ if } I_{i,j} \geq b_{min} \wedge I_{i,j} \leq b_{max}, \\ 0 \text{ else}, \end{cases} \quad (1)$$

where bmin is the minimal brightness of the pixel and bmax is the maximal. For example, take Figs. 1, 2 and set $b_{min} = 0,18$ and $b_{min} = 0,19$; $I_{width} = I_{height} = 720$. We will visualize the highlight matrix as blue pixels on the screen and draw green ellipse using the conic fitting algorithm. For these values, the result is sufficient in case of the straight tube, but in case of the curved tube these points do not make convincing elliptic shape on their own as we can notice on Fig. 7.

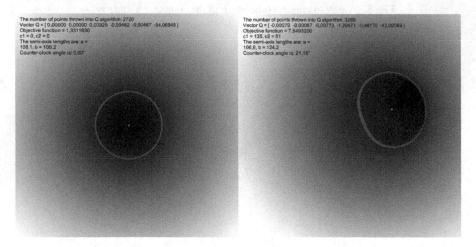

Fig. 7. First algorithm result on Figs. 1 and 2

The second algorithm of highlighting points is based on the difference in brightness between neighborhoods. Let H_d be a I_{width} X I_{height} difference in brightness highlighting matrix, where

$$H_{d i,j} = \begin{cases} 1 \text{ if } \max\{I[i-1, i, i+1; j-1, j, j+1]\} \\ \quad - \min\{I[i-1, i, i+1; j-1, j, j+1]\} > d, \\ 0 \text{ else}, \end{cases} \quad (2)$$

where d is the targeted difference in brightness. As with previous highlight matrix we take Figured 1, 2 set d $= 0{,}03$. Unfortunately, Fig. 1 is too smooth to find any points. From Fig. 8 we ca observe that the ellipse indicated in the contour, compared with the drawn ellipse, is not that precise. However, this filter can be used to extract exact ellipse parameters from Figs. 3, 4. In the next Subsection we will work with pixels selection from the matrix H_b.

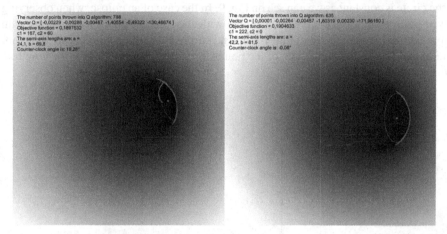

Fig. 8. Second algorithm result on Figs. 1 and 2

We start with the implementation of conic fitting algorithm by embedding points from the highlight matrix H to $\mathcal{G}_{5,3}$. Let $n = I_{\text{width}}$ and $m = I_{\text{height}}$, then the point set U is computed as follows,

$$u_{i+n(j-1)} = \begin{cases} (i - \tfrac{1}{2}n)e_1 + (j - \tfrac{1}{2}m)e_2 H_{i,j} = 1, \\ o \quad \text{else.} \end{cases}$$

Then we compute the matrix $\mathbf{P}$

$$P = \sum_{i}^{nm} BC(u_i)C(u_i)^T B, \quad u_i \in \mathbb{U}.$$

3.3   Tube Axis Recovery

If we want to recover the tube axis using the above algorithms (resulting in a single ellipse), we have to find the connection between the shape and position of the ellipse on the screen and known environment properties (camera and tube properties). We can use projective geometry in computer graphics to see how the point in 3D is projected on the screen [4].

In the computer graphics, camera has 3 main properties along with its position, rotation and resolution (FOV (field of view), the closest and the most distant point that can be projected. Now we consider that the camera has its own coordinate system (we consider that the camera is static in its own coordinate system and changes to its position and rotation are done in global coordinate system). The reason to do this is that we don't have to manipulate with the projection matrix M described below, but rather transform the rest of the space.

Note that the following assumptions are made on the orthographic projection. In the case when the generated ellipse is a circle, we can say that the e_3 coordinate o the points on the circle is constant as we can see on Fig. 9. In the case of an ellipse, when observing curved part of the tube, there exist 2 points with the same e_3 coordinates, along with ellipses center, as we can see in Fig. 10. It is no surprise that these 2 points are on major semi-axis. If we compute distance of the points $\bar{u}_{proj}$, $\bar{v}_{proj}$, we get $2a$ (a is the length of ellipses major semi-axis).

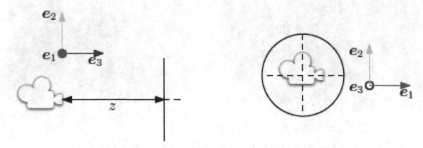

Fig. 9. Orthographic view of a circle from distance

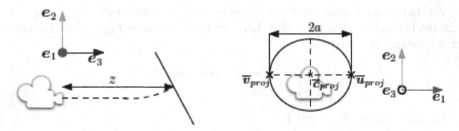

Fig. 10. Orthographic view of rotated circle around e1 axis from distance

$$\bar{u}_{proj} = (\bar{c}_{proj}[1] + a \quad \bar{c}_{proj}[2]) = \frac{1}{2u_3} \cot\left(\frac{FOV}{2}\frac{\pi}{180}\right)(u_1 I_{height} \quad u_2 I_{width}),$$

$$\bar{v}_{proj} = (\bar{c}_{proj}[1] - a \quad \bar{c}_{proj}[2]) = \frac{1}{2v_3} \cot\left(\frac{FOV}{2}\frac{\pi}{180}\right)(v_1 I_{height} \quad v_2 I_{width}),$$

where u_1, u_2, u_3 and v_1, v_2, v_3 are coefficients of 3D points u, v and a is major semi-axis length. We can use that $u_3 = v_3$, $u_2 = v_2$ and calculate an Euclidean distance of these 2 points, which is $\|*\|_2$ norm of vector $u - v$

$$\|u - v\|_2 = \sqrt{\left(\bar{c}_{proj}[1] + a - \bar{c}_{proj}[1] + a\right)^2 + \left(\bar{c}_{proj}[2] - \bar{c}_{proj}[2]\right)^2} = 2a$$

$$= \frac{1}{2u_3} \cot\left(\frac{\text{FOV}}{2}\frac{\pi}{180}\right)\sqrt{\left(u_1 I_{height} - v_1 I_{height}\right)^2 + \left(u_2 I_{width} - v_2 I_{width}\right)^2}$$

$$= \frac{I_{height}}{2u_3} \cot\left(\frac{\text{FOV}}{2}\frac{\pi}{180}\right)(u_1 - v_1), \tag{3}$$

where $u_1 - v_1 = 2r$, where r is the radius and since u_3 is the only unknown in the previous equation we can compute it directly. Note that a is semi-axis length of the ellipse in perspective view, while r is actual tube radius. Thus

$$2a = \frac{I_{height}}{2u_3} \cot\left(\frac{\text{FOV}}{2}\frac{\pi}{180}\right)2r$$

$$c_3 = u_3 = \frac{I_{height}}{2} \cot\left(\frac{\text{FOV}}{2}\frac{\pi}{180}\right)\frac{r}{a}.$$

With all this in mind we are now able to compute the center's e_3 coordinate of the conic. Now it is easy to compute the rest of the centers coordinates as follows

$$\left(\bar{c}_{proj}[1] \quad \bar{c}_{proj}[2]\right) = \frac{1}{2c_3} \cot\left(\frac{\text{FOV}}{2}\frac{\pi}{180}\right)\left(c_1 I_{height} \quad c_2 I_{width}\right)$$

$$\Leftrightarrow (c_1 \quad c_2) = 2c_3 \tan\left(\frac{\text{FOV}}{2}\frac{\pi}{180}\right)\left(\bar{c}_{proj}[1]\frac{1}{I_{height}} \quad \bar{c}_{proj}[2]\frac{1}{I_{width}}\right)$$

The computer application has a camera with the following properties: $\text{FOV} = 100$, $z_{near} = 0.3$, $z_{far} = 1000$ and $I_{height} = I_{width} = 720$. Then we approximate the ellipses center $c = (c_1, c_2, c_3) \in \mathcal{R}^3$ in camera coordinate system by

$$c_3 = 360 \cot\left(\frac{5\pi}{18}\right)\frac{r}{a},$$

$$c_1 = \frac{c_3}{360} \tan\left(\frac{5\pi}{18}\right)\bar{c}_{proj}[1] = \frac{r}{a}\bar{c}_{proj}[1],$$

$$c_2 = \frac{c_3}{360} \tan\left(\frac{5\pi}{18}\right)\bar{c}_{proj}[2] = \frac{r}{a}\bar{c}_{proj}[2], \tag{4}$$

where $\bar{c}_{proj}[1], \bar{c}_{proj}[2] \in \mathcal{R}^2$ is center of the ellipse computed by conic fitting algorithm, a is its major semi-axis length, and r is radius of the tube. Remember that this center c is related to the camera, and we have to place it into global coordinate system, which can be done using Euler angles of the camera rotation. Euler angles are commonly used in computer graphics, and they are easy to work with. Recall from linear algebra that rotation can be computed using rotation matrix for each axis

$$R_{e_1}(\theta) = \begin{pmatrix} 1 & 0 & 0 \\ 0 & \cos(\theta) & \sin(\theta) \\ 0 & -\sin(\theta) & \cos(\theta) \end{pmatrix},$$

$$R_{e_2}(\theta) = \begin{pmatrix} \cos(\theta) & 0 & -\sin(\theta) \\ 0 & 1 & 0 \\ \sin(\theta) & 0 & \cos(\theta) \end{pmatrix},$$

$$R_{e3}(\theta) = \begin{pmatrix} \cos(\theta) & \sin(\theta) & 0 \\ -\sin(\theta) & \cos(\theta) & 0 \\ 0 & 0 & 1 \end{pmatrix}. \tag{5}$$

Let $\theta_{e_1}, \theta_{e_2}, \theta_{e_3}$ be Euler angles of camera rotation in global coordinate system. Let $w = (w_1, w_2, w_3) \in \mathcal{R}^3$ be a camera position in global coordinates, then the center of the ellipse c is transformed to global coordinate system center $\hat{c}$ as follows

$$\hat{c} = w + cR_{e_1}(\theta_{e_1})R_{e_2}(\theta_{e_2})R_{e_3}(\theta_{e_3}). \tag{5}$$

Now we estimate the tube axis. Suppose that the camera is moving along an exact axis trough a part of the tube with the following restrictions. The look rotation of the camera goes with a tangent of the axis at a point where the camera is placed. Every step $I \in \{1, \ldots, n\}$ camera captures an image, from which we will obtain highlight matrix. Using conic fitting algorithm, we compute the ellipse properties. From those properties and the camera properties, we can compute the i-th point of estimated tube. Then the tube sector is divided into n points and the estimate of the axis is then set of points $\hat{c}_i \in \mathbb{R}^3$, $i = 1, \ldots, n$

$$\hat{c}_1 = w_1$$
$$\hat{c}_i = w_i + c_i R_{i,e_1}(\theta_{i,e_1})R_{i,e_2}(\theta_{i,e_2})R_{i,e_3}(\theta_{i,e_3}), \tag{6}$$

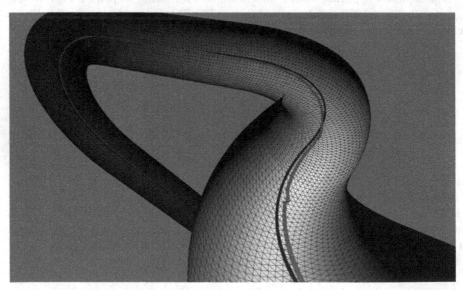

Fig. 11. Perfect scenario simulation, where the exact elliptic projection of circle is obtained from intersection of plane (distance from camera is 8/3 r) with the tube.

Note that even the perfect scenario showed in Fig. 11 does not give exact axis back. This is due to perspective projection properties, which are noticeable from Fig. 13.

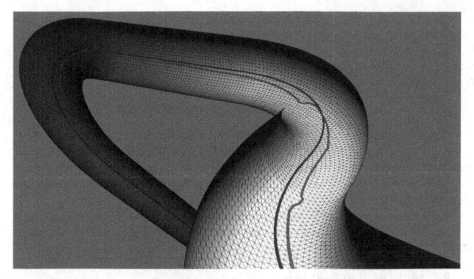

Fig. 12. The axis is computed using Hb with values bmin = 0.18, bmax = 0.19.

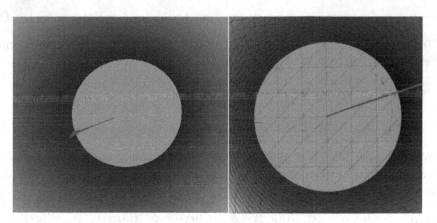

Fig. 13. Inaccuracy in perspective projection.

3.4 Transformation in C#

There are two main approaches to structures in C#. We use classes because it has no negative impact on functionality. The code alone is quite long, thus we describe only the idea behind this approach. The C# code is not supposed to work on its own, it is called by Unity.

Because it is so much easier to work with positions of the basis vectors in their basis, we define the general multivector of GAC as 256-dimensional vector of coefficients $a \in \mathcal{R}^{256}$. Each position $i \in \{1,\ldots, 256\}$ of this vector represents coefficient for basis blade $e_{S[i]}$, where $\mathcal{S} = \text{Po}(\{1,\ldots,8\})$. Each multivector is initiated as $o \in \mathcal{R}^{256}$. All functions are related to the multivectors. We do not need to introduce the basis blades in the code, because all their properties can be derived from the position in their basis. This is that we want to precompute all combinations of geometric product of two basis blades. A matrix $G \in \{1, -1, 2 -2 \ldots, 256, -256\}^{256 \times 256}$, where

$$G_{i,j} = \{l \in \mathbb{Z} : l = \text{sgn}(E_k)k\}, \text{ where } E_k = E_i E_j. \tag{7}$$

Thus, the geometric product can be computed using this matrix as follows, $E_i E_j = \text{sgn}(G_{i,j})E|_{G_{i,j}}|$. This approach reduces computation time, because in practice there are commonly hundreds or even thousands of geometric products computed in one step.

Subsequently, this section is finished by functions, that perform geometric, outer and inner products of 2 multivectors.

Furthermore, we can convert multivector in the terms of basis $\mathcal{R}^{5,3}$ to the multivector in terms of basis $\mathcal{R}^{5,3*}$. We specify this transition for vector $u \in \mathcal{R}^{5,3} \subset \mathcal{G}_{5,3}$ as function $\varnothing: \mathcal{R}^{5,3} \subset \mathcal{G}_{5,3} \to \mathcal{R}^{5,3} \subset \mathcal{G}^{5,3}$

$$u = (u_1 \ u_2 \ u_3 \ u_4 \ u_5 \ u_6 \ u_7 \ u_8),$$

$$\phi(u) =$$

$$\left(-u_1 + u_8 \ -u_2 + u_7 \ -u_3 + u_6 \ u_4 \ u_5 \ \tfrac{1}{2}(u_3 + u_6) \ \tfrac{1}{2}(u_2 + u_7) \ \tfrac{1}{2}(u_1 + u_8)\right). \tag{8}$$

Transition of vector $v \in \mathcal{R}^{5,3} \subset \mathcal{G}_{5,3}$ in terms of basis $\mathcal{R}^{5,3*}$ to the vector in terms of basis $\mathcal{R}^{5,3}$ is defined by $\varnothing^{-1}: \mathcal{R}^{5,3} \subset \mathcal{G}_{5,3} \to \mathcal{R}^{5,3} \subset \mathcal{G}_{5,3}$,

$$v = (\bar{v}_\times \ \bar{v}_- \ \bar{v}_+ \ v_1 \ v_2 \ v_+ \ v_- \ v_\times),$$

$$\phi^{-1}(v) =$$

$$\left(-\tfrac{1}{2}\bar{v}_\times + v_\times \ \ -\tfrac{1}{2}\bar{v}_- + v_- \ \ -\tfrac{1}{2}\bar{v}_+ + v_+ \ \ v_1 \ \ v_2 \ \ \tfrac{1}{2}\bar{v}_+ + v_+ \ \ \tfrac{1}{2}\bar{v}_- + v_- \ \ -\tfrac{1}{2}\bar{v}_\times + v_\times\right). \tag{9}$$

We implement IPNS and OPNS representations of conics to C# code in follow. In the case of OPNS representation we implement the conic spanned by 5 points $u_1, u_2, u_3, u_4, u_5 \in \mathcal{R}^2$ as follows

$$Q_O = \phi^{-1}(\mathcal{C}(u_1)) \wedge \phi^{-1}(\mathcal{C}(u_2)) \wedge \phi^{-1}(\mathcal{C}(u_3)) \wedge \phi^{-1}(\mathcal{C}(u_4)) \wedge \phi^{-1}(\mathcal{C}(u_5))$$

In the case of axes-aligned conic given by 4 points and one basis vector n_x,

$$Q_O^{al} = \phi^{-1}(\mathcal{C}(u_1)) \wedge \phi^{-1}(\mathcal{C}(u_2)) \wedge \phi^{-1}(\mathcal{C}(u_3)) \wedge \phi^{-1}(\mathcal{C}(u_4)) \wedge \phi^{-1}(n_\times)$$

In the case of circle spanned by 3 points and basis vector of GAC representing infinity $n_x, n_-,$

$$C_O = \phi^{-1}(\mathcal{C}(u_1)) \wedge \phi^{-1}(\mathcal{C}(u_2)) \wedge \phi^{-1}(\mathcal{C}(u_3)) \wedge \phi^{-1}(n_-) \wedge \phi^{-1}(n_\times). \tag{10}$$

Transformations in C# finishes implementations of $\mathcal{G}^{5,3}$ functionalities to C# source code. Clockwise rotation by angle α done in $\mathcal{G}_{5,3}$ is given by rotor R and its reverse $\tilde{R}$.

We will finish this section with getting conic properties from its general representation. From conic properties and parametric equations for an ellipse and hyperbola we can obtain set of points (pixels), which will be displayed as a graphical output.

4   Conclusion

This paper aimed to a tube axis estimation, which consists of projected ellipse centers into environment of the tube. Firstly, we implemented necessary algorithms to be able to perform geometric, inner and outer product.

In next section we created 3D environment including light source, camera and tube. From image data (Figs. 1 and 2) we were able to create algorithms for choosing certain points and extract an ellipse. However, only the first algorithm (using matrix H_b) was able to estimate the tube axis, that was actually going through the tube (Fig. 12). We compared that algorithm to the best scenario (Fig. 11), which took advantage of the cutting plane (Figs. 3 and 4).

The inaccuracy, even in the best scenario, is caused by projective geometry in computer graphics, where the size of the projected object depends only on e_3 coordinate. This causes that the distant objects (in e_1, e_2 coordinates) seems closer than they really are.

The next step would be an image processing to reduce the inaccuracy, or even compute the inaccuracy from the shape of the ellipse. Even considerable are self-learning algorithms that can choose points based on different tube examples and textures. The result given by matrix H_b is sufficient for demonstration of approach to autonomous navigation of a robot with camera in the tube. The result is that using three operations it is possible to determine the center of a given conic section, with all the configuration taking place in the GAC, so the result is a conic section in the GAC.

In Sect. 3.4 we implemented necessary algorithms to be able to perform geometric, inner, and outer product. Then we implemented efficient method for computing geometric product of two basis blades as a basis blade with position from the value matrix with precomputed values for the geometric product. An improvement can be made by generalizing this concept to the general geometric algebra $\mathcal{G}_{p,q}$ and move the computation of the value matrix to C#.

We defined two functions $\varnothing$ and $\varnothing^{-1}$ further, which transit vectors between the bases $\mathcal{R}^{5,3}$ and $\mathcal{R}^{5,3*}$. Then, using $\varnothing^{-1}$, we implemented inner and outer product null space representations of conics to C# code.

References

1. Artin E.: Affine and Projective Geometry (1988), [cit. 2021-05-05]. https://doi.org/10.1002/9781118164518.ch2
2. Ayoub, A.B.: The Central Conic Sections Revisited, pp. 322–325, Taylor & Francis (1993). [cit.2021-04-28]. https://doi.org/10.1080/0025570X.1993.11996157
3. Dorst, L., Fontijne, D., Mann, S.: Geometric Algebra for Computer Science (Revised Edition). Morgan Kaufmann Publishers (2007). ISBN 978-0-12-374942-0
4. Herman, I.: Projective Geometry and Computer Graphics. In: Hewitt, W. T., Grave, M., Roch, M. (eds.) Advances in Computer Graphics IV. EurographicSeminars, pp. 28–61. Springer, Berlin, Heidelberg (1991). ISBN 978-3-642-84060-9. https://doi.org/10.1007/978-3-642-84060-9_2
5. Hildenbrand, D.: Foundantions of Geometric Algebra Computing. Springer, Berlin, Heidelberg (2013). ISBN 978-3-642-31794-1. https://doi.org/10.1007/978-3-642-31794-1

6. Hrdina, J., Návrat, A., Vašík, P.: Conic fitting in geometric algebra setting. Adv. Appl. Clifford Algebras **29**(4), 1–13 (2019). https://doi.org/10.1007/s00006-019-0989-5
7. Hrdina, J., Návrat, A., Vašík, P.: Geometric algebra for conics. Adv. Appl. Clifford Algebras **28**(3), 1–21 (2018). https://doi.org/10.1007/s00006-018-0879-2
8. 3D Graphics with OpenGL, Internet site. [cit. 2021-05-05]
9. Machálek, L.: Korekce obrazových vad pomocí CGA [cit. 2021-04-08]. https://www.vutbr.cz/studenti/zav-prace/detail/109029
10. Machálek, L.: Geometric Algebra Applications. Brno (2021). MASTER'S THESIS. BRNO UNIVERSITY OF TECHNOLOGY. Vedoucí práce doc. Mgr. Petr Vašík, Ph.D.
11. Perwass, C.: Geometric Algebra with Applications in Engineering. Springer, Berlin (2009). ISBN 354089067X. https://doi.org/10.1007/978-1-4612-0159-5
12. Richter-Gebert, J.: Perspectives on Projective Geometry. Springer Publishing Company, Berlin, Heidelberg (2011). Incorporated. ISBN 978-3-642-17285-4. https://doi.org/10.1007/978-3-642-17286-1
13. Smith, C.: On Vertex-Vertex Systems and Their Use in Geometric and Biological Modelling, University of Calgary (2006). ISBN 9780494195741
14. Solomon, C.J., Breckon, T.P.: Fundamentals of Digital Image Processing: A Practical Approach with Examples in Matlab, Wiley-Blackwell, Hoboken (2010). ISBN 978-0470844731
15. Young, C.Y.: Precalculus; Chapter 9. John Wiley and Sons, Hoboken (2010). ISBN 978-0-471-75684-2

Towards Modularity: Integration Strategy of Radar into a LiDAR Based Robotics Mapping Platform

Kevin Murphy[1,2], Dylan Charter[1,2], Dylan Pasley[1,2(✉)],
Israel Lopez-Toledo[1,2], and Ahmet Soylemezoglu[1]

[1] Construction Engineering Research Lab, Champaign, IL 61801, USA
{Kevin.F.Murphy,Dylan.T.Charter,Dylan.A.Pasley,
Israel.J.LopezToledo,Ahmet.Soylemezoglu}@erdc.dren.mil
[2] University of Illinois, Champaign, IL 61801, USA

Abstract. Removing Combat Engineers, first responders, and disaster relief workers from dangerous situations remains a major motivation for researching semi-autonomous mapping platforms. The successful adoption of such systems requires the implementation of a series of complex sensors collecting, processing, and storing terabytes of data, in near real-time. Operations in uncertain and austere environments has great potential for sensor and computational hardware unavailability and damage; robustness to these difficulties requires careful planning and dedicated practices. While simulation allows for rapid creation and testing of such complicated robotic systems and algorithms, development in simulation and on hardware introduces additional complications.

This research explores these challenges and proposes a conventional workflow method for modular development of hardware and software in parallel. The Large-group Parallel Simulation-Hardware Development (LaPaSHD) workflow arose from years of US Army Corps of Engineers (USACE) Engineer Research and Development Center's (ERDC) research with Unmanned Ground Vehicles (UGV). LaPaSHD, system requirements and considerations, best practices, and the challenges motivating this workflow are introduced through a case study: incorporating radar systems into an existing LiDAR based simulated platform.

Keywords: ROS · Sensor Modularity · Scalability · Modularity · Workflow · Parallel Development · UGV

1 Introduction

1.1 Motivation

Unmanned and robotic systems are increasingly utilized to perform military mission sets. These autonomous and semi-autonomous systems heavily rely on sensors and depend on the computational hardware and software compiling the raw

J. Mazal et al. (Eds.): MESAS 2022, LNCS 13866, pp. 87–108, 2023.
https://doi.org/10.1007/978-3-031-31268-7_6

data into high-level directives. Due to the ever-changing environment, threats, improvements in technology, etc.; the hardware (sensor and compute payload) and software configuration of such systems are subject to change to include the addition of new sensing modalities to be able to perform new and emerging missions. However, creating and integrating custom sensor communications is infeasible for independent robotic system developers. To address this problem, many robotic component manufactures release software packages which translate robot communications and control into a common medium.

Robot Operating System (ROS) is an open-source framework for robotics that was created to support the need software modularity [13]. However, ROS' current implementation and common practices fall short of this goal. The rest of this paper aims to address these shortcomings through the introducing and providing a framework supporting development of independent packages and integrating them onto robotics systems. This also extends the capabilities to ease parallel development challenges on hardware and software simultaneously.

1.2   Project Background and Rationale

This research builds off two of the US Army Corps of Engineers (USACE) Engineer Research and Development Center's (ERDC) projects: Robotics for Engineer Operations (REO) and Robotic Assessment of Dams (DamBot). These two projects, referred to as REO and DamBot Teams (RaDaT), aim to enable autonomous robotic site characterization and preparation in unknown and austere environments. Benefits of these efforts include keeping combat and civil engineers out of dangerous environments, replacing hazardous manual labor, and strengthening operational capabilities against loss of communication. One example of this technology can be seen with DamBot [22], which conducts inspections on dams which are no longer safe for humans, such as after an earthquake, without the possibility of any wireless communication. Another example of the this technology is seen in the REO project where specialized platforms collect and build high-fidelity models of the environment or perform combat engineer support operations (such as terrain shaping or obstacle reduction) in navigation satellite system (GNSS)-denied, unknown environments at beyond-visual-line-of-sight standoff distances [23]. The operational environment of an austere mapping platform offers significant challenges to current robotic system development workflows and is an open research area.

RaDaT's current ROS-based mapping system relies primarily on camera and LiDAR sensors which provide a means to add ground truth to apriori satellite imagery, as well as capture additional pertinent engineering information that can only be obtained by ground platforms. Additional diversified instrumentation will increase the robustness of this system. RaDaT's research robotic platforms are actively in development, including in software, design, and instrumentation changes, from teams separated by several states. Despite the challenges discussed in Sect. 1.1, RaDaT continues to introduce new capabilities. Through years of experience and development, RaDaT has identified processes that facilitate parallel development of hardware and software with large and geographically diverse teams.

1.3   State of the Art

Modularity in service robotics is a subject that has been deeply researched and well documented. The state of the art suggests that, although the research supports the wide scale adoption of modular concepts, gaps exist in standards and production protocols that are needed to support the wide scale shift towards open modular networks and supply chains. [3] introduces this issue and discusses it in depth as well as introducing readers to the ISO publication 22166-1 which outlines some standards that can be adopted as a common stepping stone towards modularity.

While [3] does a great job at introducing and defining modularity and its shortcomings in the field of robotics, paper [8] presents one potential solution. In [8], the authors successfully design and demonstrate a hardware to software integration component for a ROS based platform. The key finding for this paper is that extensibility and flexibility can be attained on a ROS platform without compromising its efficiency. However, this is still an example of a closed system solution and showcases the interest and potential ease of designing modular systems.

A large amount of research exists for mapping and the role of modularity in this focus area. In [9] we are shown how different sensor modalities perceive different data sets as the authors work to advance the use of ground penetrating radar along side visual sensors for urban search and rescue. The authors successfully utilize simulation to display increased robustness in data collected using multiple sensor modalities.

In [10] and [11], the authors explore the use of radar for mapping purposes and pursue an interest in combining LiDAR and Radar for terrain mapping. These papers, in addition to [12] demonstrate a growing interest in, and ability to, fuse the data collected from multiple sensor modalities to produce better results.

Our paper seeks to fill a gap in the current state of the art by providing an in depth look at the conventional integration of a new sensor modality into an established robotic stack. While the research is still moving towards modularity, and towards LiDAR/Radar integration, this paper provides a path forward for researchers looking to expand the capabilities of their own previously established platforms.

1.4 Primary Contributions

The goal of this research is to increase the scalability and robustness of existing research platforms through increased system modularity achieved through the LaPaSHD workflow. The LaPaSHD workflow takes physical, computational, and data management constraints and operational requirements into consideration. An example of the delivered workflow is shown in a case study, which walks through the process of extending the capabilities of a robotic ground platform by adding an additional sensor modality to an existing ROS stack.

This exercise addresses development challenges that currently exist within the field of robotics, namely scalability, robustness, and development flexibility, thus supporting the case for advancing modularity for robotic systems and components. In addition, this paper expands the body of work relating to autonomous mapping of diverse and changing environments by examining a platform designed for such a task. Developing a process facilitating rapid adjustments in robotic infrastructure and software forms the foundation of this research.

1.5 Paper Organization

This exploration begins in Sect. 2 by providing an overview of the LaPaSHD workflow, beginning with a general overview. Software practices, hardware considerations, and system requirements supporting sensor integration in platform development are then detailed. Section 3 opens with the introduction and background for the case study, transitions to details of the study, and concludes with discussion of the results, the process, and implementation challenges. Section 4 condenses the LaPaSHD workflow in a bulleted list. Finally, this research is concluded with a discussion of the workflow, our recommendations for sensor integration, and future work efforts which are expected to improve modularity in robotics software and development.

2 LaPaSHD Workflow and Organization

2.1 Overview

The workflow detailed below focuses on developing a modular software structure. The Large-group Parallel Simulation-Hardware Development (LaPaSHD) is the workflow RaDaT utilizes to ensure system modularity. Additionally, by utilizing simulation environments, the workflow facilitates seamless development within large scale teams restricted by limited access to robotic platforms. Software practices that support modularity include the following: maintaining separate packages, utilizing environmental variables to identify and utilize the proper sensors, utilizing UDEV rules to replace system port names, utilizing machine tags to direct software nodes to specific computers, utilizing install and setup scripts, and computation expense analysis. The LaPaSHD workflow emphasises the co-design of the physical system with software, in which developers must consider the system hardware, speed, and computational requirements; which sensors, buses, and interfaces will be required; and the ease of integration of the hardware into the system. Figure 1 shows a high-level flowchart outlining holistic development using the LaPaSHD system, which consists of three main components: design variables and parameters, parallel design processes, and a suitability check. Each of the four items inside of the parallel development component represent an individual process. Each process checks design suitability of its respective component using the same set of system variables and parameters as the other parallel components. If all system requirements and specifications are met, the design is suitable. This process can also be used to optimize past suitability. The following sections review the design considerations and methods to adjust parameters utilized in the Computer Design and Platform Instrumentation components. The remaining two sections are out of scope for this work.

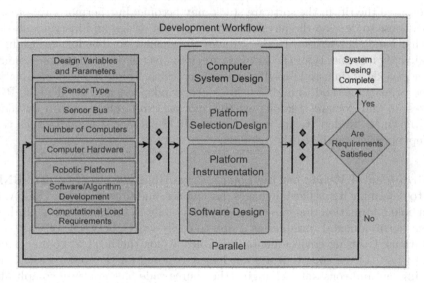

Fig. 1. High-level LaPaSHD workflow diagram outlining the for development of a software package for a robotic system.

2.2 Software Practices

Developing or converting a software package compatible with LaPaSHD requires additional structuring and components beyond meeting system requirements outlined above. These additional attributes form a standard for package interoperability and integration autonomy, which are shown by the workflow in Fig. 2. Upon reaching the end of a flowchart, the package has the following traits: single script exaction identical installation and setup, support for multiprocessing across several computers, incorporated environmental variables configuration, and package independence. The method to achieve each of these attributes are discussed in detail below.

Modular ROS Packages. While, ROS is deigned to functions as a modular framework, it relies on the developers designing the software to achieve package independence. This goal is rarely reached outside of professional development of individual packages. It is not uncommon for users to splice and co-mingle packages, thus creating new dependencies which lose the idea of modularity. While not inherently a problem, it does necessitate significant and wide spread software changes in many packages for any change in the system. Software alteration effort and potential for software defects grows disproportionately larger the more complex the system and the more packages that are altered, limiting standardization and dramatically slowing down platform development. These problems are accentuated when developing with large teams with members creating unique co-mingled/co-dependant packages independently. The more spread out the software development team is and the more limited the communication, the more exacerbated the rift in the software stack may become. Furthermore, roboticists must choose to develop the physical robotic system design and instrumentation in either parallel or series with the software via simulation. The former produces significantly more areas for the software stack to diverge while the latter requires longer periods of time and possibly several iterations. LaPaSHD uses modularity as the primary method to address the package independence. By default, ROS utilizes an xml document known as the "package.xml" along with a standard tool known as "rosdep" to try and make the ROS package standalone such that all dependencies can be easily installed.

Environmental Variables. Environmental variables [24] are a standard UNIX way to determine items like languages, hostnames, and library paths. These variables hold information that can be read by externally installed programs. RaDaT utilizes environmental variables as a way to easily switch between software configurations. Utilizing environmental variables avoids the need to comment out specific parts of the code that are not longer required for the mission set. Commenting out and constantly changing the source code files not only complicates reading the code, but also makes merging different software versions a tedious task. One example where environmental variables are used is when determining which sensors serves as the primary sensors used in forward obstacle avoidance. For example, in a highly vegetated area, a LiDAR based solution may not be the most effective. If the current system configuration assigns the LiDAR as the primary sensing modality, multiple configuration files would have manually edited without using environmental variables. All of the environmental variables are stored in an environmental variable file such that the user does not have to manually find each file in order to change the functionality of the system. Note that after environmental variable files are changed, they must be sourced in order to take effect.

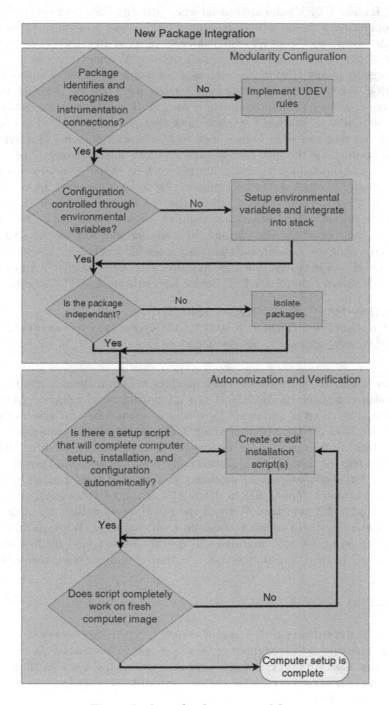

Fig. 2. Package development workflow

UDEV Rules. UDEV rules are crucial when utilizing USB devices. By default, UNIX operating systems will enumerate USB devices randomly upon boot. In simple terms, with multiple USB devices plugged in, there is no guarantee that USB1 is the same device after a reboot. Without the use of UDEV rules, plugging in any USB device such as a computer mouse can cause a failure in the ROS driver as the all of the device ports have now be changed causing the source code to read data from the wrong device. UDEV rules use device-specific attributes to provide a symbolic link that can be referenced as opposed to the device name in ROS launch files and parameter servers. This symbolic link will account for the fact that the device order might change. The UDEV daemon can also provide elevated privileges such as changing port permissions which typically reset after a system reboot. [21] System installed udev rules are located at "/usr/lib/udev/rules.d" while user created udev rules are located at "/etc/udev/rules.d." Any sensor that requires a udev rule has a "udev" folder located at the root of the ros package. In a similar way to how the setup files are parsed during a vehicle installation, any udev file located in this udev folder will be added to the custom udev location of "/etc/udev/rules.d". An example udev rule is shown below for a USB device that utilizes an FTDI adapter.

```
SUBSYSTEM=="tty", SUBSYSTEMS=="usb",
ATTRS{product}=="FT232R USB UART", ATTRS{serial}=="*******",
SYMLINK+="kvh_address", MODE="0666"
```

Machine Tags. ROS utilizes standard machine tags in roslaunch files to determine which computer the node will run on during multi-computer setup. A multi-computer setup is important for not only redundancy for system failure, but also for ensuring the required amount of computation is available for the required task. ROS1 operates on a non-real-time operating system resulting in a larger system overhead than a conventional real-time system. These machine tags allow for easy swapping of machines in case of failure. RaDaT Robotics utilizes a machine's .launch file to define the common nodes such as battery, camera, and LiDAR machines. Without the use of machine tags, the user would have to manually start the other nodes on each computer. With machine tags, the nodes running on each machine can quickly be swapped by just altering the "address" in this "machines.launch" to that of another computer as shown below.

```
<launch>

<machine name="battery"  user="****"    address="******"
  env-loader="/opt/ros/noetic/env.sh" default="false"/>
<machine name="localization" user="****" address="localhost"
  env-loader="/opt/ros/noetic/env.sh" default="false"
  timeout="10"/>
<machine name="control"  user="****" address="localhost"
  env-loader="/opt/ros/noetic/env.sh" default="false"
```

```
timeout="10"/>

</launch>
```

Setup Script. While ROS utilizes xml documents to install ROS packages dependencies, there are often standard UNIX dependencies that are not accounted for. Along with this, there are often post-installation requirements such as updating library paths and rebooting the computer that are not accomplished by standard ROS setup procedures. In order to address these issues, LaPaSHD utilizes a "setup" folder in each of its custom ROS packages. Inside of this setup folder exists a "setup.sh" bash script and a "rosinstall" file. For ROS dependencies that require compilation, a "rosinstall" file is used to add the source code of the software to the workspace. This bash script includes the installation of any non-ROS packages. When the RaDaT Robotics software stack in installed, the workspace is parsed and every setup.sh dependency script is ran to ensure all dependencies are accounted for.

Computation. While in simulation, time is relative to the computer, allowing computation requirements to be relaxed greatly. On less powerful computers, the simulations can be made to run effectively even with significantly more computationally expensive tasks. However, when implemented on hardware, these requirements come crashing back, meaning processes and algorithms that work in simulation may fail in reality. Evaluating the ability for robot hardware to meet the requirement to run onboard in real-time is nontrivial.

Sensor communications in simulation vs hardware introduce another layer of considerations for computational expense. Many sensors use proprietary or nonstandard data packets. Using point clouds as an example, the Intel RealSense 435i use the Point Cloud Library (PCL) point cloud messages, ROS uses sensor_msgs/PointCloud2 messages, and the radar simulation uses custom RadarTargetArray messages. These messages virtually convey the same information and can generally be converted back and forth; however, converting tens of thousands of points hundreds of times per second greatly increase computational load and introduces delay.

2.3   System Hardware and Requirements

In order to meet the program requirements of near real-time mapping as well as operation in a communication denied environment, RaDaT utilizes high-end computational systems to process, classify, and store data onboard. Figure 3 shows a detailed of the computer design parallel process from Fig. 1, consisting of possible design options to reach a sufficient or optimized computer hardware design. Similarly, Fig. 4 shows possible actions used to make sensor instrumentation viable for the robotic system. The items on these lists of design options are discussed in the sections below. Critical to each of those sections, and one of the most critical requirements in instrumentation selection, is the hardware interface

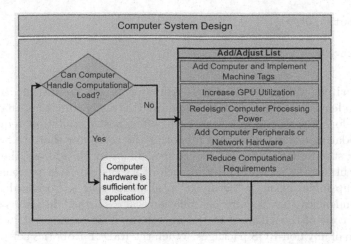

Fig. 3. Computer system design parallel LaPaSHD process, outlining considerations when verifying suitability of computational hardware in the parallel development process.

type. Two of the most common interface types are universal serial bus (USB) and Ethernet. Factors such as speed of data transmission, bandwidth, and ease of integration are considered in the selection process. USB devices require a USB host controller while Ethernet devices require Network Interface Cards (NICs).

Speed of Data Transmission. The speed of the sensor depends on its application as well as the operational speed of the robotic platform. Core sensors such as those that are responsible for aiding in the relative localization of the system such as inertial measurement units (IMUs) and wheel encoders require high update rates, due to the critical impact of these sensors on the overall system performance. Table 1 displays the interface speeds of USB generation 2 and above and Ethernet category (CAT) 6 and above. At the time of writing, USB 1.0 and 1.1 along with CAT 4 Ethernet and below are considered obsolete, and therefore they are omitted from this discussion. Identifying the true transfer speed of a particular sensor is usually not trivial, but manufacturers typically list the required USB speed or the required Ethernet speed. Both USB and Ethernet are backwards compatible meaning a USB 2.0 device will work on a USB 3.0 port, for example, so it's best to ensure the USB ports are at a minimum the required generation.

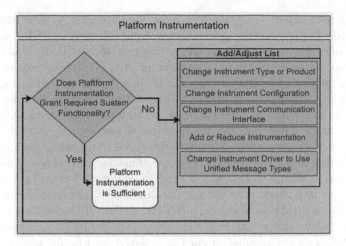

Fig. 4. Platform instrumentation design parallel LaPaSHD process, outlining considerations when verifying suitability of system instrumentation in the parallel development process.

Table 1. Interface Speeds [17, 18]

Interface Type	Speed (Megabits per second)
USB 2.0	480
USB 3.0	5000
USB 3.1	10000
USB 3.2	20000
USB 4	40000
Ethernet:CAT5e	1000
Ethernet:CAT6a	10000

Bandwidth. Bandwidth is an important factor to consider when utilizing sensors that transfer large amount of data such as cameras and LiDAR sensors or when utilizing a large amount of sensors on the same interface. Both USB host controllers and NICs have bandwidth limits that can cause issues receiving the data from the sensor if the total amount of traffic on this interface is above or near this limit. These hardware controllers are ultimately the limiting factor for bandwidth. RaDaT has experienced issues utilizing solely the motherboard integrated USB ports with a sensor suite of four 1080p USB cameras and two IMUs. The optimization of the sensor driver along with the operating system also factor into the bandwidth issue. A high-bandwidth sensor such as an USB camera can obtain a majority of the available bandwidth leaving the future devices with not enough bandwidth to even enumerate, which is the initial communication handshake and determination of the device [20].

One way to deal with many devices of the same interface type is to utilize the motherboards Peripheral Component Interconnect Express (PCIe) slot. These PCIe slots offer expansion options where one can add an USB expansion card that contains its own USB host controller or NIC. Graphics processing units (GPUs) also utilize PCIe slots on the motherboard, but the current generation of motherboards often provide extra PCIe slots that could be used for this purpose. A PCIe slot contains either 1, 4, 8, or 16 lanes which directly correlates to the amount of data that can be transferred per second as well as have a generation ranging from 1.0 to 5.0 where the speed improves at each newer generation. Caution should be taken to ensure that the motherboard used in the computational system supports the desired PCIe generation and the number of lanes. Another important note is that the amount of usable PCIe lanes is also limited by the central processing unit (CPU), so the CPU specifications should be checked. Lastly, the motherboard specifications should be checked to ensure that the PCIe slot the expansion card is inserted into is not shared with any other high bandwidth devices such as GPUs. PCIe USB expansion cards are also manufactured that take additional power directly from the power supply in order to utilize high power devices that draw more power than the PCIe slot can provide. This method is highly recommended if one is planning to utilize all of the USB ports on the card.

PCIe network interface cards are often manufactured in terms of speed such as 1 gigabit per second (Gbps), 2.5 Gbps, 5 Gbps, or 10 Gbps. For ethernet applications, instead of adding a PCIe expansion card, another option is to utilize a network switch. Utilization of a network switch allows for only one connection to the computation system with the downside that every sensor plugged into that network switch has its bandwidth limited by the up-link of the switch as well as the bandwidth of the internal NIC. A similar option is available for USB as well by utilizing USB hubs, with externally powered variants available, but the bandwidth is in the end still limited by the USB port the hub is connected to along with the integrated USB host controller.

Ease of Integration. Ease of integration is also a critical factor to development of the robotic platforms. As with any research and development, changes occur quickly and often. Sensor placement can often move due to interference from other sensors, motors, or other hardware or the desire for a change of the field of view. USB and Ethernet cables both have a maximum length before the signal degrades. CAT 6a Ethernet cable is able to achieve 10 Gbps at a distance of 100 m [18]. USB cables, however, of generation 3 are not able to obtain more than 15 m, but this can be extended to 18 m by utilizing an active cable that injects power into the system [19]. Utilizing Ethernet provides having the flexibility to move the sensors without having to worry about adding in extra powered cables. Recall these are the maximum lengths so issues can still occur, often experienced in USB, at lengths less than the maximum listed. Some USB interfaces are able to power the system from the USB port while others require external power. Ethernet devices that are not Power over Ethernet (PoE) must be powered externally; however many Ethernet sensors are Poe which mean if a PoE network card is utilized, the sensor can be powered via the Ethernet cable providing even more flexibility.

Fig. 5. Clearpath Warthog UGV [14]

3 Case Study

3.1 Case Study Introduction

By expanding the suite of onboard sensors, RaDaT can extend the utility, accuracy, and robustness of its robotic capabilities, increasing mission success assurance. In general when looking to integrate in a new sensor, simulation can be very useful for experimenting to see how the sensor will affect the desired application. While RaDaT conducts research with several Unmanned Ground Vehicle (UGV) platforms, this effort focuses on the Clearpath Robotics' Warthog UGV platform [14] shown in Fig. 5. The Warthog is designed to be an all-terrain robot that is capable of operating in various environments and weather conditions.

This section gives an overview of the case study in which RaDaT explores the advantages of the LaPaSHD workflow while integrating a new sensor modality into an existing software stack running in a Gazebo simulation developed with ROS Noetic on Ubuntu 20.04 operating system. Several challenges were encountered while working to develop an accurate simulation. In this case, radar will be integrated into a LiDAR based system. This study examines, exemplifies, and discusses common challenges faced when altering robotic infrastructure. Details how LaPaSHD overcame these challenges, highlighting the impact advanced modularity would have for bespoke robotic platforms. In the end, data collected from the simulated tests are presented and analyzed. This research effort outlines a conventional method for integrating a new modality into an existing system.

3.2   Case Study Background

One core capability of RaDaT platforms is high fidelity terrain mapping and obstacle identification in remote austere environments. The operating environment for this platform can be unpredictable, offering a range of terrain features, unreliable or nonexistent Global Navigation Satellite Systems (GNSS), and extensive biodiversity. To meet its primary objectives, the system has been designed to carry out mapping operations in GNSS denied environments with the potential of a lack of communications to the system while deployed. This design utilizes LiDAR sensors along with stereo and monochrome cameras to meet its visual mapping objectives. However, we begin to experience the limitations of this configuration when attempting to classify elements within the environment. This limitation is not unique to our system, as the requirement for utilizing multiple modalities has been highlighted in similar research efforts [5]. Similarly, our experiments provide us with evidence to suggest that adding an additional modality to our system will be the most efficient way to increase our mapping and navigation capabilities. Additionally, the plausibility of combining radar and LiDAR sensors has been thoroughly explored in [6]. It has also been demonstrated that environmental mapping can be done with both radar and LiDAR sensors in [7]. However, gaps begin to emerge in the research when you attempt to find working integrated systems that utilize both radar and LiDAR systems simultaneously.

In addition to these issues highlighted above, further challenges arise while a UGV is operated in potentially hazardous environments. In our case, due to the unpredictability and variations in the operating environment, it is highly likely that parts of the platform might sustain damage and would require rapid replacement. The current state of the art is too restricted in its ability to plug and play, or 'hot swap', different components of existing platforms. Field replacement of damaged/non-functioning sensors currently require extensive amounts of experience, time, and money. Therefore, it is highly beneficial to work towards standardized modular systems.

3.3   Case Study Problem Space

Autonomous terrain mapping of austere environments is a data intensive task which spans multiple professional and academic fields. Due to the current cost and complexity of unmanned ground platforms, many organizations have to rely on a single platform to perform this task autonomously/semi-autonomously. Challenges arise when dealing with complicated or untraversable terrain, inclement weather, or other sources of outside interference. Designing and implementing a robotic platform that is robust enough to operate in unpredictable conditions, without overloading its data storage and processing capabilities is inherently difficult. An easy solution to increasing the flexibility and robustness of a system is to add an additional sensor modularity to its existing architecture. In most cases, in which platforms are designed for specific purposes, this is a non-trivial modification [1]. The implications for such a change impact a systems physical configuration, power requirements, software stack, and operational capabilities, and therefore must be carried out with significant care and planning.

Capturing data with different sensor modalities offers a great deal of control over which elements data can be collected, and how these data can be processed. This indicates that a system with multiple sensor types will be better equipped to function more robustly [2]. Assuming the increased volume of data can be captured, stored, and processed, the result is a much richer data set.

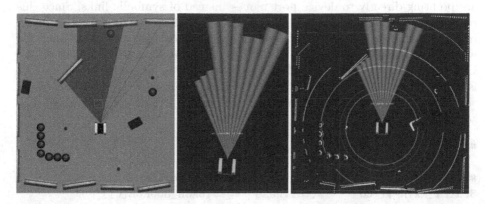

Fig. 6. Simulation implementation of the Warthog platform in the same scene. Left shows the view in Gazebo simulator with radar package visible as blue swath. Middle shows the re-implemented radar using conical grey beams and red point readings from the radar in Rviz. Right shows all of the previous measurements with the addition of LiDAR point cloud. (Color figure online)

3.4 Simulation Design

The Clearpath Robotics Warthog [14] was chosen as the simulated robotic platform for several reasons, including the ease of implementation and that RaDaT had yet to build a simulator for the that particular platform. The primary reason the Warthog was chosen is Clearpath Robotics' software stack and documentation. The installation process is well explained on their website [25] and implementing and testing the base model is user friendly. The software stack is structured with several grouped packages. Warthog_control contains configurations and implementation of the platform's driving control, Warthog_gazebo holds the simulation worlds, etc. Warthog_description, is dedicated to describing base robot including visualization and sensors. Most notably in the visualization package are the "accessories" files. Built into the Warthog base model are configurations to add and remove additional components. This same structure is followed to add additional sensors.

Simulated LiDAR uses the Toyota Research Institute's Velodyne Simulator [16] and Ainstein_radar package [15]. Sonar, radar, and LiDAR were implemented by placing the sensor visualization (URDF) and functional service (Gazebo) portions into a dedicated file which was read into the Warthog top-level URDF. This has the added benefit of letting is use the sensors as a class and reusing that code. In our case, using several sonar sensors to replicate a radar sensor only added three more lines instead of a new file per beam.

The Ainstein_radar package exists in its own modular package and does provide test launch files. However, the device ports listed in some of the launch files are pointing directly to device port names instead of symbolic links. Since this research is only simulation it does not matter in this case, but for the actual implementation a "udev" folder containing the udev rule and the launch file would be modified to use this symbolic link. There is some development on the UNIX operating system required to get the simulation environment set up that is shown in the setup script below. It is crucial that after the creation of the script that the file is made executable via "chmod +x" or else the installation script will not be ran.

```
#! /bin/bash

#Variable that holds the location of this script
SCRIPT_PATH=$( cd -- "$( dirname -- "${BASH_SOURCE[0]}" )"
    &> /dev/null && pwd )

#Holds the Workspace path from enviornmental variable
WORKSPACE_PATH=$WORKSPACE_PATH

#Create the default gazebo model directory if it does not exist
if [ ! ~/.gazebo ]; then
    mkdir ~/.gazebo
fi

#Copy the models from the ainstein_radar package to the
#default gazebo model location
cd $SCRIPT_PATH
cp -r ../models ~/.gazebo

#Delete any previous text in the .bashrc
sed -i "/## Begin gazebo_models/,/## End gazebo_models/d"
    ~/.bashrc

#Add the path to the ~/.bashrc for each terminal
cat >> ~/.bashrc <<EOL
## Begin gazebo_models
```

```
export GAZEBO_MODEL_PATH=$GAZEBO_MODEL_PATH:~/.gazebo/models
export GAZEBO_PLUGIN_PATH=$GAZEBO_PLUGIN_PATH:
   ~/$WORKSPACE_PATH/devel/lib

## End gazebo_models
EOL
```

3.5   Results

Figure 7 shows the simulation with a scenario where it is trying to choose the best path forward. This scenario is one of many that exemplify the benefits of diverse sensing. In this scene, thin objects are being missed by the LiDAR, but are however sensed by the simulated radar indicating the only way forward is outside the jersey barriers. Other scenarios that would exemplify the benefits of combined LiDAR/radar sensing include navigating around 1) transparent objects, which are not visible to LiDARs, 2) thin objects, such as a chain link fence, which may be missed depending on LiDAR configuration, 3) fast moving obstacles, where radar Doppler shift provides speed of obstacle, etc.

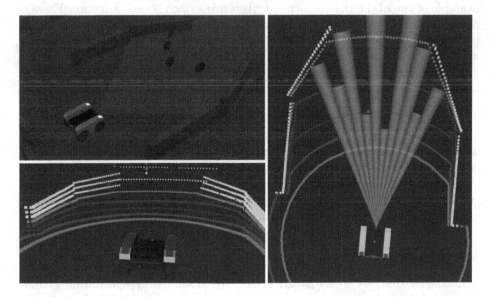

Fig. 7. Simulation implementation of the Warthog platform in the same scene, where the goal is to determine what path the robot should take to move forward. The top left shows the view in Gazebo simulator with radar package visible as blue swath. The lower left shows the LiDAR view of the scene. The right side shows the LiDAR points and simulated radar using conical grey beams in Rviz. (Color figure online)

4   Implementation Challenges Discussion

Although several commercial and open-source physics simulators exist, all of them have their own unique challenges. These issues stem from many different sources: bugs in simulator implementation, steep learning curve, difficult user interface, human error, incomplete documentation, etc. Even though each of the several challenge sources are unique, we find many of the issues fall into similar categories, suggesting that the challenges in simulation faced are representative of those throughout the field and allowing them to be extrapolated from this case study.

4.1   Broken Source Code

The first challenge encountered while conducting this research was building the radar package [15]. Even though it is one of the two radar simulators commonly used with Gazebo, this package's source code does not build initially. The first and less significant problem is incomplete reporting of required software. With tools such as CMakelist's Build Depends or .rosinstall files, code authors can specify what packages are needed to ensure a successful installation. This is an example of one of the risks associated when using open source software. There is no guarantee of functionality or support. In this case, Ainstein is a company that produces physical radars and not only is this software suite the simulation, but it is also the radar driver for the physical system [15]. When several members of a team must use the same simulation, the differing simulation environments resulting from manual installation can result in differences in software versions, functionality, and simulation results.

The more critical problem with the aforementioned radar package is incorrect library service names throughout. While these problems can be isolated and fixed with time, build error resolution, and an extensive dive into the software source code, the process of solving them is tedious and an additional barrier to use. If time is essential, finding a fully functioning driver is critical, as drivers are not trivial to develop. In some cases, it can be near impossible to develop a driver without documentation from the manufacturer on how to interpret the data.

4.2   Model Accuracy

While all simulations are by nature inaccurate to some degree, confirming simulation veracity is instrumental to gaining meaningful results. Related specifically to this paper, the radar package [15] implemented its radar with 10 rays spread across its field of view, in contrast to the conical shape of radar beams in reality. In essence, the simulated radar is a low beam count LiDAR. To overcome this problem, several sonar sensors were fused together to produce a semblance of a radar, shown in Fig. 6, where all images were taken at the same configuration and time. Notice that the orange traffic barrel is not picked up by the radar, but can be seen by the conical radar implementation and LiDAR.

Additionally, Doppler shift phenomena allow radars to determine the relative speed of the targeted object, this implementation does not produce this reading and that richness of data is lost. While numeric differentiation can be used to estimate velocity, it is noisy. Filters can reduce noise at the price of introducing delay, which may be problematic for robots in dynamic environments.

4.3 Package Independence and Co-mingling

Once working, utilizing multiple packages simultaneously presents additional challenges. This is partially caused by the fact that basic software stack implementations vary widely throughout industry and academia. Therefore, many software packages within the same simulator are incompatible out-of-the-box. Although commonly utilized due to their simplicity, non-modular, co-mingled software stacks limit future possible modifications/customizations. In these cases, adding sensor functionality requires splicing portions of code into other several files existing throughout in the stack, which commingles different packages within each other, destroying any package independence and requiring extensive manual software manipulation.

4.4 Documentation

Possibly the most pervasive concern in user simulations is the incomplete documentation of package implementation and use. Packages commonly provide examples. However, problems commonly arise from the simplistic nature of these examples. Packages without adequate documentation may have several tools, applications, and uses that users could only determine by picking apart source code. In this project, the radar's example simulation relies on the sensor's output Coordinate System (CS) defaulting to the base_link. This worked because in that example simulation the LiDAR is stationary. In contrast, when placed onto a mobile component, the sensor data refers to the wrong (default) CS and becomes erroneous. Only after comparing the source code to similarly organized sensor packages was the built-in method to specify the correct CS discovered and implemented.

5 Recommended Best Practices for Robotic Platform Modularity

Through RaDaT's experiments and robotic platform development, we present a list of best practices to guide development of simulations, the software stack, and hardware implementation. Our research recommends:

- Utilizing holistic install scripts with standard layouts and arguments
- Utilizing automated package dependency installation
- Platforms adapt standardized modular stack structure
- Thoroughly document implementation, all tools/arguments, and provide examples at basic and complex levels

- Utilize unified data messages and buses wherever possible
- Ensure your computational system has adequate bandwidth for the desired sensor interface and processing
- Utilize the GPU for parallel processing tasks such as those used in image processing
- Use simulation in development of new software implementations to obtain the initial workflow
- Utilize system-wide environmental variables to interchange sensors
- Avoid fixed assignment, connections, and processing assignment with by utilizing automated configurations, UDEV rules, and machine tags

6   Summary and Conclusion

Overall, LaPaSHD fills in the gaps that ROS leaves open in terms of modularity by adding the support for pre-compiled binaries and any other system-wide tasks such as library path sourcing. The inclusion of a standard practice such as a setup.sh bash script would allow for an easy way to replicate and automate packages ensuring modularity. The use of UDEV rules reduces the need to constantly change device port names in software once agreed upon, and the use of environment variables allows the user to easily swap the function of the software without having to make large modifications that have to be dealt with in future code merges. This framework has proven to be effective in producing better time management skills, reducing human errors, and promoting more effective collaborative development.

Through the implementation of Gazebo based Warthog simulator, the general workflow of how sensors can be modularly added to an existing platform was shown using the example of adding a radar to a LiDAR based platform. This paper proposed set of best practices for keeping the hardware and software stack operable, modular, and interchangeable. As showcased in the example, finding an out-of-the box working ROS driver can be difficult; however, careful preparation regarding the hardware can mitigate some of the challenges. In the most efficient scenario, the pros and cons of each interface type should be taken into consideration along with the additional metric of the amount of time required to develop a driver. For RaDaT applications, USB devices are less advantageous for high-bandwidth applications due to an already large array of USB sensors; however if a driver for a specific sensor only exists for USB variants, this time saved on driver development may outweigh the other downsides of potentially having to lower the sensor resolution or update frequency. One should choose sensors that are already contain the proper interface when in scenarios that the computational system is not modifiable.

Implementing the radar in simulation had its challenges and similar occurrences are not uncommon. The simulation not only exemplified ways to mitigate and overcome simulation implementation challenges, but aided in the understanding of the driver, its limitations, and its software errors. As aforementioned, simulation always included inherent accuracy issues with respect to the real world, but simulating a robotic platform remains an extremely powerful tool for debugging software issues, obtaining performance metrics for comparisons in a consistent environment, and developing the live implementation on robot hardware.

Future iterations of this research will further integrate radar into our system to enhance our data capture capabilities. Primarily, the focus will be to explore the gaps present in LiDAR data sets and fill them with radar based data. The implications of this future work will connect with efforts to enhance multi platform navigation as well as advanced UI development for operation and control of unmanned platform systems. Additionally, RaDaT will explore the qualities of feeding integrated Radar-LiDAR data into machine learning image recognition algorithms to further enhance and optimize our ability to navigate in an offline environment. By verifying these results on hardware, codifying an intuitive software stack structure that maintains clarity and enables modularity, and open-sourcing documentation for the structure, examples, and detailed instructions for use will expand on this effort.

References

1. Colosi, M., et al.: Plug-and-play SLAM: a unified SLAM architecture for modularity and ease of use. In: IEEE/RSJ International Conference on Intelligent Robot and Systems (IROS), USA, pp. 5051–5057. IEEE (2020)
2. Povendhan, A., et al.: Multi-sensor fusion incorporating adaptive transformation for reconfigurable pavement sweeping robot. In: IEEE/RSJ International Conference on Intelligent Robots and Systems (IROS), Czech Republic, pp. 300–306. IEEE (2021)
3. Zou, Y., Kim, D., Norman, P., Espinosa, J., Wang, J.-C., Virk, G.: Towards robot modularity - a review of international modularity standardization for service robots. Robot. Auton. Syst. vol. **148** (2022). https://doi.org/10.1016/j.robot.2021.103943
4. Barbanson, C., Mallet, C., Gressin, A., Frison, P., Rudant, J.: Fusion of LiDAR and radar data for land-cover mapping in natural environments. In: IEEE International Geoscience and Remote Sensing Symposium (IGRASS), Italy, pp. 3715–3718. IEEE (2015)
5. Schoffmann, C., Ubezio, B., Bohm, C., Muhlbacher-Karrer, S., Sangl, H.: Virtual radar: real-time millimeter-wave radar sensor simulation for perception-driven robotics. IEEE Robot. Autom. Lett. **6**(3), 4707–4711 (2021). https://doi.org/10.1109/LRA.2021.3068916
6. Diehl, C., Feicho, E., Schwambach, A., Dammeier, T., Mares, E., Bertram T.: Radar-based dynamic occupancy grid mapping and object detection. In: IEEE 23rd International Conference on Intelligent Transportation Systems (ITSC), Greece, pp. 1–6. IEEE (2020)
7. Clarke, B., Worrall, S., Brooker, G., Nebot, E.: Sensor modelling for radar-based occupancy mapping. In: IEEE/RSJ International Conference on Intelligent Robots and Systems, Portugal, pp. 3047–3054. IEEE (2012)
8. Robinson, C., Abubakar, S., Das, S., Popa, D.: ROSFuse: a high-modularity ROS to firmware instrumentation bridge for robotic sensors. In: IEEE 16th International Conference on Automation Science and Engineering (CASE), China, pp. 449–454. IEEE (2020)

9. Chen, J., Li, S., Liu, D., Li, X.: AiRobSim: simulating a multisensor aerial robot for urban search and rescue operation and training. Sensors **20**(18) (2020). https://doi.org/10.3390/s20185223

10. Grebner, T., Schoeder, P., Janoudi, V., Waldschmidt, C.: Radar-based mapping of the environment: occupancy grid-map versus SAR. IEEE Microwave Wirel. Components Lett. **32**(3), 253–256 (2022). https://doi.org/10.1109/LMWC.2022.3145661

11. Guerrero, J., Jaud, M., Lenain, R., Rouveure, R., Faure, P.: Towards LiDAR-RADAR based terrain mapping. In: 2015 IEEE International Workshop on Advanced Robotics and its Social Impacts (ARSO), France, pp. 1–6. IEEE (2015)

12. Merkle, D., Frey, C., Alexander, R.: Fusion of ground penetrating radar and laser scanning for infrastructure mapping. J. Appl. Geodesy **15**(1) (2021). https://doi.org/10.1515/jag-2020-0004

13. ROS. https://www.ros.org/. Accessed 4 July 2022

14. Clearpath Warthog. https://clearpathrobotics.com/warthog-unmanned-ground-vehicle-robot/. Accessed 10 Aug 2022

15. Ainstein Radar Github. https://github.com/AinsteinAI/ainstein_radar. Accessed 10 Aug 2022

16. Toyota Research Instatute Github. https://github.com/ToyotaResearchInstitute/velodyne_simulator. Accessed 10 Aug 2022

17. Sony. https://www.sony.com/electronics/support/articles/00024571. Accessed 10 Aug 2022

18. Electronic Notes. https://www.electronics-notes.com/articles/connectivity/ethernet-ieee-802-3/cables-types-pinout-cat-5-5e-6.php. Accessed 10 Aug 2022

19. Nerd Techy. https://nerdtechy.com/usb-maximum-length. Accessed 11 Aug 2022

20. Microsoft. https://learn.microsoft.com/en-us/windowshardware/drivers/usbcon/usb-bandwidth-allocation. Accessed 19 Dec 2022

21. Ubuntu Manual-UDEV. https://manpages.ubuntu.com/manpages/xenial/man7/udev.7.html. Accessed 18 Dec 2022

22. Dambot takes the lead on dangerous assessments. https://www.erdc.usace.army.mil/Media/News-Stories/Article/2530836/dambot-takes-the-lead-on-dangerous-assessments/. Accessed 27 Dec 2022

23. ERDC researchers combine robotics, imagery technology to solve problems. https://www.usace.army.mil/Media/News/NewsSearch/Article/2543278/erdc-researchers-combine-robotics-imagery-technology-to-solve-problems. Accessed 27 Dec 2022

24. EnvironmentVariables. https://help.ubuntu.com/community/EnvironmentVariables. Accessed 28 Dec 2022

25. Warthog Unmanned Ground Vehicle. https://clearpathrobotics.com/warthog-unmanned-ground-vehicle-robot/. Accessed 28 Dec 2022

Blast-Induced Deformations of the Building Entrance Part Caused by Improvised Shaped Charges

Tibor Palasiewicz(✉) [iD], Ota Rolenec [iD], Lubomír Kroupa [iD], Pavel Maňas [iD], and Dalibor Coufal [iD]

University of Defence, Kounicova 65, 662 10 Brno, Czech Republic
tibor.palasiewicz@unob.cz

Abstract. The presented results and discussion concern the behavior of a steel rectangular profile which can be found at the building entrances exposed to blast effect of military explosives. Currently, high explosives with liners are used to create armour-piercing charges to increase their effect. The article deals with the possible use of standardized TNT block demolition charges used in military practice to create improvised shaped charges to increase their penetrating effect in comparison with the concentrated or linear charges usually generated from this block demolition charges. The advantage of using the tested block demolition charges is their lower acquisition value in comparison with a special demolition charges and the speed of assembly of improvised shaped charges in field conditions. Several shaped charge types of different shapes have been designed. In the representative samples of designed shaped charge types, their effect on a structural element occurring was simulated, whereas the effect of explosive flow was further compared in these cases with simulations in the ANSYS software. The experiment performed in a live blasting area presented the effect of all charge types. The aim of the article was to verify the different effect of individual charge types on the structural element and to assess their penetrating properties. The results enable the determination of the further course of research in this area.

Keywords: Experiment · Improvised Shaped Charge · Penetrating Effect · Numerical Simulation · Steel Profile

1 Introduction

In the military environment, there are commonly used various types of metals, which perform two basic functions for combat use. One function is protective, which involves the presence of metals in protective structures and armor technology. The second function fulfills the tasks of destruction with its irreplaceable place in weapons systems and military ammunition. A similar approach can be chosen to study the behavior of metals used in buildings, where various products can be made from this material, but at the same time this material must be tested so that it can be effectively destroyed.

J. Mazal et al. (Eds.): MESAS 2022, LNCS 13866, pp. 109–130, 2023.
https://doi.org/10.1007/978-3-031-31268-7_7

The principle of shaped and hollow charges has been known for a longer time and is advantageously used, for example, by units of the Corps of Engineers (mines, shaped charges for demolishing or destroying steel and concrete or reinforced concrete elements, etc.). Shaped charges utilize directing the explosive energy in the desired direction; in comparison with concentrated or linear charges of the same mass, made of standardized block demolition charges, they allow better use of the released energy and thus a greater effect. For this reason, military units use special concentrated charges to break through high-strength or high-thickness elements [1]. These charges are usually filled with a mixture of trinitrotoluene (TNT) and a high explosive, usually Hexogen (RDX), which increases the detonation velocity of the mixture and thus the armour-piercing properties of the charge [2].

Shaped charges can be constructed on the site using a standard TNT block demolition charge or plastic explosives. Hollow charges are usually supplied as industrially-produced charges and use the principle of shaped charges. To increase the penetrating effect, the material of the metal liner is used for these charges. In order to create the greatest possible penetrating effect, not only the composition of the high explosive in the charge, especially its detonation velocity, is important, but also the shape of the charge, the geometry of the cavity and possibly the material of the liner, the stand-off distance from the demolished element, the site of initiation and other parameters. The shape of the cavities in shaped and hollow charges is most often close to the upside-down letter "V" in the cross-section and may be in the form of a cone, wedge or half-cylinder.

Hollow charges can also be prepared in an improvised manner, especially with the use of plastic explosives and pre-prepared moulds and liners. Malleable metals, most often copper [3], are used for the production of these liners and steel plate can also be used. For example, the Explosive Ordnance Disposal units use various shaped moulds for ammunition disposal serving for filling them with plastic explosives. The charge formed in this way is then placed on unexploded explosive ordnance and the explosive flow is to separate the fuse from the rest of the high explosive. Not only directing the explosive energy of a plastic explosive, but also the effect of the liner is used here, which further increases the effect of the directed explosive energy with its shape, material properties and mass.

A big problem in today's world is the number of attacks carried out using explosive devices against military as well as civilian targets. Exactly, shaped or hollow charges manufactured in an improvised manner can be misused for the activities that can lead to large human and material losses or to a reduction in the ability of the Integrated Rescue System components to act. Such a case could be a terrorist attack against individual critical infrastructure elements at the national level of the European Union. Precisely, improvised shaped or hollow charges can be used for overcoming the entry protection and for gaining the access to a given critical infrastructure object.

1.1 Motivation

At the present time, military units may face the need to use a large number of different types of shaped and hollow charges in their activities. This situation is caused mainly by the increasing share of fighting in the urban environment, the need to create passages even in populated areas and to remove IEDs (Improvised Explosive Devices) and UXOs

(Unexploded Ordnances) in contemporary operations. Various types of charges are used for urban breaching that will ensure a rapid forced entry into the required area and, at the same time, they can neutralize a potential enemy to resist for a certain period of time. Explosive devices for a forced entry into buildings are not only used by military units, but are also used by the police and Special Forces. In comparison with mechanical methods for breaking doors and windows, they require longer operator training and increased safety measures for the entire unit.

However, in the case of sustained conflicts, this type of charges can be exhausted and problems relating to replenishing or maintaining the supplies can arise. This is given by many times higher purchase cost of high explosives used for shaped or hollow charges. The high price of high explosives is the cause of a more complex production process and a price of individual components in production, when compared to the commonly used TNT, which serves as a comparative performance equivalent in testing and using all explosives. For this reason, the members of the Department of Engineer Support and the Department of Engineer Technology of the University of Defence began to deal with the possibility of using standardized TNT block demolition charges to make improvised shaped charges and thus to increase their penetrating effect. A new method of creating improvised shaped charges using TNT blocks could partially replace manufactured charges in the case of their shortage. Another reason was to verify the possibility of using mathematical modelling tools to solve the issues of designing improvised shaped and possibly hollow charges for the needs of the Corps of Engineers units.

1.2 Contribution and Organization of the Article

The benefit of this work is an original approach to assembling the charges with a directed effect. New charge types can significantly contribute to the successful completion of the required task when a manufactured shaped and hollow charges are absent. The new manner of using standardized blasting TNT blocks also means significant financial savings in comparison with the use of high-performance explosives, which, in long-term operations, can be an important argument for introducing the designed shaped charge types for use by military units when penetrating or demolishing various structural elements.

The literature review was performed before starting the investigation itself (Sect. 2). Based on the content of scientific articles, it was decided to start research and to set a scientific hypothesis. Subsequently, several types of shaped charges were designed for investigating their penetrating effect depending on the shape of the charge and cavity. Based on the shape of individual charges and the demolished element, the ANSYS 2020R2 program was used to simulate the demolished element using the explicit formulation of the Finite Element Method (Sect. 3). In the next part, an experiment was performed in a live blasting area, where the effect of all types of designed charges was tested. The results of the practical experiment were confronted with the results of simulations and appropriate conclusions were formulated using their comparison (Sect. 4). Based on the knowledge acquired, recommendations for further research in this area have been set (Sect. 5).

2   Literature Review

The use of explosives is a primary matter of the Armed Forces and mining or construction methods within the framework of industrial applications [4]. Nowadays, however, one of the most discussed topics is the increase in the number of terrorist attacks with the use of high explosives. For this reason, current scientific work aims mainly at investigating the effect of explosives on protective structures for sheltering people [5–8], the shock wave propagation in closed space [9–11], the effect of explosives on the outer building envelope [12–14] and possible added elements of building and critical infrastructure protection [15–18].

The performed modelling and experiment focused on the effect of an explosion on a selected structural element occurring at the building entrances. The article is, therefore, aimed at the area of critical infrastructure protection and various (new) uses of military explosives. The experiment was based on the theory that the charge and cavity shape influences the penetrating effect of the charge [19–21]. In the articles mentioned, the formation of a detonating wave influenced by the charge shape composed of different types of plastic explosives or, if applicable, of individual block demolition charges in the shape of a cylinder and a hemisphere, was investigated. In military practice, mostly the standardized TNT block demolition charges are used for demolitions. The authors of this article have not found any study that would examine the effect of the charge in relation to its shape, composed of several pieces of standardized TNT block demolition charges. For this reason and the abovementioned arguments, it has been decided to examine these issues.

3   Problem Formulation and Solution

At the beginning of the research, the two following hypotheses were set:

1. By changing the shape of a charge and cavity formed of a standardized TNT block demolition charges, the effect of the charge can be directed in comparison with a concentrated charge of the same mass formed of the same demolition charges.
2. By changing the shape of a charge and cavity formed of a standardized TNT block demolition charges, a greater penetrating effect can be achieved in comparison with a concentrated charge of the same mass formed of the same demolition charges.

To verify the hypotheses, numerical simulations using the ANSYS 2020R2 software and a subsequent experiment performed on June 30, 2020 in the military training area were used. Before that, however, individual charge types were designed and an element to be demolished was selected for verifying the effects of explosion.

3.1   Types of Charges and a Demolished Element

For investigating the effect of the charge and cavity shape on a generated explosive flow, a total of 6 charge types were designed. In all the charge types, the initiation is placed on the side of the charge opposite the destroyed surface in order that the detonating wave may spread through the charge against the surface of the demolished element. All charge types consist of three standardized 200g TNT blocks. This type of TNT blocks was used since it is the smallest block-shaped demolition charges introduced in the Army of the Czech Republic. Its shape allows an easy assembly of shaped charges as well. The dimensions of the block are as follows: 100 mm length, 50 mm width and 25 mm thickness.

The first type of charge was assembled into a pyramidal shape - two blocks in height along the sides of the charge, one block in the middle, in the half of the length of side blocks (see Fig. 1). The red arrow indicates the place and direction of the initiation.

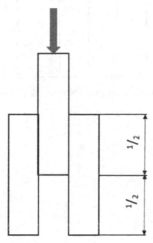

Fig. 1. Pyramid-shaped Charge with a Middle TNT Block Placed in the Half of the Length of Side Blocks.

Another charge type was also assembled into a pyramidal shape. The middle block was placed in one third of the length of side blocks from their upper edges (see Fig. 2).

The third charge type, resembling the shape of an upside-down letter "V", is initiated by the upper block. Two side blocks are in the lower part of the charge at a distance of 50 mm apart in width of a block. In the middle part, they are attached to each other and connected to another block acted as an initiation charge (see Fig. 3).

The following charge type is similar in shape to the previous one and the distance between the inner edges of blocks is 100 mm (see Fig. 4).

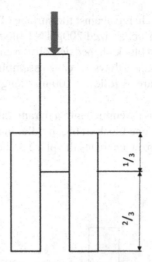

Fig. 2. Pyramid-shaped Charge with a Middle TNT Block Placed in One Third of the Length of Side Blocks.

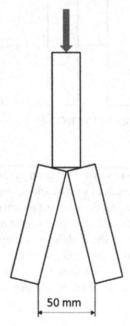

Fig. 3. A Charge with the Inner Edges of TNT Blocks at a Distance of 50 mm between Each Other.

The fifth charge type is similar to the third one with a different placement of the detonator. The detonator is placed on the upper joint of side blocks horizontally to the

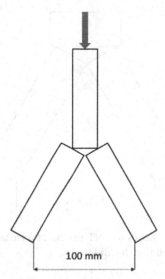

Fig. 4. A Charge with the Inner Edges of TNT Blocks at a Distance of 100 mm between Each Other.

middle. Thus, it laps over the sides of blocks (by 25 mm on each side) and the initiation is carried out from the side (see Fig. 5).

Fig. 5. A Charge with the Inner Edges of TNT Blocks at a Distance of 50 mm between Each Other; the Initiation Is Performed from the Side.

Another type of charge is of a similar design to the previous type with the difference that the distance between the inner edges of side blocks is 100 mm (see Fig. 6).

The last charge type is a standard concentrated charge composed of TNT blocks demolition charges placed side by side that are attached to each other with the largest surface (see Fig. 7). Its purpose is to create a comparative basis for the other types of

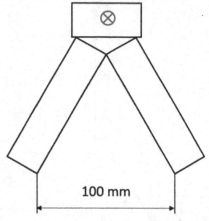

Fig. 6. A Charge with the Inner Edges of TNT Blocks at a Distance of 100 mm between Each Other; the Initiation Is Performed from the Side.

charges and to demonstrate the effect of a classically assembled charge in comparison with the shaped charge.

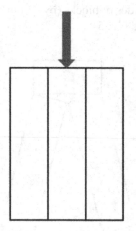

Fig. 7. Concentrated Charge with the Initiation in the Middle.

Thus, a total of 7 charge types were selected for modelling and experimentation, of which 6 charges formed the variants with the directed effect of an explosion. More variants of charges were created for the possibility of a more extensive investigating the effects on a demolished object. Individual TNT blocks were connected to each other by means of the adhesive PVC tape, and were fixed in an open position.

The "C" profile welded to a steel closed rectangular profile made of structural steel of the usual quality was selected to be a demolished object. The thickness of the steel strip used was 3.5 mm and the total height of the demolished element was 80 mm (see Fig. 8). The tested charges were attached to the elements demolished using a PVC adhesive tape, each time one charge per one element for one setting off. The demolished elements were placed on the ground and fixed in an upright position. During the tests, individual elements were arranged in such a manner that no mutual influence of elements as well as charges could happen due to the explosion of adjacent charges. At distances of approx. 0.5 m from the previous placement of the charge, other test charges were gradually placed on the individual elements and then set off in order that the material should not be affected by the explosion of the previous charge.

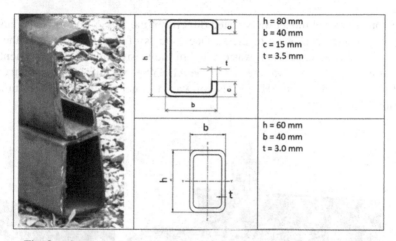

Fig. 8. Diagram and the Dimensions of the Elements Being Demolished.

Similar types of structural steel and a profile demolished can be commonly found, for example, at building entrances (gates). These are, therefore, suitable elements for testing the possibility of their demolishing by concentrated and shaped charges for their potential use in breaching.

The total mass of the charge used within the tests performed was 600 g of TNT. When using a military formula to determine the mass of a concentrated charge to demolish a steel plate specified in [1]:

$$N = 10 \times b \times h^2 \tag{1}$$

where N is the calculated mass of the charge (g), b is the width of the steel plate to be demolished (cm) and h is the thickness of the plate (cm), it is assumed that with this amount of explosive and a width of 4 cm of the element being demolished, the charge used is able to pierce a steel plate 3.8 cm thick. However, the formula calculates with a concentrated charge and a homogeneous plate and does not reflect destroying the structurally shaped element without the possibility of inserting the charge directly into the element. In military practice, the calculation of shaped charges to demolish elements is not solved, therefore, it is possible to proceed only from the above-mentioned laws.

With regard to the above-mentioned calculation, the different penetrating effect of different types of improvised shaped charges by the penetration or deformation of the element inner parts should be recognizable on this structural element without complete penetration.

3.2 Modelling the Effect of an Improvised Shaped Charge

The ANSYS 2020R2 finite element system was used for the numerical simulation of the whole process, which allows the simulation of very fast events, such as explosions, ballistic resistance, shock loading, etc. using the explicit formulation of the Finite Element Method. The results can be presented using the static images of stress and damage distribution of simulated models, graphs of important quantities or illustrative animations of the course of interaction of bodies, including the distribution of their stress and damage.

The computational model was created directly in the ANSYS/Workbench environment, the geometry consisting of the surface models of steel elements and the solid models of the charge and the soil was created in the DesignModeler environment. The computational model itself was created in the ANSYSMechanical environment and an explicit solver based on the AUTODYN software technology was used for numerical simulation (Fig. 9).

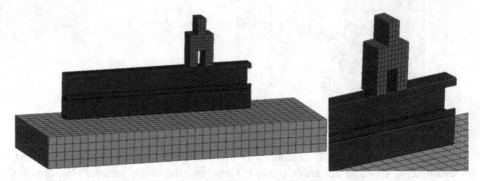

Fig. 9. Computational Model – Finite Element Network.

The finite element mesh of the computational model consists of approximately 12,000 elements and nodes, whereas the destroyed steel profiles consist of a total of 9,500 nodes and shell elements. With regard to the fact that, in similar cases, it is not possible to determine the material properties of destroyed steel profiles in advance, a relatively simple but sufficiently accurate bilinear isotropic material model of steel was selected for the simulation without considering the effect of strain rate. Of course, the results are affected by this significantly, however, the nature of deformation and the shape of damage remain.

The following figures show the results of the analysis for the representative shapes of charges that were selected due to the significant shape difference among them.

In the case of simulation of a charge with the inner edges of blocks at a distance of 100 mm between each other, an opening incurred in the upper part of the demolished element can be observed, which is very similar to the real result. As for the further transmission of the explosive flow, it is already clear that the simulation assumed a fixed structure of the element throughout the detonation. As a result, the direction of the explosive flow passage is perpendicular to the element. In the real situation, the element

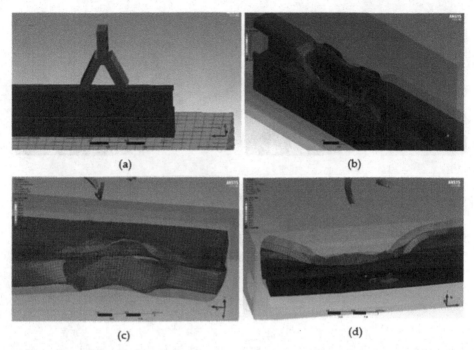

Fig. 10. Modelling the Effect of a Charge with the Inner Edges of Blocks at a Distance of 100 mm between Each Other: (a) Modelled Element; (b) Development of Deformation in Time 5×10^{-4} s; (c) Top View; (d) Bottom View.

rotation and the explosive flow deviation could have happened throughout the detonation and the inaccurate placement of the element could have played an important role. The simulation results may be affected by the initial deformations of the profiles destroyed (see Fig. 8) and by the placement on the ground. However, there is a relatively good analogy between the damage geometry of both the upper C-profile and the penetration of the lower part of the rectangular profile (see Fig. 10d) (Fig. 11).

In the case of a pyramid-shaped charge with a middle TNT block placed in the half of the length of side blocks, a similar anomaly can be observed as in the previous case. At the sight of the result of the demolished element, the penetration caused by the incoming explosive flow is very similar in shape and size to the simulated element. In the case of simulation, the wave passes in a perpendicular direction to the element and the total penetration of the element happens in the final part of the detonation. In the real situation, obviously a deviation, and thus a reduction in the directed effect occurs. The result of the simulation, in terms of the geometrical correspondence with the destroyed profiles, corresponds relatively well and the difference in the software calculation of the lower rectangular strip can be explained by the initial deformations of destroyed elements and also by the placement on the ground (Fig. 12).

In the case of a concentrated charge, it can be argued that the actual state of the demolished element is most similar to the simulation. It can be assumed that in this case the conditions of the practical experiment came closest to the theoretical basis and the

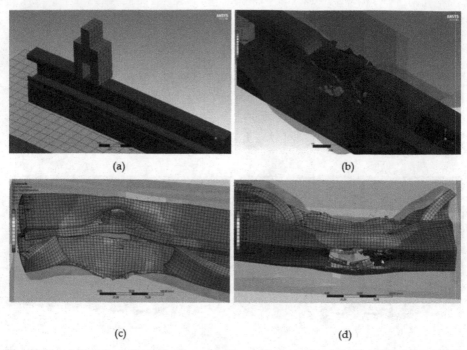

Fig. 11. Modelling the Effect of a Pyramid-shaped Charge with a Middle Block Placed in the Half of the Length of Side Blocks: (a) Modelled Element; (b) Development of Deformation in Time 1×10^{-4} s; (c) Top View; (d) Bottom View.

directed effect reached very similar values here. The penetrating effect was much more noticeable here and the phase of the bypass explosion flow was minimal.

4   Experiment and Results

In this chapter, the course of the experiment together with the attached photo documentation is described first, showing how the charges were placed on the demolished object. At the same time, the results after the setting off performed and a brief discussion related to the explosion effect are presented.

4.1   Performing an Experiment

The experiment was carried out in a live blasting area in the military training area with the aim to verify the knowledge acquired by modelling the effect of an improvised shaped charge on an element being demolished. A total of three 1m long steel elements were used. Each charge type was detonated once. Only two charges (each charge on a different element) with a minimum distance of 4 m between the charges were always used for individual set off, in order that throwing-off or sliding-down the charge from the demolished element should not take place. The charges were detonated gradually using a safety fuse. The charges were attached to the demolished element that the vertical axis

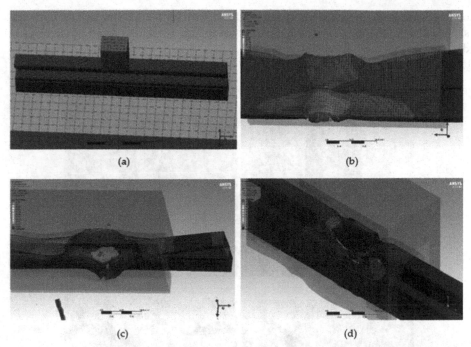

Fig. 12. Modelling the Effect of a Concentrated Charge: (a) Modelled Element; (b) Development of Deformation in Time 1.5x10-4s; (c) Top View; (d) Side View.

of the charge was perpendicular to the longitudinal axis of the demolished element at a minimum distance of 500 mm on the element between emplacement and the deformation of the element did not affect the results obtained. The charges were initiated using a safety fuse and a standard detonator containing 0.8 g of pentrite (PETN) and 0.3 g of lead azide. The detonator was inserted into the capwell of the upper TNT block that the considered initiation point was in the longitudinal axis of the block at a depth of 30 mm from the front of the block.

The charges were assembled before they were fixed to the demolished element. The practical test proved that the charge assembly itself was very fast and simple and took tens of seconds. The simplicity of the V-shaped charge assembly was also enhanced by the choice of distances between the inner edges of TNT blocks. This enabled the dimensions of TNT blocks to be used instead of a ruler, which simplified the preparation in field conditions.

4.2 Experiment Results

Furthermore, for the sake of the article clarity, the detonation results of individual charges are described in the same manner as in subchapter 3.1, even though the charges were set off in a different order in the experiment itself. However, this does not affect the results of the experiment, as described above. Figure 13 shows the placement of a pyramid-shaped charge (the diagram of which is shown in Fig. 1) and the result of the element deformation after the detonation performed.

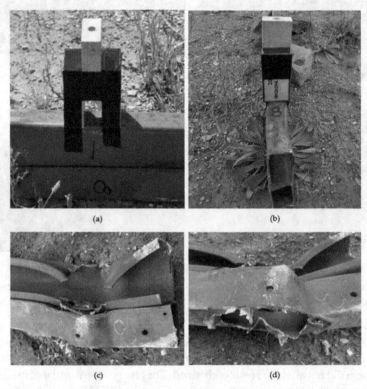

Fig. 13. The Arrangement and Result of a Pyramid-shaped Charge with the Middle Block Placed in the Half of the Length of Side Blocks: (a) Front View of the Placed Charge; (b) Side View of the Placed Charge; (c) Front View of the Element Deformation; (d) Bottom View of the Element Deformation.

After the setting off of this charge type, a complete penetration happened. At the upper part of the "C" profile, a considerable element deformation inwards in the direction of the explosion is visible. The deformation of the element lower part shows that most of the explosive energy of the charge spread along the sides of the charge. Although a penetration occurred in the middle of the element lower part, a considerable part of the material remained a part of the element and towards the side edges of the opening a significant separation of the steel strip to the sides is visible.

Next, the test result of a similar charge shape (see Fig. 14) is represented, with the difference that the middle block is placed in the upper third of the length of side blocks (the diagram is in Fig. 2).

Even in this case, the penetration of the element occurred in the direction of the detonating wave propagation through the charge; however, the resulting opening in the lower part of the rectangular profile is on the side of the open "C" profile only. The side

Fig. 14. The Arrangement and Result of a Pyramid-shaped Charge with the Placement of the Middle Block in the Upper Third of the Length of Side Blocks: (a) Front View of the Placed Charge; (b) Side View of the Placed Charge; (c) Front View of the Element Deformation; (d) Bottom View of the Element Deformation.

view again indicates that most of the explosive energy of the charge spread along the sides, although in this case a larger deformation is visible on one side only.

Figure 15 represents the placement of a charge with side blocks placed into the "V" shape (the diagram is in Fig. 3).

In this charge type, the deformation of the demolished element upper part is very pronounced. The upper steel strip of the element was completely twisted inwards. In the lower part, it is also possible to observe the penetration of the element in two places with openings smaller than in the previous cases, and thus also directing the explosive energy of the charge along the sides of the charge.

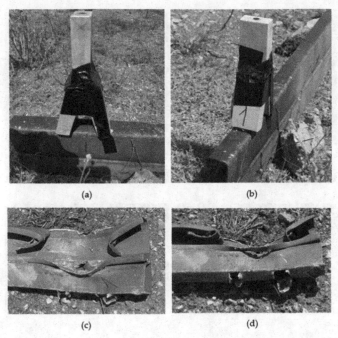

Fig. 15. The Arrangement and Result of a Charge Containing Side Blocks into the "V" Shape (length 50 mm): (a) Front View of the Placed Charge; (b) Side View of the Placed Charge; (c) Front View of the Element Deformation; (d) Bottom View of the Element Deformation.

The following charge (see Fig. 16) is of a similar shape; the lower distance between TNT blocks is 100 mm (the diagram is in Fig. 4).

When testing this shape of the charge, the required penetration of the element did not occur. In the upper part of the element, the steel strip was "cut off" like in the first two charge types, however, in its lower part there was only a small crack (marked with a red circle). Thus, the effect of the charge was spreading in another way than in the case of the previous charge type, which was the cause of an insufficient penetrating effect.

Another charge (see Fig. 17) was also in the shape reminding the letter "V", but with an upper block placed horizontally (the diagram is in Fig. 5).

At the same time, the deformation of the upper part of the demolished element shows the deformation of steel strip inwards as well as its separation from the element. In the lower part, a penetration occurred on one side only corresponding to the edge of the charge.

The last type of a shaped charge (see Fig. 18) is similar to the previous type with a longer distance between the edges of side blocks (the diagram is in Fig. 6).

The upper part of the element was again significantly deformed, analogous to the third case (see Fig. 15). In the lower part, two significant penetrations were visible corresponding to the side edges of the charge attached.

Fig. 16. The Arrangement and Result of a Charge Containing Side Blocks into the "V" Shape (100 mm): (a) Front View of the Placed Charge; (b) Side View of the Placed Charge; (c) Front View of the Element Deformation; (d) Bottom View of the Element Deformation.

The last charge of the experiment was a concentrated charge, consisting of three 200 g TNT blocks (see Fig. 19), attached to the demolished element in the same manner as in the previous cases (the diagram is in Fig. 7).

The result of the setting off of a concentrated charge shows its considerable effect on the overall destruction of the element. In the upper and the middle part, the steel strip was "cut off" and in the lower part an opening was created approximately corresponding to the width of the charge. The effect of this charge on the demolished element appears to be the most destructive.

5   Discussion

Comparison of the simulation results in the ANSYS 2020R2 software and the results of the experiment performed shows slight differences between the results achieved. In the case of a concentrated charge type, the opening incurred in the lower part of the element during the simulation is very similar to the real result obtained within the experiment. The difference is that the side steel strip was not destroyed on one side of the element. In the pyramidal shape of the charge, the difference in the shape of the opening in the lower part of the demolished element is greater; however, the simulation and the practical experiment proved piercing the element in its transverse axis. The largest difference was observed in the charge containing side TNT blocks into the "V" shape, where, within the simulation, the penetration of an opening in the element bottom part

(a)   (b)

(c)   (d)

Fig. 17. The Arrangement and Result of a Charge Containing Side Blocks into the "V" Shape (50 mm) and a Block with a Safety Fuse Placed Horizontally: (a) Front View of the Placed Charge; (b) Side View of the Placed Charge; (c) Front View of the Element Deformation; (d) Bottom View of the Element Deformation.

occurred on a larger area than in performing the experiment. The differences between the simulation and the experiment could be caused mainly by small structural deformations of the demolished element, smaller weld deposits, which were not taken into account during the simulation, after the explosive interaction of the element with the ambient environment and inaccurate placement of charges on the demolished element.

In all charge types, the penetration of the element in its transverse plane was a surprising result. Thus, the assumption stated at the beginning of subchapter 3.1 was not proved, which, based on the calculation, predicted a deformation and penetration only to a certain depth of the element. Both the experiment and the results of the simulation confirm overdesigning the formulas used in the calculation for demolishing the elements in the military environment by reason of the focus on fulfilling the given task, especially within the combat operation. At the same time, however, no complete penetration of the element took place in any case, even though the charge always exceeded the demolished element by 0.5 cm on each of its sides, when both side steel strips of the element remained intact with the exception of a concentrated charge. This effect is probably caused by the fact that the main type of element material disruption in thin-walled steel elements is the pressure effect of the explosion and vice versa; the directing of the explosive effect is suppressed by the dispersion of the directed stream of explosion products during the process of distorting the material under the charge.

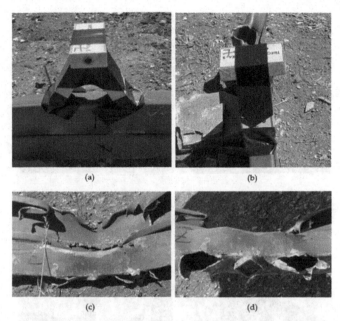

Fig. 18. The Arrangement and Result of a Charge Containing Side Blocks into the "V" Shape (100 mm) and a Block with a Safety Fuse Placed Horizontally: a) Front View of the Placed Charge; (b) Side View of the Placed Charge; (c) Front View of the Element Deformation; (d) Bottom View of the Element Deformation.

The deformation of the element lower part proved different effects of improvised shaped charges with one another, as well as in comparison with the concentrated charge. The different effect of the explosion in comparison with the concentrated charge is most notably visible in charges containing side TNT blocks into the "V" shape (Fig. 15 and 18), in which the penetration of the element corresponding with the side edges of the charges happened. Even in other types of improvised shaped charges, the effect of detonation on the demolished element was more visible towards the side edges of assembled charges. In the three types of charges (Fig. 14, 16 and 17), the explosive effect is observable towards one side edge of the charge.

The most noticeable destructive ability was demonstrated by the concentrated charge. This effect is caused by placing a charge directly on the demolished element without a transition barrier (of air) and thus the maximum explosive effect in the event of a charge explosion is guaranteed. However, even this charge type failed to cause a complete penetration since the side steel strip of the element oriented in parallel to the direction of the explosive effect propagation remained undestroyed.

It can be stated that the first hypothesis "By changing the shape of a charge and cavity formed of a standardized TNT block demolition charges, the effect of the charge can be directed in comparison with a concentrated charge of the same mass formed of the same demolition charges" was verified for thin-walled steel structural elements. Both the simulation and the experiment showed different destruction of the element in relation to individual charge types.

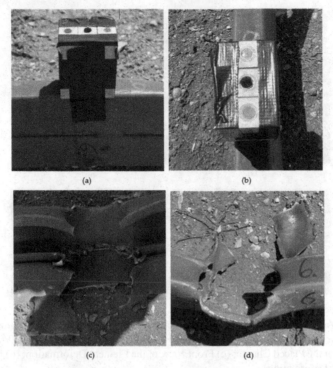

Fig. 19. The Arrangement and Result of a Concentrated Charge: (a) Front View of the Placed Charge; (b) Side View of the Placed Charge; (c) Front View of the Element Deformation; (d) Top View of the Element Deformation.

The second hypothesis "By changing the shape of a charge and cavity formed of a standardized TNT block demolition charges, a greater penetrating effect can be achieved in comparison with a concentrated charge of the same mass formed of the same demolition charges" was not verified for thin-walled steel structural elements since the results obtained in the case of the demolished element did not make it possible to demonstrate a different (greater) penetrating effect of improvised shaped charges. The demolished thin-walled steel profile did not prove to be a suitable element for measuring the penetrating effect and, therefore, it can be argued that this hypothesis was not even refuted.

6 Conclusions

The authors of the paper investigated the effect of improvised shaped charges formed of a standardized TNT block demolition charges on a common structural element. The performed simulations and the experiment proved the regularities between the charge shape composed of a standardized TNT block demolition charges and directing its effect in the course of detonation. The first hypothesis related to directing the effect of the charge was confirmed on the basis of these results. The second hypothesis dealing with the penetrating effect of the charges was neither confirmed nor refuted due to the structure of the demolished element.

This research was conceived as an initial assessment of possibilities of using standardized TNT block demolition charges to assemble improvised shaped charges as a possible replacement when high explosives or manufactured shaped charges are absent. Based on the results obtained, the authors of this article plan to continue further research and assess the penetrating effect of designed charges on steel strips of greater thickness, which would allow measuring the depth of the effect of charges by ultrasound method for the selection of their effective type.

Acknowledgment. This research was funded by the Ministry of Defence of the Czech Republic, grant LANDOPS "Conduct of Land Operations" and by the Ministry of Education, Youth and Sports of the Czech Republic under specific research grant.

References

1. Kyjovský, J., Kroupa, L.: Bojová ženijní podpora. Jednoduché trhací práce. 1st edn., pp. 12–18. University of Defence, Brno (2017)
2. Zukas, J.A., Walters, W.: Explosive Effects and Application. Springer, New York (1998). https://doi.org/10.1007/978-1-4612-0589-0
3. Jangl, Š., Kavický, V. Ochrana pred účinkami výbuchov výbusnín a nástražných výbušných systémov. 1st edn. Jana Kavická-KAVICKY, Oščadnica (2012)
4. Stanković, S., Škrlec V., Dobrilović M., Bohanek V.: Velocity of detonation of AN base blasting agent with addition of hay and recycled rubber. In: Proceedings of the 21th Seminar on New Trends in Research of Energetic Materials, pp. 1042–1050. Springer, Pardubice (2018)
5. Caçoilo, A., Mourão, R., Belkassem, B., Teixeira-Dias, F., Vantomme, J., Lecompte, D.: Blast wave assessment in a compound survival container: small-scale testing. In: The 18th International Conference on Experimental Mechanics. MDPI, Basel (2018)
6. Smith, P.: Blast walls for structural protection against high explosive threats: a review. Int. J. Protect. Struct. **1**(1), 67–84 (2010)
7. Hajek, R., Foglar, M., Fládr, J.: Influence of barrier material and barrier shape on blast wave mitigation. Constr. Build. Mater. **120**, 54–64 (2016)
8. Zezulová, E., Hasilová, K., Komárková, T., Stoniš, P., Štoller, J., Anton, O.: NDT methods suitable for evaluation the condition of military fortification construction in the field. Appl. Sci. **10**(22), 8161 (2020)
9. Caçoilo, A., Teixeira-Dias, F., Mourão, R., Belkassem, B., Vantomme, J., Lecompte, D.: Blast wave propagation in survival shelters: experimental analysis and numerical modelling. Shock Waves **28**(6), 1169–1183 (2018). https://doi.org/10.1007/s00193-018-0858-5
10. Malhotra, A., Carson, D., McFadden, S.: Blast pressure leakage into buildings and effects on humans. Proc. Eng. **210**, 386–392 (2017)
11. Karlos, V., Solomos, G., Larcher, M.: Analysis of the blast wave decay coefficient using the Kingery-Bulmash data. Int. J. Protect. Struct. **7**(3), 409–429 (2016)
12. Figuli, L., Bedon, C., Zvaková, Z., Jangl, Š, Kavický, V.: Dynamic analysis of a blast loaded steel structure. Proc. Eng. **199**, 2463–2469 (2017)
13. Cormie, D., Mays, G., Smiths, P.: Blast Effects on Buildings, 3rd edn. ICE Publishing, London (2019)
14. Shin, J., Whittaker, S.A., Cormie, D., Wilkinson, W.: Numerical modeling of close-in detonations of high explosives. Eng. Struct. **81**, 88–97 (2014)

15. Štoller, J., Dvořák, P.: Field tests of cementitious composites suitable for protective structures and critical infrastructure. Key Eng. Mater. **722**, 3–11 (2016)
16. Štoller, J., Dvořák, P.: Reinforced concrete frames under distant blast. Key Eng. Mater. **755**, 229–235 (2017)
17. Hájek, R., Fládr, J., Pachmáň, J., Štoller, J., Foglar, M.: An experimental evaluation of the blast resistance of heterogeneous concrete based composite bridge decks. Eng. Struct. **179**, 204–210 (2019)
18. Alogla, A., Helal, M., ElShafey, M.M., Fathallah, E.: Numerical analysis for critical structures protection against blast loading using metallic panels. Appl. Sci. **10**(6), 2121 (2020)
19. Guerrero, A.J., Sánchez, P.J., Dias, T.F.: Blast wave dynamics: the influence of the shape of the explosive. J. Hazard. Mater. **331**, 189–199 (2017)
20. Guo, H., Zheng, Y., Yu, Q., Ge, C., Wang, H.: Penetration behavior of reactive liner shaped charge jet impacting thick steel plates. Int. J. Impact Eng. **126**, 76–84 (2019)
21. Hryciów, Z., Borkowski, W., Rybak, P., Wysocki, J.: Influence of the shape of the explosive charge on blast profile. J. KONES Powertrain Transp. **21**(4), 169–176 (2014)

Improving Procedural Hexapod Locomotion Generation with Neural Network Decision Modules

Teymur Azayev(✉) , Jiří Hronovský, and Karel Zimmermann

Faculty of Electrical Engineering, Czech Technical University in Prague, Karlovo náměstí 13, 121 35 Praha 2, Czechia
{azayetey,hronojir,zimmerk}@fel.cvut.cz

Abstract. Hexapod robots are highly flexible and statically stable platforms that are able to traverse a wide range of terrains. The overactuated nature of the platform results in a difficult and high dimensional locomotion problem. Despite the dimensionality, the locomotion task exhibits both morphological and temporal structure. Procedural locomotion generation uses inverse kinematics and leg scheduling to move the torso towards a target location and is used extensively in graphical animation. However, kinematic approaches often fail in dynamical environments due to slippages and other unforseen effects. We propose taking such an approach and replacing the leg scheduling and other heuristic decision points with neural networks. We show that we can formulate the gait-phase decision for each leg as learnable state machines and use Evolutionary Strategies (ES) in simulation to optimize the free parameters. We also show that other useful locomotion traits, such as torso and leg height can be optimized as well. The result improves on the baseline procedural approach on difficult terrains such as stairs. Our approach attempts to inject learnable experience from simulation into an algorithm with a high inductive prior, resulting in a hybrid control policy that has superior performance on a wide range of uneven terrains.

Keywords: Legged robot locomotion · evolutionary strategies · simulation

1 Introduction

Legged robots are one of the most versatile robotic platforms due to the large variety of difficult terrain that they are capable of traversing. This has motivated many areas of research for the construction and locomotion of such platforms. Various morphologies, such as two, four, and six-legged platforms have their own advantages [12] and drawbacks. The Hexapod platform has six legs with three degrees of freedom for each

The research leading to these results has received funding from the Czech Science Foundation under Project 20-29531S. This work has been supported by the EU OP RDE funded project Research Center for Informatics; reg. No.: CZ.02.1.01/0.0./0.0./16_019/0000765. T.Azayev was also partially supported by Grant Agency of the CTU in Prague under Project SGS22/111/OHK3/2T/13.

J. Mazal et al. (Eds.): MESAS 2022, LNCS 13866, pp. 131–144, 2023.
https://doi.org/10.1007/978-3-031-31268-7_8

leg, totalling in 18 degrees of freedom. The most prominent advantage of such a configuration is static stability, meaning that locomotion can be generated kinematically, without significant consideration for the dynamics of the system. Such approaches are often used in graphics animations [6] and high-end game engines. On real robotic platforms, where slippage, obstructions and other difficulties are present, we may find that various heuristics are required to tune the algorithm to perform robustly in a given environment. Such tuning can be difficult and time-consuming. Instead what can be done is to relax the handcrafted algorithm and replace various heuristic decision points with learnable functions such as neural networks. These can then be optimized in simulation on a wide variety of complex terrains until suitable behavior is achieved. This approach is in contrast to the classical end-to-end learning paradigm where we assume that we know nothing about the problem and train a large neural network to solve the task using Reinforcement Learning (RL). Such methods are powerful and have shown impressive performance in various tasks, but require a large number of training steps and are more difficult to generalize to unknown settings, due to the lack of inductive prior of the underlying algorithm structure (Fig. 1).

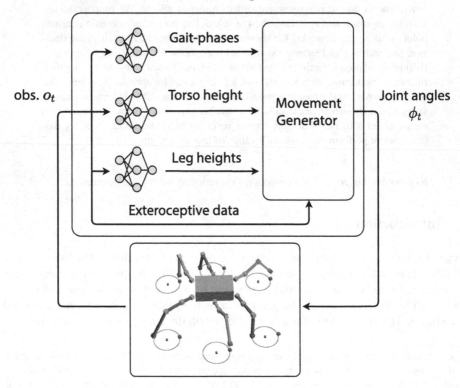

Fig. 1. .

2   Related Work

Various approaches have been developed over the past years which study hexapod loco-motion. Biologically inspired solutions are popular and mostly revolve around using Central Pattern Generators (CPG) for generating a locomotion gait. Such generators can be tuned or learned [7] according to a given reward function. CPGs have also been implemented for legged robots in analog circuits [10]. Some works have also used plain oscillators with variable frequencies for each leg with interdependent signals to generate locomotion [4]. Other approaches include using leg planning [5] and proprioceptive sensing methods for gait adaptation such as in [3]. Powerful learning methods such as Reinforcement learning (RL) can be used to generate locomotion for hexapod robots. The work of [11] uses neural networks with focus on decentralized control. Inductive priors such as graph-like structures can also be applied to neural networks in conjunction with RL for hexapod robots [14]. The work of [1] uses a heirarchical structure of expert policies that provide adaptive locomotion in difficult terrains.

Alternative, non-learning approaches include using kinematic models and procedural generation for locomotion, such as the work of [6]. These algorithms are strongly structured, perform well, but experience issues when deploying on a physical engine. Some works have attempted to model hexapod dynamics [15] to assist with this. Nevertheless, it is necessary in such methods to relax some of the heuristic parts of the algorithms and replace them with neural networks so that we can learn more complex behavior through trial and error. Black box algorithms such as Heuristic Random Search algorithms such Covariance matrix adaptation evolution strategy (CMA-ES) [8] and Augmented Random Search (ARS) [9] can be used to optimize any set of free parameters in a given algorithm by using interactions with an environment that are evaluated by a reward function. Some works such as [13] have leveraged similar algorithms to improve openloop sinusiodal locomotion generation for hexapod robots. Other works such as [2] use similar search algorithms to improve programmed algorithms by optimizing for locomotion within a constrained gait space. Our approach is similar to [2], but we propose to use Heuristic Random Search (HRS) algorithms to improve a kinematic approach similar to [6] by replacing various modules using neural networks and using black box optimization to find the parameters which improve the initial algorithm on difficult terrains such as stairs and high tiles.

Our contributions can be summarized in the following points

- A hybrid locomotion algorithm that consists of hand designed kinematic logic as well as learnable decision points.
- Training procedure and performance evaluation of the baseline procedural locomotion method against our improved version with learnable state-machine leg scheduling, and torso and leg height regression.
- A brief analysis of the training difficulties of unstructured vs structured algorithms.
- An environment of several difficult terrains in the Pybullet simulation for locomotion testing.

3   Locomotion Generation

In this section we will describe the hexapod platform in brief, particularly perception and actuation. We also breakdown the components of our procedural locomotion algorithm, and describe how we attempt to improve the performance by replacing various components with neural network modules.

4   Hexapod Environment Overview

The platform that we use is a model of the MKII Phantom X hexapod in the Pybullet simulator. This hexapod has six legs with three joints in each leg, shown in Fig. 2.

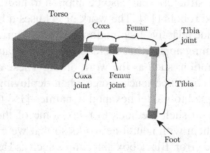

Fig. 2. Hexapod leg description.

The actuators are modeled as servos that accept target joint angles and implement control using a PID regulator. Proprioceptive observations include current joint angles and velocities, as well as torso attitude. To obtain an algorithm that can be realistically used on a real platform, we use sparse point cloud observations that could be obtained from a depth camera or lidar. From the sparse point cloud we compute a height map by dividing the point cloud regions into a regular grid, shown in Fig. 3. Empty voxel heights are calculated by interpolation from neighboring voxels.

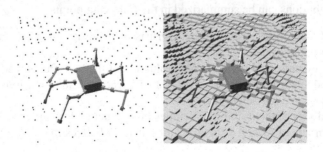

Fig. 3. Point cloud approximation by heightmap.

We also assume that we will be running an accurate localization algorithm such as ICP so in simulation we use ground truth position data for our experiments.

5 Algorithm Structure

The locomotion algorithm consists of a movement generation module which accepts a set of pre-computed gait parameters, set of observations and target control inputs. In this section we will describe all the above components.

5.1 Observations and Control Inputs

The observations and target control inputs include the following:

- Current state of the hexapod $s_t = (x_t, q_t, j_t)$ which consists of position x_t, orientation q_t and joint angles j_t
- Control inputs θ_t^{tar}, and v_t^{tar} defines the target direction angle and the xy velocity respectively. These are provided by the user or by a waypoint follower.
- Point cloud heightmap pc_t provides exteroceptive data for the algorithm, shown in Fig. 3.

5.2 Movement Generation Module

A single step of the movement generation module is described in Algorithm 1.

Algorithm 1. Movement generator step

    Estimate surface normal
    Update torso pitch and roll based on the surface normal
    if no legs are at the operating boundary **then**
        Use IKT to move torso position and yaw based on control input
    end if
    Update torso height based on input control
    Calculate torso transformation matrix
    for each leg **do**
        Update leg given precomputed gait parameters and observations (see 5.2)
    end for
    write joint angles to servos

The leg update function, mentioned in Algorithm 1 consists of calculating the target foot position using direct kinematics, and then deciding the movement depending on whether the leg is in *stance* or *swing* phase. If in *stance* phase, then the leg follows the height of the corresponding position of the terrain. If in *swing* phase, then the leg height and position is updated according to the progress of the swing. Phase decisions are described in Fig. 2.

Target Foot Position Calculation. Foot placement depends on the control input. The following examples can be seen in Fig. 4.

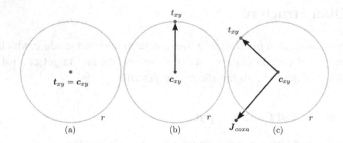

Fig. 4. Visualization of foot placement defined by Eqs. 1 and 3.

When the input control is static, the foot target t_{xy} is held in the middle c_{xy} of the boundary. Otherwise, the step-down target t_{xy} is placed within range r in the direction d of translational or rotational control, shown in Eq. 1.

$$t_{xy} = c_{xy} + r\frac{d}{\|d\|} \tag{1}$$

Turning control is shown in Eq. 3

$$w = (J_{coxa} - c) \times z_{world} \tag{2}$$

$$t_{xy} = c_{xy} + rd\frac{w_{xy}}{\|w_{xy}\|} \tag{3}$$

The leg z coordinate is then sampled from the heightmap location corresponding to the target foot position

5.3 Precomputed Gait Parameters

Precomputed gait parameters: We consider the following important three gait parameters that have a significant impact of the locomotion: a) Gait-phases: These variables decide whether a leg will transition into one of the possible $\{stance, swing\}$ phases. b) Torso height: Torso height can be important for locomotion and it is not always straightforward to decide how high it should be based on underlying terrain. c) Leg lifting height: Leg lifting can have an impact on the quality of the gait, stability as well as collision with the neighboring terrain. In the following two subsections we describe how these gait parameters are computed manually and how we propose to replace them using neural network modules.

Hand Designed Gait Parameters. At a given time, an individual leg can be in the *stance* or *swing* phase. When in the *stance* phase then the leg remains in this phase until it is nearing defined kinematic reach boundary of that given leg, where it automatically goes into the *swing* phase, described in Algorithm 2. We use a stable tripod gait which activates groups of three legs at once, shown in Fig. 5.

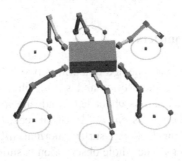

Fig. 5. Tripod gait. The leg groups can be distinguished by the red and green color. (Color figure online)

Algorithm 2. Gait-phase transition

1: **if** Group 1 is in stance phase **and** some leg from Group 2 is stuck **then**
2:     Put Group 2 in swing phase
3: **end if**
4: **if** Group 2 is in stance phase **and** some leg from Group 1 is stuck **then**
5:     Put Group 1 in swing phase
6: **end if**
7:
8: **for** leg **in** All legs **do**
9:     **if** leg distance from target foot position < some threshold **then**
10:         Put leg in stance phase
11:     **end if**
12: **end for**

The movement generator calculates the torso height as follows:

$$h_{t_z} = \frac{1}{6} \sum_{j=1}^{6} t_{j_z} + h_d + h_i \tag{4}$$

where h_{t_z} is the torso height in world coordinates, $t_{1_z}, t_{2_z}, \ldots, t_{6_z}$ are z-coordinates of the target positions, h_d is the default height value, and h_i is the torso height control parameter.

Leg height when lifting is calculated as follows:

$$h_l = h_t + h_d + h_i \tag{5}$$

where h_l is the leg height in the world coordinates, h_t is the terrain height sampled from heightmap, h_d is the default lifting height, and h_i is the leg lifting height control parameter.

Neural Network Gait Parameters

Gait Phase Decisions. We implemented a neural network for each of the 6 legs that can decide to switch between the *stance* and *swing* phases given interoceptive and exteroceptive data. The observations o_t^i for leg i and timestep t consist of current leg phases ph_t, leg tip ground contacts $cp_t \in \mathbb{R}^6$ of all legs, leg joint angles $j_t^i \in \mathbb{R}^3$, distance to the target position $d_t^i \in \mathbb{R}^3$, surface normal $sn_t^i \in \mathbb{R}^3$ and leg boundary conditions $lb_t \in \mathbb{R}^6$ of all legs. The whole observation is shown in Eq. 6.

$$leg_t^i = \{ph_t, cp_t, lb_t, j_t^i, d_t^i, sn_t^i\} \in \mathbb{R}^{25} \tag{6}$$

Each leg gets detailed information such as joint angles only of itself, but global information such as leg contact points of all other legs as well. This way the observation can stay relatively low dimensional but still be informative. The neural networks can collectively decide which legs have slipped, which are stuck and can adapt to unforseen behaviors.

The neural network is a Multi Layer Perceptron (MLP) with ReLu activation functions and a hyperbolic tangent (tanh) function at the output. Each network $pi^i >_{gait_{\theta_i}}$ maps input leg_t^i to an output $a_{t+1}^i \in \mathbb{R}$. The phase was decided according to Eq. 7

$$\text{leg phase} = \begin{cases} \text{swing-phase,} & a_1 > a_2 \\ \text{stance-phase,} & a_1 \leq a_2 \end{cases} \tag{7}$$

Figure 6 shows the structure of such a network.

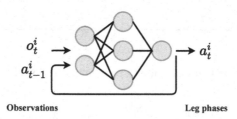

o_t^i

a_{t-1}^i

a_t^i

Observations   **Leg phases**

Fig. 6. .

Torso and Leg Height. For predicting the Torso and leg heights we use a similar neural network architecture as the gait phases, but with slightly different inputs. For the Torso height prediction the observation consists of gait phases ph_t, leg boundary conditions lb_t, leg contacts cp_t, surface normal sn_t^i, torso orientation $torso_t^{ang}$ and the torso height $torso^{hm}$ sampled from the heightmap. This totals to a dimension of 25.

For the leg height prediction of leg i we only a small 8 dimensional vector consisting of the surface normal sn_t^i, leg joint angles j_t^i, leg ground contact cp_t^i and current leg height $l_h^i eight$.

Weight Sharing Patterns for Gait Phases. Given that we will be making decisions for each leg of the hexapod robot, it makes sense to consider the structure of the morphology so as better to distribute the weights of the neural network and to avoid redundancy. We propose three options of weight sharing. The first is to allow each leg neural network module to have unique weights. This leads to a large amount of parameters and is more difficult to train. The second scheme is to use bilateral weight sharing to exploit the bilateral symmetry present in the robot. This would mean that we only have 3 sets of weights, and the rest will be mirrored. The last scheme is to use the same weights for each leg of the hexapod, resulting in only one set of weights (Fig. 7).

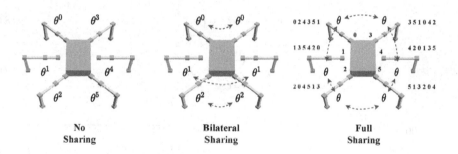

Fig. 7. Neural network weight sharing schemes.

We experimentally found that the third proposed scheme to share a single set of weights across all 6 legs works best. Some locomotion results can even be seen after a single epoch of training. The only difficulty with the bilateral and full weight sharing scheme is to correctly route the inputs of the other legs to each other input.

6   Experiments

Training and testing is done in the PyBullet simulator. The environment consists of the physics engine, hexapod robot, and the reward function. Episodes start with the robot spawned at a given position. The main goal is to achieve successful locomotion in the direction of the positive x axis, along with other criteria described below. We test three different terrains with varying difficulties and challenges, shown in Fig. 8. The rocky terrain is generated by discretizing the height of a 2 dimensional Perlin noise function.[1]

---

[1] Video: https://vimeo.com/744114592.

Fig. 8. Experimental terrains: Flat, rocks, stairs

Training is done using the CMA-ES algorithm by sampling a batch of candidate solutions from the current distribution, evaluating them for a single episode each and then then updating the candidate solutions according to the rewards. We consider three different criteria for evaluation: a) Distance travelled, which is calculated by summing the instantaneous $\dot{x}$ velocities, b) Locomotion smoothness per distance, calculated by summing torso translational and angular accelerations a_t and ϵ_t, normalized by the distance travelled, shown in Eq. 8 c) Power spent, by summing the product of instantaneous joint torques and velocities, shown in Eq. 9 (Fig. 9).

$$r_s = -\|a_i + c\epsilon_i\|^2 \tag{8}$$

$$r_p = \sum_{k=1}^{18} |\tau_k| \cdot j_k \tag{9}$$

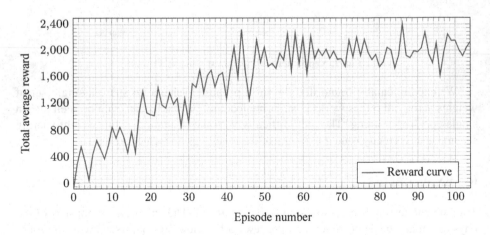

Fig. 9. A training curve of an optimization procedure of our learnable structured algorithm approach

We trained and evaluated our baseline structured algorithm (SA) approach, against the improved proposed learnable structure algorithm (LSA) and also an end-to-end

(E2E) neural network. The approaches were trained individually on all three terrains. Results are shown in Tables 1. D is the distance reached, S is the smoothness per distance, P is the power consumption per distance. The tables show that on flat terrain, the E2E policy travels the furthest and has the lowest consumption. This is, however due to the fact that the E2E policy performs jumps, rather than walking which allows it to travel further and spend less overall energy. This can also be seen in the supplementary video. We can see that on more difficult terrains, the E2E attains significantly worse scores in smoothness and power consumption in comparison to the structured policies. We also see that the LSA outperforms the SA in all terrains in both distance covered and power consumption. It does, however, come with a slight decrease in locomotion smoothness which results in the additional effort to traverse the difficult terrain.

Table 1. Evaluation comparison of the proposed approaches on three different terrains.

(a) Flat terrain   (b) Rocky terrain   (c) Steps terrain

Policy	D	S_d	P_d
SA	28.6	**-7.4**	-94.9
LSA	32.6	-9.2	-86.7
E2E	**135.2**	-339.2	**-61.9**

Policy	D	S_d	P_d
SA	16.3	**-202.7**	-262.7
LSA	**23.0**	-210.4	**-190.1**
E2E	15.3	-1906.9	-643.2

Policy	D	S_d	P_d
SA	6.9	**-251.1**	-603.4
LSA	8.2	-481.1	**-588.3**
E2E	**9.4**	-2374.0	-818.6

We can also see from Fig. 10 that our proposed learned variant (LSA) is superior to the baseline algorithm (SA) with increasing terrain difficulty in distance travelled and power consumption. This suggests that the baseline algorithm is suboptimal and admits improvement.

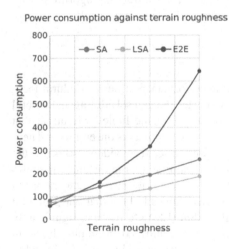
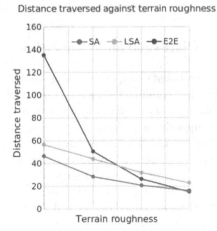

Fig. 10. Trends comparing the various policies

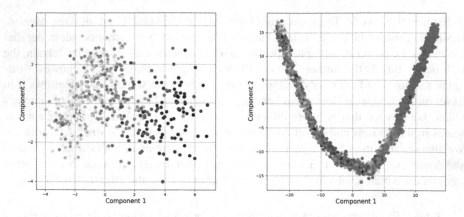

Fig. 11. Parameter vectors of the LSA (left) and E2E (right) projected to 2D with PCA. The figure suggests that the E2E reward landscape is significantly more smooth and informative than the LSA.

Reward Landscape. One interesting thing to note when training a highly structured algorithm versus a neural network is that the reward landscapes are vastly different. A small change to the weight of the E2E neural network has a smooth and roughly proportionate effect on the reward. The structured algorithm, on the other hand, is much more sensitive, especially when optimizing something like the gait phase scheduling. We attempt to show the various landscapes by projecting parameter-reward pairs to a 2 dimensional plot using Principle Component Analysis (PCA). Figure 11 shows the structured LSA algorithm on the left, and the unstructured neural network on the right. The color intensity denotes reward. We can see that in the unstructured algorithm there is quite a distinct path in 2D which leads the weight vector from the random initialization to the optimal solution. This is something that can make training algorithms with high inductive prior quite difficult using techniques such as random search.

7   Discussion and Conclusion

We proposed several experiments to compare the performance of our procedural locomotion algorithm (SA) and the variant where we replace the gait scheduling and several other control parameters with neural network modules. From the Table 1 we can see that the algorithm with the largest traversed distance and lowest power is the end-to-end neural network (E2E). This is, however misleading as we can see from video results that the hexapod cheats by making large jumps and strides, gaining a large distance. It shows that it is more difficult to train such a task without a strong prior and more work has to go into the reward function to prevent such artifacts. Tables 1 show that our proposed neural network modules alow the structured algorithm (LSA) to traverse significantly more terrain than the static variant (SA). This is also confirmed in graphs shown in Fig. 10. Figure 10 also shows that although the distance traversed by the E2E algorithm is large for smooth terrain, it is overtaken by our LSA variant in more difficult terrains. By visually inspecting the resultant locomotion policies in the supplementary video we can see that the unstructured variant is very shaky and

We also note that both approaches, structured and unstructured, that were presented have their own difficulties during training. The unstructured approach (E2E) requires more involved reward engineering due to the lack of inductive prior in the policy structure. The structured variant, however, can be more difficult to train due to the noisier reward landscape. This can be seen in the two dimensional structure of candidate parameter vectors of the CMA-ES algorithm, obtained by PCA projection, shown in Fig. 11.

As future work, it would be interesting to analyze gait adaptation and recovery to external disturbances to the legs and torso. In general there is some room for improvement to the whole architecture of our approach. It would also be useful to confirm the experimental results on a real platform on a similar batch of terrains (flat ground, scattered bricks, stairs). One limitation of this approach is that we rely on leg tip contact information available in simulation. On the real platform this is more difficult to do as a reliable sensors would have to be installed, or the detection would have to be done in software. In conclusion, we have shown that we can improve already programmed locomotion algorithms by replacing various decision points by neural network modules. We think that this approach is useful not only for legged robots, but for other platforms where we can make use of a mix of problem domain knowledge and learned experience.

References

1. Azayev, T., Zimmerman, K.: Blind hexapod locomotion in complex terrain with gait adaptation using deep reinforcement learning and classification. J. Intell. Robot. Syst. **99**(3), 659–671 (2020). https://doi.org/10.1007/s10846-020-01162-8
2. Belter, D., Skrzypczynski, P.: A biologically inspired approach to feasible gait learning for a hexapod robot. Appl. Math. Comput. Sci. **20**, 69–84 (2010). https://doi.org/10.2478/v10006-010-0005-7
3. Bjelonic, M., Kottege, N., Beckerle, P.: Proprioceptive control of an over-actuated hexapod robot in unstructured terrain. In: 2016 IEEE/RSJ International Conference on Intelligent Robots and Systems (IROS), pp. 2042–2049. IEEE (2016). https://doi.org/10.1109/IROS.2016.7759321
4. Campos, R., Matos, V., Santos, C.: Hexapod locomotion. In: IECON 2010–36th Annual Conference on IEEE Industrial Electronics Society, pp. 1546–1551. IEEE, Glendale, AZ, USA (2010)
5. Cizek, P., Masri, D., Faigl, J.: Foothold placement planning with a hexapod crawling robot. In: 2017 IEEE/RSJ International Conference on Intelligent Robots and Systems (IROS), pp. 4096–4101. IEEE, Vancouver, BC, Canada (2017)
6. Karim, A.A., Gaudin, T., Meyer, A., Buendia, A., Bouakaz, S.: Procedural locomotion of multilegged characters in dynamic environments. Comput. Anim. Virtual Worlds **24**(1), 3–15 (2013). https://doi.org/10.1002/cav.1467
7. Lele, A.S., Fang, Y., Ting, J., Raychowdhury, A.: Online reward-based training of spiking central pattern generator for hexapod locomotion. In: 2020 IFIP/IEEE 28th International Conference on Very Large Scale Integration (VLSI-SOC), pp. 208–209 (2020). https://doi.org/10.1109/VLSI-SOC46417.2020.9344100
8. Loshchilov, I., Hutter, F.: CMA-ES for hyperparameter optimization of deep neural networks. CoRR abs/1604.07269 (2016)
9. Mania, H., Guy, A., Recht, B.: Simple random search of static linear policies is competitive for reinforcement learning. In: Bengio, S., Wallach, H., Larochelle, H., Grauman, K., Cesa-Bianchi, N., Garnett, R. (eds.) Advances in Neural Information Processing Systems. vol. 31. Curran Associates, Inc. (2018). https://doi.org/10.48550/arXiv.1803.07055

10. Minati, L., Frasca, M., Yoshimura, N., Koike, Y.: Versatile locomotion control of a hexapod robot using a hierarchical network of nonlinear oscillator circuits. IEEE Access **6**, 8042–8065 (2018). https://doi.org/10.1109/ACCESS.2018.2799145
11. Schilling, M., Konen, K., Ohl, F.W., Korthals, T.: Decentralized deep reinforcement learning for a distributed and adaptive locomotion controller of a hexapod robot. In: 2020 IEEE/RSJ International Conference on Intelligent Robots and Systems (IROS), pp. 5335–5342. IEEE (2020). https://doi.org/10.1109/IROS45743.2020.9341754
12. Todd, D.J.: Walking Machines: An Introduction to Legged Robots. Springer, Cham (2013)
13. Vice, J., Sukthankar, G., Douglas, P.K.: Leveraging evolutionary algorithms for feasible hexapod locomotion across uneven terrain. arXiv preprint arXiv:2203.15948 (2022). 10.48550/arXiv. 2203.15948
14. Wang, T., Liao, R., Ba, J., Fidler, S.: Nervenet: learning structured policy with graph neural networks. In: International Conference on Learning Representations (2018)
15. Zangrandi, M., Arrigoni, S., Braghin, F.: Control of a hexapod robot considering terrain interaction. CoRR abs/2112.10206 (2021). https://doi.org/10.48550/arXiv.2112.10206

Artificial Intelligence Support to the Paradigm Shift from Reactive to Anticipatory Action in Humanitarian Responses

Walter David[1]([✉]), Beatriz Garmendia-Doval[2], and Michelle King-Okoye[1,3]

[1] Ronin Institute, Montclair, NJ 07043, USA
`walter.david@roninstitute.org`
[2] Masa Group SA, Group, 75002 Paris, France
`beatriz.garmendia-doval@masagroup.net`
[3] University of Edinburgh, Edinburgh EH8 9JS, UK
`Michelle.King-Okoye@ed.ac.uk`

Abstract. Climate change impact factors, drought, food insecurity, exacerbate existing vulnerabilities, with security implications as often they generate opportunities for insurgence and complicate peacebuilding efforts. Humanitarian anticipatory action is an innovative approach which systematically links early warnings to actions designed to provide protection ahead of a hazard. Leveraging authors' experience in stabilization, this article investigates the role that artificial intelligence (AI) and modelling & simulation (M&S) can play to support early actions. As a proof of concept, the Expert.ai Cogito hybrid natural language processing and machine learning platform and the AI supported MASA SYNERGY system have been tested, to collect open sources information and to simulate the use case of deployment of unmanned aerial vehicles (UAVs), or drones, in a region affected by violence and natural disasters. Different prepositioning of cargo drones and resources can be tested and compared. In fact, a network of cargo drones set up in the optimal locations, ready to be deployed, can make a difference in establishing action plans and relief aid delivery.

Scenario exercise and brainstorming have captured the value of AI and M&S to improve situational awareness and early actions prior to the onset of a shock. AI and M&S tools shows the ability to support decision making and anticipatory action by training crisis cells, verifying the impact of disaster, and testing contingency plans for significantly faster and more cost-effective responses, compared with the traditional reactive approach.

Keywords: Artificial Intelligence · Simulation · Anticipatory Action

1 Background

Armed conflicts, energy crisis, climate change, drought, pandemic, hunger, displacement, never has the world seen such complex mega crises [1]. While we observe a trend for longer crises [2, 3], infectious diseases and epidemics add a further layer of complexity to humanitarian response [4, 5].

J. Mazal et al. (Eds.): MESAS 2022, LNCS 13866, pp. 145–162, 2023.
https://doi.org/10.1007/978-3-031-31268-7_9

1.1 Climate and (in)security

Conflicts, economic shocks, and weather extremes are the main drivers affecting 193 million people by food insecurity [6]. Many factors and compounding drivers lead to armed conflicts but among the countries most vulnerable to climate change, many are involved in conflicts and less able to cope [4, 5, 7].

Environmental scholars and advisors consider climate change as a conflict multiplier [8] that exacerbates vulnerabilities, causes displacement and huge humanitarian needs with negative implications for security [9].

The climate-security link is obvious to international actors deployed [5], including authors and stakeholders of this research, in the Global South. Horn of Africa communities face the threat of starvation after four consecutive failed rainy seasons including the last, the driest in the last 70 years [10]. In Somalia, severe drought has already affected, as of July 2022, at least 7 million people, of whom 918,000 are internally displaced persons (IDPs) in search of water, food, and pasture [11]. Lack of water, food insecurity and poverty create opportunities for the al-Shabaab insurgence that controls the countryside where they collect taxes. They spread corruption even in government held areas where they act as a mafia. Climate change effects empower insurgence force generation as poverty pushes many to join [12–14], influence the ongoing conflict and complicate the efforts of the international community to build peace and develop institutions.

In North-Eastern Nigeria, the insurgency has displaced over 2.2 million people, devastated agriculture and cut off people from essential services [4, 5, 15, 16]. High temperatures, wildfires, drought, tropical storms, flooding, and diseases are leading to food insecurity [16–19]. Hundreds of thousands of IDPs live in congested, garrison towns protected by the Nigerian Army [15, 17–19]. Many aid workers have been abducted or killed [5, 17] and access is a major concern because often insurgence attacks or flooding cut off remote communities, urging humanitarian officers to use helicopters. Requirements have been identified for data sets and IT tools to improve information management, early warning, surveillance, and monitoring at the tactical level (camp-like local level) [5].

Military Contribution. According to NATO Standard AJP-3.26, the primary objective of humanitarian assistance is to alleviate human suffering during and after disasters and crises. NATO military forces may be deployed in support of civil authorities overseeing the emergency [20]. Stabilization activities as described in NATO AJP 3.28 [21], should be focused on mitigating the immediate sources of instability and should help establish the foundation for long-term stability. Such activities require supporting local and regional actors to reduce violence, ensure basic security and facilitate peaceful political deal-making.

1.2 Catching the Black Swan

Ukraine War Impact Effects. An increasingly uncertain world was already grappling with the COVID-19 pandemic and climate change but, due to the consequences of the war in Ukraine and economic sanctions, people globally are facing a cost-of-living crisis not seen in more than a generation, with escalating price shocks in food and energy [22]. Today, about 60 percent of the world's workforce is estimated to have lower incomes than before the pandemic. World Food Programme (WFP), the United Nations (UN) logistic agency estimates that severely food insecure persons doubled from 135 million pre-pandemic to 276 million over just two years; this number is likely to increase up to 323 million in 2022 [22, 23].

Black Swan Events. So-called black swan events (e.g., pandemic, Ukraine war, etc.) [24], are so rare that even the possibility that one of them might occur is unknown, have a catastrophic impact when they do occur but they are explained in hindsight, as if they were actually predictable [25]. For extremely rare events, Taleb argues that the standard tools of probability and prediction, such as the normal distribution, do not apply since they depend on large population and past sample sizes that are never available for rare events by definition [25, 26].

While black swans are hard to catch, it is estimated that half of today's crises are somewhat predictable and 20 per cent are highly predictable. Recently, the humanitarian community has actively pursued ways to get ahead of crises by helping people earlier, as soon as they see problems coming, exploring disruptive technologies, and taking early actions [27]. The intent is to move from the traditional approach, where they observe the disaster, decide the response, and then mobilize funds and resources, to an anticipatory approach, where they plan, in advance for the next crises, preparing response plans and funds, release money and mobilize the response as soon as they are needed [28].

Risk is Global, Resilience is Local. Lessons identified from the pandemic, when airplanes where grounded, travels and international staff movements restricted, suggest the need for more dynamic risk assessment tools, investments in early warning and analytics and localization of leadership. In fact, while risk is global, resilience is local, and involves the engagement of the local community, calling for shifting the focus from managing risk to building resilience, and early action [29].

Initiatives include the WeRobotics sponsored Flying Labs, locally led robotics knowledge hubs networks across Africa, Asia, Latin America, focusing on local effective, sustainable solutions to strengthen local expertise in the use of drones, robotics, data, and AI for positive social change [30].

1.3 Methodology

This paper is informed by scholarly literature but, due to the rapidly evolving attitude to innovative technologies among humanitarian organizations, also by reports from UN working groups and missions.

In fact, the humanitarian community is exploring new approaches, cost-efficient project designs and programming and is open to explore the opportunities that innovative technologies can provide. Recently, big data analytics, AI, and machine learning (ML) have supported a better understanding of some events and have contributed to the response to COVID-19 pandemic [31, 32].

Aim. Leveraging authors' and partners' experience from deployment in the field, this article aims to present application concepts for promoting a discussion on the role of AI and modelling and simulation (M&S) to support humanitarian action. Due to their different organizational culture, learning approach, and skill sets, emergency and humanitarian organisations have not exploited the potential of computer simulation as the armed forces where computer assisted exercises (CAX) are routine in staff and headquarters training.

Objectives. The approach includes presenting and testing selected AI and M&S tools to explore their potential in tackling some of the tough operational challenges posed by climate change, conflict and displacement, and their nexus. Realistic scenarios of a humanitarian operating theatre have been created, discussed, and validated with the support of subject matter experts (SMEs) and decision-makers. In particular, in a real crisis scenario, the AI powered SINERGY simulation system has been tested to understand its potential in supporting decision making on the use of cargo drones and their optimal deployment in a dangerous region.

Scenario Exercise. A cargo drone simulation use case has been proposed. A Northeast Nigeria scenario has been generated to simulate a vaccines delivery contingency plan to support IDPs camps located in Borno state. As a proof of concept, two commercial tools have been tested. The Expert.ai Cogito tool, supported by natural language understanding (NLU) and machine learning (ML) technologies [4, 33] has been deployed in the humanitarian setting to produce open sources intelligence.

A scenario exercise has been conducted with the application of the MASA SYNERGY AI powered constructive simulation system to simulate efficient ways, including the deployment of Unmanned Aerial Vehicles (UAVs), commonly known as drones, to transport and deliver medical items to remote locations in a difficult access region, affected both by insurgence armed attacks and natural disasters.

Obviously, a network of cargo drones set up in the optimal locations, ready to be pre-deployed, ahead of a hazard, can make a huge difference in the times needed to establish action plans and start sending relief aid.

Humanitarian experts, academia, think tanks, non-governmental organizations, and the private sector have participated in an ad hoc session that authors have organized at the UN OCHA HNPW 2022 conference. Discussions have spotlighted the role that AI, M&S and robotics can play to support anticipation and mitigation of climate-induced hazards impact, and compounding drivers (e.g., armed conflict) of humanitarian needs across multiple regions including Somalia, Nigeria and Mozambique.

2   Anticipatory Action

Anticipatory action is an innovative approach linking systematically early warnings to actions designed to provide protection ahead of a hazard in response to a trigger (before the manifestation of humanitarian need), aiming to prevent and mitigate the shock impact of a foreseen hazard such as drought, floods, and cyclones, to reduce humanitarian needs and enhance resilience [34, 35].

Global and Local Data. The occurrence and impact of some shocks can be predicted with increasing confidence, by combining different analytical approaches [34] supporting decision-makers to take early action, in the humanitarian, development, and peace-building sectors and their interlinkages (known in the humanitarian sector as the *HDP Triple Nexus*).

Analysis is 'data hungry', meaning large amounts of data are needed to forecast hazards, understand vulnerabilities and risk, and calculate potential impacts. Global datasets are created in data centers, such as the recently established OCHA Centre for Humanitarian Data [1], but often lack the resolution needed to take actions at the tactical and local levels.

Local data are key in disaster response and disaster risk reduction. In fact, in the time of crisis, closer to the centre of the crisis, the more information you need, in more detail and in real-time, in particular for tactical level information required by ground response teams [36]. Local data are also critical for building community ownership and improving resilience.

Early Actions. Working on data and predictive analytics to support evidence-based decision-making during the time window between the forecast, prediction or warning and the hazard onset (extreme event) facilitates the implementation of mitigating measures. For example, before drought impacts on livelihoods and lives, cash can be provided and water points can be built to prevent competition among pastoralists for scarce water resources [29].

Early actions fill the gap between traditional disaster risk reduction, aiming to reduce vulnerability to hazards over the long-term, and humanitarian response, which provides relief after the occurrence of an event. Early actions can be pre-identified to proactively mitigate the projected humanitarian impact (*forecast-based actions*) to protect people before a disaster strikes. These actions could include refreshing staff training, works to strengthen houses and shelters, distribution of cash, and deployment of resources [35]. Still, to be effective, early actions require the meaningful engagement and the cooperation with the at-risk communities [37].

2.1 Robotics Supporting Humanitarian Action

Unmanned Aerial Vehicles (UAVs), commonly known as drones, have the potential to play a crucial role in early action, enabling real time capture and processing of local data, and performing emergency logistics tasks [38]. The UN OCHA Unmanned Aerial Vehicles (UAVs) in Humanitarian Response Policy Paper 3 registered the increasing use of drones, in six categories [39] identified by the Swiss Foundation for Mine Action Report Drones in Humanitarian Action [40]:

- mapping,
- delivery of essential products to remote or hard-to-reach locations;
- search and rescue,
- support for damage assessment,
- increased situational awareness,

- monitoring changes (urban and camp growth, agricultural use, construction of roads or infrastructure).

As previously mentioned, local data are key in disaster response and disaster risk reduction and UAVs can provide the resolution and the timing required to take appropriate actions at the tactical and local levels. In fact, the improved performance in visual analytics enables the production of aerial drone imagery [39], more detailed compared with available satellite imagery. The generalization of deep learning methods, significantly improve drone visual recognition and image analysis, letting UAVs further capture their operating environment and perform more complex missions while reducing required manning [39].

Drones are rapidly becoming cheaper and affordable to humanitarian agencies and even small non-governmental organizations. Authors believe that the convergence of AI and robotics technologies has the potential to facilitate the adoption of drones and, increasing autonomy simplifies their operation in the context of humanitarian early actions.

2.2 Medical and Security Threats Analysis

In an increasingly connected and digital world, affected communities become a valuable source of relevant information [41]. Authors and SMEs have explored the use of an evolved medical intelligence platform (MIP) supported by the Expert.ai Cogito engine [4], able to processes, in addition to scientific literature, national and local press, tweets and other social media data [42–45] available on the surface, deep and dark web [42, 46, 47].

In fact, the Cogito hybrid cross-lingual cognitive engine combines deep semantic natural language understanding (NLU) and machine learning (ML), exploits (un)structured real world text data, resolves text ambiguity, captures contextualized meanings of texts *the way people do*, producing knowledge, insight and actionable intelligence, saving the analyst time-consuming manual work [4].

Key indicators are generated for data clustering, to discover even weak signals, for outbreaks early detection and data driven decision-making, both for prevention actions aiming to anticipate events (ex-ante analysis) and to analyze historical situations to mitigate future events by using past experiences (ex- post analysis) [4].

I the present research, the Cogito engine has been tested beyond the digital detection of diseases [48, 49], for the evaluation of risks to humanitarian workers in a region affected by armed groups' insurgence and violence.

2.3 AI Supported Simulation

With the aim to bridge the capacity gap between humanitarian and military simulation and show case to UN decision-makers, authors have selected, for a proof of concept, MASA SYNERGY constructive simulation system.

The reason for this choice is twofold: the system is powered by the same AI engine of SWORD, used for military staff training, concept development and experimentation, and it provides the ability to model disasters and human behavior, groups, and doctrines in the context of crisis. Such features show SYNERGY as very promising for training crisis cells and teams, but also for analyzing disasters' impacts and loss on population and infrastructures, for studying the introduction of new equipment, and for testing contingency plans.

Scenario Representation. In SYNERGY the information is represented in different layers (see Fig. 1). Entities represent and perform the work of units, teams, groups, or assets (e.g., firefighters, police patrols, a crowd, a helicopter, etc.) but the simulation is performed at a lower level, where the equipment are modelled from those really used by those units when calculating speed movement or capabilities [50].

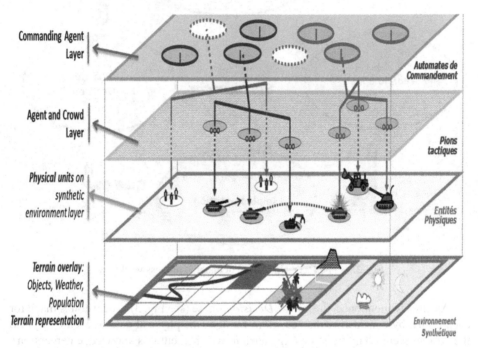

Fig. 1. Information layers in a SYNERGY scenario.

2.4 SYNERGY Decisional Process

At each simulation tick, for each entity, its perception is updated, i.e., the knowledge that each entity has of the situation depending on its location, its sensors, the terrain, the weather. Consequently, for each entity, the system computes its next action, depending on default behavior and current mission. The actions are implemented, and the scenario updated (reference needed).

The decisional process [50] comprises four steps (see Fig. 2). During the *Perception* phase, simulation agents perceive their own situation, build their knowledge of terrain, of other agents, and of their own physical capabilities. During the *Decision* phase, each agent makes decisions based on its own knowledge and its mission. In this phase the actions to be performed are selected. During the *Implementation,* the effects of the actions are computed. Finally, during the *Scenario update*, the effects are applied to the scenario representation.

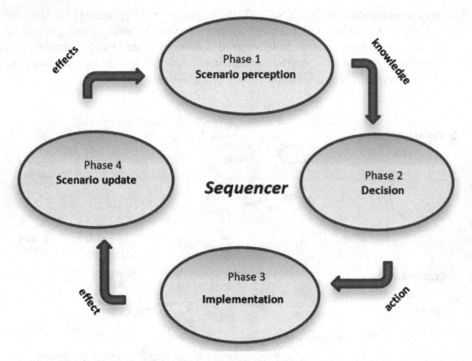

Fig. 2. SYNERGY simulation decisional process workflow.

As already mentioned, during the *Decision* phase (see Fig. 3), a decision is made for each entity, by considering the behaviour models, the physical data of each entity and the current scenario information (e.g., terrain, weather, entity's knowledge perception).

The DirectAI Brain. The MASA DirectAI engine is the core of the SYNERGY simulation system. It is configured and used to integrate decisional processes in simulation agents. Such agents are created to perform several different tasks, but they must choose their actions in dynamic and unpredictable environments and their tasks may conflict the allocation of resources (e.g., if the situation requires to extinguish a fire and to transport injured people at the same time) [50].

The DirectAI brain implements an action selection policy, based on drives and representations. Its architecture comprises two layers; a decision layer propagates decisional information to an action layer that performs the most appropriate action according to the current situation. A graph of nodes represents the brain, with nodes able to receive activity from other nodes or from external drives; they can consult representations to modulate their output activity. The graph's leaves correspond to action nodes and the most activated actions compete for the control of the agent's actuators [50].

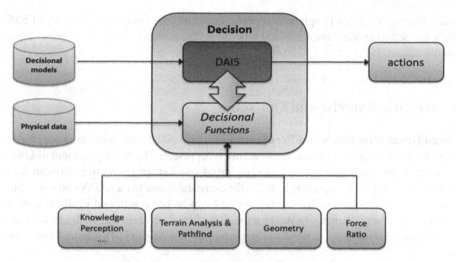

Fig. 3. The decision algorithm in SYNERGY.

Direct AI Paradigm: A Two-level Language. The complexity of defining the behavior depends on the level of abstraction of the atomic actions. For example, the driving a car behavior is easier to implement when split in atomic actions such as go straight, turn left, turn right. Therefore, it is possible to reduce the complexity by providing more abstract atomic actions (atomic behaviors) (see Fig. 4).

Because in a brain information can flow freely, a powerful paradigm is used for selecting actions, such as the *Free-Flow Hierarchy* (FFH), to create atomic behaviors

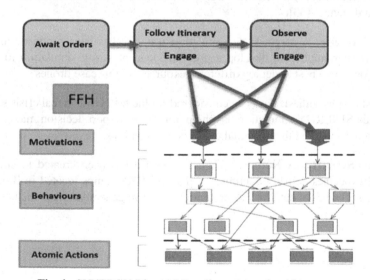

Fig. 4. SYNERGY DirectAI Paradigm: A two-level language.

while an easy to read (and implement) paradigm, such as the *Finite State Machine* - FSM – like), is used to create complex behaviors, using the activation of atomic behaviors as atomic actions [50].

3   Scenario Exercise and Outcomes

Cargo Drone Simulation and Prepositioning.   One of the most interesting use cases of robotics in the context of humanitarian action is represented by the deployment of UAVs, both for mapping and monitoring following rapid-onset emergencies like hurricanes and earthquakes, and for transporting light but time-critical loads. In fact, UAVs do not require extensive infrastructure such as runaways and can be pre-positioned in disaster-prone regions as a complementary tool when the use of land vehicles like 4x4s, motorbikes, and airplanes is restricted, slow, or too expensive for fast deliver [54], among other items, of:

- critical medical supply when roads are impassable,
- samples from field clinics to testing labs,
- health supply for unpredictable needs, such as anti-venom.

In fact, one of the recurrent issues in a disaster is the delivery where resources are needed to mitigate the situation, but main supply routes could be affected and the movement in general could be almost impossible. Even, cargo drones able to carry heavy loads for meaningful distances are becoming available. WFP is to test a Remotely Piloted Aircraft System (RPAS) which could transport almost 2 tonnes of humanitarian aid over significant distances [53].

Scenario Exercise.   A cargo drone simulation use case has been proposed and SINERGY has been applied to develop a proof of concept: using simulation to support decisions on where best to deploy different resources, in this case drones.

Hypothesis.   A hypothesis has been considered for the test. Given a real crisis scenario, AI powered SINERGY simulation has the potential to support decision making on the use of cargo drones and their optimal deployment locations.

Simulation Scenario.   A Northeast Nigeria scenario has been created to simulate a COVID-19 vaccines delivery contingency plan for IDPs camps located in Borno state (see Fig. 5). The initial data for the simulation scenario generation have included:

- hospitals,
- IDPs camps,
- population,
- roads,
- logistic units to distribute food items, water, fuel, etc.

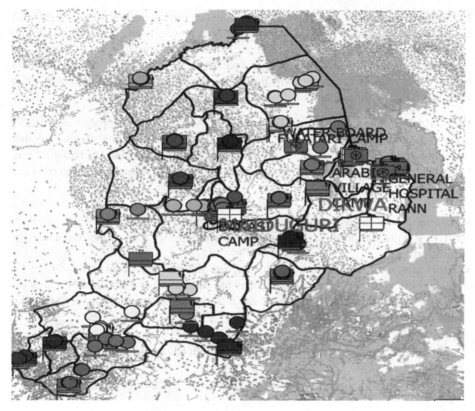

Fig. 5. SYNERGY Borno scenario.

IDPs camps data retrieved from official sources have been supplemented with data of informal camps-like settings that have been discovered after the deployment of the Cogito intelligence analysis tool, thus updating the SYNERGY scenario [4]. In addition, Cogito has been configured to identify critical situations in real time (e.g., insurgence activity, alarms affecting the area, i.e., armed attacks, blocked roads or landslides).

The simulation has been run to analyze the logistics associated with camps: food, water, shelter, plus security issues. Both trucks convoys and drones have been modelled. It has been simulated the deployment of 6 drones at the central hospital (Rann General Hospital) and 6 drones at Gajiram.

Initially, truck transportation has been simulated. Vaccines arrive to Rann General Hospital, a central regional hub from where they are delivered to different remote IDPs camps sites by standard trucks. Several itineraries have been investigated. Multiple simulation instances have been run, each one with its own course of action.

Finally, the use of standard trucks has been compared with that of cargo drones. Drones have been deployed in two locations, at the central hospital hub and at another site, centrally located with respect to most of the delivery sites. In the second use case, trucks have been only used to transport the vaccines from the central hospital to the drones' site.

Boundary Conditions. It is assumed that drones can transport much less weight than trucks (one fourth) so it was necessary to perform several drone trips compared with just one trip required by trucks. Each drone can carry maximum 1 ton of weight and maximum 1 m3 of volume, 1,000 vaccines a payload –1 ton each. The defined speed has been set at 220 km/h. To compare with the trucks, they can drive a maximum of 60 km/h but they can carry a maximum of 12 ton and a maximum of 14.1 m3.

Results' Discussion. Two courses of actions (COA) have been compared: only trucks versus six drones in Ngazai plus six drones at the General Hospital Rann. Vaccines are either distributed all to the hospital or some to the hospital, some to Ngazai. From there they can be delivered to different locations (Kala/Balge, Maiduguri, Monguno and Ngala).

- **Trucks**: trucks can deliver everything with just one trip to each camp site; vaccines arrive soon to the hospital but then it takes a long time to reach the remote camps locations.
- **Drones**: several trips are needed to complete the delivery. It takes some time for vaccines to arrive to Ngazai but once they are there the use of the drones makes the distribution of the 120,000 vaccines quite fast, completing the delivery 1:30 h earlier in a 6:00 h scenario.

The following graph compares the results of both COAs (see Fig. 6):

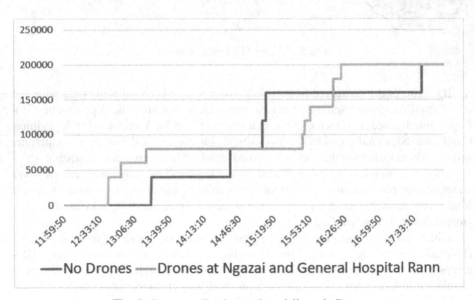

Fig. 6. Drones vs Trucks vaccines delivery in Borno.

Simulation Findings. Performed tests highlight a 25% reduction in delivery time in case of transportation by drones compared with the delivery performed using only trucks.

This is a very specific example. It is important to emphasize that a real scenario, in our case Northeast Nigeria, has been recreated in SINERGY; the simulation can be used to support the decision on the feasibility of the drones' deployment and on the optimal location for their deployment, depending on the final destinations of transportation and the available locations.

A Monte Carlo tool allows to compare several simulations of the same exercise considering, at each iteration, the outcomes due to different probabilities. However, in our case the Monte Carlo did not add much information because there was not so much difference between the different runs. Tested 10 times but got a very similar result each time.

On the other hand, Monte Carlo has the potential to add value when in the exercise scenario comprises terrorist attacks, random breakages, road problems or other negative events, when the probability of delivering everything with just one trip of each truck is almost impossible due to the unstable conditions on the roads. That can be simulated with probabilities of the convoys being destroyed or at least damaged, compared with the small probability of a drone being destroyed. In such instance, the Monte Carlo tool will be able to provide a general picture of the expected outcome when using trucks driving safer but longer routes, drones, and different drones' deployments.

It is possible to use SYNERGY to create scores to compare the different outcomes, considering not simply the time to complete all the deliveries but also to highlight the fact that the destruction of a truck is an event definitely more traumatic than the destruction of a drone as in the first case we have most probably human casualties.

Anticipatory Action and Drones Simulation. SYNERGY has proved the ability to simulate cargo drones, their movement and load capacity. Different prepositioning of drones and resources that may be needed in that scenario can be tested and compared using the MASA Analysis Tool so that the best use and location for the drones can be planned, making the cargo drones ready to be used when the actual shock/event occurs.

In fact, a network of cargo drones set up in the best locations ready to be used when needed in emergency situations can make a huge difference in the times needed to establish action plans and start sending relief aid.

In addition, it has to be highlighted, the potential to reduce the need to allocate military escorts for the protection of medical supplies convoys.

In this research, Cogito has been deployed and used by humanitarian SMEs in the field, for evaluating its capabilities to improve situational awareness. Cogito and SYNERGY interoperability could evolve by implementing an automatic transfer of MIP real time intelligence with key elements and locations (JSON files) rapidly transferred to SYNERGY to modify the exercise scenario [4].

An additional benefit from the application of SYNERGY is the ability to process actual data, if available, imported from external specialised predictive and expert tools including forest fire [51], flooding or gas contamination [4, 52]. Recently, authors have linked SYNERGY with the Spatio-Temporal Epidemic Modeller (STEM) [4, 52] to provide a realistic simulation of the virus spread, while in case of lack of actual data, past data can be used, e.g., the flood can be simulated from a previous event.

3.1 Ethical Considerations

Discussions have identified critical areas related to improving targeted approaches for diverse populations. These include ethnic minorities, under researched and under represented groups. In fact, there is a requirement to support people from deprived backgrounds and also increase, through research, the visibility of these crises across different nations.

The use of AI for humanitarian anticipatory action has demonstrated groundbreaking potential towards early warning, analytics, and faster response to natural disasters. One example of this is evidenced in Mozambique following the cyclone in 2019 when AI-supported disaster mapping was implemented as a successful humanitarian emergency response [55, 56].

However, despite the powerful role that AI plays towards humanitarian response, ethical considerations are critical to guide implementation and processes. in relation to the use of AI including artificial intelligent drones. This is due to the potential risks involved, including algorithmic bias and privacy concerns.

Algorithmic Bias. With regard to algorithmic bias, it is of great concern that AI systems do not adequately reflect differing ethnicities and abilities, which can lead to lack of data representativeness and in turn lack of impartiality [57–59]. This is particularly important for decision making and triage regarding humanitarian aid in identifying the specific needs of individuals.

For example, for persons in need of assistive equipment or those with learning disabilities. Without representative data sets, AI will be faced with shortcomings in meeting these needs, which promotes discrimination and further perpetuate existing inequalities.

Data Privacy and Data Protection. To protect vulnerable populations, the use of AI for humanitarian anticipatory action calls for data governance and data protection. Although there are legislations that guide the use of and sharing of data, there are existing loopholes that can cause potential harm to vulnerable populations.

In emergency situations, both governments and humanitarian organisations may use their 'political power' to access and process personal data without individuals' consent [60, 61]. This also has implications for individuals who may not wish to give consent but are coerced to do so to access humanitarian aid, such as food, clothing and shelter.

In summary, AI plays a significant role in humanitarian anticipatory action. Measures to protect data, enhance data privacy and reduce algorithmic bias are fundamental and the humanitarian community to safeguard vulnerable populations in emergency response, must systematically take them into account. These aspects are just as important as the technical ones, and require careful consideration however, such complex topics would require further research, beyond the scope of this paper.

4   Conclusions

In an increasingly uncertain world, armed conflicts, energy crisis, drought, pandemic, hunger, displacement, never we have seen such complex crises. Climate change impacts factors are likely to exacerbate existing vulnerabilities and reduce people's livelihood options, with negative implications for peace and stabilization efforts.

The humanitarian community is looking for new approaches, cost-efficient project designs and programming. The intent to shift from the traditional reaction to crises to new anticipatory action approaches requires a digital transformation, creative solutions, exploitation of data and predictive analytics.

M&S systems have been used by the military since decades, with lower costs compared to *live* exercises and more realism than tabletop exercises, to train commanders and staff, while humanitarian organizations traditionally rely on games and tabletop exercises for staff training.

Authors have provided the humanitarian community with a proof of concept of an use case of possible AI and M&S application in the context of anticipatory action in a demanding operating environment. An exercise scenario has been generated to simulate cargo drones' pre-deployment and operation in Borno, where both armed insurgence and frequent natural disasters affect population and restrict movement; drone and truck transportation have been compared.

The Expert.ai NLU and ML hybrid Cogito has been applied for updating the initial simulation scenario data and detecting actionable intelligence useful to enhance both situational awareness and to update the simulation scenario. The AI supported simulation MASA SYNERGY has proved very promising to simulate cargo drones pre-positioning, in disaster-prone regions to replace vehicles where terrain conditions or violence restrict road movements.

Seminar workshop and discussions have highlighted the awareness, in the humanitarian community, that deciding and acting prior to the onset of a predictable shock, will improve resource allocation, efficiency and (cost-)effectiveness of responses and operations, compared with the traditional reactive approach.

Tests and demo have captured the relevance and highlighted the consensus that AI and simulation enable humanitarian actors to efficiently prepare emergency management scenarios, rehearse procedures, and validate emergency plans, finally supporting faster decisions, real time monitoring and situational awareness.

Ethical considerations, algorithmic bias, data privacy and protection aspects are as important as the technical ones and require careful consideration to guide implementation and processes, in relation to the use of AI.

In summary, in the context of anticipatory action, SYNERGY can be used to simulate events with the aim of establishing action plans ready to be used in face of the occurrence of such events. MASA Analysis Tool allows the execution of different simulations and the comparison of those simulations using measurements and graphs. In preparedness, SYNERGY contributes to prevent and mitigate risks by improving the quality of crisis cell training within a reality - training – reality cycle, by testing contingency plans and simulating the impact of disaster on people, the environment, and infrastructures; during the response, it minimizes risks and supports decision-making process.

References

1. OCHA Centre for Humanitarian Data Website. https://centre.humdata.org/. Accessed 13 Aug 2022

2. ICRC website: When rain turns to dust: understanding and responding to the combined impact of armed conflicts and the climate and environment crisis on people's lives. https://shop.icrc.org/when-rain-turns-to-dust-pdf-en.html. Accessed 11 Aug 2022
3. Institute for Economics & Peace (IEP): Ecological Threat Report 2021. https://www.visionofhumanity.org/wp-content/uploads/2021/10/ETR-2021-web.pdf. Accessed 13 Aug 2022
4. David, W., et al.: Operationalizing a medical intelligence platform for humanitarian security in protracted crises. In: Mazal, J., et al. (eds.) MESAS 2021. LNCS, vol. 13207, pp. 397–416. Springer, Cham (2022). https://doi.org/10.1007/978-3-030-98260-7_25
5. David, W., King-Okoye, M., Mugambwa, I.: The climate change, conflict and migration nexus in the global security context. In: CMDR COE Proceedings 2021, pp. 107–142. CMDR COE, Sofia (2021)
6. World Food Programme (WFP) website. https://www.wfp.org/publications/global-report-food-crises-2022. Accessed 11 July 2022/07/11
7. ND-GAIN Index Country Rankings. https://gain.nd.edu/our-work/country-index/rankings/. Accessed 13 June 2022
8. UN website, https://operationalsupport.un.org/en/climate-change-recognized-threat-multiplier-un-security-council-debates-its-impact-peacey. Accessed 16 June 2022
9. Abel, G., Brottrager, M., Crespo Cuaresma, J., Muttarak, R.: Climate, conflict and forced migration. Glob. Environ. Chang. **54**, 239–249 (2019)
10. Reliefweb website. https://reliefweb.int/report/ethiopia/horn-africa-drought-regional-humanitarian-overview-call-action-revised-24-august-2022. Accessed 11 July 2022
11. Reliefweb website. https://reliefweb.int/report/somalia/somalia-drought-response-and-famine-prevention-situation-report-no-9-31-july-2022. Accessed 28 Aug 2022
12. Mongabay website. https://news.mongabay.com/2022/03/as-the-horn-of-africa-heats-up-the-risks-of-insecurity-are-rising-commentary/amp/. Accessed 13 Aug 2022
13. Norsk Utenrikspolitisk Institutt (NUPI) website. https://www.nupi.no/en/News/Climate-Peace-and-Security-Fact-Sheet-Somalia. Accessed 13 July 2022
14. BBC website: Somalia conflict: Al-Shabab 'collects more revenue than government'. https://www.bbc.com/news/world-africa-54690561. Accessed 16 July 2022
15. IOM website. https://dtm.iom.int/reports/nigeria-%E2%80%94-displacement-report-37-august-2021. Accessed 11 July 2022
16. IOM website, World Migration Report 2020: Chapter 9 Human Mobility and Adaptation to Environmental Change. https://publications.iom.int/books/world-migration-report-2020-chapter-9. Accessed 11 June 2022
17. Reliefweb website. https://reliefweb.int/report/nigeria/nigeria-humanitarian-needs-overview-2022-february-2022. Accessed 11 June 2022
18. UNHCR website: Climate change and disaster displacement. https://www.unhcr.org/protection/environment/596f25467/unhcr-climate-change-disasters-displacement.html. Accessed 16 June 2022
19. IOM website: Human mobility in the context of environmental and climate change March 2020. https://dtm.iom.int/sites/g/files/tmzbdl1461/files/reports/Human%20Mobility%20in%20the%20context%20of%20Environmental%20and%20Climate%20Change%20DTM-MECC.pdf. Accessed 17 June 2022
20. NATO Standard AJP-3.26 Allied Joint Doctrine for The Military Contribution to Humanitarian Assistance, Edition A, version 1
21. NATO Standard AJP- 3.28 Allied Joint Doctrine for the Military Contribution to Stabilization
22. Reliefweb website. https://reliefweb.int/report/world/global-impact-war-ukraine-billions-people-face-greatest-cost-living-crisis-generation. Accessed 11 June 2022
23. OCHA website: OCHA Global Humanitarian Overview 2022. https://gho.unocha.org/. Accessed 11 July 2022

24. Coloradonewsline website. https://coloradonewsline.com/2022/04/18/ukraine-is-another-black-swan/. Accessed 11 June 2022
25. Taleb, N.N.: The Black Swan, Random House Trade Paperbacks (2010)
26. Investopedia website. https://www.investopedia.com/terms/b/blackswan.asp. Accessed 11 July 2022/07/11
27. OCHA website. https://anticipatory-action-toolkit.unocha.org. Accessed 19 Aug 2022
28. UN website. https://cerf.un.org/sites/default/files/resources/Thesaurus_single%20column_WORKING_DRAFT.pdf. Accessed 19 Aug 2022
29. . Mishra, P.K.: COVID-19, black swan events and the future of disaster risk management in India. Progress Disaster Sci. **8**, 100137 (2020). ISSN 2590-0617. https://doi.org/10.1016/j.pdisas.2020.100137
30. WeRobotics website, https://werobotics.org/flying-labs/, last accessed 2022/08/25
31. Informaconnect website, https://informaconnect.com/can-models-predict-black-swan-events/, last accessed 2022/08/11
32. David, W., King-Okoye, M.: Artificial Intelligence and Robotics Addressing COVID-19 Pandemic's Challenges. In: Mazal, J., Fagiolini, A., Vasik, P., Turi, M. (eds.) MESAS 2020. LNCS, vol. 12619, pp. 279–293. Springer, Cham (2021). https://doi.org/10.1007/978-3-030-70740-8_18
33. Expert System website. https://expertsystem.com/products/medical-intelligence-platform/. Accessed 13 June 2022
34. Anticipation Hub website. https://www.anticipation-hub.org/experience/early-action/early-action-database/ea-list. Accessed 19 Aug 2022
35. OCHA website. https://www.unocha.org/our-work/humanitarian-financing/anticipatory-action. Accessed 19 Aug 2022
36. UN Office of Information and Communications Technology website. https://unite.un.org/blog/data-time-crisis. Accessed 21 Aug 2022
37. International Federation of Red Cross (IFRC) website. https://www.ifrc.org/early-warning-early-action#:~:text=Early%20action%2C%20also%20known%20as,engagement%20with%20at%2Drisk%20communities. Accessed 19 Aug 2022
38. Humanitarian Library website. https://www.humanitarianlibrary.org/sites/default/files/2022/03/Artificial%20Intelligence%20Applied%20to%20Unmanned%20Aerial%20Vehicles%20And%20its%20Impact%20on%20Humanitarian%20Action%20-%20May%202020.pdf. Accessed 19 Aug 2022
39. OCHA website. https://www.unocha.org/sites/unocha/files/Unmanned%20Aerial%20Vehicles%20in%20Humanitarian%20Response%20OCHA%20July%202014.pdf. Accessed 19 Aug 2022
40. Fondation Suisse de Deminage website. https://fsd.ch/en/mine-action/innovation-technology/. Accessed 29 Aug 2022
41. Meier, P.: New information technologies and their impact on the humanitarian sector. Int. Rev. Red Cross **93**(884) (2011)
42. David, W., King-Okoye, M., Capone, A., Sensidoni, G., Piovan, S.E.: Harvesting social media with artificial intelligence for medical threats mapping and analytics. Proc. Int. Cartogr. Assoc. **4**, 24 (2021). https://doi.org/10.5194/ica-proc-4-24-2021
43. Kusumasari, B., Prabowo, N.P.A.: Scraping social media data for disaster communication: how the pattern of Twitter users affects disasters in Asia and the Pacific. Nat. Hazards **103**(3), 3415–3435 (2020). https://doi.org/10.1007/s11069-020-04136-z
44. Huang, X., Li, Z., Jiang, Y., Li, X., Porter, D.: Twitter reveals human mobility dynamics during the COVID-19 pandemic. PloS one **15**(11) (2020)
45. Seddighi, H., Salmani, I., Seddighi, S.: Saving lives and changing minds with Twitter in disasters and pandemics: a Literature Review. J. Media **1**, 59–77 (2020)

46. Liang, H., Zhu, J.J.H.: Big data, collection of (social media, harvesting). In: The International Encyclopedia of Communication Research Methods. Wiley, Hoboken (2017)

47. Zhang, D., Yin, C., Zeng, J., et al.: Combining structured and unstructured data for predictive models: a deep learning approach. BMC Med. Inform. Decis. Mak. **20**, 280 (2020)

48. Brownstein, J.S., Freifeld, C.C., Madoff, L.C.: Digital disease detection - harnessing the web for public health surveillance. N. Engl. J. Med. **360**(21), 2153–2157 (2009). https://doi.org/10.1056/nejmp0900702

49. The Data Steps website. https://www.thedatasteps.com/post/data-science-in-healthcare. Accessed 13 June 2022

50. David, W., King-Okoye, M., Mugambwa, I., Garmendia Doval, B.: An artificial intelligence and simulation approach to climate-conflict-migration driven security issues. In: Dobrinkova, N., Nikolov, O. (eds.) Environmental Protection and Disaster Risks. EnviroRISKs 2022. Lecture Notes in Networks and Systems, vol. 638. Springer, Cham (2023). https://doi.org/10.1007/978-3-031-26754-3_13

51. David, W., Giannino, F., Heathfield, D., Hubervic, A., Aknai, A., Sfetsos, A.: Giving life to the map can save more lives. Wildfire scenario with interoperable simulations. Adv. Cartogr. GIScience Int. Cartogr. Assoc. **1**, 4 (2019). https://doi.org/10.5194/ica-adv-1-4-2019

52. David, W., Baldassi, F., Piovan, S.E., Hubervic, A., Le Corre, E.: Combining epidemiological and constructive simulations for robotics and autonomous systems supporting logistic supply in infectious diseases affected areas. In: Mazal, J., Fagiolini, A., Vasik, P., Turi, M. (eds.) MESAS 2020. LNCS, vol. 12619, pp. 86–107. Springer, Cham (2021). https://doi.org/10.1007/978-3-030-70740-8_6

53. World Food Programme (WFP) website. https://drones.wfp.org/updates/using-drones-deliver-critical-humanitarian-aid. Accessed 23 Aug 2022

54. WeRobotics blog. https://blog.werobotics.org/2021/01/12/teaming-up-with-pfizer-on-new-cargo-drone-project/. Accessed 14 Aug 2022

55. Reliefweb website. https://reliefweb.int/report/mozambique/2018-2019-mozambique-humanitarian-response-plan-revised-following-cyclones-idai. Accessed 19 Aug 2022

56. Reliefweb website. https://reliefweb.int/report/mozambique/joining-dots-how-ai-and-drones-are-transforming-emergencies. Accessed 19 Aug 2022

57. Sharkey, N.: The Impact of Gender and Race Bias in AI, Humanitarian Law and Policy Blog, 28 August 2018. https://blogs.icrc.org/law-and-policy/2018/08/28/impact-gender-race-bia. Accessed 19 Aug 2022

58. UN Secretary-General's High-Level Panel on Digital Cooperation, The Age of Digital Interdependence, New York (2019). www.un.org/en/pdfs/DigitalCooperation-report-for%20web.pdf. Accessed 19 Aug 2022

59. UN General Assembly, Report of the Special Rapporteur Tendayi Achiume on Contemporary Forms of Racism, Racial Discrimination, Xenophobia and Related Intolerance, UN Doc A/75/590, 10 November 2020

60. Madianou, M.: Technocolonialism: digital innovation and data practices in the humanitarian response to refugee crises. Soc. Media Soc. **5**(3), 1–13 (2019). ISSN: 2056-3051

61. Couldry, N., Mejias, U.A.: Data colonialism: rethinking big data's relation to the contemporary subject. Telev. New Media **20**(4), 336–349 (2019). https://doi.org/10.1177/1527476419879.6632

Towards a Digital Twin Architecture with Formal Analysis Capabilities for Learning-Enabled Autonomous Systems

Anastasios Temperekidis[1], Nikolaos Kekatos[1], Panagiotis Katsaros[1(✉)], Weicheng He[2], Saddek Bensalem[2], Hisham AbdElSabour[3], Mohamed AbdElSalam[3], and Ashraf Salem[3]

[1] Aristotle University of Thessaloniki, Thessaloniki, Greece
{anastemp,nkekatos,katsaros}@csd.auth.gr
[2] VERIMAG, Université Grenoble Alpes, Grenoble, France
{weicheng.he,saddek.bensalem}@univ-grenoble-alpes.fr
[3] Siemens EDA, Cairo, Egypt
{hisham_abdelsabour,mohamed_abdelsalam,ashraf_salem}@mentor.com

Abstract. Digital twins are increasingly used to test and verify complex cyber-physical systems. The main reason is their flexibility in combining multiple behavior domains to faithfully model all effects of the computing elements, their physical counterparts, and the system interactions in various environments and diverse execution scenarios. However, for autonomous systems with learning-enabled components (LECs), there are still open challenges to be addressed. In these cases, we are particularly interested in analyzing the system's safety, security, and performance in complex and unpredictable environments. In addition to having continuously evolving requirements, we also need to allow for LEC updates and support the continuous testing/verification of the system under design. To this end, we propose a compositional architecture for digital twins that allows mixing model-based and LEC components through extending the executable formal modeling language BIP. The architecture is based on an interconnect fabric enabling heterogeneous client connections and co-simulation of the integrated models/simulators. Two alternatives are introduced to integrate extended BIP models with other simulation components that may represent the physical dynamics of the system, its environment, and sensors. Our co-simulation approach is equipped with formal analysis capabilities of the requirements by runtime verification of the system under design. We present results from a self-driving use case that has been tested in a set of scenarios with varying weather conditions.

Keywords: digital twins · formal analysis · runtime verification · autonomous systems · learning-enabled systems · co-simulation

This work has received funding from the European Union's Horizon 2020 research and innovation programme under grant agreement No 956123 (FOCETA).

1   Introduction

Simulation-based verification of complex cyber-physical systems relies on the integration of heterogeneous components like sensing, control, actuation, the system's physical dynamics, and all interactions with its environment. We are interested in mixing model components at various levels of abstraction that are usually designed with different tools and frameworks, as well as to allow the integration of discrete modeling for computing elements with continuous modeling for physical components.

For autonomous systems, we face the additional challenge of integration of advanced decision-making functions that depend on learning-enabled, i.e. data-driven components (LECs). In these cases, the system's design usually evolves, as an ever-increasing set of scenarios must be considered. We foresee the need for LEC updates and continuous testing of the system, in response to emerging requirements from new scenarios, imperfect knowledge of the machine learning models (noise in data observations) or contextual misbehavior of the LECs, due to e.g., modifications in their operational design domain. It is necessary to cover as many critical scenarios as possible, whereas some scenarios may be very costly or even impossible to realize, when the system operates in its environment. Therefore, simulation-based testing/verification - possibly with interfaced physical components - may be the only existing means towards this goal. Unlike real-world conditions, simulated conditions can be fully quantified and controlled.

Multi-modeling and compositional simulation (or co-simulation) in a *digital twin* (DT) is a promising perspective [13]. DTs [17] are virtual models used to analyze and diagnose a system's operation in real-time. For autonomous systems testing/verification, it is necessary to *integrate model-based and data-driven components* to analyze the system's safety, security, and performance, in complex and unpredictable environments. This priority is a fundamental prerequisite towards deploying autonomous systems with LECs in safety-critical applications, e.g. in transportation, healthcare, etc. To the best of our knowledge, the problem has not been addressed so far in related works.

Our Approach. In this work, we propose a compositional simulation architecture for building digital twins for learning-enabled autonomous systems. The architecture is based on an interconnect fabric (PAVE360-VSI [31]) that enables heterogeneous client connections and it is responsible for the synchronization of the simulation/physical components in discrete time, as well as for their network communication and the transfer of data among them. This enables the integration of multiple behavior domains (physics, discrete dynamics, environment sensing, etc.) and models of diverse scales, while offering increased control over the system's environment. Our contributions allow for integrating executable models (in the BIP language [3]) with formal semantics, which can be used for modeling the LECs of the system under design. Formal analysis takes place through runtime verification. The range of verification targets that are supported spans the whole system development cycle through Model-in-the-Loop (MiL), Software-in-the-Loop (SiL), or even Hardware-in-the-Loop (HiL) verification [8].

Contributions. The concrete contributions of this work are:

- an extendable compositional simulation architecture that is centered around the PAVE360-VSI ecosystem and it can be used to build DTs,
- the extension of the BIP language that allows mixing model-based and data-driven components (LECs),
- the integration of formal analysis capabilities within the compositional simulation architecture via the extended BIP (two alternatives provided) and runtime verification tools,
- a case study that showcases the robustness analysis of perception LECs in diverse self-driving scenarios.

Related Work. DT technologies [18] have gained attention from academia and industry, and have been used in many application areas [22,28]. However, DTs entail several challenges as they must be indistinguishable from their physical counterparts [29]. These challenges can be application-specific and specifically, for autonomous cyber-physical systems, they are: 1) The theoretical framework, e.g. formal definition, and practical implementations of DTs can be improved [30]. 2) DT operations should be fully autonomous with no human intervention, whereas real-time monitoring is also needed [22]. 3) Interoperability with existing software and LECs integration has to be improved [29].

There is only limited work on the integration of formal analysis techniques with a DT. The potential of runtime verification in DTs is discussed in [10], whereas in [11] runtime verification has been used for anomaly detection. Another solution proposed for runtime verification is the Digital Shadows [5]. In [12], Kalman filters were used to monitor an incubator DT. In this work, we focus on properties in first-order LTL (Linear Temporal Logic) [4], whereas there are related works on runtime verification of Signal Temporal Logic properties [37,38].

Co-simulation plays a key role in the design and analysis of DTs. It can be integrated or distributed, with or without support of a standardized interface [24]. Distributed co-simulation, mainly focuses on the communication level, and is supported by the High-Level Architecture standard and the Distributed Co-simulation Protocol [23]. Integrated co-simulation focuses on the system-level operation; it can follow the FMI standard [35].

Several co-simulation frameworks have been proposed in the literature, see [24] and references therein. However, they are mainly centered around an FMI master algorithm and FMI-compatible models. Vico [19] is an architecture that supports the integration of both FMI and non-FMI components. Unlike these frameworks, our architecture leverages formal methods and supports LECs and HiL. A DT architecture that relies on co-simulation and the *Open Simulation Platform* toolchain is proposed in [20]. This work can assist in designing digital twin ships. However, there is no provision for formal analysis and it is unclear how LECs can be handled. Runtime verification approaches for FMI-based co-simulation have been recently proposed in [34].

Outline. The rest of the paper is structured as follows. In Sect. 2, we refer to vital technologies for the architecture proposed for the development of DTs, including languages and standards that enable the smooth integration and the formal analysis of autonomous systems with LECs. Section 3 focuses on the compositional simulation architecture and the integration of its constituent simulators. Section 4 describes the integration steps needed to extend BIP to support co-simulation and LECs. Section 5 presents the results of the self-driving use case, for a set of scenarios with varying weather conditions that affect the system's perception. The paper concludes with a summary of our contributions and future research prospects.

2   Background

2.1   Languages and Standards

The compositional simulation architecture for DTs is based on two well-established industrial standards, for model interoperability, namely the Functional Mock-up Interface and the Transaction Level Modeling. Moreover, it features formal analysis capabilities, for system requirements expressed in a first-order temporal logic language.

Functional Mock-up Interface (FMI). The FMI standard defines an Application Programming Interface (API) and the model components, known as Functional Mock-up Units (FMUs) that respect this API. Each FMU can be seen as a black box that implements the methods defined in the FMI API. Some methods are optional, whereas others are compulsory and must be implemented by all FMUs. The FMUs are passive objects, i.e. they do not execute, therefore, they are also called *slaves*. To execute a set of coupled FMUs, we need a master algorithm (FMI Master), whose role is to coordinate their execution. According to the latest release (FMI 3.0), the FMI defines three interface types:

- Co-simulation (CS), where the FMU typically contains its own solver or scheduler.
- Model Exchange (ME), which requires the importer to perform numerical integration, and
- Scheduled Execution (SE), where the importer triggers the execution of the model partitions.

FMI for co-simulation allows to import and co-simulate, within a single framework, model components which have been designed with different modeling formalisms, languages, and tools. This functionality plays a vital role in the design of modern cyber-physical systems, which often involves several design teams coming from different disciplines and using diverse modeling environments [35].

Transaction Level Modeling (TLM). The TLM 2.0 standard is already supported by two IEEE standards, which are commonly used in industrial simulation models, namely the IEEE 1800 SystemVerilog standard and the IEEE 1666 SystemC standard. In a TLM model, the details of communication among computing components are separated from the details of computation. Communication is modeled by channels and all unnecessary details of communication and computation are hidden. This speeds up simulation and allows validating design alternatives at the higher level of abstraction [7]. Transaction requests take place by calling interface functions of the channel models.

The TLM transaction API is based on the notion of a *"generic payload"* transaction. Such a generic payload transaction can be applied over virtually any type of application domain. Thus, TLM is a suitable framework for carrying any sort of transaction information across some backplane based "interconnect fabric", in both digital and analog simulation domains, as well as across many types of digital communication protocols, such as CAN, Ethernet, AXI, PCIe.

Past-Time First-Order Linear Temporal Logic (LTL). Any specification in first-order LTL [4] is defined over a set of tuples $p(a_1, \ldots, a_n)$, where p is a *predicate* or a *relation* over domains $\mathcal{D}_1, \ldots, \mathcal{D}_n$ and for $1 \leq i \leq n$, $a_i \in \mathcal{D}_i$ is a value from some domain $\mathcal{D}_i$, which can be, e.g., the integers, the reals or strings. It is also possible to refer to (state-dependent) Boolean variables, which are perceived as a degenerate predicate with 0 parameters. The syntax of the past-time fragment of first-order LTL is defined as follows, where a is a constant representing a value in some domain $\mathcal{D}$, and x denotes a variable over the same domain $domain(x)$.

$$\varphi ::= true \mid false \mid p(x_1, \ldots, x_n) \mid (\varphi \vee \psi) \mid (\varphi \wedge \psi) \mid$$
$$\neg\varphi \mid (\varphi \, S \, \psi) \mid \ominus \varphi \mid \exists x \, \varphi \mid \forall x \, \varphi \mid e \sim e$$

where $\sim \in \{<, \leq, >, \geq, =, \neq\}$ and

$$e ::= x \mid a \mid e + e \mid e - e \mid e \times e \mid e \, / \, e.$$

The *Since* operator, for e.g. $\varphi \, S \, \psi$ means that "ψ was true in the past, and since then, including that point in time, p has been true". Operator $\ominus \varphi$ specifies that "in the previous state p was true". The following relationships also hold: $false = \neg true$, $\forall x \, \varphi = \neg \exists x \, \neg\varphi$, and $\varphi \vee \psi = \neg(\neg\varphi \wedge \neg\psi)$. Some additional operators that are useful in property specifications are: $P\varphi = true \, S \, \varphi$ (for "previously"), $\varphi \, R \, \psi = \neg(\neg\varphi \, S \, \neg\psi)$ (the dual of the Since operator), and $H\varphi = (false \, R \, \varphi)$ (for "always in the past").

2.2   Tools

Any standards-based simulator may be integrated into our DT architecture, but the formal analysis capabilities that are currently provided are based on the BIP tools for building executable component-based models and the DejaVu tool for the synthesis of runtime monitors. We also refer to the Simcenter Prescan simulator, which has been used in the case study.

Behavior, Interaction, Priority (BIP). BIP is a component modeling framework for rigorous system design [3]. The BIP language [27] enables building complex systems by coordinating the behavior of a set of atomic components.

BIP *atomic components* are transition systems extended with a set of *ports* and *variables*. An atomic component C is defined as a tuple (Q, X, P, T), where Q is a set of *control locations*, X is a set of variables, P is a set of communication ports, and T is a set of *transitions*. Each transition τ is of the form (q, p, g, f, q') where $q, q' \in Q$ are control locations, $p \in P$ is a port, g is a *guard* and f is the *update function* of τ. g is a predicate defined over variables in X and f is a function (BIP can invoke functions written in C/C++) that computes new values for X, based on their current values. By using the composition of multiple atomic components, we can build *composite components*. Interactions between components are specified by *connectors*, which define sets of interactions.

During the execution of a BIP interaction, all components that participate in the interaction, i.e., have an associated port that is part of the interaction, must execute their corresponding transitions simultaneously. All components that do not participate in the interaction, do not execute any transition and thus remain in the same control location.

Runtime Verification (DejaVu). DejaVu is a runtime verification tool[1], designed in Scala, which can synthesize runtime monitors for past-time first-order LTL specifications [4]. Starting with a user-defined formula/property, the tool parses the formula and generates an abstract syntax tree, which is then traversed and translated into a monitor program. A trace is fed into the monitor that returns a verdict.

Simcenter Prescan. Prescan [33] provides a physics-based simulation platform to prototype, test, and validate advanced driver assistance systems.

3   Compositional Architecture for Digital Twins of Autonomous Systems

Autonomous systems integrate computations with physical processes. Due to continuously evolving requirements and the need for LEC updates, it is essential to support the continuous testing/verification of the system at design time. Moreover, when the systems are based on SoC (System-on-Chip) and AI accelerators, pre-silicon verification is necessary to ensure that there are no bugs or risk of failure. These matters along with critical safety demands [14] raise the importance of verification. DTs provide a valuable means for pre-silicon verification [1,17] and continuous testing/verification.

PAVE360-VSI [31] is a network interconnect with hardware emulation capabilities that has been used for the verification of hardware and software associated with the control of autonomous systems. It provides cyber-physical ports

---

[1] https://github.com/havelund/dejavu.

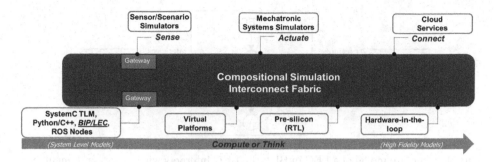

Fig. 1. Compositional Simulation Architecture for Digital Twins of Learning-enabled Autonomous Systems

that enable heterogeneous client connections. Additionally, PAVE360-VSI offers protocol-agnostic, as well as protocol-aware connections between mixed-fidelity models and allows sharing them for MiL, SiL and HiL verification.

In essence, PAVE360-VSI acts as the core of our compositional architecture, in which simulation progresses in discrete time steps. The overall simulation architecture is visualized in Fig. 1. The interconnect fabric enables interoperability between the various components of a DT, synchronizes the network communication and enables the data transfer via various protocols. A client connection is feasible, if it complies with the electronic design automation standards supported: TLM 2.0 [15], FMI 2.0 [26], and Inter Process communication. Such clients include, sensor/scenario simulators [32], mechatronic system simulators [33], cloud services and models at different abstraction levels, including C/C++, Python, virtual platforms and hardware emulation.

The presumption is that each of these external simulators and foreign models supports a third-party API. This application-specific API then can be coupled with a TLM fabric portal interface [2] - called Gateway - which gives access to the interconnect fabric backplane for transactional communication purposes, as well as for mutual time advancement coordination. Each third-party simulator or foreign model is assumed to be a client process that hangs on the common backplane interconnect. The backplane is the keeper of time and is responsible for all time advance operations that are coordinated across the client processes, thus maintaining full determinism.

4   Integration of BIP Formal Models with LECs and Runtime Verification

4.1   BIP Extension for LECs

BIP has been extended to model systems with LECs. A LEC is represented as an atomic component, which can make machine learning inference. Similar to the classic atomic components in BIP, LECs are also described as labeled transition systems extended with variables that store "local" data. A *learning function*,

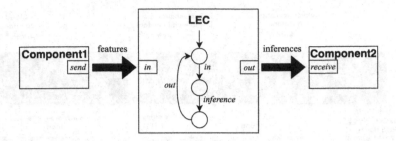

Fig. 2. Template model of a LEC in BIP; the LEC interacts with other components via ports and connectors. Two ports are needed; for receiving inputs and sending outputs. An *inference* transition performs the ML inference via external C++ functions.

called ML, is associated with a transition designed for making *inference*. The learning function is actually a trained neural network model, which can make inferences based on inputs.

We need to guarantee that LEC components can perform at least three actions: (i) get the inputs from the environment, (ii) pass the inputs to the ML function, and (iii) send the outputs to another component. Figure 2 shows a template model of a LEC. Three specific transitions exist in every LEC. The first transition named *in* gets the features, i.e., the inputs from other components. The second transition, named *inference*, passes the features into the ML function, which returns the inference results. Function ML is a wrapper function written in C++ that generates the commands with inputs to execute ML programs written in Python or C++. Finally, the third transition named *out* sends the inference results to other components.

4.2   Integration of BIP Models

The architecture for building DTs can be seen as an interconnect framework with gateways that are customized, for external simulations and models interoperability. BIP formal models can be integrated using either a BIP gateway or an FMI Master gateway. The BIP gateway option can be faster, since it can handle high bandwidth traffic efficiently. The FMI-based approach is suitable when the aim is to reuse the BIP FMUs with custom FMI master algorithms and toolchains. FMI version 2 supports simple data types, which implies difficulties, when more complex data have to be communicated. This limitation is addressed in FMI version 3, but most tools currently do not support this standard.

BIP Gateway. The role of the gateway that we have developed is to enable the BIP model connection with the interconnect fabric server, from one side, and to convert the BIP model data to SystemC TLM generic payloads. The gateway code is integrated with the BIP model and takes the form of generated C++ code upon calling the BIP compiler [36]. Most of the gateway implementation is generic and reusable for different BIP models and simulated systems. Figure 3 shows an example gateway that receives RGB camera feed, for a BIP model that executes control actions via brake and throttle adjustments.

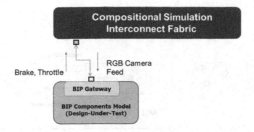

Fig. 3. BIP Model Integration via a Gateway

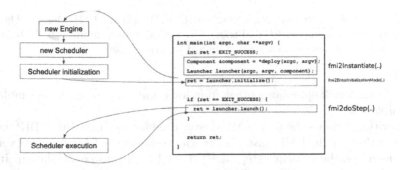

Fig. 4. Abstract representation of the mapping of BIP model and engine to FMI functions; the boxes on the left correspond to basic BIP engine operations, the code snippet in the middle is the *main* function of the C++ generated code of a BIP model.

FMI Master Gateway. The BIP model is encapsulated into an FMU for co-simulation, which is called/triggered via an FMI Master Gateway. To this end, an FMU generator for BIP models has been developed and the BIP execution engine has been modified such that the BIP function calls are mapped to functions from the FMI standard (Fig. 4). The modified BIP engine essentially runs only one execution step (BIP components interaction) at a time, when the `fmi2doStep` function is called (Fig. 5).

Generation of an FMU for a BIP model takes place as follows (the process has been automated). First, the C++ code for the BIP model is generated using the BIP compiler. The generated code is then compiled with the modified BIP engine and results in a dynamic library (shared object). An XML file is also generated, from the BIP model, which specifies its structure and the variables used. All these files are packaged into an `.fmu` file as specified in the FMI standard.

Co-simulation and data exchange of the BIP FMU with the rest of the DT architecture take place using an FMI Master gateway. The gateway converts FMU data into SystemC TLM generic payloads, which are transported through the compositional interconnection fabric. The FMI Master takes the FMU as input, reads its XML file and loads the dynamic library. The FMI functions to create the FMU instance are then called and the model variables are initialized. Once everything is setup and initialized, the master algorithm executes itera-

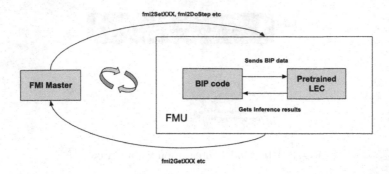

Fig. 5. Scheme for co-simulating a single BIP FMU via an FMI Master. The BIP FMU internally contains a LEC and triggers it with different inputs. The FMI Master orchestrates the sequence of calls via standard functions like fmi2Set.

tively the `fmi2doStep`, among other functions, until all steps of the simulation are completed.

Algorithm 1 shows the basic FMI Master used for co-simulating a BIP model. The algorithm for the FMI Master is generic, respects the FMI standard version 2 and describes the principle steps needed for FMI-based co-simulation. It can be modified and extended. Our FMI Master follows the steps proposed in [6,9] to guarantee determinacy and termination.

The algorithm is divided into three main parts: 1) instantiation and initialization of FMUs, where the FMU instances, variables, simulation parameters are created and set, 2) data propagation and step-wise simulation of FMUs, where the inputs-outputs connections are specified and the FMUs are co-simulated in the right order, and 3) termination, where the analysis is completed and the memory is released. The calls in black are from the standard and have been implemented (via our newly designed BIP FMU generator[2]) to match the BIP features. The functions in color are non-standard calls. The calls in green (lines 8–10, 14) are mapped to the BIP model structure and its execution control. Function `set_inverted_maps` is parsing, extracting and mapping the BIP variables to the variables described in `ModelDescription.xml`. There are also checks that the BIP model's state machine has not reached a terminal state or a deadlock. The calls in blue (lines 4, 16) are specific to PAVE360: i) an `fmiTransport` API is used that setups the interconnect according to TLM (session, channel) and imports the FMUs, and ii) the user can choose how to connect the FMUs and specify the inputs. Note that the variables u, v, y that appear in the algorithm correspond to inputs, exposed variables, and outputs respectively (notation used in the standard).

---

[2] The generator is written in C++ as an open source tool accessible at: https://depend.csd.auth.gr:8443/anastast/bip_fmu.

Algorithm 1: FMI master algorithm for co-simulating BIP with integrated runtime verification

---

```
    /* Cosimulation parameters */
 1  tCurrent: current simulation time; tStart: start time; tStop: stop time
 2  h: simulation step; nSteps: number of steps; nStepsMax: max. nSteps
    /* Instantiate and initialize FMUs */
 3  foreach FMU c ∈ C do
 4  │   fmiTransportFMU();                                    /* PAVE360-VSI */
 5  │   fmi2Instantiate();
 6  │   fmi2SetupExperiment(tStart, tStop);
 7  │   fmi2EnterInitializationMode();
 8  │   foreach variable in c.variables() do
 9  │   │   set_inverted_map(c, variable.id, variable.name);
10  │   end
11  │   fmi2ExitInitializationMode();
12  end
    /* Instantiate and Initialize Monitor */
13  DejaVuSetup();
    /* Step-wise simulation */
14  while tCurrent<tStop & !deadlock & nStep ≤ nStepMax do
15  │   foreach connection between an input u and an output y do
16  │   │   callInputSignals()                               /* PAVE360-VSI */
17  │   │   fmi2SetXXX(u,v)            /* Real, Integer, Boolean, String */
18  │   │   fmi2doStep(h);
19  │   │   fmi2GetXXX(y);
20  │   end
21  │   DejaVuVerification();
22  │   tCurrent=tCurrent+h; nStep=nStep+1;
23  end
    /* Termination */
24  foreach FMU c ∈ C do
25  │   fmi2Terminate();
26  end
```

4.3   Runtime Verification

There are several ways to integrate a runtime verification tool into our co-simulation architecture. It can be done online or offline, with or without FMI, via a gateway or at the interconnect level. In this article, we have used the DejaVu tool and Algorithm 1 shows abstractly the calls for coupling the runtime verification in pink (lines 13 & 21). DejaVu runtime monitors are first initialized in the FMI master and are then called iteratively after the fmi2doStep call.

5   Application Examples

In this section, we develop and present a software-in-the-loop autonomous driving case study. Our goal is to demonstrate how the proposed DT architecture

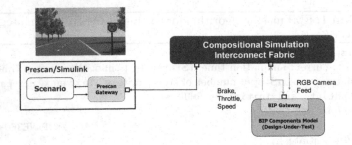

Fig. 6. Application Example: Software-in-the-Loop containing a Prescan model and a BIP model. The interaction and synchronization are performed via PAVE360-VSI.

can integrate a LEC, formally modeled in BIP, into a system model and perform co-simulation and formal analysis. Prescan and BIP tools are used to model different parts of the system, and they need to interoperate using PAVE360-VSI. BIP models the perception and control modules, whereas Prescan models the environment and the vehicle model. The vehicle has an RGB camera sensor. The camera feed is sent to the BIP model for classification of speed signs, and the controller component takes the action of acceleration/deceleration of the vehicle based on the speed sign detected. We opt for connecting the BIP model to the interconnect fabric via a gateway. The structure and the connections of the case study are shown in Fig. 6.

5.1   Simcenter Prescan Experiment

Prescan was used to specify the driving scenario. We assume that there is a single vehicle which moves along a straight way and it has a camera that captures the environment. A standard vehicle model was chosen, for which the default dynamics was generated by Prescan and imported into Simulink [25]. The Prescan gateway is a *S-function*. A video frame from an RGB camera sensor mounted on the ego vehicle is sent by Prescan, as the vehicle moves on.

5.2   BIP Model and Gateway

The BIP tools consist of a compiler for generating code from BIP sources, and an execution engine used as a scheduler for executing the generated code. The BIP model in Fig. 7 contains two components, i.e., the perception and a simple controller. The perception module performs object detection and classification on the image received via external C++ functions. The controller updates the throttle/brake values and sends these values back to Prescan. Figure 8 demonstrates the synchronization and communication between the BIP model and the Prescan experiment through their gateways and our compositional simulation interconnect, to which all clients are connected to.

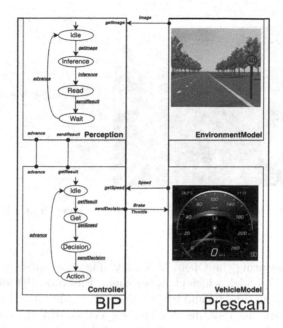

Fig. 7. SiL example – BIP Model w/ LECs and control); BIP Model: performs object detection and classification on the image received, updates and send throttle/brake values to Prescan. Prescan Model: updates vehicle speed according to throttle/brake values received and sends new video frame captured from the RGB camera sensor.

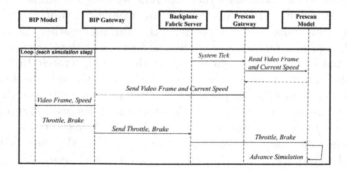

Fig. 8. SiL example – Synchronization & Communication between PAVE360 & clients.

5.3   Implementation and Execution

The video frames from the Prescan RGB camera sensor are captured and sent to the BIP model as SystemC TLM generic payloads; in each time step, an image from the video frame is passed to a sign detection YOLO model [16] trained using the GTSDB [21] and Tsinghua-Tencent 100K datasets [39]. The video frames are sent as 1D payload consisting of all 4 RGBA arrays, but flattened, with this 1D array being split into 4 RGBA channels. Inside BIP, images are constructed

Fig. 9. A simulation snapshot of the SiL example; 3D image from Prescan and execution log from BIP.

from video frames using the OpenCV library. They are subsequently passed to the trained YOLO model, which classifies them. Based on the identified "traffic sign speed limit" the throttle and brake values are updated and are then sent to the Prescan scenario for updating the vehicle speed according to the new throttle and brake values. Figure 9 shows a snapshot of the entire system simulation.

5.4   Scenario Generation and Testing

Our tests focused on the impact that different weather conditions can have on traffic sign detection and the overall system behavior. Evaluating all possible scenarios in a brute-force way is not realistic. Various weather conditions may be selected, e.g., fog, rain, or snow, whereas there are other types of perturbation/noise that can blur the traffic signs, e.g. dust, mud, scratch. In addition, all these so-called imperfections can have different coverage, and intensity/opacity.

The tests took place by implementing different scenarios through changing the types of imperfection in Prescan. A set of examples was executed and the findings in all these cases are reported in Table 1. As expected, the accuracy decreases when increasing the coverage of imperfection. Also, our YOLO model appears to be i) robust against low-coverage scratch and snow, and ii) sensitive against high-coverage mud and snow. Figure 10 shows how the classification of a specific traffic sign is affected via imperfections of varying coverage. Finally, Fig. 11 shows an incorrect prediction made displayed via a bounding box.

5.5   Runtime Verification

The following properties have been evaluated via runtime verification:

P_1: "The vehicle should always identify the traffic sign value correctly and the vehicle's speed should be always smaller or equal to the current speed limit."

P_2: "If the vehicle detects a new speed limit, the speed should not exceed this speed limit by more than ϵ for T_1 time units after detection, where ϵ is a given percentage.".

Table 1. Testing different driving scenarios/Prescan traffic signs at runtime; four types of imperfection on traffic signs from 30 to 130 km/h; *low* and *high* refer to coverage and opacity levels; # Runs are the total number of simulations with the specific traffic sign; # Misclass: the number of traffic sign misclassifications.

	Dust		Mud		Scratch		Snow	
	low	high	low	high	low	high	low	high
# Runs	8	6	8	8	8	6	8	5
# Misclass.	4	4	4	7	2	3	2	5

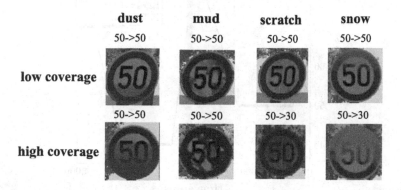

Fig. 10. Evaluating the impact of noise on a specific traffic sign. Experiments with different imperfections indicate the misclassifications.

Fig. 11. Visualization of a misclassification result

The properties are expressed in past-time first-order LTL as

$$P_1 : \forall t, \ v_{sign}(t) = v_{rec}(t) \wedge v_{sim}(t) \leq v_{rec}(t)$$
$$P_2 : \forall t, \ \neg(v_{sim}(t) \leq v_{rec}(t) + \epsilon \cdot v_{rec}(t)) \rightarrow \neg\exists t', \ t' \leq t$$
$$\wedge \ \mathbf{H}_{\leq T_1} v_{rec}(t'-1) \neq v_{rec}(t')$$

Table 2. Runtime Verification Results with DejaVU

Property	Param.	Param.	Synth. [s]	#Events	#Violat.	Anal. [s]
Rule 1	-	-	0.401 s	4001	**1063**	0.415 s
Rule 2	$\epsilon = 15\%$	$T = 20$	1.104 s	4001	**42**	0.317 s
Rule 2	$\epsilon = 30\%$	$T = 20$	1.149 s	4001	**21**	0.301 s

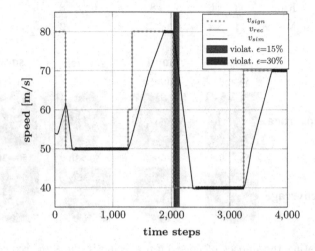

Fig. 12. A trace of the SiL example co-simulated for an horizon of 4001 time units. The violating events of property/traffic rule 2 are shown in red. (Color figure online)

with v_{sign} denoting the actual speed limit, v_{rec} the recognized/detected speed limit and v_{sim} the (simulated) vehicle's speed.

For a set of six traffic signs, we co-simulated the entire system and performed runtime verification by a monitor synthesized by DejaVu. The results are shown in Table 2. The first property is violated 1063 times, although all traffic signs have been correctly identified. The violations occur 1) when there is a new traffic sign that changes the speed limit from a higher to a lower value, and 2) due to oscillations of the vehicle speed, when reaching a new speed limit.

The second property aims to ameliorate this transition error by providing the vehicle extra time to stabilize its speed. Figure 12 shows the simulation trace over the entire time horizon. The violations occur at the time points after a speed limit change from a higher to a lower speed and we observe how tighter bounds increase the number of violations.

6   Conclusion and Outlook

Simulation environments and digital twins play a vital role in the continuous development and operations cycle of autonomous systems with learning-enabled components. We presented an architecture that allows integrating components for both Model-in-The-Loop (MiL) and Software-in-The-Loop (SiL) verification and validation activities.

Typically, in the industry, most projects start from MiL, move into SiL and end up with HiL using some of the mature commercial tools for modeling multi-domain systems and for physics-based simulation. All these heterogeneous components can be easily integrated into our compositional simulation architecture, which is based on an optimized interconnect framework for mixed fidelity modeling, compliant with well-established electronic design automation standards. In this paper, we showed how it is possible to integrate BIP models, i.e., model components with formal semantics that can utilize learning-enabled components, as well as runtime verification.

As a future work plan, we intend to address the need for evaluating the impact of adversarial attacks and defenses for learning components, allow the connection with Robot Operating System (ROS) subsystems using a dedicated gateway and apply our approach to more sophisticated Prescan experiments.

References

1. AbdElSalam, M., Khalil, K., Stickley, J., Salem, A., Loye, B.: Verification of advanced driver assistance systems and autonomous vehicles with hardware emulation-in-the-loop a case study with multiple ECUs. IJAE **10**(2), 197–204 (2019)
2. Erickson, A., Stickley, J.: UVM-Connect primer. https://verificationacademy.com/courses/uvm-connect
3. Basu, A., Bensalem, S., Bozga, M., Bourgos, P., Sifakis, J.: Rigorous system design: the BIP approach. In: Kotásek, Z., Bouda, J., Černá, I., Sekanina, L., Vojnar, T., Antoš, D. (eds.) MEMICS 2011. LNCS, vol. 7119, pp. 1–19. Springer, Heidelberg (2012). https://doi.org/10.1007/978-3-642-25929-6_1
4. Bensalem, S., et al.: Formal specification for learning-enabled autonomous systems. In: Isac, O., Ivanov, R., Katz, G., Narodytska, N., Nenzi, L. (eds.) Software Verification and Formal Methods for ML-Enabled Autonomous Systems, pp. 131–143. Springer, Cham (2022). https://doi.org/10.1007/978-3-031-21222-2_8
5. Brecher, C., Dalibor, M., Rumpe, B., Schilling, K., Wortmann, A.: An ecosystem for digital shadows in manufacturing. Procedia CIRP **104**, 833–838 (2021)
6. Broman, D., et al.: Determinate composition of FMUs for co-simulation. In: 2013 Proceedings of the International Conference on Embedded Software (EMSOFT), pp. 1–12. IEEE (2013)
7. Cai, L., Gajski, D.: Transaction level modeling: an overview. In: International Conference on Hardware/Software Codesign and Systems Synthesis, pp. 19–24. IEEE (2003)
8. Corbier, F., Loembe, S., Clark, B.: FMI technology for validation of embedded electronic systems. In: Embedded Real Time Software and Systems (ERTS 2014) (2014)
9. Cremona, F., Lohstroh, M., Broman, D., Lee, E.A., Masin, M., Tripakis, S.: Hybrid co-simulation: it's about time. Softw. Syst. Model. **18**(3), 1655–1679 (2019)
10. Esterle, L., Porter, B., Woodcock, J.: Verification and uncertainties in self-integrating system. In: 2021 IEEE International Conference on Autonomic Computing and Self-Organizing Systems Companion (ACSOS-C), pp. 220–225. IEEE (2021)

11. Feng, H., Gomes, C., Thule, C., Lausdahl, K., Iosifidis, A., Larsen, P.G.: Intro-duction to digital twin engineering. In: 2021 Annual Modeling and Simulation Conference (ANNSIM), pp. 1–12. IEEE (2021)

12. Feng, H., Gomes, C., Thule, C., Lausdahl, K., Sandberg, M., Larsen, P.G.: The Incubator Case Study for Digital Twin Engineering. arXiv (2021)

13. Fitzgerald, J., Larsen, P.G., Pierce, K.: Multi-modelling and co-simulation in the engineering of cyber-physical systems: towards the digital twin. In: ter Beek, M.H., Fantechi, A., Semini, L. (eds.) From Software Engineering to Formal Methods and Tools, and Back. LNCS, vol. 11865, pp. 40–55. Springer, Cham (2019). https://doi.org/10.1007/978-3-030-30985-5_4

14. International Organization for Standardization (ISO). 26262:2018 Road vehicles - Functional safety (2018)

15. Frank, G.: Transaction-Level Modeling with SystemC: TLM Concepts and Applications for Embedded Systems. Springer, New York (2005). https://doi.org/10.1007/b137175

16. Ge, Z., Liu, S., Wang, F., Li, Z., Sun, J.: Yolox: exceeding yolo series in 2021. arXiv preprint arXiv:2107.08430 (2021)

17. Grieves, M.: Digital Twin: Manufacturing Excellence through Virtual Factory Replication-A Whitepaper by Dr. Michael Grieves. White Paper, pp. 1–7 (2015)

18. Grieves, M.: Origins of the digital twin concept. Florida Institute of Technology, vol. 8 (2016)

19. Hatledal, L.I., Chu, Y., Styve, A., Zhang, H.: Vico: an entity-component-system based co-simulation framework. Simul. Model. Pract. Theory **108**, 102243 (2021)

20. Hatledal, L.I., Skulstad, R., Li, G., Styve, A., Zhang, H.: Co-simulation as a fundamental technology for twin ships. Model. Ident. Control **41**(4), 297–311 (2020)

21. Houben, S., Stallkamp, J., Salmen, J., Schlipsing, M., Igel, C.: Detection of traffic signs in real-world images: the German traffic sign detection benchmark. In: International Joint Conference on Neural Networks (IJCNN), pp. 1–8. IEEE (2013)

22. Jones, D., Snider, C., Nassehi, A., Yon, J., Hicks, B.: Characterising the digital twin: a systematic literature review. CIRP J. Manuf. Sci. Technol. **29**, 36–52 (2020)

23. Krammer, M., et al.: The distributed co-simulation protocol for the integration of real-time systems and simulation environments. In: Proceedings of the 50th Computer Simulation Conference, pp. 1–14 (2018)

24. Li, Y., Chen, J., Zhenchao, H., Zhang, H., Jinzhi, L., Kiritsis, D.: Co-simulation of complex engineered systems enabled by a cognitive twin architecture. Int. J. Prod. Res. **60**, 1–22 (2021)

25. MathWorks. MATLAB/Simulink®. https://www.mathworks.com/products/simulink.html

26. MODELISAR Consortium. Functional Mock-up Interface for Co-Simulation, Version 2.0 (2021). http://fmi-standard.org/

27. Nouri, A., Bozga, M., Molnos, A., Legay, A., Bensalem, S.: Astrolabe: a rigorous approach for system-level performance modeling and analysis. ACM Trans. Embed. Comput. Syst. (TECS) **15**(2), 1–26 (2016)

28. Qi, Q., et al.: Enabling technologies and tools for digital twin. J. Manuf. Syst. **58**, 3–21 (2021)

29. Rasheed, A., San, O., Kvamsdal, T.: Digital twin: values, challenges and enablers from a modeling perspective. IEEE Access **8**, 21980–22012 (2020)

30. Sharma, A., Kosasih, E., Zhang, J., Brintrup, A., Calinescu, A.: Digital twins: state of the art theory and practice, challenges, and open research questions. J. Ind. Inf. Integr. 100383 (2022)

31. Siemens EDA. Veloce®. https://eda.sw.siemens.com/en-US/ic/veloce/
32. Siemens PLM Software. Simcenter Amesim. https://www.plm.automation.sieme
    ns.com/en/products/lms/imagine-lab/amesim/
33. Siemens PLM Software. Simcenter PreScan. https://www.plm.automation.sieme
    ns.com/global/en/products/simulation-test/active-safety-system-simulation.html
34. Temperekidis, A., Kekatos, N., Katsaros, P.: Runtime verification for FMI-based
    co-simulation. In: Dang, T., Stolz, V. (eds.) Runtime Verification, pp. 304–313.
    Springer, Heidelberg (2022). https://doi.org/10.1007/978-3-031-17196-3_19
35. Tripakis, S.: Bridging the semantic gap between heterogeneous modeling for-
    malisms and FMI. In: 2015 International Conference on Embedded Computer Sys-
    tems: Architectures, Modeling, and Simulation (SAMOS), pp. 60–69. IEEE (2015)
36. Verimag Laboratory. BIP Compiler. https://www-verimag.imag.fr/New-BIP-
    tools.html
37. Woodcock, J., Gomes, C., Macedo, H.D., Larsen, P.G.: Uncertainty quantification
    and runtime monitoring using environment-aware digital twins. In: Margaria, T.,
    Steffen, B. (eds.) ISoLA 2020. LNCS, vol. 12479, pp. 72–87. Springer, Cham (2021).
    https://doi.org/10.1007/978-3-030-83723-5_6
38. Zapridou, E., Bartocci, E., Katsaros, P.: Runtime verification of autonomous driv-
    ing systems in CARLA. In: Runtime Verification - 20th International Conference,
    RV 2020, Los Angeles, CA, USA, 6–9 October 2020, Proceedings, pp. 172–183
    (2020)
39. Zhu, Z., Liang, D., Zhang, S., Huang, X., Li, B., Hu, S.: Traffic-sign detection and
    classification in the wild. In: Proceedings of the IEEE Conference on Computer
    Vision and Pattern Recognition, pp. 2110–2118 (2016)

Airborne Sensor and Perception Management

Context-Based Selection of Specialized CNNs to Ensure Reliable and Trustworthy Object Detection

Martin Ruß[(✉)] and Peter Stütz

Institute of Flight Systems, Bundeswehr University Munich, Neubiberg, Germany
martin.russ@unibw.de, peter.stuetz@unbiw.de

Abstract. Despite algorithmic advances in the field of image processing as well as modern computer architectures, automated sensor data processing that guarantees reliable and robust information retrieval in dynamic environmental and varying flight conditions is still a challenging task within unmanned surveillance and reconnaissance missions. In our paper we will elaborate the reasons and propose a promising way out by adapting to variable environmental conditions and states of the UAS platform in terms of the dedicated usage of specialized sensor data processing chains.

However, these specialized chains must be used within their operation space. Otherwise, their performance in terms of detection precision and recall will degrade. To overcome this drawback, we propose to apply chain performance models based on Bayesian Networks (BNs). The evaluation of the BNs takes place during the flight depending on environmental influences. Accordingly, a performance probability can be predicted for each chain, which is used for an automatic chain selection.

We validate our approach within a real flight Search and Rescue scenario (SAR). To compare generalized and specialized chains, we conducted several flight experiments with an EO/IR mission sensor setup: a) to annotated and prese-lect/filter training-datasets, used for transfer-learning of the Convolutional Neural Networks (CNNs), and b) to derive test datasets in different environmental situations and with varying platform/sensor states. The sensor data comprises variations in illumination and meteorological conditions, photographic conditions (e.g., different sensor elevation angles and ground sample distances) as well as topographic conditions. We provide a comprehensive insight into the detection results derived. Based on these results we conclude that a targeted use of specialized CNNs can outperform generalized CNNs.

Keywords: Sensor and Perception Management · Context-based reasoning · Bayesian detection performance modeling

1 Introduction and Object of Research

Objection detection is one of the key applications for future UAS deployments. From surveillance to inspection and agriculture, most applications need accurate object detection to serve their purpose or to plan and monitor the course of action during UAS

J. Mazal et al. (Eds.): MESAS 2022, LNCS 13866, pp. 182–206, 2023.
https://doi.org/10.1007/978-3-031-31268-7_11

missions. Object Detection is used to identify and describe the contents of an image along with the location the objects. Due to their high detection accuracy and their inherent generalization capability, deep convolutional neural networks (CNN) have outperformed traditional image processing techniques such as geometry-based blob detectors and shallow learning approaches e.g., SVMs. State-of-the-art CNNs such as Efficient-Det [1], RetinaNet [2] or YOLO [3–5] achieve reliable results on reference datasets such as COCO [6], ImageNet [7] or Pascal Visual Object Classes (VOC) [8]. Such object detection systems can be used to classify between multiple classes e.g., vehicles, traffic signs and buildings, trees, and pedestrians. The best CNNs (e.g. YOLOv7-E6E) achieve Average Precision AP up to 74,4% [5].

On the one hand, these confident results are reproducible for frontal/fixed camera setups e.g., ground based surveillance camera. But on the other hand, object detection and tracking tasks in the UAV remote sensing video face many challenges, such as image degradation due to illumination and weather changes and real-time problems such as perspective specificity, background complexity, scale, and direction diversity problems [9]. This makes current object detection methods used for fixed camera unsuitable for UAV platform [10].

One obvious approach might be to adapt current CNNs to the needs of UAV platform by using larger CNNs[1], that might be trained for all conceivable circumstances in terms of environmental and platform states. But this approach will come along inherently with the following drawbacks [9, 11, 12]:

- Large CNNs need more labeled training data.
- They require more computing resources, which are only available to a limited extent on a UAV.
- Varying environmental conditions and situations can influence each other, resulting in unpredictable or incorrect conditions for object recognition.

To reduce the effort to record and annotate the training data as well as to establish trust in such image processing systems an alternative approach to adapt to environmental and platform challenges during UAV flights seems to be of interest.

2 Methodology

Environmental and relevant mission-sensor states such as daytime, weather conditions, depression-angle, Field-of-View (FoV) or ground sampling distance (GSD) can be measured. Consequently, it might be feasible to switch between explicitly corner-/edge cases instead of integrating the adaptation to corner-/edge cases into the CNNs, which would result in larger CNNs.

The basic idea behind our approach is to use specialized chains in a targeted manner to increase object detection/classification performance. Possible and desired adaptations of the image processing algorithms to environmental and platform parameters should be explicitly developed, trained, or specified by experts for this purpose. Such operational

---

[1] Larger CNNs refers to networks with higher resolution or multimodal input images and a denser network structure (increased number of nodes, layers).

areas are derived from the color or structure of the background, the temperature, the time of day and lighting conditions or from specific sensor parameters such as perspective, resolution/GSD and sensor footprint/overlap.

These specializations/permutations of a chain prototype are expected to achieve higher chain performance thanks to adapted parameters and specialized training-data sets compared to generalized/generic chains. Since the operational area is explicitly limited, the CNN-network architecture can be dimensioned smaller compared to generic chains, e.g., image-input size, number of layers. Therefore, less training data and less computing resources are needed.

On the other hand, the detection performance of these chains might drop when they leave their designated area of use. Thus, the expected useability of individual chains needs to be modeled (Sect. 2.1) in a way that the detection performance can be predicted and evaluated as a function of environmental and platform parameters. An additional chain management and scheduling (Sect. 2.2) is needed to select the best suited chains during the flight and enables automated, situation-optimal sensor deployment and processing for real UAS missions.

2.1 Chain Performance Modelling with Bayesian Networks

The goal of chain performance modelling is to predict the expected performance of individual chains as a function of (uncertain) environmental variables to enable the optimal chain selection during the flight.

A common representation of all chains implies modeling over all integrated sensors and algorithms, as well as their interrelationships, parameterization and boundary conditions. Modeling as a monolithic system with a central knowledge base is not advisable for the following reasons:

- Expert knowledge about the use of the different sensors and algorithms is always only selective/specific.
- The complexity and the effort to create and verify the knowledge base increases with the number of chains considered.
- If changes are made to chains, new chains are integrated, or chains are removed from the system, then with a central knowledge representation all connections would have to be checked again for correctness, consistency, and freedom from contradiction.
- Contexts and assumptions about the adaptability and robustness of algorithms with respect to environmental parameters are often chain-specific.

Chain-specific modeling, on the other hand, can help to reduce complexity and thus improve traceability/verifiability by using dedicated knowledge units for each chain instead of monolithic modeling.

Moreover, our chain performance modelling takes into account the following aspects:

- Extensibility and modularity should be guaranteed to integrate new chains or environmental parameters.
- The measurements of environmental conditions such as weather or sensor states (e.g., pose/position from GPS) might be inaccurate.

• The modeling should be transparent and comprehensible to developers and users.

Therefore, a graphical, probabilistic approach with a *Bayesian Network* (BN) for each chain was introduced in [13] to model qualitative and quantitative knowledge about perception chains. Possible and desired adaptations of the image processing algorithms to environmental parameters should be explicitly developed, trained, or specified for this purpose. These specializations/permutations of a chain prototype usually achieve a high chain performance (*"Chain Performance"*), due to adapted parameters and preselected/filtered datasets. However, this is only achieved for defined environmental parameters (*"Processing Adaptation"*). Their range of application is therefore limited, and the chains often also have special requirements regarding the sensor data (*"Sensor Requirements"*)[2].

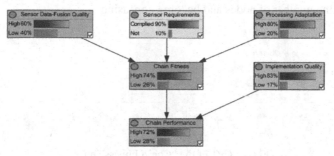

Fig. 1. Core elements of modeling chain performance via BNs.

As depicted in the Core-BN model in Fig. 1, the reliability/fitness (*"Chain Fitness"*) of chains depends on the adaptation of the algorithms e.g. due to dedicated training datasets (*"Processing Adaptation"*), on the compliance with sensor requirements (*"Sensor Requirements"*) and additionally on the expected sensor data quality (*"Sensor Data-Fusion Quality"*).

An extra node is introduced in the BN. This node serves on the one hand to normalize over all chains and on the other hand to scale the chain fitness to possible performance metrics[3]. Besides the fitness/adaptability to environmental parameters ("Chain Fitness"), the absolute performance of the chains (*"Chain Performance"*) additionally depends on the implementation of the chains (*"Implementation Quality"*).

The respective influences/dependencies are chain-specific and are defined in the form of conditional probability tables (CPTs, $P(X_i|Parent(X_i))$, [14]). An initial estimate can

---

[2] The ideas of specialized chains can furthermore be used to cope with the limited computational capacities on UAVs. Additionally adapted sensor requirements (e.g. reduced resolution/GSD, sampling/frame rate, number of channels/spectra, color depth) can be used to form runtime-optimized chain specializations/permutations but with usually lower performance.

[3] Depending on the application/use, separate metrics may also have different relevance with respect to an actual, situation-optimal evaluation of chain performance. For example, the selected threshold value of the classification generally influences the precision/false positive rate on the one hand and the recall on the other. A distinction of different performance criteria is therefore useful for the use of UAVs especially in safety-critical missions [21].

usually already be made by developers during chain development. Afterwards, the CPTs are successively verified based on representative training/test data and, if necessary, readjusted/improved. Ideally, these selected data sets should cover a high degree of possible environmental variations to enable a generalization of the model development.

For intuitive/and error-reducing specification of the probabilities, the input nodes (e.g., in Fig. 2: "Sensor Requirements", "Processing Adaptation", Sensor Data-Fusion Quality") can be sorted according to their expected influence strength. Likewise, the respective state variables should be named and sorted expressively. In this way, a clear structure can often be achieved, with the "most favorable" case at the top-left (here: "Complied" + "High" + "High") and the "unfavorable" case at the bottom-right (here: "Not Complied" + "Low" + "Low"). The influences/probabilities for the favorable case thus often decrease continuously from left-to-right. This procedure is especially helpful for large BNs and nodes with many input variables, since the scope of CPTs can increase rapidly with the number of nodes and become confusing.

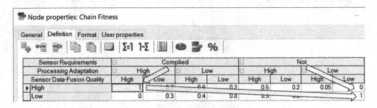

Fig. 2. CPT of the "Chain Fitness" node.

To model the environmental influences the causal order should be maintained, so that the cause comes before the effect, since this usually results in more compact and easier to model networks. The procedure will first be explained using the simplified BN for modeling the suitability of the mission sensors ("*Suitability*") as shown in Fig. 3. Hereby, the environmental states and variables can be divided into the following categories:

- Platform states (gray): These include the distance/altitude to the observation point or speed of the aircraft.
- Sensor system states (blue and turquoise): In addition to a general assessment of the sensor system (e.g., chip + optics), additional parameters such as ground resolution (GSD), ground coverage, sampling rates, and sensor orientation are considered.
- Weather and environmental conditions (green): These categories include weather, cloud spacing, temperature, and time of year and day.
- Topographic features (brown): In addition to the type/color of the subsurface, the condition of the subsurface as well as the slope and surface texture/ruggedness might have direct influence on sensor quality e.g., for distance sensors such as LIDAR.

The respective influences/dependencies are chain-specific. The quantitative expert knowledge about the strength of the influences varies for each chain and is stated within the CPTs. The values are initialized by the developers and can iteratively be adapted by comparing the results perception chains with annotated sensor streams.

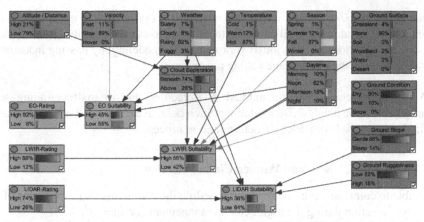

Fig. 3. Simplified BN for mapping the suitability of sensors ("Suitability") as a function of platform condition (gray), weather and environmental conditions (green), topographic conditions (brown), and an evaluation of the sensor system ("Rating", blue) (Color figure online).

The model knowledge for estimating the usability/reliability of individual sensors, algorithms or entire chains is to be successively expanded and refined in a multi-stage, iterative modeling and adaptation process. Our proposed BN modelling workflow comprises three phases as shown in Fig. 4:

- In *the development phase*, the requirements/limitations, and quality-rating of the selected sensors as well as the CNN architecture and specialties of the training shall be used to derive initial BN-models for each chain.
- In *the training and test phases*, these initial models are to be adapted, checked and, if necessary, improved. In the operation phase, the user should be given opportunities for "fine-tuning" the models.

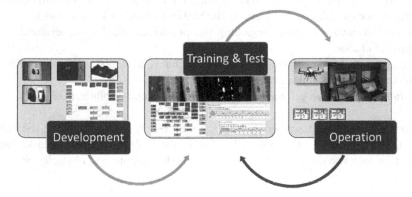

Fig. 4. Chain performance modelling workflow

- *During active operation*, the user should be given the opportunity to make fine adjustments. This should enable adjustments to be made to current conditions and, if necessary, to conditions not previously foreseen in the modeling, by passing inadequate models through the training and testing phase again.

Additionally, chains can be marked as defective, due to malfunctioning sensor/hardware or due to unprecise modelling. Such defective chains will not be evaluated within the automated winner-chain determination process.

2.2 Chain Management and Winner-Chain Selection

To be able to compare, rank, monitor and schedule the competing chains in terms of an optimized selection during the flight, chain management is required[4].

Thereby, scalability, expandability, and robustness with regards to failures of chains a high degree of modularity must be taking into account. Chains shall be connected, disconnected or started/stopped without inferring each other or locking the overall system. Therefore, a distributed architecture was proposed in [13]. The current implementation comprises:

- A *message broker*, which is transparently distributing messages between clients according to the publisher-subscriber principle [15] and
- *Clients*, which are publishing and subscribing messages through the broker and never communicate directly with each other.

Clients are, on the one hand, a chain-monitoring *"Processing Coordinator"* (PC) and, on the other hand, all possible chains and their permutations adapted to environmental conditions. Components and message flow of the chain management are shown as UML sequence diagram in Fig. 5. It comprises the following main tasks:

- *Capability Collection* (green) a query of all chain capabilities in order to be able to aggregate the overall capability across the SPMS (operational framework),
- *Winner-Determination* (blue) regarding the pre-selection/selection, evaluation and ranking of chains,
- *Runtime Control* (orange) to stop last running chains, to start new winner-chains and to allocate resources and sensors, and
- *Monitoring* (purple) to get alarmed due to environmental or platform changes.

Perception Tasks are described by the perception-task type[5], a sensor type, the surface type e.g., road or grass and an optional task-priority. Multiple perception tasks can be assigned for each waypoint, e.g., to search for vehicles, people, and obstacles on a road.

---

[4] Chain management was primary described within our Sensor-Perception-Management System approach (SPMS, [22]).

[5] In addition to the transmission of sensor images, detection, identification or tracking of objects (vehicles, persons, obstacles) can be selected as perception-task types.

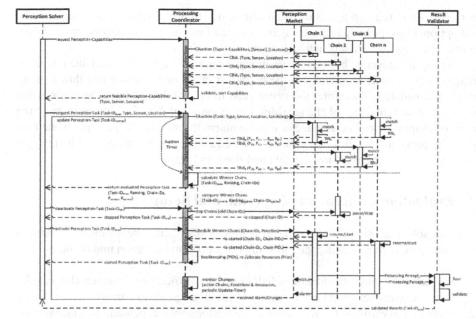

Fig. 5. Sequence diagram illustrating the chain management flow control.

For sequence and processing control unique task-IDs, chain-IDs and process-IDs were mandatory.

The query of all perception capabilities (*Capability Collection*, task = any, green) and the evaluation of suitable chains (*Winner-Determination*, blue) proceed analogously in *Perception Auctions*[6]:

- All chains subscribe to the request for *Perception Tasks*. They are notified by the broker if either a concrete perception task or the query of all perception capabilities is published by the PC. For pre-filtering chains, tasks can have optional constraints with respect to their task type, sensor type, or deployment location. Here, chains will only participate in the auction if the task-constraints are fulfilled (green arrows).
- In return, the PC subscribes to *Perception Bids*. The bids are calculated by each chain applying its internal performance model. Afterwards, the bid is published into the market. For the runtime-scheduling, the Perception-Bid are additionally provided with the corresponding task-ID and chain-ID.

After the auction deadline has expired, the received bids of participating chains are evaluated by the PC (*Winner-Chain-Determination*, WCD, blue). Each bid contains the predicted chain performance P_i and the expected resource requirements R_i. An optimal chain-ranking is created, filtering bids by min-max thresholds and setting the predicted

---

[6] Requests for a specific perception task or the query of perception capabilities are regarded as an auction (Multi-Attribute Reverse Auction, [23–25]). The auctions have an expiration time and for each auction the task-ID is incremented or randomized via a unique hash value.

performance in relation to resource consumption [16]. Finally, the current ranking and the optional task-priority is used to derive the runtime parameters (status, process PID, process priority) for already active and new winner-chains[7].

During the mission, both the environmental parameters and the available resources may change to such an extent that the predicted chain performance and thus ranking might be outdated. Therefore, the system can monitor relevant input parameters and detect their changes/rates of change (Monitoring, purple in Fig. 5). If the changes or the rates of change exceed percentage or relative alarm thresholds, the perception auctions with the previous task IDs are restarted. Consequently, chain ranking will be updated considering the current environmental conditions and resources.

3 Evaluation Concept and Experimental Setup

Our Sensor-Perception-Management-System (SPMS), shall be evaluated within a representative scenario taking the following objects of investigation into account:

1. Specialized chains should assembled/trained for difficult environmental constellations (edge/corner cases) and used in a targeted and profitable manner.
2. Modeling to estimate the respective chain performance depending on current environmental parameters is the prerequisite for the targeted use of specialized chains. For this purpose, the SPMS shall evaluate the respective models and establish a current ranking of suitable chains/chains adapted to the environment.
3. Automated object detection can be used reliably/trustworthy during a surveillance UAS mission even at different times of day, seasons, weather conditions as well as for varying geographical backgrounds.

Thereby, the added value of using the SPMS concept in the context of a sample scenario (Fig. 6) shall be quantified.

In addition to the implementation of the SPMS concept (Sect. 2.1 Chain Performance Modelling with Bayesian Networks, Sect. 2.2 Chain Management and Winner-Chain Selection) a suitable experimental environment setup had to be built. This setup includes:

- the airframe and the mission-sensor-payload (Sect. 3.2) and
- the implementation and the training of specialized chains (Sect. 3.3).

3.1 Mission Scenario and Flight Planning

A suitable scenario would be airborne traffic monitoring. Traffic monitoring and coordination of rescue forces is still largely carried out with the help of manned aircraft (rescue/police helicopters). In the future however, a supporting, automated use

---

[7] For targeted stopping, starting, and prioritizing of chains, in addition to runtime parameters, task IDs, chain IDs and the currently available resources are stored by the PC in a database (bookkeeping). During the de-/activation of perception tasks via the perception solver as well as during the updating of auctions, these databases are evaluated for the scheduling of the chains, e.g., by stopping or prioritizing the executed processes (chain PIDs) for each task ID.

of (autonomous) rescue drones would also be conceivable. This could lead to shorter response times, more extensive and simultaneous observation of multiple critical points/regions, and a reduction in costs.

Application framework was tailored down to a small sized toy-scenario that could be conducted at our test-flight premises. The route of the UAV was planned based on waypoints and individual waypoints were linked to concrete perception tasks such as person or vehicle detection. The flight patterns comprise a combination of low, straight overflies and meander search patterns. Altitude and velocity vary according to mission needs and sensor limitations.

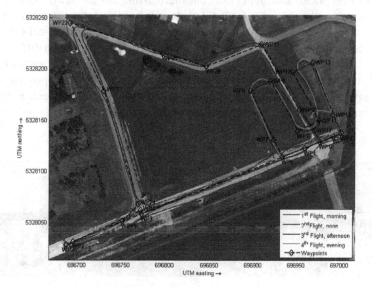

Fig. 6. Waypoints and flight trajectories of the first summer-flight campaign.

To compare generalized and specialized chains (CNNs), we conducted several real flight experiments with an EO/IR mission sensor setup to capture training and test data in different environmental situations and with varying platform/sensor states.

The sensor data should include variability in time of day, illumination, temperature, photographic conditions (GSD, FoV) and topographic conditions (asphalt/road, grass). Therefore, starting from spring season in 2013 until winter in 2021 we repeated the main scenario (WP6-WP19) about 40 times and split the test-flights into two categories: While the first ones were conducted for the implementation and the training of the chains, the remaining test-flights were used for an overall system proof-of-concept (Fig. 13).

3.2 Airframe and Mission-Payload

To conduct the test-flights, a suitable flight vehicle and a modular sensor-computer payload were designed and integrated. The selection and adaptations of a possible test vehicle should take place according to the needs and conditions of the bespoke scenario, our test site and varying weather and environmental conditions:

- A *Multicopter VTOL platform* (Fig. 7) was selected due to ease of operation, its hovering and slow flight capabilities, and flight-regulation issues. Maximum air speed is around 40 km/h and an endurance is up to 15 min with a payload weight ranging between 1.5–2.0 kg. To monitor the flight conditions and to send and switch between individual waypoints, a serial communication between the mission computer and the flight control was programmed and used during the test flights in the example scenario.
- The *SOMA mission sensor payload* (*Sensor Oriented Mission Avionics*) was designed as a modular, vibration damped and lightweight payload concept. SOMA is mounted below the rotor/propeller level of the VTOL-UAV (Fig. 8). The sensor payload comprises electro-optical cameras (4x EO), one thermal imaging camera (LWIR), a LIDAR range-sensor[8], and an accurate GPS-aided attitude heading reference system (AHRS) in the center of gravity for image registration tasks. The electro-optical cameras are well suited for daytime detection and tracking. They are equipped with different lenses enabling multiple ground sampling distances and aperture numbers within the same flight. Furthermore, different viewing directions and sensor-typical optimized presets (e.g., white balance, contrast, or exposure time) can be set for the each EO-camera. The thermal imaging camera was integrated for low-light and night vision capabilities.

Fig. 7. A Multicopter-VTOL platform was equipped with the SOMA payload and was used within evaluation scenario at the UniBwM test-premises in Neubiberg/Germany.

The use of the mission-payload SOMA offers advantages during the generation of test-data and during the evaluation flights. Due to its multisensory setup and multiple configurations/presets options, four different adaptations of the EO-sensor to environmental conditions and an additional LWIR sensor stream can be captured simultaneously. In particular, less test-flights were needed for the generation of training and test-data sets.

3.3   Implementation and Training of Chains

For the evaluation of the SPMS concept, specialized chains must be implemented and trained for difficult environmental constellations (edge/corner cases).

---

[8] Optional algorithms for object and obstacle detection are using to the LIDAR range-sensor, but not relevant for the evaluation within this paper.

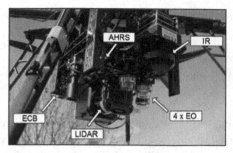

Fig. 8. The SOMA sensor payload (Sensor Oriented Mission Avionics) comprises a mission computer (ECB), multiple cameras (4x EO) with different lenses, a thermal LWIR, a range sensor (LIDAR), and a position/altitude sensor (AHRS).

In contrast to traditional methods[9], the key idea behind deep learning (DL) is that object models, properties and features are learned directly from raw/source images. Therefore, they can generalize better and have a wider scope of application [11]. However, SOTA- or Image Transformers [17] require large datasets to train the models and computer architectures that runs computationally intensive machine learning algorithms fast and efficiently. Thanks to modern GPUs and FPGAs and due to the availability of large scales labeled datasets, DL methods like CNNs outperformed traditional methods in recent computer vision contests e.g. COCO [6], ImageNet [7] or Pascal Visual Object Classes (VOC) [8].

CNN based object detection methods can categorized into two-step (region-based) and single-step approaches [2, 3, 18]:

- *Two-step approaches*: These region-based algorithms like R-CNN and Fast(er) R-CNN first identify regions where objects are expected and then detect objects only in those regions using convnet.
- Single-step approaches: Single shot detectors (SSDs) like YOLO or RetinaNet use a fully convolutional approach[10] in which the network can find all objects within an image in one pass ('single-shot' or 'look once') through the convnet.

Region-based models have a slightly higher accuracy, whereas single-shot algorithms are more efficient (higher speed and less memory requirement) and still have good accuracy. To cope with challenges in deploying the vision and intelligence capabilities on a UAV platform [19]:

---

[9] Traditional object recognition and detection methods for UAVs are using dedicated features such as SIFT (Scale-Invariant Feature Transform, [26, 27]), SURF (Speeded-Up Robust Features, [28]), and HOG (Histogram of Oriented Gradient, [29, 30]) or rely on the evaluation the foreground/background (e.g., color or edge based) and geometry constraints (BLOB, [31]). These methods use local features, thresholds and assumptions regarding the environment that were created by hand. Therefore, traditional image processing methods are error-sensitive or generally only valid for a very limited state space ([32]).

[10] Consequently, there are neither separate classification or detection modules that should be synchronized with each other nor region proposals necessary.

- consume minimal power to minimize its effect on battery consumption and flight time of the drone
- require less memory footprint and computational power as typical UAV has resource limitation
- process the input data from its camera with low latency and perform faster to make critical decisions

SSDs are more suitable for an employment in UAVs. Therefore, we decided to implement the specialized chains based on YOLOv4, which is very efficient C + + implementation of a state-of-the-art SSD [4]. The chain setup for the evaluation of the SPMS concept should include generic EO- and IR-chains (*ch-eo*, *ch-ir*) on the one hand and chains specific to environmental parameters (*ch-eo-night*, *ch-eo-snow*, *ch-eo-gray*, *ch-ir-winter*), or low resource consumption (*ch-*-tiny*) on the other.

For each chain the YOLO object detector was pre-trained on the COCO dataset with two classes (persons and cars) and later specialized by transfer learning with dedicated training sets. These data sets were created from the training flights (flight planning in **Fehler! Verweisquelle konnte nicht gefunden werden.**) by manually labeling 4 different EO images and one IR image each (see Fig. 8) per frame.

4   Results and Evaluation

Taking the objects of investigation (evaluation concept in Sect. 3) into account, we will evaluate:

- in Sect. 4.1, if specialized chains can be assembled/trained for difficult environmental constellations (edge/corner cases) and
- in Sect. 4.2, if these specialized chains can be used in a targeted and profitable manner by using the SPMS concept within the sample scenario.

For the evaluation of the detection results we adapted the performance metric from Pascal VOC Challenge [8]:

- The area under the Precision-Recall (PR) curve at a specific Intersection over Union (IoU) is the Average Precision (AP) per class.
- IoU describes the overlap ratio between detection and ground truth boxes. IoU was set to 0.4 for small objects (persons) and 0.6 for larger objects (cars).
- The detection threshold of the CNNs was set to 0.5.
- Mean Average Precision (mAP) is the average of AP over all detected classes:
  $mAP = \frac{1}{n} \cdot \sum_{i=1}^{n} AP_i$, where n is the number of classes.

In the context of this paper, primarily the results of the person detection are considered for reasons of space. The results of the vehicle detection are not listed, but they are included in the calculation of the mAPs. The mAPs are given in brackets in the evaluation curves.

Within the thumbnail images, all labeled ground truth boxes (persons and cars) are green, whereas by chains detected persons are drawn red and detected cars are drawn blue.

4.1 Performance Analysis of Specialized Chains

4.1.1 Generic vs. Efficient Chains (Ch-*-Tiny)

In [20] a novel CNN-model scaling technique was developed proposed and evaluated based on YOLOv4. They showed upper and lower bounds of linear scaling up/down models, and respectively analyzed the issues that need to be considered in model scaling for small models and large models.

Due to the promising results (performance ~ AP_{50}, efficiency ~ FPS) on ground based reference data (COCO, [6]), these models were used for our chain implementations. Parameters and results of the models are listed according to [20] in Table 1:

Table 1. Comparison of state-of-the-art YOLOv4 based object detectors in accordance with [20] and evaluated on COCO [6] using a NVIDIA RTX 2070 GPU.

Model	HW-Platform	Input Size	AP_{50}	FPS
YOLOv4-CSP	Workstation GPUs	640 × 640	66.2%	73
YOLOv4-P5	High-End GPUs	896 × 896	70.3%	41
YOLOv4-P7	Server/Cloud GPUs	1536 × 1536	73.4%	16
YOLOv4-tiny	Embedded GPUs (NVIDIA Jetson)	41 × x416	40.2%	330

- The *YOLOv4-CSP* achieve the best trade-off between speed and accuracy.
- Large CNNs like *YOLOv4-P5/P7* achieve slightly better accuracy but require high-end GPUs. Therefore, they would not be computed in real-time with low latency (high FPS) onboard of small and medium sized UAVs due to limited resources.
- *YOLOv4-tiny* is a promising option, when efficiency is more relevant than accuracy, e.g., if GPU-resources are shared[11] or if only embedded GPUs are available.

Consequently, for an evaluation within airborne traffic surveillance application we trained and deployed the YOLOv4-CSP and the YOLOv4-tiny models. Both model types were used for the implementation of generic chains, which were trained for different environmental situations and backgrounds, as well as for specialized chains (*ch-eo-night, ch-eo-snow, ch-ir-winter*).

The detection performance AP (Fig. 9), especially with regard to efficient CNNs (*ch-*-tiny*), is significantly better in the flight tests compared to the evaluation on COCO. This is due, among other things, to the fact that in the trials:

- Only 2 classes and not 80 classes as in COCO had to be learned and distinguished.
- For better reproducibility/comparability of different specializations, possible influence factors should be able to be considered on their own, therefore perspective was kept constant (top-down view).

---

[11] E.g., with path-planning from a Mission-Management-system [13].

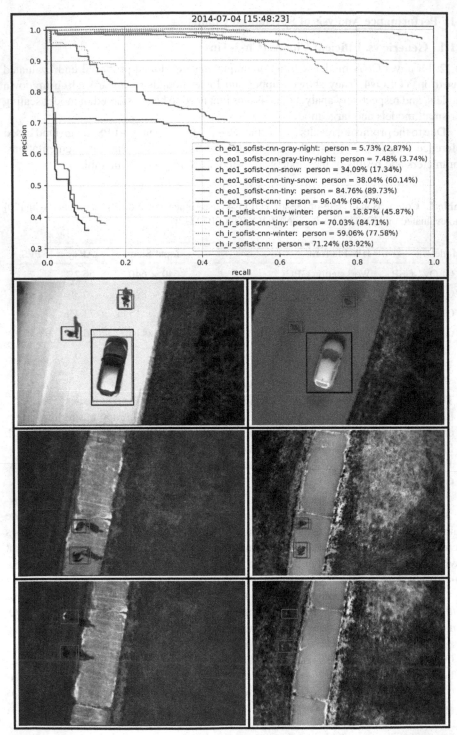

Fig. 9. Precision-Recall curve, AP and detections (EO, LWIR) for a flight in summer (afternoon, sunny conditions, hot temperature).

The evaluation of the test series and the detection results confirmed that the performance of generically trained chains also varies depending on the environmental parameters. Weather, temperature, lighting conditions but also the type, color, or roughness of the surface[12] influence the sensor quality. Besides obvious dependencies like the range limitation of active sensors and distance sensors, or the daylight dependency of EO cameras, more complex relationships were found and modeled. For example, there is a causal relationship between usability of thermal IR images and the temperature and type of background on the other hand:

- Thermal LWIR images are readily usable at high temperatures in summer over homogeneous surfaces (including asphalt).
- In contrast, LWIR images on hot days over unstructured terrain or vegetation (e.g., grass) are not/barely usable and lead to poor detection results.
- Such examples of good (asphalt) and poor results (grass) of the thermal infrared person detection chain are depicted in Fig. 9.

These causal dependencies in the sense of a prediction of the chain performance were modelled with Bayesian networks (Sect. 2.1) and will be exploited during the flight for the winner-chain determination within the monitor traffic scenario (Sect. 4.2).

4.1.2 EO-Night: Low-Light Conditions

A typical edge-case is the deteriorating sensor quality in unfavorable lighting conditions, e.g., during twilight. However, by manually adjusting brightness and contrast (Fig. 10), a noisy and tinged image can be restored even in almost complete darkness, from which the human eye can make out objects.

Compared to nighttime infrared sensors, EO sensors are mostly cheaper, not export-restricted, and often smaller and lighter, which simplifies integration on UAVs. Therefore, an extended operational range EO sensors would have a great practical benefit. We tried to automate the described procedure by creating specialized single-shot-detectors:

- First, we used transfer-learning only with twilight datasets to adapt the generic, color-based EO-chains. But it failed due to the tinged and faded colors
- In the second experiment, the COCO dataset and our own residual light datasets were first converted to gray-scale images before repeating the training.

---

[12] Both foreground and background.

The results of the gray-value based EO night experts are only slightly inferior to LWIR cameras at dusk (top, Fig. 10) and are still acceptable even after sunset (second graph in Fig. 10). However, it is also clear from the bottom plot in Fig. 10 that deliberately overtrained experts need to be deployed very targeted.

Compared to the generic EO-chains, an improvement of 21.2% or 16.7% for the efficient tiny implementation could be achieved at twilight conditions.

4.1.3   EO-Snow: White Surface

To explore if and to what extend adaptation to dedicated surfaces can be realized, we picked snowy winter scenes from our dataset for the transfer learning. The results and detection thumbnails are giving in Fig. 11.

Compared to the generic EO-chains, an improvement of about 7% or 5% for the efficient tiny implementation could be achieved. Also evident is discrimination, which is not as strong as with the low-light EO-chains (compare Fig. 10).

4.1.4   IR-Winter: Cold Temperatures

In winter there are distinctive temperature differences between foreground and background. But in contrast to hot summer days (Fig. 9), the quality of LWIR images is suitable for object detection over asphalt and over vegetation e.g., grassland as depicted in Fig. 12. Therefore, we trained IR-chains scenes with low-temperatures of the surface/background.

A resulting performance gain of AP of about 11.7% and about 12.5% for the tiny CNN model could be achieved. In contrast to the EO chains, the adaptation to distinct conditions is less pronounced.

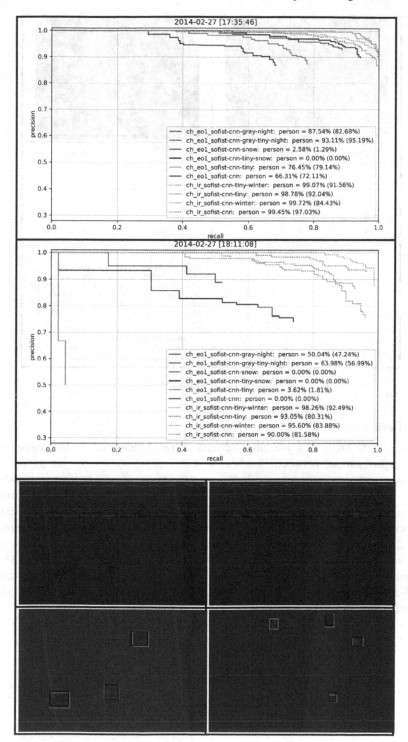

Fig. 10. Results and detections of the low-light EO-chains at dusk and after sunset.

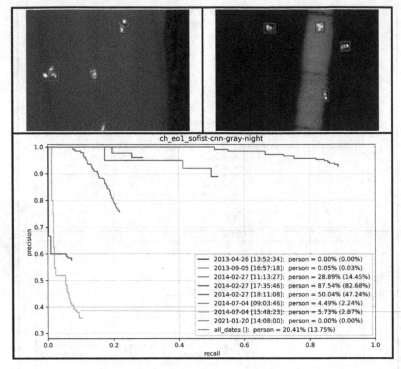

Fig. 10. (*continued*)

4.1.5 Review

As shown in the previous subsections, specialization of chains can indeed increase the detection performance between 5%–21%.

However, discrimination is a side effect of the intended adaptation to corner/edge operational states: It has also been shown that specialized chains might have very limited operating ranges. Outside these limits, they should not or only be used to a limited extent.

Somewhat surprisingly, it can also be concluded from the test series that smaller CNNs do not only have runtime advantages: Compared to larger CNNs, their detection performance was even better in some corner cases (compare EO-snow in Fig. 11 and IR-Winter). The reasons for this are the smaller input image size and a reduced number of nodes and layers, which sometimes favor targeted adaptation but also unintentional discrimination, especially if only small datasets are available for training.

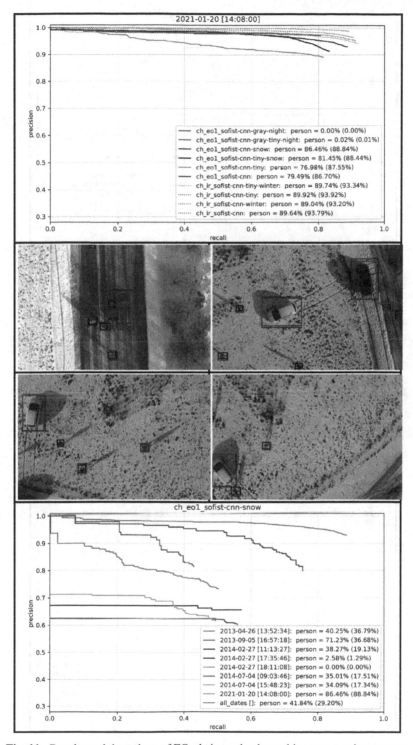

Fig. 11. Results and detections of EO-chains trained on white, snowy winter scenes.

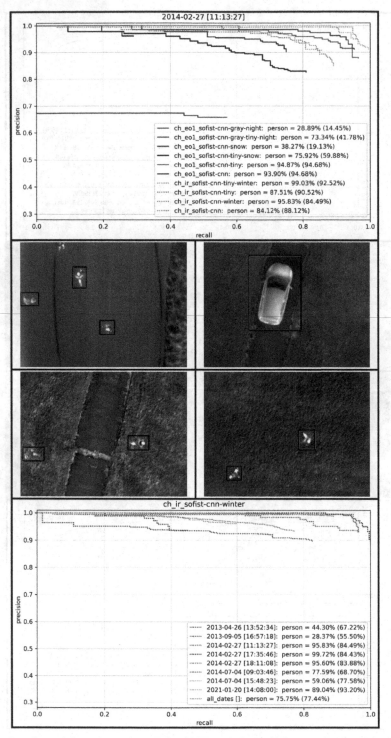

Fig. 12. Results and detections of specialized LWIR-chains, which are trained and deployed at low temperatures during winter season.

4.2 SPMS-Performance Within the Surveillance Scenario

Finally, we want to assess whether an improvement in detection performance can also be achieved by using the SPMS concept in the context of a potential surveillance UAS application. To guarantee a high variability in environmental conditions – season, weather, time of day or year, exposure, temperature, background surface – several evaluation flights (Fig. 13) were selected and excluded from training of chains (CNNs).

Fig. 13. Flight trajectories, dates and daytime used for the evaluation.

In addition to explicitly trained chains, sensor properties and limitations were also modeled. During the replay of the evaluation flights, a prediction of the chain performance was possible. A ranking was derived from the chain performance, which ultimately enabled targeted switching between chains.

Compared to the best chains, an increase in AP of about 10% to almost 92% was achieved by using the SPMS (magenta in Fig. 14).

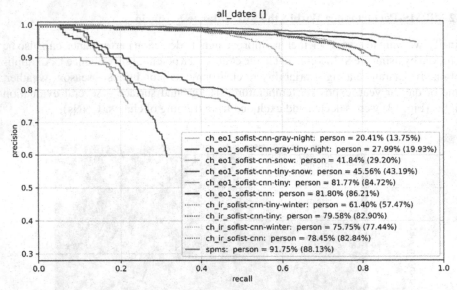

Fig. 14. SPMS-Performance within the surveillance scenario, summarized over all evaluation flights (Fig. 13).

5   Conclusion

Instead of using large CNNs, we proposed medium sized CNNs in combination of specialized CNNs for edge/corner use-cases (dedicated configuration spaces). We trained and tested SOTA image processing algorithms on real flight sensor data and provided a comprehensive insight into the detection results derived. Based on these results we conclude that a set of specialized CNNs can outperform generalized CNNs. However, these specialized CNNs must be used within their operation space. Otherwise, their performance in terms of detection precision and recall will degrade.

Therefore, our SPMS comprises of a chain useability model considering environmental and platform states to predict each chain performance and situational awareness scheduler ("processing coordinator"), that will select the best suited CNNs during the flight.

The future work will focus on the integration and evaluation of more specialized chains. On the one hand, we want to profitably adapt the architecture of CNNs and, on the other hand, train, deploy and evaluate experts for different perspectives.

References

1. Tan, M., Pang, R., Le, Q.V.: EfficientDet: scalable and efficient object detection. In: Proceedings of the IEEE/CVF Conference on Computer Vision and Pattern Recognition, pp. 10778–10787 (2020). https://doi.org/10.1109/CVPR42600.2020.01079
2. Lin, T.Y., Goyal, P., Girshick, R., He, K., Dollar, P.: Focal loss for dense object detection. IEEE Trans. Pattern Anal. Mach. Intell. **42**, 318–327 (2017). https://doi.org/10.48550/arxiv.1708.02002

3. Redmon, J., Divvala, S., Girshick, R., Farhadi, A.: You only look once: unified, real-time object detection. In: Proceedings of the IEEE Conference on Computer Vision and Pattern Recognition, pp. 779–788 (2015). https://doi.org/10.48550/arxiv.1506.02640

4. Bochkovskiy, A., Wang, C.-Y., Liao, H.-Y.M.: YOLOv4: optimal speed and accuracy of object detection (2020). https://doi.org/10.48550/arxiv.2004.10934

5. Wang, C.-Y., Bochkovskiy, A., Liao, H.-Y.M.: YOLOv7: trainable bag-of-freebies sets new state-of-the-art for real-time object detectors (2022). https://doi.org/10.48550/arxiv.2207.02696

6. Lin, T.-Y., et al.: Microsoft COCO: common objects in context. In: Fleet, D., Pajdla, T., Schiele, B., Tuytelaars, T. (eds.) ECCV 2014. LNCS, vol. 8693, pp. 740–755. Springer, Cham (2014). https://doi.org/10.1007/978-3-319-10602-1_48

7. Deng, J., Dong, W., Socher, R., Li, L.-J., Li, K., Fei-Fei, L.: ImageNet: a large-scale hierarchical image database, pp. 248–255 (2010). https://doi.org/10.1109/CVPR.2009.5206848

8. Everingham, M., Van Gool, L., Williams, C.K.I., Winn, J., Zisserman, A.: The pascal visual object classes (VOC) challenge. Int. J. Comput. Vis. **88**, 303–338 (2010). https://doi.org/10.1007/S11263-009-0275-4

9. Wu, X., Li, W., Hong, D., Tao, R., Du, Q.: Deep learning for UAV-based object detection and tracking: a survey. IEEE Geosci. Remote Sens. Mag. **10**, 91–124 (2021). https://doi.org/10.1109/mgrs.2021.3115137

10. Valappil, N.K., Memon, Q.A.: CNN-SVM based vehicle detection for UAV platform. Int. J. Hybrid Intell. Syst. **17**, 59–70 (2021). https://doi.org/10.3233/HIS-210003

11. Srivastava, S., Narayan, S., Mittal, S.: A survey of deep learning techniques for vehicle detection from UAV images. J. Syst. Archit. **117** (2021). https://doi.org/10.1016/J.SYSARC.2021.102152

12. Tian, G., Liu, J., Yang, W.: A dual neural network for object detection in UAV images. Neurocomputing **443**, 292–301 (2021). https://doi.org/10.1016/J.NEUCOM.2021.03.016

13. Russ, M., Stütz, P.: Application of a probabilistic market-based approach in UAV sensor & perception management. In: Information Fusion (16th FUSION) (2013)

14. Russell, S., Norvig, P.: Artificial Intelligence: A Modern Approach (2020)

15. Tanenbaum, A.S., van Steen, M.: Distributed Systems. CreateSpace Independent Publishing Platform (2017)

16. Russ, M., Schmitt, M., Hellert, C., Stütz, P.: Airborne sensor and perception management: experiments and results for surveillance UAS. In: AIAA Infotech@aerosp. Conference, pp. 1–16 (2013). https://doi.org/10.2514/6.2013-5144

17. Touvron, H., Cord, M., Sablayrolles, A., Synnaeve, G., Jégou, H.: Going deeper with image transformers. In: Proceedings of the IEEE/CVF International Conference on Computer Vision, pp. 32–42 (2021). https://doi.org/10.48550/arxiv.2103.17239

18. Khan, A., Sohail, A., Zahoora, U., Qureshi, A.S.: A survey of the recent architectures of deep convolutional neural networks. Artif. Intell. Rev. **53**(8), 5455–5516 (2020). https://doi.org/10.1007/s10462-020-09825-6

19. Vaddi, S., Kim, D., Kumar, C., Shad, S., Jannesari, A.: Efficient object detection model for real-time UAV application. Comput. Inf. Sci. **14**, 45 (2021). https://doi.org/10.5539/CIS.V14N1P45

20. Wang, C.-Y., Bochkovskiy, A., Liao, H.-Y.M.: Scaled-YOLOv4: Scaling Cross Stage Partial Network (2021)

21. Hrabia, C.E., Hessler, A., Xu, Y., Brehmer, J., Albayrak, S.: EffFeu project: efficient operation of unmanned aerial vehicles for industrial fire fighters. In: Proceedings of the 2018 ACM International Conference on Mobile Systems, Applications and Services, DroNet 2018, pp. 33–38 (2018). https://doi.org/10.1145/3213526.3213533

22. Russ, M., Stütz, P.: Airborne sensor and perception management: a conceptual approach for surveillance UAS. In: Information Fusion (15th FUSION) (2012)

23. Sadaoui, S., Shil, S.K.: A multi-attribute auction mechanism based on conditional constraints and conditional qualitative preferences. J. Theor. Appl. Electron. Commer. Res. **11**, 1–25 (2016). https://doi.org/10.4067/S0718-18762016000100002

24. Shil, S.K., Mouhoub, M., Sadaoui, S.: Winner determination in multi-attribute combinatorial reverse auctions. In: Arik, S., Huang, T., Lai, W.K., Liu, Q. (eds.) ICONIP 2015. LNCS, vol. 9491, pp. 645–652. Springer, Cham (2015). https://doi.org/10.1007/978-3-319-26555-1_73

25. Bichler, M., Kalagnanam, J.: Configurable offers and winner determination in multi-attribute auctions. Eur. J. Oper. Res. **160**, 380–394 (2005). https://doi.org/10.1016/j.ejor.2003.07.014

26. Xi, C.J., Guo, S.X.: Image target identification of UAV based on SIFT. Procedia Eng. **15**, 3205–3209 (2011). https://doi.org/10.1016/J.PROENG.2011.08.602

27. Chen, X., Meng, Q.: Vehicle detection from UAVs by using SIFT with implicit shape model. In: Proceedings of the 2013 IEEE International Conference on Systems, Man, and Cybernetics, SMC 2013, pp. 3139–3144 (2013). https://doi.org/10.1109/SMC.2013.535

28. Zhao, Y., Pei, H.: An improved vision-based algorithm for unmanned aerial vehicles autonomous landing. Phys. Procedia **33**, 935–941 (2012). https://doi.org/10.1016/J.PHPRO.2012.05.157

29. Blondel, P., Potelle, A., Pégard, C., Lozano, R.: How to improve the HOG detector in the UAV context. IFAC Proc. **46**, 46–51 (2013). https://doi.org/10.3182/20131120-3-FR-4045.00009

30. Zhang, G., Gao, F., Liu, C., Liu, W.: A pedestrian detection method based on SVM classifier and optimized Histograms of Oriented Gradients feature. In: 2010 Sixth International Conference on Natural Computation, pp. pp. 3257–3260. IEEE (2010). https://doi.org/10.1109/ICNC.2010.5582537

31. Jędrasiak, K., Nawrat, A.: Image recognition technique for unmanned aerial vehicles. In: Bolc, L., Kulikowski, J.L., Wojciechowski, K. (eds.) ICCVG 2008. LNCS, vol. 5337, pp. 391–399. Springer, Heidelberg (2009). https://doi.org/10.1007/978-3-642-02345-3_38

32. Ramachandran, A., Sangaiah, A.K.: A review on object detection in unmanned aerial vehicle surveillance. Int. J. Cogn. Comput. Eng. **2**, 215–228 (2021). https://doi.org/10.1016/J.IJCCE.2021.11.005

AxS/AI in Context of Future Warfare and Security Environment

Swarm Maneuver of Combat UGVs on the Future Digital Battlefield

Jan Nohel$^{(\boxtimes)}$, Petr Stodola , Zdeněk Flasar , Dana Křišťálová ,
Pavel Zahradníček , and Luděk Rak

University of Defense, 662 10 Brno, Czech Republic
{jan.nohel,petr.stodola,zdenek.flasar,pavel.zahradnicek,
ludek.rak}@unob.cz, dana.kristalova@unob.czm

Abstract. The article describes the possibilities of the effective use of combat unmanned ground vehicle swarms in performing offensive tasks on the battlefield. An integral part of the effective tactical use of these robotic weapon systems is the planning of the axes of their coordinated maneuvers towards a single or group of targets. The Maneuver Control System CZ was used to calculate the axes of the offensive maneuver of the entire swarm of combat unmanned ground vehicles, which evaluates the combination of surface and terrain, weather and also the influence of enemy and friendly units deployment. The basis for the system's calculations is a digital territory model, a digital relief model, weather forecasts, and information on the deployments of forces on both sides. The possibilities of the effective use of the Maneuver Control System CZ in planning the axes of a swarm maneuver of unmanned ground vehicles are demonstrated in three scenarios of simulated tactical situations. The calculated axes of the maneuvers were then checked in the field by an ATV.

Keywords: Automation · Maneuver Model · Offensive Maneuver · Swarm · Unmanned Ground Vehicle

1 Introduction

Information processes automation and the use of weapon systems, robotization, use of high-precision weapons, and an overview of the situation on the battlefield in real-time are characteristic elements of current and future military operations. Their purpose is to use military forces effectively and in the required time and space, from tactically advantageous positions, in order to achieve dominance on the battlefield and meet the objectives of the operation. The use of Unmanned Aerial Vehicles (UAVs) and Unmanned Ground Vehicles (UGVs) to gather information is more frequent. The key factors for their development and effective operation on the battlefield are battlefield situational overview, command and control system, firepower, trafficability and maneuverability, as well as sustainability and resilience. The distribution of information in order to create an overview of the battlefield situation, as well as the transmission of commands and orders, can be implemented in the environment of a digitized and computer-linked

J. Mazal et al. (Eds.): MESAS 2022, LNCS 13866, pp. 209–230, 2023.
https://doi.org/10.1007/978-3-031-31268-7_12

battlefield. It consists of information sensors, decision-making authorities and a means of action, interconnected in a network of computer stations, see [1–5]. There are also some cases where the target is kinetically affected by the same remote-controlled vehicle that identified it and constantly monitors it, using carried weapon systems. The speed, efficiency, and effectiveness of this target destruction then depend only on the speed of creating an overview of the situation on the battlefield and the decisions of commanders and operators. The degree of automation of the activities of UGVs and their weapon systems can then include planning the axis of their movement, direct navigation in the microrelief of the terrain, automatic target identification, up to autonomous or semi-autonomous destruction of the identified target. The greater this automation, the smaller the requirements for the control of activities and autonomous vehicles by operators.

Masked enemy infantry that effectively uses the covering properties of the terrain, however, still represents a dangerous adversary for these autonomous systems. One way to eliminate this threat and make use of autonomous systems on the modern battlefield more effective is to deploy them in greater numbers. A swarm of several combat UGVs could observe, search and control the jeopardized area from the distance of observation sensors visibility and effective fire of carried weapon systems, including the possible implementation of a coordinated attack.

The maneuver of the UGV swarm to a defined target can be planned autonomously, as well as the direct navigation in the field and circumvention of identified obstacles. To identify obstacles, digital tactical-geographical battlefield data, satellite navigation, LIDAR – high-resolution laser radar, and other vehicle sensors can be used. Target destruction can then be performed in an automated mode after target identification via an automatic target recognition system, see [6], or semi-automatically after approval by the vehicle operator. A key element of the effective use of the C-UGV swarm will be in the methods for quickly planning an effective offensive and coordinating maneuvers for an entire combat UGV swarm, taking into account the tactical principles of movement on the battlefield and approach to the target.

The aim of the article is to identify the tactical and technical parameters and required capabilities of the C-UGV and the possibilities of their effective use on the battlefield, based on the analysis of professional literature and interviews with experts. Routes of C-UGV offensive maneuvers, evaluated as one of its effective uses, were calculated by the Maneuver Control System CZ (MCS CZ) program. The results of the calculations were subsequently verified by practical tests in the field and described in case studies in the text of the thesis.

2   Literature Review

A number of publications deal with the issue of automation and robotization of unmanned systems, motion modelling and obstacle avoidance. The characteristics of different types of UGVs in the world can be observed in [7–9]. The use of robotic and autonomous systems, artificial intelligence, and their implementation on the battlefield are described in [10–12]. The strategy for the deployment and integration of robotic and autonomous systems in future US military operations and the associated psychological, humanitarian, and legal context can be found in [13–15]. Artillery reconnaissance to secure autonomous weapon systems is described in [16]. Creating terrain trafficability maps by autonomous vehicles and terrain natural cover trafficability is described in [17, 18]. The model proposed in these articles minimizes the threat to maneuver elements and optimizes the length of the maneuver axis. The analysis of surface, soils and forest for passability of personnel armored vehicles and wheeled vehicles based on remote sensors screening and technical parameters of vehicles are described in [19–21]. Autonomous navigation of robots with legs in broken terrain that is impenetrable for vehicles with wheels and caterpillar chassis is considered in [22–26]. Here, the potential of autonomous navigation of robots with legs is shown. The navigation system was integrated and tested on four-legged and two-legged robots.

The modelling and simulation of the movement of forces and resources in urban battlefields of the 21st century and the degree of autonomy of unmanned systems is addressed in [27–29]. These articles further describe the possible use of autonomous systems on the battlefield, including the degree of autonomy and human control in the control of unmanned systems. The capabilities of ground UGVs and their levels of autonomy are defined on practical examples. The possibilities of increasing the effectiveness of units by deploying unmanned systems and their integration into military operations are discussed in [30, 31]. The specific use of combat UGVs is also described here, including the specification of their technical parameters and types of carried weapons. The mathematical-algorithmic model of maneuver planning, usable in military operations and in the deployment of UGV, is specified in [32, 33].

The modelling, use of simulations, and training of automotive systems are described in [34–36]. The technological development of combat UGVs, future development trends, implementation into military armaments and training are discussed in [37]. The definition of tactics and effectiveness of the use of small units in ground unit operations and the aspect description of the decision-making process of commanders in military operations for the effective use of UGVs can be found in [38, 39]. The nature of the tactical situation, geographical conditions, route finding algorithms and vehicle types are the most important factors that affect the effectiveness of UGVs. The article also describes field experiments using UGV TAROS. In [40, 41], the possibilities of using UGVs in ground forces, their equipment, and control are discussed. Travel planning, avoiding obstacles including practical testing and control of the trajectory of diverse swarms of air, land, and sea unmanned vehicles is described in [42, 43].

3   The Tactical Situations of the Combat Use of the UGV Swarm

Before analysing the possibilities of using an effective and coordinated maneuver of a combat UGV swarm on the battlefield, it is necessary to specify the tactical and technical parameters and required capabilities of the C-UGV. The specifications of combat UGVs, optimized on the basis of the conduct of current military operations, transport options, logistical sustainability and combat effectiveness is described in detail in [7–9, 44]. Current combat UGVs use a wheel or tracked chassis, diesel or hybrid electric drives with a maximum speed of up to 77 km.h^{-1} with a range of 20 to 300 km. Target identification and monitoring of the surrounding area are provided by various optoelectronic and radar sensors carried by the vehicle. To eliminate the target, 7.62- to 12.7-mm calibre machine guns and anti-tank guided missiles are usually used. Other weapons of combat UGVs can alternatively consist of, for example, a 30-mm cannon, mortar, smoke grenades or land mines. Significant progress can also be observed in the development of humanoid robotic systems that do not yet have the defence and ability to conduct effective combat operations.

As part of ongoing research into the use of the C-UGVs, 8 current or former commanders of reconnaissance, motorized, mechanized and tank units with experience in foreign military operations in Iraq and Afghanistan were contacted and interviewed using a semi-structured interview. The commanders were asked about the tactical and technical requirements of the vehicles in a UGV swarm, with regard to the methods of conducting current military operations and the aim to develop previously identified characteristics. The commanders also considered the effective weapon system of the vehicle, methods of control, tasking and navigation on the battlefield. An equally important part of the questions focused on the possibilities of using a C-UGV swarm in current operations, or to predict their use in the future and to address tactical situations in Sect. 4.

In terms of flexibility and variability of use, the most efficient setup for mobility that was proposed consisted of a combined chassis, consisting of a caterpillar chassis as a base, supplemented by retractable wheels for moving on roads or robotic legs for moving over very rough terrain. Minimum noise and maximum range of the vehicle will be ensured by using a hybrid drive, consisting of a gas and electric motor. The batteries will be recharged by solar panels; their power will be increased by telescopic unfolding to the sides. Sensory equipment must include optoelectronic, thermal and night vision devices, laser rangefinders and laser radar for direct field navigation. The effective destruction of priority targets will ensure an anti-tank set of guided missiles in combination with a machine gun, with semi-automated fire control. Similarly, the UGV swarm activity control will be in a semi-autonomous mode with the swarm operator specifying the sub-objectives of the activities. The use of combat UGVs is the most effective in tactical activities where their main role is oriented around speed, loss of life, risk, and coordination of maneuvers. It is a maneuver defence, the implementation of a trap, reconnaissance and diversionary activities in the rear of the enemy, or leading the enemy into a trap. As a tactical advantage, some commanders suggested including different types of C-UGVs in each swarm group. The reason was mainly the different types and number of carried weapon systems on the vehicle, usable for specific tactical activities.

4   The Offensive Maneuvers of MCS CZ

The Maneuver control system CZ (MCS CZ), developed at the University of Defense of the Army of the Czech Republic, can be used to plan the axes of the coordinated maneuvers of the C-UGV swarm. MCS CZ allows for the calculation of tactical maneuver axes that can be used for autonomous vehicles or unit maneuvers on the battlefield. It uses a raster representation of tactical and geographical data from the area of operation, based on the Digital Model of Territory and Digital Model of Relief, see [45–47]. Rapid space evaluation is performed using mathematical algorithms and criterion evaluations of the Model of the optimal maneuver route, described in [31]. The model calculates the cost surface of trafficability including a combined influence of important factors of the situation. The model of the optimal maneuver route uses the Tactical Decision Support System (TDSS), developed at the University of Defense in 2006, see [48], as the basis for the calculation of maneuver axes.

The model of optimal maneuver route evaluates the area trafficability of the operation based on the raster layers of the effects of the battlefield situation, as shown in Fig. 1. The basis for calculating the Cumulative Cost Surface (CCS) is the Cost Surface of the surface and terrain vegetation (CS_1), which includes the effect of different types of terrain. Each of these surface terrain types allows for different UGV maneuver velocities, specific military techniques or units. Specific velocities on different types of surfaces of specific military equipment or units can be stored in a database. The influence of terrain relief in the CCS calculation is implemented by the Altimetry Vertical Factor (VF_2). VF_2 expresses both the marginal trafficability slopes for the considered types of military units and machinery, as well as the degree of acceleration or deceleration of the maneuver on the slope. The impacts of the weather on the overall trafficability of the area, in terms of rain and snow, are included in the model using the Horizontal Weather Factor (HF_3). The Horizontal Factor of Enemy Influence (HF_4) defines the areas endangered by enemy units. The Horizontal Factor of Own Units (HF_5) represents the supporting effect of friendly units in a military operation on the terrain trafficability through tasked maneuvered units. Military weapon systems units of both friendly and enemy forces can also be stored in a database, characterized by the distance of the effective range of weapons. In combination with other mathematical models, the model of optimal maneuver route then calculates the final axis of the tactical maneuver in MCS CZ, see the equation below (1).

$$CCS = \frac{CS_1}{VF_2 \cdot HF_3 \cdot \min(1, HF_4 \cdot HF_5)} \tag{1}$$

To do this, it uses raster models of digital data, criteria evaluation of individual effects of the situation on the battlefield and map algebra to calculate their combined effect on the overall trafficability of the terrain. The characteristic information of individual raster layers can be constantly actualized based on their indented development. The combined effect of all raster layers of battlefield situation effects is expressed in the cost surface of the trafficability in the form of a numerical matrix. The numerical value of each cell of the matrix then indicates the calculated time required to overcome it, expressed in hundredths of a second. If a matrix cell is evaluated as impassable by a combined calculation of all influences, for example due to exceeding the terrain slope or a waterlogged terrain surface, its value is "infinitely high". Based on the cell values of the CCS trafficability matrix, the model calculates a time-optimized safe maneuver axis, using the algorithm for finding the shortest path. For this, TDSS uses the combination of Floyd-Warshall and Dijkstra's principle, described in [49–51].

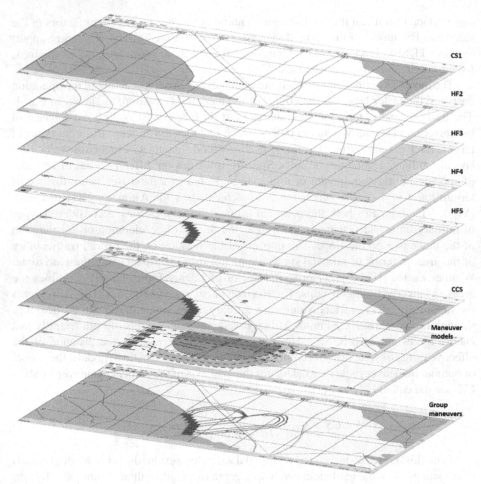

Fig. 1. Layers of the MCS CZ swarm maneuver model

The MCS CZ offers a calculation of four types of offensive maneuvers: envelopment, turning movement, frontal attack and attack by fire, which are described in Sect. 4.1 in detail. The course of their time-optimized and safe axis is specified by an invisible layer of impassable CS. The shape of the invisible impassable CS depends on the type of offensive maneuver and the distance D between the task maneuver unit of friendly forces and the target units of the enemy. Due to the necessary cooperation of frontal units and units performing offensive maneuvers, the maximum distance $D \leq 1$ km. When calculating the envelope maneuver axis, the impenetrable space of the invisible layer is in the shape of a circle with a diameter of $D \leq 1$ km, between the positions of the maneuver units and the enemy's target unit. The impassable space specifying the turning movement maneuver has the shape of two semi-ellipsoids intersecting in the distance $D \leq 1$ km, and having the length 1.3D and width 0.5D. The attack by fire maneuver represents the fastest and safest axis of movement to the nearest edge of direct visibility to the target object or enemy unit. The last offensive maneuver is a frontal attack, which uses the Model of the optimal maneuver route to calculate its axis. The result is therefore the fastest and safest axis of the maneuver to the position of the enemy target unit on which the attack is aimed. If the offensive maneuver is calculated by MCS CZ for the same object or enemy unit for more maneuver units, then their individual axes in the final phase of the maneuver are guided in tactical width. The spacing between the individual axes is adjustable based on the size of the maneuver units, at a pre-set distance from the position of the target enemy.

4.1   The Swarm Offensive Maneuvers of MCS CZ

The swarm maneuver represents a joint maneuver of a group of units (organic companies, platoons, teams, or a group of UGVs), in order to coordinate the approach to the target object. The maneuver is planned for the whole unit (task force), with up to nine separate elements. The individual maneuver axes are then calculated on the basis of the subordination or organizational division of individual elements. The model is designed to calculate the maneuver of a swarm of units cooperating in a three-piece set of combat elements in the first sequence. Defined forces and resources can be organized into three groups of three elements.

Before starting the maneuver calculation, it is necessary to define the organizational structure of the three three-member sets of elements and the target area of the maneuver, or the object of the attack. Based on the size or type of the element (company, platoon or UGV), it is then necessary to adjust the width of the restricted zone, located on the sides of the routes of the unit's individual entities. The defined restricted zone creates tactical spacings of the formation maneuver axes. Its width should be set for each element separately. The total width of the impassable zone on both sides of the calculated maneuver route can take values such as 50 m for a UGV, 100 m for a squad or tank, 200 m for a platoon, and 400 m for a company. The distance of this restricted zone on the sides of the maneuver axis from the target position of the enemy can be set depending on the requirement to adhere to the tactical spacing of the formation.

It is possible to use all types of MCS CZ maneuvers for the C-UGV swarm maneuver, i.e., frontal attack, envelopment, turning movement and support by fire, see [33]. The spatial specifications of the calculation of all maneuvers remain the same as for the original MCS CZ maneuver models. However, the initial deployment of a C-UGV swarm may not always be in line with regular spacing, as is in the case study in Sect. 4. The tasked vehicles can be deployed over a larger area and distance. Furthermore, individual groups of vehicles can be tasked to perform various tactical maneuvers. As a solution, the exact specification of the distribution structure of up to three three-member groups is offered for the calculation of the maneuver of the whole swarm. A fixed position in the group structure is important for the order of calculation of the axes of individual vehicles. To start the calculation of maneuver variants, the number 1 belongs to the leading element of the whole group/unit. Numbers 2 and 3 belong to the right and left neighbour of the three-member subgroup of the centre element of the unit maneuver. Number 4 is for the central element of the wing subgroup, according to the considered variant of the unit formation. Numbers 5 and 6 are assigned to their right and left neighbour in this first/right subgroup. Number 7 then belongs to the centre element of the second wing three-member subgroup of the unit maneuver. Numbers 8 and 9 are assigned to the right and left elements of this subgroup.

The C-UGV swarm maneuver can be calculated for three individual groups of elements, for each of which a different MSC CZ maneuver can be selected, as shown in Fig. 2. The maneuver calculation of each subgroup starts with the axis of the centre element of each subgroup. The order of calculation of subgroup maneuvers can be chosen arbitrarily. Restricted zones in the vicinity of already calculated maneuver axes are included in the calculation of maneuver axes of other elements of the group. In the case of choosing the same type of maneuver for all three individual groups, the tactical distance of individual elements maneuvers of each swarm group can be met.

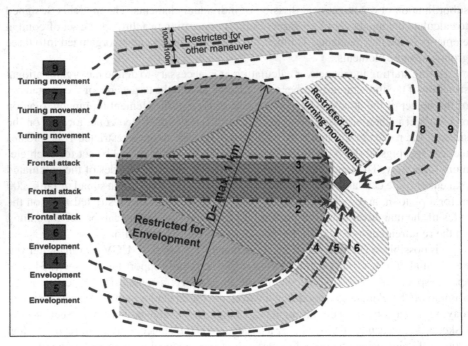

Fig. 2. Variant of multiple swarm maneuver models calculation of the MCS CZ

This means that a swarm of nine elements can also maneuver uniformly on a common target object, using one type of common maneuver. The calculation of the axes of the common type maneuver of the whole swarm then takes place according to the division into groups and in the order of numerical order of the unit's elements, from the leading central element with number 1 and then with numbers 2, 3, 4–6 and 7–9. In the case of deployment of autonomous vehicles which achieve the maximum effect by mass deployment of the entire swarm on a common goal, the calculations of the maneuver axes can be performed in order from the leading centre element with number 1 in sequence to number 9.

4.2   The Swarm Offensive Maneuver Models of MCS CZ

The least complicated calculation is the frontal attack maneuver. In the model, the maneuver calculation is initiated by calculating the maneuver axis of the central leading element of the unit formation, which imaginarily divides the calculated maneuver space into right and left parts, see Fig. 3, part A. After that, the calculation of the maneuver of the elements according to their organic and numerical classification into the unit's formation is carried out. The maneuver calculation begins by number 1 belonging to the leading centre element of the group/unit with its axis pointing through the centre of the formation directly to the target enemy. The right and left neighbours of a three-member subgroup of the centre element carry the numbers 2 and 3. Their routes are calculated to the right (element 2) and to the left (element 3) of the leading centre element (1). The number 4 belongs to the centre element of the first or right subgroup, depending on the considered variant of the unit formation. MCS CZ calculates its axis to the right of element 2. Numbers 5 and 6 are assigned to the elements in this first/right subgroup and their axes are calculated to the right of number 4. Number 7 represents the central element of the third/left three-member subgroup. The axis of number 7 is calculated to the left of element number 3. The axes of elements number 8 and 9 are then calculated to the left of number 7.

The axis of each calculated maneuver becomes impassable for the other elements of the unit, at a set distance or 1000 m from the target enemy or closer. In MCS CZ, envelopment is defined by an impassable space with a diameter D, equal to the distance between the central guide element (1) of the unit formation, but not greater than 1000 m. In the case of the envelopment maneuver calculation for element groups, the diameter of the impassable space between the centre element of the unit formation is also equal to or less than 1000 m. After calculating the maneuver of the centre element, the impermeable space of diameter/width D widens perpendicular to the straight distance between the centre element and the target point, on the opposite side to the first calculated maneuver of the centre element. This procedure will ensure a side-oriented envelopment maneuver of all elements of the group. This will be followed by the calculation of the maneuver of the elements of the whole unit according to their order in the organizational structure of the unit, in the order of calculation 2, 3, 4–6 and 7–9, see Fig. 3, part B.

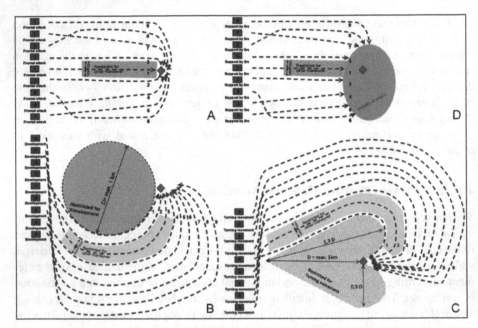

Fig. 3. Swarm variant of multiple maneuver models of the MCS CZ

The turning movement in MCS CZ is defined by the impassable space of a semi-ellipsoid with a length equal to 1.3 D and a width with a value of 0.5 D. The maximum distance D is set to 1 km. The calculation of the turning movement maneuver axis is started by the central element (1) of the group of unit's elements or three-member subgroup. After calculating the axis of the centre element, a space with width D will expand to the unfinished distance, on the opposite side to the course of the turning movement maneuver, and will be counted as impassable in further calculations. The axes of the turning movement maneuvers of the other elements of the unit will therefore be led to the same side from the direct distance between the unit position and the target area as the maneuver of the central leading element of the unit, in the calculation order 2, 3, 4–6 and 7–9, see Fig. 3, part C.

Support by fire is defined in MCS CZ as the shortest path to the nearest edge of direct visibility of the target enemy, in the distance of effective firing of own forces and resources. The calculation of its axis will start again by calculating the axis of the central leading element of the unit. This will be followed by calculations of maneuvers of other elements in the unit, according to the order in the structure of the unit and with respect to tactical distances between elements, in the form of restricted spaces, in the order of calculation 2, 3, 4–6 and 7–9, see Fig. 3, part D.

5   Case Studies of the Combat Use of the UGV Group

In the case studies, tactical scenarios will be simulated and modelled, in which the possibility of using a group of nine C-UGVs as a separate combat element on the battlefield in conducting offensive operations will be verified. The velocities on the individual types of surfaces for the C-UGV (practical tests performed by the Yamaha Grizzly 700 EPS ATV) were set to values enabling safe vehicle control, navigation and orientation in the surrounding situation, maneuvering in formation and effective use of the weapon system. A value of 0.5 km.h^{-1} was set for all types of paved and unpaved roads. Any prolonged road movement in the scenarios described below is not tactically appropriate. By setting this velocity, the priority of road usage was suppressed. In the built-up area, all movement was restricted due to significant restrictions and disadvantages resulting from the deployment of current C-UGVs in these areas. Likewise, movement on water areas that do not allow the C-UGVs to effectively conduct combat operations was restricted. For forests, the average velocity was set to 1 km.h^{-1}, 7 km.h^{-1} for green fields and pastures and 10 km.h-1 for fields.

5.1   Case Study 1

In the first tactical scenario, the Intelligence Surveillance Reconnaissance (ISR) identified the SAM (Surface to Air Missile) anti-aircraft missile system in a pre-built fire position. The swarm (platoon) of C-UGVs moving along an unpaved road at the edge of the forest in a north-easterly direction, has been tasked with the immediate destruction of this anti-aircraft system. The missile system has not yet opened fire. The commander-operator of the C-UGV swarm decided to quickly divide the swarm into three groups. Using MCS CZ, they calculated a different swarm maneuver for each of the groups, in the form of a frontal attack for the middle group, envelopment for the left-wing group and turning movement for the right-wing group. The spatial course of the C-UGV maneuvers is shown in Fig. 4.

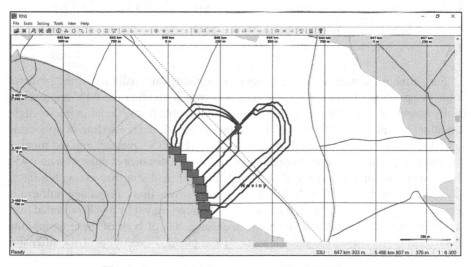

Fig. 4. Swarm multiple maneuver of the C-UGV group

The maneuvering times of individual vehicles, direct and real distance, as well as the time measured by the ATV in the field calculated by MCS CZ are given in Table 1. MCS CZ performed the calculation of the axes of the coordinated maneuver of the C-UGV swarm in 2 min. Pre-calculated maneuver times can be used to time-synchronize the maneuver of individual groups and C-UGVs so that they act on the anti-aircraft missile system in the required time and space. However, with regard to visibility from the position of the enemy calculated by MCS CZ, see Fig. 5, all C-UGVs initiate the maneuver at the same time.

Table 1. Characteristics of the swarm multiple maneuver of the C-UGV group

C-UGV No.	Enemy unit	C-UGV maneuver	Direct distance (meter)	Maneuver distance (meter)	Calculated time of maneuver	Real time in terrain
1	SAM	Turning movement	441	976	5:42	6:15
2	SAM	Turning movement	407	888	5:04	5:22
3	SAM	Turning movement	373	805	4:28	4:43
4	SAM	Frontal attack	341	347	1:53	1:48
5	SAM	Frontal attack	316	316	1:37	1:35
6	SAM	Frontal attack	309	309	1:32	1:27
7	SAM	Envelopment	306	483	3:52	3:43
8	SAM	Envelopment	314	511	3:34	3:35
9	SAM	Envelopment	323	515	3:23	3:20

Furthermore, by measuring the subjective audibility and visibility of the observer in the fire position of the anti-aircraft system, it was found that the ATV approach is faintly audible at a distance of about 500 m and noticeable from 300 m, in line-of-sight conditions and at up to 4000 rpm of the engine. In Fig. 5, the borderline of noticeable audibility is represented by a yellow dashed line. The ATV approaching and moving was observed, without the use of optical instruments, at a distance of approximately 450 m on the surface of a grassy meadow and agricultural field after harvest with a forest background. The height of an ATV with crouching driver in a camouflage uniform is approximately 160 cm. In Fig. 5, the line of sight is represented by a yellow dotted line. The above-described results of subjective measurements of both of these unmasking characteristics supported the effectiveness of the planned execution of the offensive maneuver of C-UGV group.

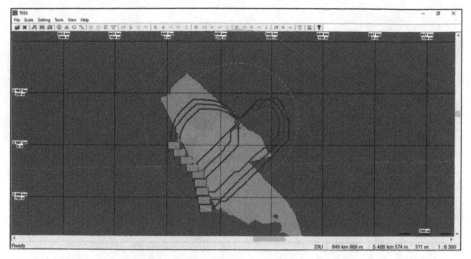

Fig. 5. Areas of enemy visibility and audibility of three C-UGV maneuvers

During the practical implementation of the scenario, the observer at the firing place observed and heard almost all C-UGVs only after they came out of the forest. They were not, however, able to predict the intent of their maneuver. Under the pressure of approaching vehicles, the observer began to move faster to the northeast, where they would be caught up with the C-UGV No. 3.

After getting acquainted with the scenario of the tactical situation and geographical characteristics of the terrain, the addressed unit commanders evaluated the maneuver calculated by MCS CZ as feasible and tactically effective. The decision-making process to plan the same UGV swarm maneuver would take them 10 to 20 min. Its final design would be highly dependent on information regarding the current position of the anti-aircraft missile system and the movement of enemy units in the vicinity. In the opinion of the unit commanders, the control of each C-UGV would have to be handled by an operator who would receive the axis of the planned maneuver from the C-UGV unit commander. Operators would use vehicle sensors, satellite navigation and real-time transmission of vehicle position data to the control computer station to accurately implement the axis of each tactical spacing maneuver. It would be effective if the commander of the C-UGV unit would share the planned maneuver axis with the control computer stations of the operators.

5.2 Case Study 2

The second tactical scenario is based on the same situation of the identified enemy anti-aircraft missile system and friendly group of C-UGVs. However, the missile system is ready to fire and the priority of its immediate destruction is very high. The commander-operator, therefore, decided on the fastest possible approach for the destruction of the missile system. For all C-UGVs, the frontal attack maneuver was chosen, see Fig. 6.

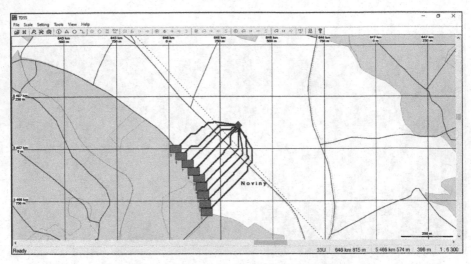

Fig. 6. Swarm single maneuver of the C-UGV group

The successful destruction of the enemy missile system by a friendly swarm of C-UGVs depends on the element of surprise and the mass deployment of all nine vehicles in a width of approximately 400 m. The distance between the C-UGVs and the enemy missile system is between 309–441 m. The MCS CZ calculated the axes of the coordinated maneuver of the C-UGV in 70 s. Vehicles from the centre and right-wing group of C-UGVs are the first to arrive in the area of firing position or in the presumed area of retreating targets, see Table 2.

Table 2. Characteristics of the swarm single maneuver of the C-UGV group

C-UGV No.	Enemy unit	C-UGV maneuver	Direct distance (meter)	Maneuver distance (meter)	Calculated time of maneuver	Real time in terrain
1	SAM	Frontal attack	441	553	3:56	4:07
2	SAM	Frontal attack	407	488	2:55	2:58
3	SAM	Frontal attack	373	439	2:28	2:23
4	SAM	Frontal attack	341	347	1:53	1:48
5	SAM	Frontal attack	316	316	1:37	1:35

(continued)

Table 2. (*continued*)

C-UGV No.	Enemy unit	C-UGV maneuver	Direct distance (meter)	Maneuver distance (meter)	Calculated time of maneuver	Real time in terrain
6	SAM	Frontal attack	309	309	1:32	1:27
7	SAM	Frontal attack	306	320	1:34	1:30
8	SAM	Frontal attack	314	322	1:51	1:56
9	SAM	Frontal attack	323	360	2:02	2:11

The enemy observes the approaching friendly C-UGV immediately after it leaves the wooded area, see Fig. 7. In the case of the enemy remaining in the firing position, the time of their destruction and approach to the firing position conducted by the friendly C-UGV is the same. The advantage of this option is the execution simplicity, without the need for further calculations and coordination with other types of tactical offensive maneuvers. The disadvantage, however, is the one-sided frontal attack of the C-UGV swarm, lacking in a depth of maneuver. If the enemy reacted immediately and rapidly, the anti-aircraft system of the enemy could get away.

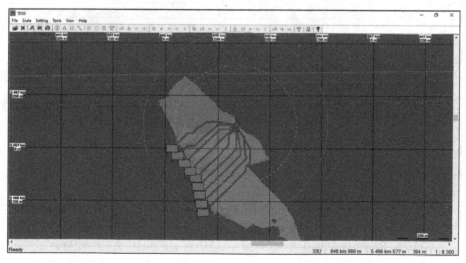

Fig. 7. Areas of enemy visibility and audibility of a single C-UGV maneuver

After getting acquainted with the time specifics of this tactical scenario, the addressed unit commanders evaluated the maneuver calculated by MCS CZ as feasible and very tactically effective. The decision-making process to plan the axes of the same UGV swarm maneuver would take them 4 to 7 min. As in the previous tactical scenario, the control of each C-UGV would have to be handled by an operator who would primarily receive the position of the target, the initial direction of the maneuver, and coordination instructions for its implementation from the C-UGV unit commander. To implement the maneuver of each vehicle and to maintain tactical distances, operators would use vehicle sensors, satellite navigation, real-time transmission of vehicle position data to control computer stations and intuitive coordination of vehicle movement during a frontal attack maneuver. The operator's intuitive coordination of vehicle movement could cause irregular frontal attack line-ups and excessive clustering or delaying of vehicles in the line-up.

5.3   Case Study 3

In another tactical scenario simulation, the C-UGV group (platoon) moves along an unpaved road at the edge of the forest in a north-easterly direction, in the same position as in the previous two cases. At the same time, air reconnaissance aircraft identified three enemy armoured vehicles moving north. The enemy's vehicles suddenly stopped in open terrain due to a technical defect in one of them. The commander/operator of the C-UGV group decided to destroy the standing armoured vehicles. Using MCS CZ, they quickly created the axes of a coordinated group maneuver, in order to attack the enemy, see Fig. 8.

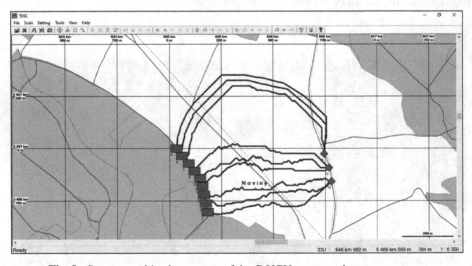

Fig. 8. Swarm combined maneuver of the C-UGV group against a group target

The distance between the C-UGV group and the enemy vehicles is between 613–713 m. The calculation of the axes of the coordinated maneuver of the C-UGV swarm took 3 min. This scenario was practically only partially verified, always only for the centre

Table 3. Characteristics of the swarm combined maneuver against a group target

C-UGV No.	Enemy unit No.	C-UGV maneuver	Direct distance (meter)	Maneuver distance (meter)	Calculated time of maneuver	Real time in terrain
1	13	Frontal attack	613	675	2:20	none
2	13	Frontal attack	613	694	2:55	3:16
3	13	Frontal attack	617	678	2:56	none
4	12	Frontal attack	617	696	2:34	none
5	12	Frontal attack	625	727	2:03	2:10
6	12	Frontal attack	650	772	2:46	none
7	11	Envelopment	656	1103	3:35	none
8	11	Envelopment	686	1169	3:27	3:44
9	11	Envelopment	713	1255	3:29	none

vehicle axis of each of the C-UGV groups. The maneuver times and distances of the individual vehicles are listed in Table 3.

According to MCS CZ calculations, the centre group friendly C-UGV will be the first to approach the convoy of enemy vehicles. The maneuver of the right-wing group will be a few tens of seconds slower. However, the approach of both groups at the same time is more tactically appropriate, which means that the commander-operator must deliberately delay the maneuver of the middle group by approximately 17 s. The terrain is open yet slightly undulating, which affects the visibility of the enemy and allows a hidden approach of the C-UGV group in 30–60% of their maneuver axis, see Fig. 9. Together with the ability to detect the motion of the C-UGV (at a distance of 450 m), the terrain allows the centre group a covert approach within approximately 50% of the calculated maneuver and to both wing groups within approximately 50% of the length of their maneuver.

The visibility and maneuverability borderline of the C-UGV maneuver are other elements that, if exceeded coordinately, can achieve the simultaneous approach of all C-UGV vehicles into the enemy convoy area from different directions and take advantage of the destructive effects of all weapon systems at the same time. After getting acquainted with the scenario of the tactical situation, the addressed unit commanders evaluated the maneuver calculated by MCS CZ as feasible and tactically achievable. The decision-making process to plan the same UGV swarm maneuver would take them 15 to 25 min. As in previous tactical scenarios, the control of each C-UGV would have to be handled by an operator who would receive the planned maneuver axis from the C-UGV unit commander to the computer control station. The final execution of the C-UGV swarm maneuver would again depend on information regarding the current position of the enemy vehicles convoy and the movement of enemy units in the vicinity. The critical element of the C-UGV swarm maneuver in this case will be the uncertainty of the enemy

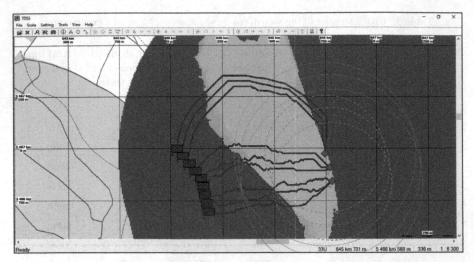

Fig. 9. Areas of enemy visibility and audibility of swarm C-UGV maneuvers

forces' actions in solving the technical defect on one of the vehicles and in observing the approaching C-UGV, as well as the greater maneuvering distance.

6 Conclusion

Effective coordinated use of the C-UGV swarm, as well as the maneuver of the entire swarm on the battlefield, could be performed using MCS CZ. The case studies described above show possible tactical situations that can be solved by effectively using the C-UGV swarm with maneuver axes calculated by MCS CZ. With its help, the commanders can obtain an effective tool for their command and control system that is able to evaluate the tactical situation on the battlefield in terms of trafficability very quickly and on this basis generate maneuver axes of the C-UGV swarm. Its importance increases mainly in situations with high time requirements for creating time and safety-optimized decisions. In the case studies, the times of the C-UGV swarm maneuver axes calculation using MCS CZ, compared to the fastest times of the commander's decision-making process, MCS CZ took 20–30% less time. At the same time, the calculated maneuver axes of individual C-UGVs uploaded into their control units represent, with the use of GPS, a very effective way of controlling vehicles on the battlefield. MCS CZ, in cooperation with onboard sensors and the operation of modern weapon systems of autonomous robotic systems, can bring considerable operational efficiency to the 21st-century battlefield, which in many areas of combat control exceeds the capabilities of people-soldiers-commanders. More C-UGV deployments to perform risky and time-consuming tasks can be expected in future military operations. However, the tactics of using C-UGVs currently have a number of critical shortcomings that need to be addressed. The most prominent of these are the continuous secure connection between the operator-commander and all C-UGV swarms on the battlefield, as well as their long-term sustainability in the operation.

An encrypted satellite connection is offered as an effective option for performing dynamic tasks in various types of terrain, as well as for possible deployment in the rear of enemy units. Especially the last option of C-UGV deployment places considerable demands on long-term sustainability, especially in terms of performing operational maintenance and ammunition replenishment. Autonomy in performing partial tactical activities, including precise navigation in very rough terrain, can be seen as a challenge in the combat use of the C-UGV. To achieve the autonomy of C-UGV activities, artificial intelligence algorithms will be used, which will be critically dependent on sufficiently relevant tactical-geographical data of the situation in the operational area. Perhaps the biggest challenge in the area of autonomous combat use of the C-UGV will be the decision-making process on target elimination. Will the vehicle system decide based on information from onboard sensors, enemy target databases and fire control system parameters? From the point of view of the deployed C-UGV swarm operator-commander workload, this would be an effective solution, if only the corresponding enemy targets are always selected for destruction.

Sub-algorithms for planning of detour or retreating route, as well as routes for offensive maneuvers, can be implemented in the activity planning system of existing robotic platforms. With its use, it is possible to model and choose a route of movement, optimized according to the technical state of the robotic systems, speed and safety. In the future, the continuation of research in this area will be focused on the practical testing of algorithms implemented in the robotic systems used, as well as the use of geographical data currently captured, for example, by LIDAR sensors onboard UAVs. The paper also can be used for further research in the field of tactical use of combat unmanned ground vehicles as well as for starting to work on training and doctrinal publications.

References

1. Federated Mission Networking. NATO Allied Command Transformation. Brussels (2015). https://web.archive.org/web/20190128083216/https://www.act.nato.int/fmn
2. Brannsten, M.R., Johnsen, F.T., Bloebaum, T.H., Lund, K.: Toward federated mission networking in the tactical domain. Commun. Mag. **53**, 52–58 (2015). https://doi.org/10.1109/MCOM.2015.7295463
3. Siegel, N.G., Madni A.M.: The digital battlefield: a behind the scenes Look from the systems perspective. Proc. Comput. Sci. **28**, pp. 799–808 (2014). https://doi.org/10.1016/j.procs.2014.03.095
4. Steen-Tveit, K., Munkvold, B.E.: From common operational picture to common situational understanding: an analysis based on practitioner perspectives. Saf. Sci. **142**, 105381 (2021). https://doi.org/10.1016/j.ssci.2021.105381
5. Sophronides, P., Papadopoulou, C., Giaoutzi, M., Scholten, H.: A common operational picture in support of situational awareness for efficient emergency response operations. J. Future Internet **2**, 10–35 (2017). https://doi.org/10.18488/journal.102.2017.21.10.35
6. Schachter, B.J.: Automatic target recognition, no. 3, p. 330. SPIE Press, Bellingham (2018). https://doi.org/10.1117/3.2315926. ISBN 9781510618572
7. The Buzz. [Top 10 Unmanned Ground Combat Vehicles (UGCVs), Top Military Robots in the World (2019)] In: YouTube, 23 November 2019
8. Top 10 military robots and unmanned ground vehicles in the world. RoboticsBiz. 19 March 2020. https://roboticsbiz.com/top-10-military-robots-and-unmanned-ground-vehicles-in-the-world/
9. Top 10 best military robots in the world, Auto journalism, Jim Carrey, 7 June 2021. https://autojournalism.com/top-10-best-military-robots-in-the-world/

10. Feickert, A., Kapp, L., Elsea, J.K., Harris, L.A.: U.S. ground forces robotics and autonomous systems (RAS) and artificial intelligence (AI): considerations for congress, Washington D.C., pp. 47 (2018). https://digital.library.unt.edu/ark:/67531/metadc1442984/m1/

11. Bērziņa, I., et al.: Digital infantry battlefield solution, research and innovation, part III, Milrem robotics, Tallinn, Estonia, p. 120 (2019). ISBN 978-9934-567-37-7

12. Andžāns, M., et al.: Digital infantry battlefield solution, introduction to ground robotics, part I, Milrem robotics, Tallinn, Estonia, p. 128 (2016). ISBN 978-9984-583-92-1

13. The U.S. Army Robotic and Autonomous Systems Strategy, U.S. Army Training and Doctrine Command, p. 43. Fort Eustis (2017)

14. Unmanned Systems Integrated Roadmap FY2017-2042, p. 58 (2017). https://www.defenseda ily.com/wp-content/uploads/post_attachment/206477.pdf

15. Harder, B.R.: Automated battle planning for combat models with maneuver and fire support, Dissertation, p. 477. Naval Postgraduate School, Monterey, California (2017)

16. Ivan, J., Potužák, J., Šotnar, J.: Dělostřelecká rekognoskace pro zabezpečení činnosti autonomních zbraňových systémů a základní požadavky na rekognoskační jednotky. Vojenské rozhledy 28(4), 063–077 (2019). ISSN 1210-3292 (print), pp. 2336–2995. www.vojenskerozhledy.cz, https://doi.org/10.3849/2336-2995.28.2019.04.063-077

17. Pokonieczny, K., Rybansky, M.: Method of developing the maps of passability for unmanned ground vehicles. In: 9th IGRSM International Conference and Exhibition on Geospatial & Remote Sensing (IGRSM 2018), p. 169. IOP Conference Series: Earth and Environmental Science, Kuala Lumpur (2018). https://doi.org/10.1088/1755-1315/169/1/012027. ISSN 1755-1307

18. Rybansky, M.: Trafficability analysis through vegetation. In: Conference Proceedings of ICMT 2017, pp. 207–210. Institute of Electrical and Electronics Engineers Inc., Piscataway (2017). https://doi.org/10.1109/MILTECHS.2017.7988757. ISBN 978-1-5386-1988-9

19. Rada, J., Rybansky, M., Dohnal, F.: The impact of the accuracy of terrain surface data on the navigation of off-road vehicles. ISPRS Int. J. Geo-Inf. 10, 106 (2021). https://doi.org/10.3390/ijgi10030106

20. Rada, J., Rybansky, M., Dohnal, F.: Influence of quality of remote sensing data on vegetation passability by terrain vehicles. ISPRS Int. J. Geo-Inf. 9, 684 (2020). https://doi.org/10.3390/ijgi9110684

21. Rybansky, M.: Determination the ability of military vehicles to override vegetation. J. Terrramech. 91, 129–138 (2020). https://doi.org/10.1016/j.jterra.2020.06.004

22. Wermelinger, M., Fankhauser, P., Diethelm, R., Krüsi, P., Siegwart, R., Hutter, M.: Navigation planning for legged robots in challenging terrain. Daejeon, South Korea, pp. 1184–1189 (2016). https://doi.org/10.1109/IROS.2016.7759199

23. Kanoulas, D., Tsagarakis, N., Vona, M.: Curved patch mapping and tracking for irregular terrain modeling: application to bipedal robot foot placement. Robot. Auton. Syst. 13–30 (2019). https://doi.org/10.1016/j.robot.2019.05.012

24. Li, Z., Zeng, J., Chen, S., Sreenath, K.: Vision-aided autonomous navigation of bipedal robots in height-constrained environments. arXiv e-prints (2021). arxiv:2109.05714

25. Gilroy, S., et al.: Autonomous navigation for quadrupedal robots with optimized jumping through constrained obstacles. In: 2021 IEEE 17th International Conference on Automation Science and Engineering (CASE), pp. 2132–2139 (2021). https://doi.org/10.1109/CASE49 439.2021.9551524

26. Suryamurthy, V., Raghavan, V., Laurenzi, A., Tsagarakis, N., Kanoulas, D.: Terrain segmentation and roughness estimation using rgb data: path planning application on the CENTAURO robot. In: The 19th IEEE/RAS International Conference on Humanoid Robots, Humanoids (2019). https://doi.org/10.1109/Humanoids43949.2019.9035009

27. Hodický, J., Castrogiovanni, R., Lo Presti, A.: Modelling and simulation challenges in the urbanized area. In: Proceedings of the 2016 17th International Conference on Mechatronics - Mechatronika (ME), pp. 429–432. Czech Technical University in Prague, Prague (2016). ISBN 978-80-01-05882-4

28. Hodický, J., Procházka, D.: Challenges in the implementation of autonomous systems into the battlefield. In: Proceedings of the 2017 International Conference on Military Technologies (ICMT), pp. 743–747. Institute of Electrical and Electronics Engineers Inc., Piscataway (2017). https://doi.org/10.1109/MILTECHS.2017.7988855. ISBN 978-1-5386-1988-9

29. Braun, W.G., Nossal, K.R., Hlatky, S.: Robotics and military operations. In.: Kingston Conference on International Security, p. 77. U.S. Army War College, New York (2018). https://doi.org/10.1117/12.720422. ISBN 1-58487-780-4

30. Tilenni, G.: Unmanned ground vehicles for combat support. European Security & Defence, pp. 74–77. Mittler Report Verlag, Bonn (2019). ISSN 1617-7983. https://euro-sd.com/2019/11/articles/15191/unmanned-ground-vehicles-for-combat-support/

31. Nohel, J.: Possibilities of raster mathematical algorithmic models utilization as an information support of military decision making process. In: Mazal, J. (ed.) MESAS 2018. LNCS, vol. 11472, pp. 553–565. Springer, Cham (2019). https://doi.org/10.1007/978-3-030-14984-0_41. ISSN 0302-9743, ISBN 978-3-030-14984-0

32. Nohel, J., Stodola, P., Flasar, Z.: Model of the optimal maneuver route [online first], pp. 79–100. IntechOpen, London (2019). https://doi.org/10.5772/intechopen.85566. https://www.intechopen.com/online-first/model-of-the-optimal-maneuver-route

33. Nohel, J., Flasar, Z.: Maneuver control system CZ. In: Mazal, J., Fagiolini, A., Vasik, P. (eds.) MESAS 2019. LNCS, vol. 11995, pp. 379–388. Springer, Cham (2020). https://doi.org/10.1007/978-3-030-43890-6_31. ISBN 978-3-030-43889-0

34. Hodický, J., Procházka, D., Procházka, J.: Training with and of autonomous system - modelling and simulation approach. In: Mazal, J. (ed.) MESAS 2017. LNCS, vol. 10756, pp. 383–391. Springer, Cham (2018). https://doi.org/10.1007/978-3-319-76072-8_27. ISSN 0302-9743, ISBN 978-3-319-76071-1

35. Hodicky, J., Prochazka, D.: Modelling and simulation paradigms to support autonomous system operationalization. In: Mazal, J., Fagiolini, A., Vasik, P. (eds.) MESAS 2019. LNCS, vol. 11995, pp. 361–371. Springer, Cham (2020). https://doi.org/10.1007/978-3-030-43890-6_29. ISSN 0302-9743. ISBN 978-303043889-0

36. Drozd, J., Stodola, P., Rak, L., Zahradníček, P., Hodický, J.: Effectiveness evaluation of aerial reconnaissance in battalion force protection operation using the constructive simulation. J. Defense Model. Simul. 1–15 (2021). https://doi.org/10.1177/15485129211040373. ISSN 1548-5129

37. Zahradnicek, P., Rak, L.: Combat UGV: the challenge of their implementation in combat units. In: International Conference Knowledge-Based Organization, vol. 27, pp. 105–109 (2021). https://doi.org/10.2478/kbo-2021-0096

38. Rak, L., Zahranicek, P., Polach, M.: The effectiveness of infantry squad combat and pre-combat formations for warfighting. In: International Conference Knowledge-Based Organization, vol. 27, no. 1, pp.106–111 (2021). https://doi.org/10.2478/kbo-2021-0017

39. Kristalova, D., et al.: Geographical data and algorithms usable for decision-making process. In: Hodicky, J. (ed.) MESAS 2016. LNCS, vol. 9991, pp. 226–241. Springer, Cham (2016). https://doi.org/10.1007/978-3-319-47605-6_19

40. Matejka, J.: Robot as a member of combat unit – an utopia or reality for ground forces? Adv. Milit. Technol. 15(1), 7–24 (2019). https://doi.org/10.3849/aimt.01332

41. Vichore, H., Gurumurthi, J., Nair, A., Choudhary, M., Ladge, L.: Self driven UGV for military requirements. In: Saini, H.S., Sayal, R., Govardhan, A., Buyya, R. (eds.) Innovations in Computer Science and Engineering. LNNS, vol. 171, pp. 87–98. Springer, Singapore (2021). https://doi.org/10.1007/978-981-33-4543-0_11

42. Thoresen, M., Nielsen, N.H., Mathiassen, K., Pettersen, K.Y.: Path planning for UGVs based on traversability hybrid A*. IEEE Robot. Autom. Lett. **6**(2), 1216–1223 (2021). https://doi.org/10.1109/LRA.2021.3056028

43. Stolfi, D.H., Brust, M., Danoy, G., Bouvry, P.: UAV-UGV-UMV multi-swarms for cooperative surveillance. Front. Robot. AI **8**, 1–11 (2021). https://doi.org/10.3389/frobt.2021.616950

44. Nohel, J., Stodola, P., Flasar, Z.: Combat UGV support of company task force operations. In: Mazal, J., Fagiolini, A., Vasik, P., Turi, M. (eds.) MESAS 2020. LNCS, vol. 12619, pp. 29–42. Springer, Cham (2021). https://doi.org/10.1007/978-3-030-70740-8_3. ISBN 978-3-030-70739-2

45. Wang, M., Chang, J., Zhang, J.: A review of digital relief generation techniques. In: ICCET 2010 - 2010 International Conference on Computer Engineering and Technology, Proceedings, p. 4 (2010). https://doi.org/10.1109/ICCET.2010.5485636

46. Hirt, C.: Digital terrain models. In: Grafarend, E. (eds.) Encyclopedia of Geodesy, pp. 1–6. Springer, Cham (2014). https://doi.org/10.1007/978-3-319-02370-0_31-1

47. Galin, E., et al.: A review of digital terrain modeling. Comput. Graph. Forum. **38**(2), 553–577 (2019). https://doi.org/10.1111/cgf.13657

48. Stodola, P., Mazal, J.: Tactical decision support system to aid commanders in their decision-making. In: Hodicky, J. (ed.) MESAS 2016. LNCS, vol. 9991, pp. 396–406. Springer, Cham (2016). https://doi.org/10.1007/978-3-319-47605-6_32. ISBN 978-3-319-47605-6

49. Risald, R., Mirino, A., Suyoto, S.: Best routes selection using Dijkstra and Floyd-Warshall algorithm, pp. 155–158. Indonesia, Surabaya (2017). https://doi.org/10.1109/ICTS.2017.8265662

50. Pradhan, A., Kumar, M.G.: Finding all-pairs shortest path for a large-scale transportation network using parallel Floyd-Warshall and parallel Dijkstra algorithms. J. Comput. Civ. Eng. **27**(3), 263–273 (2013). https://doi.org/10.1061/(ASCE)CP.1943-5487.0000220

51. Stodola, P., Mazal, J.: Planning algorithm and its modifications for tactical decision support systems. Int. J. Math. Comput. Simul. **6**(1), pp. 99–106 (2012). ISSN 1998-0159. http://www.naun.org/journals/mcs/17-474.pdf

Cooperative Use of Autonomous Systems to Monitor Toxic Industrial Materials and Face Accidents & Contamination Crises

Agostino G. Bruzzone[1,2,3](✉), Tommaso Vairo[4], Elvezia Maria Cepolina[2],
Marina Massei[1,2,3], Alberto De Paoli[1,2], Roberto Ferrari[1,2], Antonio Giovannetti[1,2],
and Massimo Pedemonte[2]

[1] DIME, Genoa University, via Opera Pia 15, 16145 Genova, Italy
agostino.bruzzone@simulationteam.com
[2] Springer Simulation Team, via Cadorna 2, 17100 Savona, Italy
[3] SIM4Future, via Trento 34, 16145 Genova, Italy
[4] ASL3, via Bertani 4, 16145 Genova, Italy
https://www.itim.unige.it, https://www.simulationteam.com,
https://www.sim4future.com, https://www.asl3.liguria.it/

Abstract. The use of Autonomous Systems to monitor pollution of TIC/TIM (Toxic Industrial Materials/Toxic Industrial Chemical) or to track a CBRN (Chemical, Biological, Radiological and Nuclear) crisis could help to quickly and effectively assess the risks, in addition the combination of these assets with Simulation and Artificial Intelligence further reinforces their effectiveness. This paper proposes an approach to apply their coordinated uses combining the Simulation results of diffusion models able to suggest where to go and what to measure with a Smart Control based on Intelligent Agents to direct their movements and actions. In this paper scenario are proposed different potential cases related to release of contaminants; the hypotheses move from an industrial Plants to hazardous material spill during transportations, while the specific case analyzed is related to Maritime Logistics. In this paper, it is introduced the scheme of the AI solution to be adopted in joint cooperation with simulation to control the drones devoted to assess the situation and improve reliable evaluation of crisis evolution.

Keywords: Modeling & Simulation · Autonomous Systems · CBRN & TIC/TIM Crisis

1 Introduction

In modern age the presence of TIC (Toxic Industrial Chemical) and TIM (Toxic Industrial Material) in proximity of urban areas represent a major threat and it should be required the use of innovative approach to develop sustainable plans that could be effectively activated to prevent and mitigate a crisis. It is evident that a spill of hazardous material in atmosphere in an industrial area not far from a Town, could require to evacuate a large part of it, transforming the Standing Operation Procedures in good practices with

J. Mazal et al. (Eds.): MESAS 2022, LNCS 13866, pp. 231–242, 2023.
https://doi.org/10.1007/978-3-031-31268-7_13

mostly no possibility to be put them in place due to the size of the problem and the time available. In addition, the resources equipped with sensors and vehicles to address this kind of crisis could have big problems to be deployed due to traffic congestion, limited number, availability, time to be activated, location, etc. Hereafter the authors propose the idea to use autonomous vehicles such as Rotary Wing UAV (unmanned aerial vehicle) to continuously monitor an area respect potential pollution source and CBRN (Chemical, biological, radiological and nuclear) threats. The idea is to use AI (Artificial Intelligence) to determine the actions and paths of UAV to optimize their reconnaissance as well as to combine it with simulation models devoted to predict the contaminant behavior to direct the drones on the expected contaminated perimeter while the real measures are used to correct the model parameters and hypotheses and to properly estimate the real effective situation as well as its expected evolution.

2 State of the Art

Several researches have been conducted in recent decades on the use of UAVs to monitor pollution and contaminants. The application of mobile robots to find the source of odor has become one of the hottest research topics. Compared with traditional robots, unmanned aerial vehicles (UAVs) are more flexible and safer, while low speed and dimension support a better performance on measurements by sensors. Therefore, the use of multi-UAVs to solve pollution source tracking is also a significant study [1]. In similar way, also the monitoring the water environment is also an important part of environmental monitoring. Hence, remote sensing of UAVs is a very promising approach for investigating water pollution in the regional area, as it takes into account both accuracy and spatial coverage [2].

Being able to determine the best trajectory and coordination of the multiple UAVs in these scenarios is crucial in order to optimize the timing, in case of a crisis prompt action is needed, and the efficiency of the data collected, the batteries in these instruments are often limited and wasting time collecting unnecessary data can be detrimental. The use of algorithms and simulations for this purpose is expected to be necessary to obtain real optimizations on these multiple aspects [3]. Obviously, the modeling and structure of drones plays a strong role in this regard. In similar way, the location and type of sensors to be equipped to the drone can radically change the impact the drone has on the mission [4].

The use of multiple drones in the field can be a further improvement to speed up the sensor deployment and data acquisition. Therefore, it should be outlined that as the number of drones increases, it turns more and more difficult their control and coordination, which can no longer be considered as a group of individual drones, but as a flock [5–7]. The need for coordination between the various means is increasingly driving us to the massive use of machine learning and AI processes [8, 9] and surely the addition of 3D simulation processes will lead to a broader view of the problem. Research has also taken many steps forward for modeling the diffusion of elements in the environment: several oil spill simulation models exist in the literature, which are used worldwide to simulate the evolution of an oil slick created from marine traffic, petroleum production, or other sources [10]; For air contaminant dispersion, simulations takes into account phenomenologically 3D wind flow and turbulence around buildings and using a stochastic Lagrangian particle dispersion model [11]. In facts, the authors have carried out research in this field as well as developed models such as IDRASS, T-REX and ALACRES2 that are used in this research as virtual experimental framework [12–14]. These scenarios already address CBRN problems in relation to use of Autonomous Systems and specifically of UAVs, AUVs (Autonomous Underwater Vehicles) and UGVs (unmanned Ground Vehicles) and allow the team to start from an established knowledge of the problem. The concepts proposed in this paper are inspired by innovative discipline defined as Strategic Engineering that uses AI, Modeling and Simulation (M&S) and Data analytics in closed loop with big data arriving from the field to support decisions [15].

3 The Problem and Innovative Solutions

Release of contaminants is subjected to many effects including transportation strongly depending on their own chemical and physical characteristics and weather conditions; in addition deposit on ground, dispersion and dissolution should be taken in consideration and also in this case the environmental conditions and component characteristics change drastically the behavior, without mentioning that the analysis of boundary conditions could include quite sophisticated models such as three dimensional wind equations, thermal inversion over towns, effect of orography and building respect the transportation that usually require to adopt hypotheses on some parameters; due to these elements a proper data flow subjected to analytics should be activated to properly understand the situation and correct potential misunderstandings and improper estimations on the above mentioned elements. Furthermore, even the characteristics of the contaminant are not always very well known, both in case of accidents and release of TIM as well as for the case of pollutants; this aspect is due to the fact that usually these events are not really expected so are consequences of improper operations, accidents, design errors, unfair management resulting into evidences for potentially accountable people that could be motivated to alter data or available information. In addition, in the case of accidents, it is evident that the emergency forces to react and eventually to compromise evidences to save lives and infrastructures, altering the data. Due to these reasons, even quantities and thermochemical characteristics of the contaminant are affected by uncertainty as all the other boundary conditions. In facts, it is necessary usually to adopt precautionary models devoted to face these crises in conservative way to be used in order to guarantee safety of people; therefore these choices could require to protect and/or evacuate areas so wide that it turns almost impossible to execute these operations in short time: in these case it could be useful to have also more reliable and precise measures and models of current dynamic status of the crisis as well as related forecasts. Due to these reasons, it is proposed an integrated approach where the classic procedures are still operational, but, on short terms, the combined use of AI, Simulation with UAV equipped with proper sensors are able to identify properly dangerous areas and to track their evolution and movement with good reliability and precision.

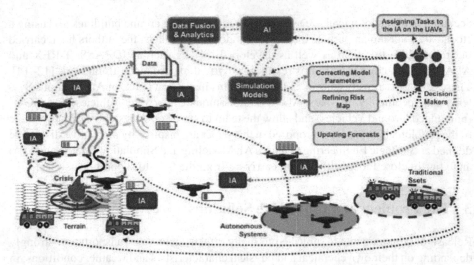

Fig. 1. General Architecture

The concept is that a swarm of small rotary wing drones is maintained in standby in the area ready to take off and proceed in cloud tracking directed by AI operating in synergy with simulation models and operational people on the field. The simulation models estimate the evolution of the contaminant and determine the dangerous areas, the AI identify the most critical points where to conduct measures by detectors and/or by sampling material on ground, while the Intelligent Agents directing each UAV provide a plan to operate in coordinated way on these investigations as proposed in Fig. 1. For instance, identified the edges of the contamination at the time the UAV are supposed to arrive in the area, each of them received a path to follow the evolving cloud starting from equally distributed points on the perimeter, so while they proceed they close the surveillance quickly and at the same time expand the range based on simulation estimations; therefore the results of the measures provided by the UAV probably will not match exactly simulation forecasts and the AI should correct the parameters of the simulation and the related contamination estimates in order to improve the result reliability. By this approach it turns possible to get better estimates on the contamination. It is evident that a similar approach could be used also for conducting routine check on pollutant levels in an area and that the creation of UAV Swarm and its location should affect the logic to propose sustainable and persistent monitoring during a crisis; indeed, in case of 6 drones, may be the time to fly the zone and return could guarantee to stay on the are just for 10 min and could suggest to deploy just 2 to be substituted at right time by other 2 and so on, while returning drones get their batteries recharged on the docking stations.

4 Alacres 2 and the Scenario

A contamination scenario has been defined in relation to the case of ALACRES2 Virtual Laboratory for Port Crisis Simulation in which it is possible to simulate and test a continuous monitoring of a TIM Crisis. In this simulator it turns possible to release toxic materials from tanks, ships, port plants and facilities inside the area that include also a large part of a town over different regional areas (South France, Mediterranean Areas), but it can also quickly extended to new locations [12]. Different algorithms could be used to analyze the situation and proceed to define the actions to be carried out by drones as well as the correction to models to be adopted. In this preliminary part of the research the authors define the scenario to be simulated and addressed by UAV swarm that focus on a simple release of oil and toxic component produced as result of a fire. Indeed, as amply known, the release of oil in case of ship accident is considered one of the most serious threats to coastal and marine environment exerting immediate and potential long-term consequences. The ALACRES2 platform is ready to be used to assess possible environmental consequences along the coast, to identify the possible causes of damage to the ship leading to loss of containment, to quantify the physical effects through fire consequence modeling in terms of radiation and toxic/pollutant/flammable dispersion. The consequences evaluation arising from the development of a fire on board of a ships was performed making reference to the source points corresponding to the identified ship location. As amply reported, rate and amount of smoke produced during a fire scenario depend upon the type and quality of material involved in the fire, combustion rate and the rate at which air is entrained into the plume.

4.1 Experimentation

For the accidental scenario evaluation, the 2F weather stability class was adopted for the consequence modelling, considering worst-case consequence in connection with flammable gas dispersion. The scenario is the random rupture of ship fuel tank causing the release of a flammable and toxic substance. The fuel characteristics are as follows:

- Flash Point 325 K;
- LFL (Lower Flammable Limit) 1.3%;
- UFL (Upper Flammable Limit) 6%;
- Vapor Pressure 2.17 mm Hg at 294 K;
- Specific Gravity 0.841 at 289 K;
- Boiling Point 556–611 K at 760 mm Hg;
- H_2O Solubility < 1 mg/mL at 294 K

Based on historical data, hole sizes corresponding to medium size leak and catastrophic failure were considered and a qualitative estimation of the frequency of each loss of containment event and associated scenarios was calculated using a combination of API 581 standard and event tree technique [16]. The corresponding fire evolution scenarios at each point were evaluated considering as well the propagation of the combustion fumes resulting from fire. A multi-method approach to effect evaluation was performed, utilizing standard software: EFFECTS 8 (TNO) for the evaluation of the impact zones of a fire; ALOFT-FT 3.1 (A Large Outdoor Fire plume Trajectory) of NIST, for the propagation of smoke caused by the fire and MIKE3 (DHI) for the marine dispersion of the spill. In the following figures the simulation results are represented. The scenario corresponding to a catastrophic leakage and subsequent fire was based on a maximum release rate corresponding to 4,000 kg/min. It can be argued that the maximum downwind extension of the hazardous area at 10% LFL is calculated as corresponding to 477 m. The whole numerical modelling study considered following combustion products on the basis of the utilized fuel: PM10; PM2.5; CO; CO2; SO2; VOC. The plume rises and extension concerning the combustion products referred to the worst-case event, impacting the environment are reproduced in Fig. 2. In Figs. 3 and 4, the heat radiation contour and the heat radiation versus distance, in Fig. 5 the radiation isopleth, and in Figs. 6, 7 and 8 the impact on people, represented by first, second and third degrees burning (Fig. 9).

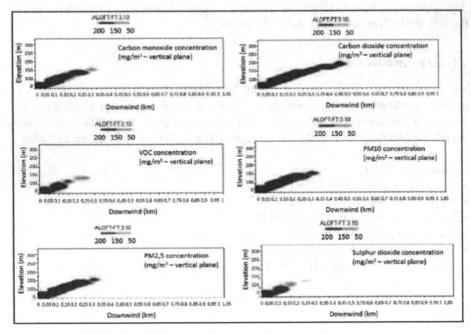

Fig. 2. Downwind concentration profiles of combustion products

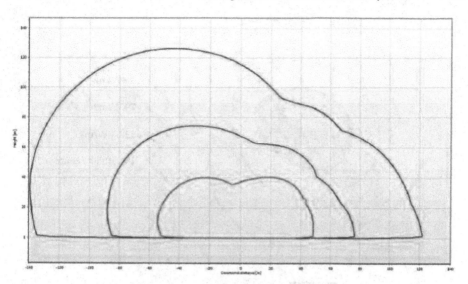

Fig. 3. Heat Radiation contour

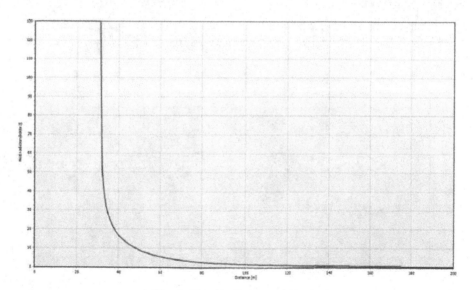

Fig. 4. Heat Radiation vs Distance

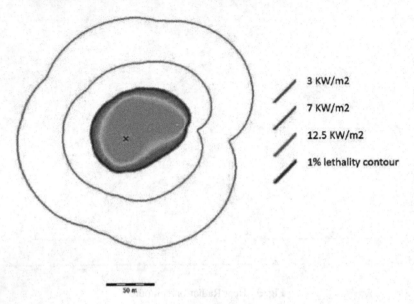

Fig. 5. Heat Radiation isopleth

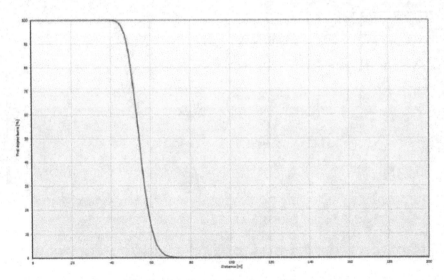

Fig. 6. First Degree Burning vs Distance

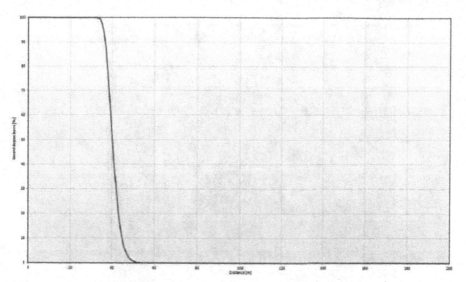

Fig. 7. Second Degree Burning vs Distance

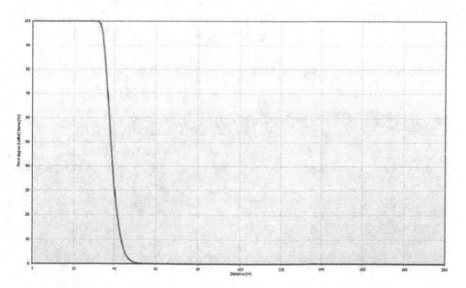

Fig. 8. Third Degree Burning vs Distance

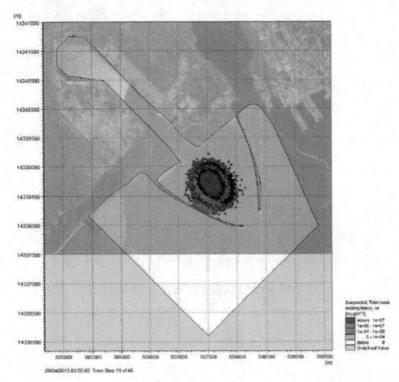

Fig. 9. Oil Spill

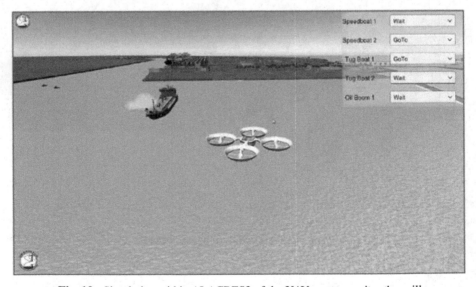

Fig. 10. Simulation within ALACRES2 of the UAV use to monitor the spill

The scenario corresponding to a catastrophic leakage and subsequent fire was based on a maximum release rate corresponding to 4,000 kg/min.

The evolution of the event could be monitored by means of drones equipped with multispectral sensors to measure: atmospheric concentration of hazardous substances, dispersion of pollutants into the sea. Currently the authors are reproducing the use of the UAV and their activities for conducting the test on the AI driving them in order to refine the collaboration modes and to validate and verify the models as proposed in Fig. 10.

5 Conclusions

This is a preliminary part of our research on this topic and we get benefits from using available models to simulate the dispersion of contaminant and its evolution. The idea to create this integrated intelligent approach resulted from applying Strategic Engineering approach to the case of the CBRN and it seems pretty promising based on preliminary tests.

Currently the authors are focusing on further develop the models to cover a wide spectrum of TIM/TIC and to improve the efficiency and effectiveness of the AI as well as the retune of the simulation based on collected data. It should be outlined the importance to guarantee interoperability among models and real Command and Control Systems to enhance the potential impacts of this research in improving Safety and Security around Industrial Plants and Critical Infra-structures.

References

1. Fu, Z., Chen, Y., Ding, Y., He, D.: pollution source localization based on multi-UAV cooperative communication. IEEE Access **7**, 29304–29312 (2019). https://doi.org/10.1109/ACCESS.2019.2900475
2. Zang, W., Lin, J., Wang, Y., Tao, H.: Investigating small-scale water pollution with UAV remote sensing technology. World Autom. Congr. **2012**, 1–4 (2012)
3. Liu, T., Han, D., Lin, Y., Liu, K.: Distributed multi-UAV trajectory optimization over directed networks. J. Franklin Inst. **358**(10), 5470–5487 (2021). ISSN 0016–0032
4. Villa, T.F., Salimi, F., Morton, K., Morawska, L., Gonzalez, F.: Development and validation of a UAV based system for air pollution measurements. Sensors **16**, 2202 (2016). https://doi.org/10.3390/s16122202
5. Altshuler, Y., Yanovsky, V., Wagner, I.A., Bruckstein, A.M.: The cooper- ative hunters-efficient cooperative search for smart targets using UAV swarms. In: Second In- ternational Conference on Informatics in Control, Automation and Robotics (ICINCO), the First International Workshop on Multi-Agent Robotic Systems (MARS), pp. 165–170 (2005)
6. Kolling, A., Kleiner, A.: Multi-UAV Trajectory planning for guaranteed search. In: 12th International Conference on Autonomous Agents and Multiagent Systems (AAMAS 2013), pp. 79–86. The International Foundation for Autonomous Agents and Multiagent Sys- tems (IFAAMAS) (2013)
7. Stodola, Petr, Mazal, Jan: Tactical decision support system to aid commanders in their decision-making. In: Hodicky, J. (ed.) MESAS 2016. LNCS, vol. 9991, pp. 396–406. Springer, Cham (2016). https://doi.org/10.1007/978-3-319-47605-6_32

8. Kung, C.M., Yang, W.S., Wei, T.Y., Chao, S.T.:The fast flight trajectory verification algorithm for drone dance system. In: 2020 IEEE International Conference on Industry 4.0, Artificial Intelligence, and Communications Technology (IAICT), pp. 97–101 (2020). https://doi.org/10.1109/IAICT50021.2020

9. D'Ursol, F., Grasso, C., Santoro, C., Santoro, F.F., Schembra, G.: The tactile internet for the flight control of UAV flocks. In: 2018 4th IEEE Conference on Network Softwarization and Workshops (NetSoft), pp. 470–475 (2018). https://doi.org/10.1109/NETSOFT.2018.8458493

10. Keramea, P., Spanoudaki, K., Zodiatis, G., Gikas, G., Sylaios, G.:Oil spill modeling: a critical review on current trends, perspectives, and challenges. J. Mar. Sci. Eng. **9**(2), 181 (2021)

11. Gomez, F., Ribstein, B., Makké, L., Armand, P., Moussafir, J., Nibart, M.: Simulation of a dense gas chlorine release with a Lagrangian particle dispersion mod- el (LPDM). Atmos. Environ. 244, 117791 (2021). ISSN 1352-2310 9172016

12. Bruzzone, A.G., et al.: Innovative virtual lab for improving safety and port operations. In: Proc. of HMS, Rome (2022)

13. Bruzzone, A.G., Massei, M., Di Matteo, R., Kutej, L.: Introducing intelligence and autonomy into industrial robots to address operations into dangerous area. In: Mazal, J. (ed.) Modelling and Simulation for Autonomous Systems. MESAS 2018. Lecture Notes in Computer Science, vol 11472, pp. 433–444. Springer, Cham (2018). https://doi.org/10.1007/978-3-030-14984-0_32

14. Bruzzone, A.G., Massei, M.: Simulation-based military training. In: Mittal, S., Durak, U., Ören, T. (eds.) Guide to Simulation-Based Disciplines, Simulation Foundations, Methods and Applications, pp. 315–361. Springer, Cham (2017). https://doi.org/10.1007/978-3-319-61264-5_14

15. Bruzzone, A.G., Massei, M., Sinelshchikov, K., Giovannetti, A., Gadupuri, B.K.: Strategic engineering applied to complex systems within marine environment. In: 2021 Annual Modeling and Simulation Conference, Proc. of ANNSIM IEEE, July, pp. 1–10 2021

16. Vairo, T., Quagliati, M., Del Giudice, T., Barbucci, A., Fabiano, B.: From land-to water-use-planning: a consequence based case-study related to cruise ship risk. Saf. Sci. **97**, 120–133 (2017)

Unmanned Surface Vehicle Chase a Moving Target Remotely Controlled

Camilla Fruzzetti(✉) and Michele Martelli

Department of Naval Architecture, Electric, Electronic and Telecommunication Engineering
(DITEN), University of Genoa, 16145 Genoa, Italy
camilla.fruzzetti@edu.unige.it

Abstract. Shortly, it is expected to have hybrid marine scenarios in which manned and unmanned vehicles navigate in the same environment. The study of the interactions between autonomous and human-controlled vessels becomes essential to improve and make the control systems more resilient. For such a reason, this paper shows a simulation architecture to test the effectiveness of a guidance law in a target tracking scenario for surface navigation. The guidance logic is based on the idea of reaching and following a target when the future motion is unknown and only the instantaneous position and speed are available. The adopted guidance law can handle both the chasing and the following phases minimising the time needed to reach the chased vehicles. The actuators' set-point generation is ensured by speed and heading controls, properly developed for this aim.

A cyber-physical testing scenario has been developed and can run in real-time. Both target and interceptor dynamics are based on detailed mathematical models in which the parameters have been validated by dedicated tank experiments. An operator remotely controls the target through a human-machine interface and tries to leave behind the autonomously controlled interceptor to make the simulation's results more realistic.

At the end of the paper, the results are reported for investigation and the conclusions are drawn.

Keywords: Human in the loop · Target tracking · Guidance · Autonomous Surface Vessel

1 Introduction

In recent years, automatic systems have become essential in many different applications and areas. In the maritime field, there is a demand for an even greater level of complexity and autonomy in onboard systems with the increase of the computational power needed, which leads to moving towards an ever higher level of automation. The process towards full automation goes through several steps and over the years several classifications with different levels of automation have been proposed, from the first one proposed by Sheridan in 1978 [24] to the one proposed in [22] that also evaluates the transport environment. Also the International Maritime Organization (IMO) during the

J. Mazal et al. (Eds.): MESAS 2022, LNCS 13866, pp. 243–254, 2023.
https://doi.org/10.1007/978-3-031-31268-7_14

99th, [14], and 100th, [15], sessions of the Marine Safety Committee (MSC) proposed four level of autonomy. Since the 1990s s several Autonomous Surface Vehicles (ASV) with different levels of autonomy have been developed and an exhaustive analysis of the existing model is shown in [23]. During the years lots of progress has been made and lots of names have been used for identifying the smart/autonomous ships, hence to clarify at the 98th MSC session, [16], the IMO defined the concept of Maritime Autonomous Surface Ships (MASS).

Increasing the automation level all ship systems need to be re-thinked and modified, but a focus needs to be paid to the autonomous handling of the units, hence it is the motion control system that becomes paramount. It is usually designed as three independent modules: Guidance, Navigation, and Control (GNC) systems [9]. Such systems have been developed together with the diffusion of the inertial system [8] and interact with each other. A review of the GNC systems is shown in [17] and a review of the state of the art of the MASS is given in [28].

In fact, this paper is focusing on testing a guidance law for a target tracking scenario for surface navigation thanks to a simulation architecture, hence it lies within the guidance system. The Guidance system has the role of computing the path processing the reference data of the ship together with the data collected from the Navigation system and other information. Usually, this system can be split into several sub-systems. The first one is a high-level path planner that defines a route based on geometrical parameters, the weather, or user-defined mission, [26]. The second one is a collision-avoidance system, that avoids the risk of collision, [13] and [27]. At this stage, the Guidance system demands the use of different motion control scenarios, the last sub-system. Clearly, there are lots of motion control scenarios, like the path following, without the temporal constrain [10] and with [2], the dynamic positioning, [1], the follow-the-leader, [21], the target tracking, [5,11], etc. The last one is the one investigated in this paper and regards following a target of which only the instantaneous position and velocity are known; hence the motion evolution is unknown. In [4,9] three different guidance logics to satisfy the target tracking scenario have been proposed: the Line-Of-Sight, the Pure Pursuit, and the Constant Bearing guidance. This paper focuses on the last one, in particular, it has adopted a properly modified Constant bearing guidance law (proposed in [11]) that tends to converge to a path parallel to the target one. Such laws have been derived from the missile guidance studies, [25].

The logic has been implemented into a properly developed simulation platform that reproduces the dynamic behaviour of the model-scale tugboat named "Tito Neri", fully validated and presented in [12]. Simulation allows for estimating the performance of a system under any operating condition. The behaviour of the system in the time-domain is described by using mathematical and logical models on a digital computer, [6]. Traditionally, the simulation is used as the digital copy of the system for the design and testing of a new improvement or control logic, in this way a simulator is a stand-alone object. Subsequently, the introduction inside the simulation loop of a real part has been introduced for testing the functionality of the specific system or for the development of a mathematical model, these are the hardware in the loop and software in the loop techniques. A new trend is the introduction of the human inside the loop [20]. In this way, the human interacts with the simulator, and he can make some errors, hence it is possible to test the reaction of the system to the wrong input. An additional benefit of this technique is the use of the simulator for training purposes. This paper proposes manually controlling the target, which tries to leave behind the automatically controlled interceptor. In this way, it is possible to test the guidance logic and it is possible to have more realistic results.

The paper is organised as follows. The simulation platform and the guidance laws adopted are presented in Sect. 2. The Human-In-the-Loop architecture is shown in Sect. 3. The simulation results for validating the guidance law are shown in Sect. 4 and the conclusion are drawn in Section 5.

2 Simulation Platform

Simulation is a technique that allows the prediction of the vehicle response in both design and off-design conditions. This means that system behaviour can be simulated for all conditions and sets of input parameters without full-scale tests. The ship simulator implements a mathematical model, i.e. a set of differential or algebraic equations, which represents the various elements of the physical systems. It is like a digital copy of the real model. The simulation model used in the present work represents the dynamics of a tugboat model called "Tito Neri" with the overall length (L_{OA}) equal to $0.97\,m$ in three degrees of freedom. Indeed, only the motion in the horizontal plane has been taken into account, or rather, the motions of surge, sway, and yaw.

The tugboat propulsion model implemented in this simulator is composed of two DC motors that drive two azimuth ducted propellers, one for each shaft-line. In addition, a bow-thruster, driven by a separate DC motor, is present and it is necessary to improve the manoeuvrability at slow speed. Within the simulation platform, the bow-thruster model is not implemented. Hence, the model is an underactuated one in the horizontal plane with two independent actuators.

The layout of the whole simulation platform is shown in Fig. 1. Here, inside the dotted line, there is the ship model, essential for the development of the presented guidance logic and explained below.

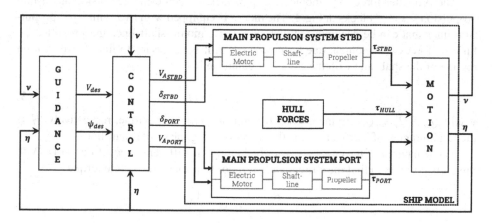

Fig. 1. Tugboat Layout

2.1 Ship Model

The dynamic of the ship can be solved with the equation of motion 1, which is derived from the Newton-Euler formulation.

$$(M_{RB} + M_A)\dot{v} + C(v)v = \tau_{stbd} + \tau_{port} + \tau_{hull} \tag{1}$$

where M_{RB} and M_A are the inertial and added mass matrices, respectively; $C(v)$ is the Coriolis matrix; v is the velocity $v = [u,v,r]$; τ represent the external forces and moment, the general τ is defined as $\tau = [X,Y,N]^T$ and the subscripts $stbd$, $port$, and $hull$ refer to the starboard azimuthal thruster, to the port azimuthal thruster, and to the hull force, respectively. Hence, the Eq. (1) gives as output the kinematics of the model in terms of the velocity v and, after an appropriate integration, of the position $\eta = [x,y,\psi]$. Hence, it is necessary to determine the hull and the propeller forces.

The hull forces and moment have been evaluated with the Oltmann & Sharma model [19]. As presented in [18], this method for evaluating the hull forces is comparable to the use of Computational Fluid Dynamics (CFD) techniques for the control design. In this model the total hydrodynamic force is composed of three main contributions: the Ideal Fluid Force, which is assessed by using the potential theory, i.e. neglecting the effects of viscosity; the Lift Force, which is assessed by comparing the hull with a low aspect ratio wing; and the Cross Flow Drag, it represents the resistance due to the viscous forces generated by a moving body in a real fluid. Besides, the hull resistance is considered as a separate term. The formulation of the hull forces and moments is presented in Eq. (2).

$$\tau_{hull} = \begin{cases} X_{hull} = & X_I + X_{HL} - R_T \\ Y_{hull} = & Y_I + Y_{HL} + Y_{HC} \\ N_{hull} = & N_I + N_{HL} + N_{HC} \end{cases} \tag{2}$$

where R_T is the hull resistance and the subscript I, HL, and HC refer to the Ideal Fluid Force, to the Lift Force, and to the Cross Flow Drag, respectively.

The propeller forces and moment, $\tau_{port,stbd}$, have been evaluated inside the "Main propulsion system" blocks in Fig. 1. The model is equipped with two symmetric propulsion lines that can be decomposed into an electric motor, shaft line, and propeller. To find the forces and moment due to the propeller, it is necessary to find the revolution regime of the shaft line with the shaft line equation in (3).

$$I_T \dot{n} = Q_{eng} - Q_{fric} - Q_o \tag{3}$$

where Q_{eng}, Q_{fric}, Q_o are the engine, friction and propeller torque, respectively, I_T is the total moment of inertia, and n is the revolution regime of the shaft line.

The behaviour of the engine is described using the differential equation in (4). With this, it is possible to find the current and, as a consequence, the engine torque.

$$\frac{di}{dt} = \frac{R}{L}i - \frac{1}{L}K_e\omega + \frac{1}{L}V_a \tag{4}$$

where R is the resistance, L is the inductance, i is the current, K_e is a constant of the electric engine, ω is the engine speed, and V_a is the applied voltage.

With the revolution regime n it is possible to find the value of the advance angle and, as a consequence, the working point of the propeller inside the open water diagram that gives as output the propeller torque Q_o and thrust T with the formulations in (5).

$$C_T = \frac{T}{\frac{1}{2}\rho\pi\frac{D^2}{4}V_r^2} \qquad C_Q = \frac{Q}{\frac{1}{2}\rho\pi\frac{D^3}{4}V_r^2} \tag{5}$$

where ρ is the water density, D is the propeller diameter, and V_r is the incoming velocity.

The azimuth angle δ is modelled with a limit on the first derivative of the signal to take into account that the azimuthal thruster can rotate with a maximum given speed. At this point, with the knowledge of the azimuth angle δ, it is possible to find the propeller forces and moment as shown in (6).

$$\tau_{port,stbd} = \begin{cases} X_p = & T\cos\delta \\ Y_p = & T\sin\delta \\ N_p = & x_pY_p - y_pX_p \end{cases} \tag{6}$$

At this stage, all the terms inside Eq. (1) have been defined and it is possible to solve it and to give as output the kinematics of the model. It is the output of the Ship model put inside the dotted line in Fig. 1.

However, a dynamic system, besides the process part, has a controller. Hence, there is an additional differential equation that describes the model. The aim of it is to find the correct input for the processing system that nullifies the error between the set-point and the feedback values. In this ship model, besides the control system block in Fig. 1, a local governor is also present inside the engine system. All the governors inside the model are Proportional Integrative Derivative (PID) controllers represented with the equation in (7).

$$u = K_P e + K_I \int_0^t e d\tau + K_D \frac{de}{dt} \tag{7}$$

where e is the generic error defined as the difference between the set-point and the feedback, K_P, K_I, and K_D are the proportional, integral and derivative gains, respectively.

2.2 Speed Pilot and Autopilot

The control system determines the proper action to be provided by the ship to satisfy the control objective provided by the guidance. In this case, the guidance outputs are the desired heading angle ψ and the desired speed V_{des}, as will be shown in Sect. 2.3. Indeed, the target tracking scenario's control objective tends to nullify the distance between the target and the interceptor. The interceptor is considered to be an under-actuated ship in the horizontal plane and an autopilot with a speed controller has been developed to obtain the target tracking motion control objective. The controller has been developed as proposed in [7] and as the one in [3], here proof of the controller's stability has been shown. The two controllers are modelled as PID controllers with the equation shown in (7). The output of this equation is the value that nullifies the error between the feedback and the desired value.

The first controller is a speed pilot. The speed controller aims to maintain a desirable ship speed and correct the difference from this value. The second one is an Autopilot, for the heading control. Hence, the controllers need as input two time-varying set-points, the desired heading angle ψ_{des} and the desired ship speed V_{des}, and give as output the speed and heading angle that nullifies the errors. Since the ship model requires the voltage value, as shown in Fig. 1, the set-point value of the speed is transformed, with a suitable gain, into a voltage value.

2.3 Guidance

The motion control scenario is the target tracking one, where the aim is following a moving object without information on the future motion and the control objective tends to nullify the distance between the target and the interceptor. The necessary condition to fulfil the mission's goal is that the chasing ship's full speed, named interceptor, is greater than the chased one's full speed, called target. The scenario can be divided into two parts: the first one regards the approach phase, where the interceptor needs to reach the target, while the second one is the following phase, where the interceptor has reached the target and is required to follow it. In this paper, the Constant Bearing guidance law has been adopted.

The Constant Bearing guidance law is based on parallel navigation. Indeed, the interceptor is required to keep a path parallel to the target one and the required distance vector is a user-defined input that can be chosen as desired. In this logic, the interceptor corrects the path as long as the distance between the target and the interceptor is greater than the desired. A speed and a heading law have been implemented to give as input the desired distances $e_{des} \in \mathbb{R}$ and $s_{des} \in \mathbb{R}$ along $\underline{f}$ basis. The guidance geometrical scheme is shown in Fig. 2.

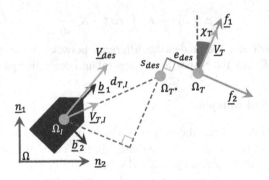

Fig. 2. Geometrical Sketch of the CB Guidance.

In this case, the relative interceptor-target velocity is the key control variable and is along the vector between the target and the interceptor. Hence, in the following part, the interceptor perceives the target at a constant bearing and a constant distance.

The speed law is defined as the module of the velocity in Eq. (8). This law consists of the sum of two components: the target velocity $\underline{V}_T$, which nullifies the relative velocity between the interceptor and the target, and the relative interceptor-target velocity $\underline{V}_{T,I}$, that is the key control variable of this law. Indeed, the relative interceptor-target velocity lets to reach the target with a smooth behaviour thanks to the ξ_{CB} parameter and, when the desired distance is reached, this part is equal to zero and the following phase begin.

$$\underline{V}_{des} = \underline{V}_T + \underline{V}_{T,I} = \underline{V}_T + K_{CB}\frac{\underline{d}_{T,I}}{\sqrt{\underline{d}_{T,I}^2 + \xi_{CB}^2}}$$

$$\underline{d}_{T,I} = (x_T - x_I)\,\underline{n}_1 + (y_T - y_I)\,\underline{n}_2 + e_{des}\,\underline{f}_2 + s_{des}\,\underline{f}_1 \tag{8}$$

$$K_{CB} = V_{I_{max}} - V_T^*$$

where $\underline{V}_T$ is the target velocity, $\underline{V}_{T,I}$ is the velocity aligned along the LOS vector, $\underline{d}_{T,I}$ is the vector between the interceptor and the target, $K_{CB} \in \mathbb{R}^+$ is a speed gain and is set equal to the maximum speed ($V_{I_{max}}$) minus the maximum target speed in a previous time interval (V_T^*), $\xi_{CB} \in \mathbb{R}^+$ is the main parameter that affects the chasing phase, $\Omega_T = (x_T, y_T)$ is the target position, and $\Omega_I = (x_I, y_I)$ is the interceptor position.

The heading law is taken according to the law in (9) and is outlined in Fig. 3. It is obtained as the difference between the desired course angle χ_{des} and the drift angle of the interceptor β. The core of the heading law is the angle χ_{corr} that depends on the desired distance e_{des}. Indeed, until the distance along $\underline{f}_2$ is different from the desired one, it corrects the heading, while when it is equal, the following phase on the parallel path begins.

$$\psi_{des} = \chi_{des} - \beta$$

$$\beta = \arctan\frac{v}{u} \qquad \chi_{des} = \chi_T + \chi_{corr}$$

$$\chi_T = \arctan\frac{\dot{y}_T}{\dot{x}_T} \qquad \chi_{corr} = \arctan\frac{e_{corr}}{\Delta} \tag{9}$$

$$e_{corr} = e + e_{des} \qquad e = (\Omega_T - \Omega_I) \cdot \underline{f}_2$$

where χ_{corr} is defined according to the sketch in Fig. 3, e is the geometrical distance between the interceptor and the target along $\underline{f}_2$, and $\Delta \in \mathbb{R}^+$ is a constant that guarantee the smooth behaviour of the interceptor.

3 Human-in-the-loop Architecture

The architecture used to simulate the scenario is drawn in Fig. 4. The human is introduced inside the simulation loop in this architecture, however, he interacts with the simulator and the reaction of the autonomous system can be tested. In particular, in this architecture, the target is manually controlled and tries to leave behind the automatically controlled interceptor. In this way, it is possible to test the guidance logic and have more realistic results.

Here, the target set-points are given manually by an operator via a human-machine interface. Since the target has two azimuthal thrusters, the manual set-points are the voltage and the azimuthal angle of each azimuthal. The signals are processed through

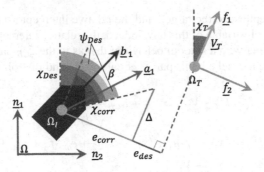

Fig. 3. CB heading law.

the ship model of Sect. 2.1 that computes the trajectory of the target and sends it to the interceptor.

The interceptor, instead, is an autonomous ship model like the one in Fig. 1. It automatically computes the course through the guidance module described in Sect. 2.3, and computes a speed and heading set-points to be sent to the control module. At this stage, the interceptor implements the guidance outputs through the control module described in Sect. 2.2. In the end, the ship model described in Sect. 2.1 computes the interceptor trajectory that follows the target.

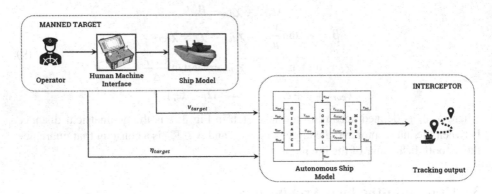

Fig. 4. Simulation Loop Framework

4   Simulation Results

The guidance law described in Sect. 2.3 is tested through the architecture shown in Sect. 3. The target is remotely controlled by an operator and it tries to leave behind the chasing vehicle, which operates autonomously. In this simulation the distances e_{des} and s_{des} along the $\underline{f}$ basis are set equal to $2L_{PP}$ and $-2L_{PP}$, respectively, where L_{PP} is the length between the perpendiculars. Below the simulation results are shown.

In Fig. 5 it is possible to note the trajectory covered during the simulation by the target, in red, and the interceptor, in blue, while the yellow lines are used to connect the target and interceptor positions at the same time step.

In Fig. 6 and Fig. 7 the inputs given manually to the target are shown. As shown in Fig. 1 the inputs required by the two shaft lines are the voltages, required for setting the speed, and the azimuth angles δ, required for setting the heading angles. The inputs are required for the starboard and portside azimuth thrusters, but in this case, the choice was to couple the starboard and portside signals, and mimic a navigation situation.

In Fig. 8 the speeds of the target and the interceptor have been shown. In particular, in red is shown the target speed as the result of the manual inputs, in green is shown the maximum speed available for the interceptor, in orange, the desired value finds by the guidance law, and in blue is the speed assumed by the interceptor in reaction to the set-point given by the guidance.

In Fig. 9 the heading set-point given by the guidance law, in orange, and the real value, in blue, have been shown.

In Fig. 10 the distances between the interceptor and the target have been shown. The distances are taken according to Sect. 2.3 and in particular, the distance e is shown in yellow, while the distance s is shown in purple.

The simulation has a duration of 1000 s and, as it is possible to see in Fig. 7, it has been tried to keep the maximum speed available for the target to leave behind the interceptor, and to stop the voltage inputs of the target, about around 700 s, to see how the guidance logic reacts when the target stops. As it is possible to see from the target path in Fig. 5, the trajectory given as input through the azimuth angles in Fig. 6 has several changes of direction and ends with a straight path to see the following part. Indeed in the final part, the interceptor speed is set equal to the target one, as shown in Fig. 8, and the distances are set equal to the desired values, as shown in Fig. 10. From the results, it is also possible to note that when the speed target goes to zero, also the interceptor stops to wait for the target, as highlighted in Fig. 8, and that the interceptor, thanks to the guidance law, reacts at each change of direction in a proper manner.

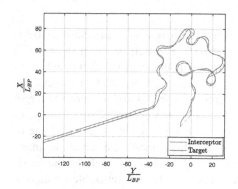

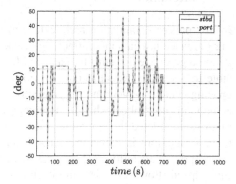

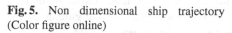

Fig. 5. Non dimensional ship trajectory (Color figure online)

Fig. 6. Target manual input - Azimuth angles (Color figure online)

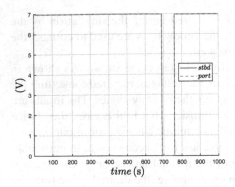

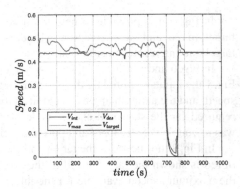

Fig. 7. Target manual input - Voltages

Fig. 8. Interceptor and Target speed (Color figure online)

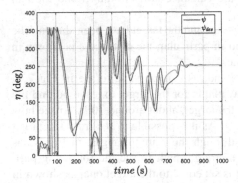

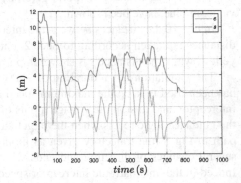

Fig. 9. Interceptor heading angle (Color figure online)

Fig. 10. Interceptor distances (Color figure online)

5   Conclusion

In this paper, a simulation architecture to test the effectiveness of the constant bearing guidance law in a target tracking scenario for surface vessels has been shown. The adopted guidance law aims to reach and follow a moving object of which it is only possible to know the instantaneous position and speed. Hence, there are two objects: the chasing vehicle (target) and the chased one (interceptor). In this architecture, the target is manually controlled, while the interceptor is autonomously controlled. In several simulations conducted the human operator never leaves behind the interceptor and one of these simulations is shown in Sect. 4 as an example; this demonstrates an autonomous interceptor's capability to always reach a human-handled marine vehicle (if the maximum speed allows that). The architecture is developed inside a customizable simulation scenario where the interceptor and the target are modelled through detailed mathematical models. Simulation outputs are reported to show the validity of the guidance law, and they can be used for debriefing after a training session. Future activities will regard the testing in a relevant environment by using a remote control station and two drones to get feedback on the guidance module behaviour under disturbances.

References

1. Alessandri, A., et al.: Dynamic positioning system of a vessel with conventional propulsion configuration: modeling and simulation, pp. 725–734 (2015). https://doi.org/10.1201/b17494-97
2. Alessandri, A., Donnarumma, S., Martelli, M., Vignolo, S.: Motion control for autonomous navigation in blue and narrow waters using switched controllers. J. Mar. Sci. Eng. 7(6), 196 (2019)
3. Altosole, M., Campora, U., Donnarumma, S., Zaccone, R.: Simulation techniques for design and control of a waste heat recovery system in marine natural gas propulsion applications. J. Mar. Sci. Eng. 7(11), 397 (2019). https://doi.org/10.3390/jmse7110397
4. Breivik, M., Hovstein, V., Fossen, T.: Straight-line target tracking for unmanned surface vehicles. MIC—Model. Identif. Control 29(4), 131–149 (2008). https://doi.org/10.4173/mic.2008.4.2
5. Breivik, M.: Topics in guided motion control of marine vehicles. Ph.D. thesis (2010)
6. Donnarumma, S., Figari, M., Martelli, M., Zaccone, R.: Simulation of the guidance and control systems for underactuated vessels. In: Mazal, J., Fagiolini, A., Vasik, P. (eds.) MESAS 2019. LNCS, vol. 11995, pp. 108–119. Springer, Cham (2020). https://doi.org/10.1007/978-3-030-43890-6_9
7. Donnarumma, S., Zacearían, L., Alessandri, A., Vignolo, S.: Anti-windup synthesis of heading and speed regulators for ship control with actuator saturation. In: 2016 European Control Conference (ECC), pp. 1284–1290 (2016). https://doi.org/10.1109/ECC.2016.7810466
8. Draper, C.: Control, navigation, and guidance. IEEE Control Syst. Mag. 1(4), 4–17 (1981)
9. Fossen, T.I.: Handbook of Marine Craft Hydrodynamics and Motion Control. Wiley, Hoboken (2011)
10. Fossen, T.I., Breivik, M., Skjetne, R.: Line-of-sight path following of underactuated marine craft. IFAC Proc. Volumes 36(21), 211–216 (2003)
11. Fruzzetti, C., Donnarumma, S., Martelli, M.: Dynamic target chasing: parameters and performance indicators assessment. J. Mar. Sci. Technol. (Japan) 27(1), 712–729 (2022). https://doi.org/10.1007/s00773-021-00865-3
12. Haseltala, A., et al.: The collaborative autonomous shipping experiment (case): motivations, theory, infrastructure, and experimental challenges. In: International Ship Control Systems Symposium (iSCSS 2020). IMaReST (2020)
13. Huang, Y., Chen, L., Chen, P., Negenborn, R.R., Van Gelder, P.: Ship collision avoidance methods: state-of-the-art. Saf. Sci. 121, 451–473 (2020)
14. IMO: Maritime Safety Committee (MSC), 99th session (16-25 May 2018). https://www.imo.org/en/MediaCentre/MeetingSummaries/Pages/MSC-99th-session.aspx. Accessed 28 June 2021
15. IMO: Maritime Safety Committee (MSC), 100th session (3-7 December 2018). https://www.imo.org/en/MediaCentre/MeetingSummaries/Pages/MSC-100th-session.aspx. Accessed 28 June 2021
16. IMO: Maritime Safety Committee (MSC), 98th session (7-16 June 2017). https://www.imo.org/en/MediaCentre/MeetingSummaries/Pages/MSC-98th-session.aspx. Accessed 28 June 2021
17. Liu, Z., Zhang, Y., Yu, X., Yuan, C.: Unmanned surface vehicles: an overview of developments and challenges. Annu. Rev. Control 41, 71–93 (2016)

18. Martelli, M., Villa, D., Viviani, M., Donnarumma, S., Figari, M.: The use of computational fluid dynamic technique in ship control design. Ships Offshore Struct. **16**(1), 31–45 (2021). https://doi.org/10.1080/17445302.2019.1706908
19. Oltmann, P., Sharma, S.D.: Simulation of combined engine and rudder maneuvers using an improved model of hull-propeller-rudder interactions. Technical report (1984)
20. Pedersen, N., Bojsen, T., Madsen, J.: Co-simulation of cyber physical systems with hmi for human in the loop investigations. In: Proceedings of the Symposium on Theory of Modeling & Simulation, pp. 1–12 (2017)
21. Piaggio, B., Garofano, V., Donnarumma, S., Alessandri, A., Negenborn, R., Martelli, M.: Follow-the-leader control strategy for azimuth propulsion system on surface vessels. In: Proceedings of the 2020 International Ship Control Systems Symposium (iSCSS 2020). Delft, The Netherlands (2020). https://doi.org/10.24868/issn.2631-8741.2020.004
22. Schiaretti, M., Chen, L., Negenborn, R.R.: Survey on autonomous surface vessels: Part I - a new detailed definition of autonomy levels. In: ICCL 2017. LNCS, vol. 10572, pp. 219–233. Springer, Cham (2017). https://doi.org/10.1007/978-3-319-68496-3_15
23. Schiaretti, M., Chen, L., Negenborn, R.R.: Survey on autonomous surface vessels: Part II - categorization of 60 prototypes and future applications. In: ICCL 2017. LNCS, vol. 10572, pp. 234–252. Springer, Cham (2017). https://doi.org/10.1007/978-3-319-68496-3_16
24. Sheridan, T.B., Verplank, W.L.: Human and computer control of undersea teleoperators. Technical report, Massachusetts Inst of Tech Cambridge Man-Machine Systems Lab (1978)
25. Shneydor, N.A.: Missile Guidance and Pursuit: Kinematics, Dynamics and Control. Elsevier, Amsterdam (1998)
26. Singh, Y., Sharma, S., Hatton, D., Sutton, R.: Optimal path planning of unmanned surface vehicles. Indian J. Geo-Mar. Sci. **47**(7), 1325–1334 (2018)
27. Tam, C., Bucknall, R., Greig, A.: Review of collision avoidance and path planning methods for ships in close range encounters. J. Navig. **62**(3), 455 (2009)
28. Wang, L., Wu, Q., Liu, J., Li, S., Negenborn, R.: State-of-the-art research on motion control of maritime autonomous surface ships. J. Mar. Sci. Eng. **7**(12), 438 (2019)

Aerial Target System Design for Effective Air Defence Training

Vadim Starý$^{(\boxtimes)}$, Lukáš Gacho , and Marek Maňák

University of Defence, Kounicova 65, 662 10 Brno, Czech Republic
{vadim.stary,lukas.gacho,marek.manak}@unob.cz

Abstract. The paper Aerial target system design for effective air defence training deals with the design and definition of on-board components of Unmanned
Aerial System (UAS) used for training ground-based air defence (GBAD) units.
The main goal of the paper is to define the essential requirements of UAS to be
applicable as an aerial target system (ATS). Fundamental elements and the most
common autopilots are described, analysed, and compared. The analysis results
are implemented over specific scenarios for GBAD units training in the tactical
simulator environment (Re-PLAN). The tactical simulator environment is specifically designed for GBAD capabilities evaluation and includes the various options
of scenario settings and verification (e.g. optical visibility evaluation, radar, fire
unit effectivity, etc.) The obtained results are summarized and implemented into
exercise variants using the target drone and the proposed onboard system, which
is suitable for different types of GBAD system principles (visual, IR, radar).

Keywords: Unmanned aerial vehicles · UAV · UAS · GBAD · target drone ·
on-board system · autopilot · M&S · Modelling and Simulation

1 Introduction and Main Goal

The effective training is an evergreen in connection with personnel preparation in all the
possible branches [1]. It should be effective and also economical.

Presented paper provides analysis and suggestion of possible design of ATS so
called Target drone, which could be used for effective training and preparation of not
only GBAD units [2, 3].

The suggested ATS is based on commercial on-board control systems (autopilots)
to assure the economic aspects of the solution.

1.1 State of Art

In connection with GBAD units training, number of ATS has been already used. These
systems come from different categories of UAS and they are modified accord-ing to the
GBAD system type and principle. Based on these principles, the ATS can be divided
into following categories.

J. Mazal et al. (Eds.): MESAS 2022, LNCS 13866, pp. 255–266, 2023.
https://doi.org/10.1007/978-3-031-31268-7_15

- ATS for visual or IR detection used by very short-range air defence (VSHORAD) systems e.g. MISS TRACTOR [4].
- ATS for radar or radio frequency (RF) detection used by SHORAD or medium and long-range surface to air missile (M/L SAM) systems, e.g. BQM-177A [5].
- ATS for universal usage.

The ATS can be also categorized in a same way as UAS according to its construction, propulsion type, etc. For example, fixed wing (FW), rotary wing (RW), with electric motor, jet motor, combustion motor.

1.2 Main Goal

The paper is mainly focused on VSHORAD category ATS design, with possible modification for SHORAD and consider primarily usage of electrical motor for FW and RW.

The main goal is to provide system design and verification of possible type of UAS, which can be effectively used as an ATS. Particularly the paper deals with on-board control systems requirements and scenarios for VSHORAD and SHORAD units training.

2 Aerial Target System Requirements Analysis

The ATS requirements have to reflect following prerequisites:

- GBAD units training type
- Technical and principal aspects of GBAD system
- Possible and effective implementation to UAS

2.1 GBAD Units Training Type

This prerequisite comes from the training procedures and defines the type of exercise, number and type of GBAD units and sensors, way of command and control (C2), identification procedures, etc.

The training type also refer to unit level of training and preparation and according to this the scenario is designed (selected).

For example, the rookie training with no manoeuvrable slow target scenario, or for the more experienced operator (unit), manoeuvrable fast target with complex chain of command.

Suggested scenarios are in Sub-sect. 4.1.

2.2 Technical and Principal Aspects of GBAD System

These aspects are defined by the GBAD missile guidance system type [6], detection type and other tactical and technical limitations of the GBAD system. In general, ATS have to fulfil technical requirements for:

- detection and tracking,
- missile guidance system,

  - passive (IR/optical detector),
  - active/semi active (radar transponder or sufficient Radar Cross Section – RCS).

2.3 Possible and Effective Implementation to UAS

All the previous prerequisites have to be possibly implemented on a UAS, to keep the effectiveness and efficiency of the ATS. These prerequisites could by divided as:

- Flight attributes,

  - min. and max. velocity,
  - min. and max. altitude,
  - min. and max. acceleration,
  - min. and max. manoeuvre,
  - flight time and operational range.

- Physical attributes,

  - RCS.
  - Visibility.

- Other requirements,

  - possibility to carry payload,
  - modularity/universal use.

2.4 ATS Requirements Example

For the basic target detection, tracking and firing with VSHORAD man-portable (MAN-PAD) based on IR passive missile guidance system (e.g. STINGER, SA-7 Grail), the ATS system requirements are in Table 1.

Table 1. ATS system requirements example

Param (min/max)	Velocity [m/s]	Distance [km]	Altitude AGL [m]	Manoeuvre [G]	Visibility distance [km]	Payload
	0–200	0,8–4,2	50–2000	2	5+	IR emitter

This defines the basic requirements for ATS flight scenario to be able to successfully engage the ATS by the IR MANPAD missile system. The scenario layout is on Fig. 1. Scenario has 3 phases, in phase 1 ATS starts in distance 8 km, reach the altitude 1 km with velocity 100 m/s. In phase 2, ATS is visually detected and tracked by the operator of SA-7, and in phase 3 the ATS could or could not be tracked and engaged by IR guided missile.

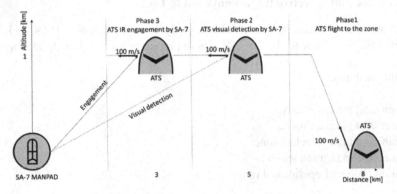

Fig. 1. ATS scenario layout example

3 ATS Control System Design and Comparison

System design of ATS is based on system structure of general UAS and it is modified according to the system requirements, which were described in Sect. 2.

Main focus is on the control system of the UAS, which can be divided by the level of man control to:

- Manual control – ATS is full controlled by the operator.
- Semiautomatic control – Operator control the flight; stabilization or particular parts of flight are controlled by autopilot (onboard control system).
- Automatic control – ATS follows the route which is predefined before (during) the flight by rout waypoints (WP).

For the GBAD units training the semiautomatic and automatic control with pre-set flight route according to a scenario is primarily used [7, 8].

3.1 Commercial Autopilots Analysis and Comparison

For the purpose of the paper, several most common autopilots compared by PATTERN [9] multi-criteria analysis with Saaty Scale Rating Matrix, see Tables 2, 3 and 4.

Following types of autopilots and their attributes were compared:

- MicroPilot - MP2128
- UAV Navigation SL - VECTOR-400
- Collins Aerospace - PICCOLO II
- PX4 Development Team and Community – Pixhawk 4
- General reference autopilot (GRA)
- Autopilot comparison

Table 2. Autopilot comparison

Type Criteria	MP2128	VECTOR-400	PICCOLO II	PX 4	GRA
1 Supported UAV types	FW, RW, multi-copters	FW, RW, multi-copters	FW, RW, multi-copters	FW, RW, multi-copters	FW, RW, multi-copters
2 Control modes	Man/Semi/ Auto	Man/Semi/ Auto	Man/Semi/ Auto	Man/Semi/ Auto	Man/Semi/ Auto
3 Availability	Low	Low	Low	High	High
4 Control accuracy	±2°	≤1°	≤1°	±0.5°	±1°
5 Software	Yes	No	No	Yes	Yes
6 Operation temperature	−20 °C +65 °C	−40 °C +85 °C	−30 °C +80 °C	−5 °C +60 °C	0 °C +60 °C
7 Mass	28 g	210 g	200 g	38 g	max 30 g
8 Price	7500 USD	6500 USD	7500 USD	210 USD	max 450 USD

Criteria scales were set as following. Value 1: Same prefer, Value 3: Weak prefer, Value 5: Strong prefer, Value 7: Very strong prefer, Value 9: Absolute prefer.

$$q_i = \frac{\sum (q_{ij} / \sum q_n)}{n} \tag{1}$$

Table 3. Saaty Criteria Scale Matrix

q_i/q_j	1	2	3	4	5	6	7	8	q_i
1	1,00	1,00	0,20	1,00	1,00	9,00	7,00	1,00	0,114
2	1,00	1,00	1,00	1,00	0,33	7,00	9,00	5,00	0,184
3	5,00	1,00	1,00	5,00	3,00	9,00	5,00	1,00	0,250
4	1,00	1,00	0,20	1,00	5,00	9,00	7,00	1,00	0,149
5	1,00	3,00	0,33	0,20	1,00	9,00	0,33	1,00	0,117
6	0,11	0,14	0,11	0,11	0,11	1,00	0,20	0,11	0,014
7	0,14	0,11	0,20	0,14	3,00	5,00	1,00	0,20	0,054
8	1,00	0,20	1,00	1,00	1,00	9,00	5,00	1,00	0,118
$\sum q_n$	10,25	7,45	4,04	9,45	14,44	58,00	34,53	10,31	$\sum=1$

The autopilots comparison by PATTERN method with the Saaty Criteria Scale Matrix and the final rank is in the Table 4. The table shown the final rank of the autopilots, as the best and optimal solution according to the Saaty Criteria Scale Matrix is the Pixhawk PX4, second is MP2128, third is Vector-400 and forth the Piccolo II.

The results show noticeable difference between PX4 and the other solutions, because of its good availability and price. The PX4 is one of the most popular commercial on-board control systems and the following system design is inspired by the PX4 solution.

The price difference is also done by the PX4 development politics, where the Pixhawk uses open standard based on BSD-3 and Creative Commons licence [10].

Table 4. PATTERN analysis results

Autopilot Criteria	MP2128	VECTOR-400	PICCOLO II	PX 4
1	0,113874354	0,113874354	0,113874654	0,113874
2	0,184250815	0,184250815	0,184250815	0,184251
3	0,125158696	0,125158696	0,125158696	0,250317
4	0,074244869	0,148489739	0,148489739	0,14849
5	0,116825572	0,058412786	0,058412786	0,116826
6	0,01384095	0,01384095	0,013840095	0,013841
7	0,054456605	0,018152202	0,018152202	0,036304
8	0,039314858	0,039314858	0,039314858	0,117945
Sum	0,721966719	0,7014944	0,701493845	0,981848
Rank	2	3	4	1

3.2 System Design

As it was mentioned, the system concept is inspired by the Pixhawk PX4 autopilot, which is modified according to the ATS requirements.

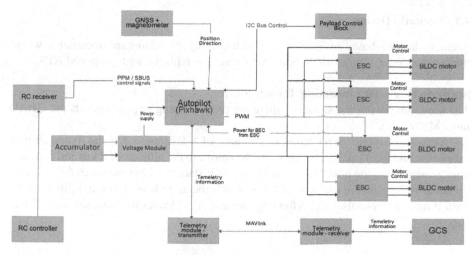

Fig. 2. ATS system design

Figure 2 illustrates system design of ATS based on UAV type quadcopter, using PX4 autopilot. The functionality is secured by the ATS construction, dimensions and flight itself and also by the Payload Control Block (PCB), which is control via I2C bus and telemetry MAVlink module.

Payload Control Block

This block controls the additional on-board equipment, which serves for the detection and tracking of the ATS. PCB is controlled via I2C bus and an onboard equipment type depends on the type of GBAD system principle. PCB can control following types of equipment:

- IR or visible point light source for optical and IR detection and tracking. In the simplest variant it is an emitting IR diode or LED with variable light intensity.
- For the radar detection, PCB could control the secondary surveillance transponder (SSR) or automated dependent surveillance broadcast (ADS-B) device. However, for radar detection, the simplest variant is to secure sufficient RCS by the ATS dimensions, materials or by on-board corner reflector.

4   System Design Verification

System design was verified by with the special simulation software tool called Re-PLAN [11], which was developed by the Retia company. The simulator is used for GBAD units planning and effectivity evaluation and allows to create and evaluate various types of scenarios even with command and control (C2) procedures [12].

4.1 Scenario Design

Scenario design is based on Czech GBAD unit training procedures and documents, where the standard type of target (helicopter, jet aircraft) is replaced with proposed ATS.

Scenario One – Two Incoming Targets SA-7
The scenario imitates the situation, there are two incoming targets towards the GBAD unit (MANPAD).

ATSs flight route: ATS1 starts in distance of 8 km and reach the 1 km altitude (above ground level - AGL), in distance 3 km move to the altitude of 2 km and provides engagement to the fire post. Engagement ends in distance of 1 km, and then ATS1 leaves the area. ATS2 starts in distance of 8 km, reach the altitude of 4 km and provides the patrolling and reconnaissance. After engagement ATS2 leaves the area, see Table 5 and Fig. 3.

Table 5. ATS Flight parameters – Scenario 1

FU	ATS Flight parameters				
	ATS type	Start distance	Velocity	Course parameter	Altitude
SA-7	FW radio controlled	8 km	80 m/s	0,5–1 km	1–4 km AGL

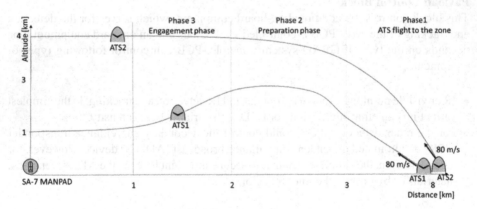

Fig. 3. Scenario 1 layout

Scenario Two – Two Low Altitude Targets RBS-70
The scenario two imitates 2 incoming drones in low altitude, which provides surveillance and the GBAD is represented by fire unit (FU) with RBS-70 system.

ATSs flight route: ATS1 and ATS2 flies as a tandem. They start in distance of 8 km with altitude 100 m (AGL) and flies with the course parameter from 500 m to 1 km from the FU see Table 6 and Fig. 4.

Table 6. ATS Flight parameters – Scenario 2

FU	ATS Flight parameters				
	ATS type	Start distance	Velocity	Course parameter	Altitude
RBS-70	FW radio controlled	8 km	80 m/s	0,5–1 km	100 m AGL

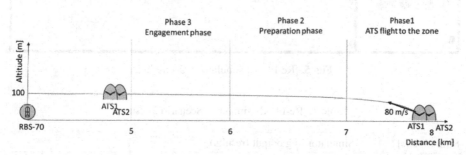

Fig. 4. Scenario 2 layout

4.2 Simulation Results

The scenario two was implemented into the Re-PLAN simulation environment and verified. Due to the simulator restriction, several simplifications were made. The maximum velocity of the target is 75 m/s and for detection the entity of air observer was added.

Simulator is based on deterministic model, it means if all the conditions of detection and possible engagement are met, the target is successfully engaged and destroyed. Simulator screen with scenario 2 layout is on the Fig. 5 and the results from the simulation in Table 7.

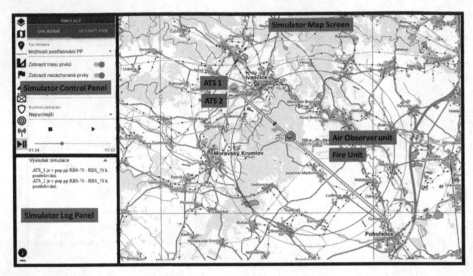

Fig. 5. Re-PLAN simulator – Scenario 2

Table 7. Re-PLAN simulator Scenario 2 results

Sim. time [s]	Simulator Log output (results)
0	ATS_1 and ATS_2 Start (D = 8,2 km)
61	ATS_1 is detected and tracked by Air observer unit (D = 3,7 km)
62	ATS_2 is detected and tracked by Air observer unit (D = 3,7 km)
62	ATS_1 is designated for engagement to FU
66	ATS_1 is engaged by FU (D = 3,63 km)
75	ATS_1 is destroyed by FU (D = 2,85 km)
76	ATS_2 is designated for engagement to FU (D = 2,8 km)
80	ATS_2 is engaged by FU (D = 2,75 km)
87	ATS_2 is destroyed by FU (D = 2,17 km)

The results of the scenario correspond with the assumptions, where the both targets are successfully detected, engaged and destroyed. It should be noticed that the results are significantly affected by the terrain profile, the ATS could be theoretically detected at 8 km, however because of their AGL altitude and the terrain profile, they are detected much closer to the unit (3,7 km). The engagement procedure also corresponds with the simulator algorithm and the results is acceptable.

5 Conclusion

The presented paper is focused on aerial target system design in connection with GBAD units training. Two training scenarios are proposed and designed ATS is tested in the Re-PLAN simulator environment over the training scenario.

The paper includes general description of ATS requirements and parameters and comparison of the most common commercial autopilots which can be used as an on-board control system of ATS.

Implementation of the ATS with designated parameters over the training scenario and its verification in the simulator, contributes to the more effective and optimized scenario and ATS settings and it should lead to the more effective GBAD units training.

5.1 Way Ahead

The next step is to implement algorithms of path modelling into the simulator [13] and practically realized the real target system, and verified its behaviour and effectivity during the live exercise or firings with the real fire unit and different GBAD systems [14].

References

1. Fletcher, J.D., Chatelier, P.R.: An Overview of Military Training (2000)
2. Maňák, M.: Návrh palubního systému vzdušného cíle pro cvičení obsluh prostředků PVO (thesis, Czech). Univerzita obrany, Brno (2022)
3. Kacer, J., et al.: Physiological data monitoring of members of air forces during training on simulators. In: Lhotska, L., Sukupova, L., Lacković, I., Ibbott, G.S. (eds.) World Congress on Medical Physics and Biomedical Engineering 2018. IP, vol. 68/3, pp. 855–860. Springer, Singapore (2019). https://doi.org/10.1007/978-981-10-9023-3_154
4. VTU homepage - Robotsystem 70 against Miss Tractor. https://www.vtusp.cz/en/uncategor ized/robotsystem-70-proti-bezpilotnimu-prostredku-iss-ractor/. Accessed 21 July 2022
5. Kratos aerial targets. https://www.kratosdefense.com/systems-and-platforms/unmanned-sys tems/aerial/aerial-targets. Accessed 21 July 2022
6. Siouris, G.M.: Missile Guidance and Control Systems [Online]. Springer, Heidelberg (2004). https://doi.org/10.1007/b97614
7. Stefek, A., Casar, J., Stary, V., Gacho, L.: Coupling of ODE and DES Models for Simulation of Air Defence in War-Gaming Experiment (2022). https://doi.org/10.2507/ijsimm21-1-586
8. Stefek, A., Casar, J., Stary, V.: Flight route generator for simulation-supported wargaming (2020). https://doi.org/10.1109/ME49197.2020.9286646
9. Sigford, J.V., Parvin, R.H.: Project pattern: a methodology for determining relevance in complex decision-making (1965). https://doi.org/10.1109/TEM.1965.6446433
10. PX4 autopilot user guide. http://docs.px4.io/main/en/. Accessed 21 July 2022
11. Retia – Replan C4I simulator [CZ]. https://retia.cz/vojenske-a-bezpecnostni-systemy/sys temy-veleni-a-rizeni-c4i2/c4i-vshorad/replan/. Accessed 21 July 2022
12. Stary, V., Farlik, J.: Aspects of air defence units C2 system modelling and simulation. In: Mazal, J., Fagiolini, A., Vasik, P. (eds.) MESAS 2019. LNCS, vol. 11995, pp. 351–360. Springer, Cham (2020). https://doi.org/10.1007/978-3-030-43890-6_28
13. Author, F.: Article title. Journal 2(5), 99–110 (2016)

14. Author, F., Author, S.: Title of a proceedings paper. In: Editor, F., Editor, S. (eds.) Conference 2016. LNCS, vol. 9999, pp. 1–13. Springer, Heidelberg (2016)
15. Author, F., Author, S., Author, T.: Book Title, 2nd edn. Publisher, Location (1999)
16. Author, F.: Contribution title. In: 9th International Proceedings, pp. 1–2. Publisher, Location (2010)
17. LNCS Homepage. http://www.springer.com/lncs. Accessed 21 Nov 2016

Future Challenges of Advanced M&S Technology

Modelling and Simulation and Artificial Intelligence for Strategic Political-Military Decision-Making Process: Case Study

Jan Hodicky[✉] and Volkan Kucuk

HQ Supreme Allied Commander Transformation, Virginia Beach, VA 23551, USA
{jan.hodicky,volkan.kucuk}@act.nato.int

Abstract. The strategic political-military decision-making process consists of sequential phases starting from Indications up to Termination. Four questions throughout the process have been identified as the key moment requesting political consensus informed by the military advice. They are as mainly: "What is happening?", "Why it is happening and what are the implications?", "What are our response options?", and "End-state achieved?". The paper analyzed the role of Artificial Intelligence (AI) and Modelling and Simulation (M&S) in answering these specific questions in the context of complex environment of political military decision-making. It brings an AI use case that studies the relationship between the quality of military capabilities, percentage of gross domestic product (GDP) spent in military budget and the power index score of each nation. To get there, data gathered from JANES database was analyzed, cleaned, normalized and Neural Network models have been implemented to predict the value of a single political level indicator called Calculated PowerIndex (CPIV). CPIV has been used to exercise the what-if analysis to understand consequences of modification of military capabilities or budget of selected country in the ranked order of all countries. It can serve as a political-military decision-making tool with ability to better explain the way the CPIV is expressed in comparison to the existing black box methodology of PowerIndex (PIV) available from Open Source.

Keywords: Artificial Intelligence · Modelling and Simulation · Strategic Level Decision-Making

1 Introduction

In the current global dynamic geopolitical situation, dealing with threats and taking appropriate actions is the uppermost responsibility of any nations and international organization. Before and during a crisis decisions are made based on incomplete information under high-level of uncertainty. Management of the crisis brings a mechanism to deal with a crisis in holistic manner to reduce the risk in decision-making process.

In NATO, crisis management is understood as the coordinated action taken to defuse crisis, prevent their escalation into armed conflict and contain hostilities if they should results [1]. NATO Crisis Response System (NCRS), that is phased based, starting from

J. Mazal et al. (Eds.): MESAS 2022, LNCS 13866, pp. 269–281, 2023.
https://doi.org/10.1007/978-3-031-31268-7_16

Indications & Warning, followed by Political and Military Assessment, centralized about Planning and escalating in Execution and concluded by Termination, covered one part of the NATO crisis management effort and is manly focused on the strategic political-military level of decisions [2].

In the article, in the introduction chapter, the strategic political-military decision making process (SPMDMP) is described followed by proclamation on M&S as an independent discipline and AI as being part of Emerging Disruptive Technologies in the military context. The second chapter contains proposed generic approach to AI and M&S employment in the SPMDMP. The third chapter brings a Use Case on the use of modelling techniques to support SPMDMP while benefit of an AI algorithm. The closing chapter summarize the AI prototype functionality and drawbacks and define the way-ahead and potential operational use.

1.1 Strategic Political-Military Decision-Making Process

This section described NCRS and identifies the main decision points the political level is faced with.

Decision-making is a complex task with high level of abstraction embraced by the dynamic iterative process of decisions made at different level of command [3]. Traditionally, well know decision-making process in the military domain is expressed as Observe, Orient, Decide Act (OODA) model [4]. The OODA approach heavily depends on the availability of data and information. Open Source data offers unique opportunity to get unlimited resource of information that can be harvested in automated fashion. However it doesn't guarantee that a human or organization can capitalize on it and make their decisions.

NCRS is in principle similar to OODA, however there are two key elements making it even more complex system to be supported by current and future technologies. NCRS is about consensus making in NATO, therefore the basic principle in applied OODA, that commander makes his own decision based on informed situational awareness is not applicable. NATO Nations needs to reach unanimous accord on any NATO activity, no single voice can prevail. Even when situation update is made and confirmed by independent entity, it can be disregard because of its political sensitivity. Another issue is that most of the time data or information is not shared effectively among Nations. Therefore reaching common understanding of the problem is based on the will to share and inform. That's not a case in military domain applied OODA. Sub-ordinated and commanding entities provides data and information as needed.

NCRS consists of sequential phases already starting from Indications up to Termination. When analyzed and elevated at the solely strategic political-military level, the four questions throughout the process can be identified. These questions are central points for NATO leaders to reach the consensus and lately make uniform decision. Therefore, it defines the main decision points in NATO crisis management.

Questions to be answered during NCRS are:

1. What is Happening?
2. Why It is Happening and What Are the Implications?
3. What are our response options?

4. End-state achieved?

These questions drive the whole discussion on the M&S and AI use in SPMDMP.

1.2 M&S and AI

M&S is a scientific discipline that develops and/or uses models, simulations and simulation systems in its lifecycle. The M&S lifecycle commence with design of the model followed by its execution called simulation; all with unique objective to solve defined problem. Model is a physical, mathematical or otherwise logical representation of a system, entity, phenomenon, or process. Simulation is the execution of a system model over time, and finally, simulation system is a combination of interacting elements or components organized to provide a representation of a system or of a part of the real world for an intended use [1].

M&S has been acknowledged as a scientific discipline in accordance with five academic characteristics [5].

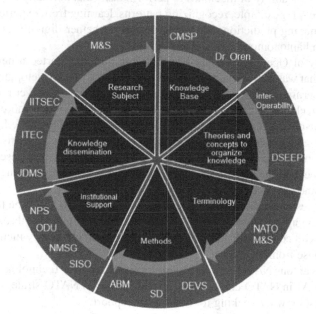

Fig. 1. Six characteristic of a discipline applied in M&S domain.

First and uppermost, a subject of research must exist. That is M&S lifecycle. Then explicit Body of Knowledge (BoK) related to research subject must be recognized. In M&S case, BoK is expressed in Dr. Oren academic classification [6] or by the content of Certified Modeling & Simulation Professional (CMSP) certification program acknowledged by the majority of M&S industry. There is a need to have theories and concepts that can organize knowledge effectively. There is M&S specific theory on Conceptual Interoperability [7] or Distributed Simulation Engineering and Execution Process (DSEEP) is a standardized concept for building federations of computer simulations [8]. A discipline requires to have its own terminology that can be represented by NATO approved M&S Glossary of Terms.

It is request to have developed particular methods. Agent Based modelling (ABM), System Dynamics (SD) or Discrete Event Simulation (DEVS) represent a family of M&S paradigms. Institutional manifestation of a subject taught at universities in graduated programs is demonstrated by Naval Postgraduate School (NPS) or Old Dominium University (ODU). NATO Modelling and Simulation Group (NMSG) and Simulation Interoperability Standards Organization (SISO) organizations assure international institutional support.

Previously described approach to recognize an academic discipline is expanded by adding known mechanisms to disseminate knowledge [9]. In case on M&S, international conferences like Inter-service/Industry Training, Simulation and Education Conference (I/ITSEC) or International Training Technology Exhibition & Conference (ITEC) are organized and a specific M&S Journal of Defense Modelling and Simulation exists. Figure 1 describes the six characteristics of M&S discipline.

AI refers to the ability of machines to perform tasks that normally require human.

intelligence – for example, recognizing patterns, learning from experience, drawing conclusions, making predictions, or taking action – whether digitally or as the smart software behind autonomous physical systems [10].

Availability of Open Source and Big Data big data has started a new path of AI development that was introduced in mid-1950s. Main todays AI development are related to Machine Learning with special attention to Deep Learning, however the scope of AI methods and techniques that are for last 70 years used, is much more broader and shouldn't be disregard. It differs from knowledge based techniques like Expert System and enumerative techniques like Dynamic Programming and Decision Trees up to Fuzzy Logic and Probabilistic methods for uncertain reasoning. Detailed description of AI techniques is beyond the content of the paper, but there are many resources describing classification and examples of AI techniques and methods [11].

AI techniques/methods support three basic activities blocks based on the replication of human behavior that AI is replicating. It starts with ability to sense, through reasoning up to engage with common denominator of learning in all previously mentioned blocks and synergy wise from all blocks.

AI belongs among NATO defined Emerging and Disruptive Technologies. Therefore, application of AI in NATO environment is understood as NATO strategic activity and should be consider when seeking for SPMDMP support.

2   Role of AI and M&S in SPMDMP

Generally speaking the role of AI and M&S in SPMDMP is to reduce uncertainty in a complex environment. We have passed the time when we are seeking more information and more data. Quite the opposed, it is estimated that in 2025 approximately 463 quintillion data will be created every day. We are not short of information and data. We are overwhelmed by it. Not all of the information and data is, however, relevant. It is no longer about who will have more but who will be able to filter through the information most effectively and in a timely manner. The power is in turning data into knowledge, which, in turn, will reduce our uncertainty.

M&S together with AI can bring tailored strategic level data aggregation and visualization on demand and doing so to support understanding of potential intended and unintended effects of strategic decisions. Common denominator is the interoperable synthetic environment with the ability to integrate various data, to perform what-if scenarios across multiple domains including hybrid warfare environment and to run a simulation of cascading effects steaming from strategic decision. Critical factor is to visualize synthetic environment input and output data in aggregated manners through executive dashboard developed for the strategic level that is able to depict, among others, a status of a diplomatic or military mission by aggregating hundreds of different data feed including videos and pictures.

Machine learning techniques can help us to build new models in the synthetic environment when employing Big Training Data from Open Source. Constraints of such models use needs to be articulated in the way it reflects the fact that these models can be used only in the scope of the task relevant to the training scope. Otherwise, the validity of the synthetic environment may be questioned.

When training data is not available, a new model for synthetic environment can be built from design of experiments with the current federated models. By composing two models, new Big Data set can be generated and it can serve as the training data set for a new model. Another approach can be to define the ontology of the specific domain of the model being developed. The anthology would serve as the bases for associate data collection. Collected data would again serve as the training set.

Synthetic environment needs to provide answers to the strategic questions just in time. Potential solution, form system of system point of view, is to replacing detailed physics based models by aggregated ones, without losing the model resolution and its validity. The models from low level of echelon can serve as inputs for the machine learning techniques without supervision to get aggregated model that can finally produce faster answers to the what –if type analysis. The following sub-chapters describe uniqueness of M&S and AI in the specific strategic questions of SPMDMP.

2.1 What is Happening?

Having timely and effective Indications and Warnings is crucial as it can provide the decisive advantage over potential adversaries. If the intelligence indicates potential crisis or an event that NATO needs to respond to, it is at this time the NAC sits together and makes a decision on what to do. It basically about finding any evidence serving to answer the question of: "What to do with the indicators and warning reports?."

To identify quickly what is happening, the situational awareness at the highest strategic level is the ultimate objective. While getting the intelligence is crucial, it is equally important to present decision-makers with digestible and actionable advice appropriate for their level. Reports and analyses about security situations need to be tailored to difference audiences – political leaders will have different requirements than the military authorities. At the same time, they do not operate separately. Providing more effective sharing among them as well as with their capitals is the key here.

Therefore, we need to understand political-military needs. Again, Big Data, one of the key areas from the emerging and disruptive technologies roadmap together with M&S and AI has potential to enhance situational awareness to early identify and analyse potential threats to NATO. Synthetic environment is again the key enabler, it offers the digital replication of NATO environment. It includes human and cognitive dimensions with the ability to analyse sentiment drawn from social media in real time reflecting what people are feeling and saying. However the specificity of this phase is to identify the indicators and warning parameters that would serve to inform the whole SPMDMP.

M&S can, for example, to help to identify the key Indications and Warning parameters for the SPMDMP by running the sensitivity analysis type of experiment that would cover the whole spectrum of (PMESII/ASCOPE) factors in the operation environment.

These key parameters would be used to enhance a crisis anticipation by multi-source fusion and analysis to build indicators and warning including automation, alerting trend and strategic changes by using their unique methodology and a vast application of AI.

Again, having synthetic environment that would fuse, analyse and visualize data would help the staff officers to focus on translating the outcomes into a digestible form rather than analysing and visualising it separately.

2.2   Why it is Happening and What are the Implications?

Once we know what is happening it is now critical to ask why the situation is happening and what the implications are. Having a comprehensive and relevant situational aware-ness is not always enough. For leaders to make a decision on what to do with data and information, they must have regular assessments of the unfolding situation. If faced with an adversary, understanding their intent and goal is an integral part of assessment and analysis. We must also focus on various angles beyond the military domain alone. The focus should be done using PMESII factors. This helps in classifying Indications and Warning and analysing them. To support SPMDMP, it is essential to visualize interde-pendencies among these factors, and analyse and assess the trends. How do changes in Economic and Societal affect the Political and how does this relate to the adversary's goals?

Digital Twin and a federation of Digital Twins seems to be one activity enabling NATO to comprehend and analyse all PMESII aspects of the security environment, especially bringing analysis of adversary intent.

The real-time translation of data with the real-time assessment of activity levels at every spot on the globe can identify how events that are happening affect regional stability. It requires transforming raw information into actionable intelligence.

Analysts should be able to use geospatial services and tools while understanding seeing how the AI engine gathers information through the modelling of this process in informal and formal way. That would bring better understanding and mostly it would increase the trust to the AI black boxes.

To get understanding what may be implications of some events, M&S needs to bring the what – if capacity to describe the second and third order effects. These effects needs to be again translated at strategic level, otherwise it would become tactical appli-cation not suitable for political military leadership. Strategic dashboards depicting the effects of strategic shocks such as electricity blackout, cyber-attack, big human movement, and pandemics) and generic events on the baseline requirements (communication, transportation, energy supplies, food and water, mass casualties, uncontrolled population movement, and continuity of government) through various scenarios can be taken as examples. This particular domain is well described by NATO in the Aggregated Resilience model enabling to understand the implications of strategic shocks for NATO [12].

2.3 What are Our Options?

The next strategic question is covering the phase of NCRS dealing with the response options. Compared to the previous phases, response options development is prescriptive in its purpose but predictive in its character. The key here is to assist the political and military leaders in what a response could be and to provide information supporting the response options development.

Developing a response strategy for the Alliance should not be, once again, limited only to the political and military areas. Instead, it needs to utilize a broader DIME-FIL framework – response options across Diplomatic, Information, Military, Economic, Financial, Intelligence and Law enforcement. In other words, DIMEFIL helps us to classify the actions recommended to the NAC and MC.

M&S plays important role in providing rigorous assessment of potential DIMEFIL courses of action and responses for the consideration of NATO decision-makers.

Developing response options is the most comprehensive tasking because all the information and data that has been collected assessed and analysed feed into the capabilities in order to be able to perform such a task. Therefore there are dependencies on the previous strategic questions.

The already identified Indicators can serve as the foundation when building the M&S services to support Course of Action (CoA) development. It is very similar to the process of operation planning, however political dimension shall not be omitted. Therefore M&S cerates environment where CoA can be firstly designed and communicated in accordance with the strategic objectives driven by key Indictors. Then these CoA can be wargamed to identify the most suitable CoA for the objectives expressed in the form of values of selected Indicators. Simulation together with AI bring the predictive character of these activities. Design of simulation support of WG is essential and needs to employ the maximum level of automation of WG elements to reach the close to real time decision making support. Finding symbiosis between WG for strategic level and its simulation support is the fundamental activity to reach the ultimate goal of reducing uncertainty in decision making process [13].

The last question about achieving the expected end-state, is similar to the assessment moment, when Indicators values are confronted with the expected values defined for the strategic end-state.

3 AI and M&S Use Case for SPMDMP

This part describes the use case demonstrating the value of modelling and AI in the SPMDMP, especially related to the identification of Indications and Warning parameters in SPMDMP. It describes a prototype that employ the AI model to predict the value of such parameter for what-if type analysis through simulation.

When searching for parameters that would be adequate to the strategic political military level decision, the *Global Fire Power Index Value* [14] was identified. It is generally described as the value collected about Nations describing national power scores and their ranking across globe. This Nations' power scores were used as outputs to train neural networks.

As there is no publicly available and approved single dataset to create an AI model for SPMDMP, we created our dataset by employing JANES dataset [15] It is used to collect nations' military capabilities and financial indicators. These data types were used as features (inputs) to train neural networks.

After combining and pre-processing of data, different types of neural networks were created to predict a nation's power index value based on military capabilities and budget info that is published in JANES database.

Following sections provide detailed information about on the model training and testing.

3.1 JANES Database

JANES is a subscription based service that provides nations' military capabilities and basic financial indicators that are collected from open sources.

In JANES Database, the individual military capabilities of each nation are represented by color codes which are black, yellow, orange and green, respectively. (*Meanings: Black- There is no capability to Green-The capability is sufficient*) To create our model, we choose 21 types of military capability and 2 types of financial indicators as shown in Table 1.

Color codes were converted in to numeric scale (*0-black, 1-red, 2-orange, 3-yellow, 4-green*) and the data was normalized in to 0–1 scale for the sake of simplicity.

The two financial indicators (TDB, GDP) are used as is, but they are also included in to same normalization process.

3.2 Global Firepower Ranking

Global Firepower Ranking is a web site that publishes nation's overall military power scores (defined as *PowerIndex* rest of this paper) and rankings annually. Basically, the nations' ranking are based on order of *PowerIndex* values of nations. But, the algorithms and models that Global Firepower uses to calculate *PowerIndex value* are not publicly available, therefore in their website it is stated as following;

> *"The finalized Global Firepower ranking below utilizes over 50 individual factors to determine a given nation's PowerIndex ('PwrIndx') score with categories ranging from military might and financials to logistical capability and geography."*

As a result, the calculation methods and the "50 individual factors" are "black boxes" for researchers, but calculated *PowerIndex* value *(PIV)* is publicly available. It is also stated in their website that, 0 value for the *PIV* is a perfect score, which means that the more closer to 0 (zero), the more power a country has. (*i.e. the U.S.A has a PIV score 0.00453, and 1st Ranking*). Therefore the use case is about computing our own PIV that would serve as one of the Indicator for SPMDMP while being as close as possible to behaviour of already published *PowerIndex* values.

3.3 Neural Network (NN) Setup

As stated in Sect. 3.2, the algorithms and the models are not publicly available in Global Firepower website, as a result, we wanted to create our own model to predict a nation's *PIV* value *(defined as CPIV – Calculated Power Index Value rest of the paper)* and its military ranking regarding to this calculation. We assumed that, creating a Neural Network (NN) would be the best option to predict *CPIVs*, and that requires solving a regression problem, so that, we set up a NN model that has 23 nodes (Table 1) for inputs and one node for output. (Fig. 2).

To create AI models, we selected 20 nations for training, and 11 nations for testing, respectively, and ordered these 31 countries based on their *PIV* scores among each other.

WEKA [16] was used to create NNs and conduct tests. WEKA is an open source, Java based software that provides a collection of machine learning algorithms for data mining tasks.

Table 1. Input Data Types for Proposed Model

MC_i	Military Capability (*MC*)	Capability Domain
1	Air-to-Air Warfare	Air Defense
2	Ground Based Air Defense	Air Defense
3	Maritime Anti-Air Warfare	Air Defense
4	Offensive Air Support	Fire Support
5	Indirect Fire	Fire Support
6	Naval Surface Fire Support	Fire Support
7	Air (Space) Recon	ISR
8	Ground Recon	ISR
9	Maritime Surveillance	ISR
10	Aerial Refueling	Logistics
11	Airlift	Logistics
12	Maritime Transport	Logistics
13	A SuW – Airborne	Anti-surface Warfare
14	A SuW – Surface	Anti-surface Warfare
15	A SuW- Submarine	Anti-surface Warfare

(continued)

Table 1. (*continued*)

MC_i	Military Capability (*MC*)	Capability Domain
16	ASW – Airborne	Anti-Submarine Warfare
17	ASW – Surface	Anti-Submarine Warfare
18	ASW- Submarine	Anti-Submarine Warfare
19	Armored Warfare	Direct Ground Combat
20	Infantry Ops	Direct Ground Combat
21	Combat Engineering	Direct Ground Combat
22	Total Defense Budget - TDB	Financial
23	Gross Domestic Product – GDP	Financial

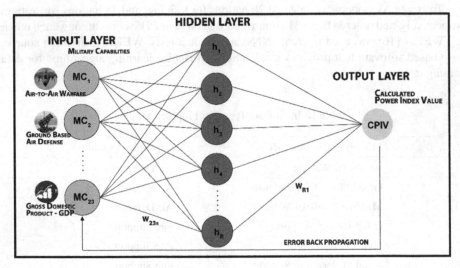

Fig. 2. Neural Network Representation

3.4 Test Results

The best NN model was selected based on correlation coefficient and Mean Square.
Error (MSE) results, as shown in Table 2.

In order to reach the best results we tested our NN setup with different no. of hidden nodes, learning rate, momentum and epochs parameters. As shown in Table 2, test no.2 has the best results based on correlation coefficient and MSE.

Table 2. NN Test Setups with Different Parameters

Test #	Hidden Layer Nodes	Learning Rate	Momentum	Epoch	Correlation Coefficient	Mean Square Error
1	2	0.3	0.2	1500	0.9218	0.1365
2	2	0.2	0.2	2500	0.9530	0.1298
3	4	0.2	0.2	2500	0.9106	0.1492
4	4	0.1	0.2	3500	0.9144	0.1534
5	4	0.1	0.2	5500	0. 9144	0. 1534

The following table (Table 3) shows the predicted values on our testing dataset.

Table 3. Testing Data Set Results Based on NN setup no 2 in Table 2.

Country	CPIV	PIV
1	0.458	1
2	0.012	0.031832
3	0.074	0.071681
4	0.035	0.051699
5	0.560	0.85545
6	0.449	0.6378
7	0.046	0.001841
8	0.043	0.002224
9	0.028	0.144895
10	0.272	0.328527
11	0.004	0.107885

3.5 Use Case Scenario

For the use case scenario, our motivation was to answer the following question:

"How much will a nation's power index/ranking be effected when one or more of its military capabilities/financial indicators change?".

In order to demonstrate our use case, we selected a nation from our test dataset as reference, and in order not to disclose its name we named it as Skolkan.

Skolkan's predicted CPIV is 0.449 and it is 29th in ranking order among 31 nations composed of *Nations in Training Dataset + Testing Datasets*.

Table 4. Effects of changed values of selected parameters of input data in the overall ranking.

Use Case	Modification	CPIV **after** modification	Ranking **after** modification
1	↑ TDB	0.428	29 --
2	↑ GDP	0.42	28 ↑
3	↑ TDB & ↑ GDP	0.42	28 ↑
3	↑ Air-to-Air Warfare	0.288	25 ↑
4	↑ Air-to-Air Warfare & ↑ TDB	0.288	25 ↑
5	↑ Air-to-Air Warfare & ↑ GDP	0.254	24 ↑

Then, we modified Skolkan's TDB, GDP and Air-to-Air Warfare values to see how these values will affect Skolkan's CPIV and ranking order.

As shown in Table 4, when we increase Skolkan's Air-to-Air Warfare capability, TDB and GDP, Skolkan's CPIV and ranking has increased significantly. Further tests can be conducted with changing different capabilities with different reference values. In this manner the what-if analysis can be conducted and expected effects of power index behaviour can predicted.

4   Conclusion

The variety and high level of ambiguity of questions related to SPMDMP shows that the NCRS cannot be replicated by a single monolithic solution for which one synthetic environment can be pre- created and support different granularity questions. Ultimately, support NCRS will depend on already established framework formed from M&S and AI services plus ad hoc designed and implemented modules serving the specific needs of decision needed to be taken in that moment. All in all, each decision should be supported by a different M&S/AI services or federation of already existing services with a new ones build from the scratch. However, common agreed Indicators from PMESSI/ASCOPE should be identified, agreed and mostly screened in any moment of the SPMDMP. The whole lifecycle of a crisis description should be driven by these validated Indicators.

The Use Case identified Indicator CPIV that may be seen as a good candidate to describe the power of Nation related to military capabilities and budget. It is predicted based on the input data aggregated from JANES. The main shortcomings of the Use Case is limited number of training and testing data that brought relatively high level of Mean Square Error. However, it doesn't degraded the main idea behind the Use Case to use NN based on the available open source data to predict values of single political level decision making indicator based on military capabilities and budget data.

References

1. AAP-06. Edition 2021. NATO glossary of terms and definitions
2. Maciej, M.: NATO crisis mangement system as a subject of research under the security studies in Poland. in book: Person. Nation. State. Interdisciplinary Research in Security Studies editors Cezary Smuniewski, Agostino Massa, Andrea Zanini, pp.72–100 (2021)
3. Roberts, K.H., Stout, S.K., Halpern, J.J.: Decision dynamics in two high reliability military organizations. Manage. Sci. **40**(5), 614–624 (1994)
4. Boyd, J.: A discourse on winning and losing. Maxwell Air Force Base, AL: Air University Library Document No. M-U 43947 (Briefing slides) (1987)
5. Krishnan, A.: What are academic disciplines? some observations on the disciplinarity vs. interdisciplinarity debate (2009)
6. Ören, T.I.: Toward the body of knowledge of modeling and simulation (M&SBOK). In: Proc. of I/ITSEC (Interservice/Industry Training, Simulation Conference). Nov. 28–Dec. 1, Orlando, Florida; paper, pp. 1–19 (2025)
7. Tolk, A., Muguira, J.A.: The levels of conceptual interoperability model (LCIM). In: Proceedings of the IEEE Fall Simulation Interoperability Workshop; 2003. IEEE CS Press; (2003)
8. Pratoomma, P., Tepkunchorn, K., Tanvilaipong, N., Kraikhow, J.: Analysis and design using distributed simulation engineering and execution process (DSEEP) as a system development life cycle of iLVC simulators. In: 2016 Second Asian Conference on Defence Technology (ACDT), pp. 84–88 (2016). https://doi.org/10.1109/ACDT.2016.7437648
9. Lenoir, T.: Instituting Science: The Cultural Production of Scientific Disciplines. Stanford University Press, Stanford (1997)
10. USAF. USAF AI Annex to DoD AI Strategy. Technical report, United States Air Force (2019). https://www.af.mil/Portals/1/documents/5/USAF-AI-Annex-to-DoD-AI-Strategy.pdf.
11. Hamilton, S., Jakeman, A.J., Norton, J.: Artificial intelligence techniques: an introduction to their use for modelling environmental systems. Math. Comput. Simul. **78**, 379–400 (2008). https://doi.org/10.1016/j.matcom.2008.01.028
12. Hodicky, J., Özkan, G., Özdemir, H., Stodola, P., Drozd, J., Buck, W.: Analytic hierarchy process (AHP)-based aggregation mechanism for resilience measurement: NATO aggregated resilience decision support model. Entropy **22**, 1037 (2020). https://doi.org/10.3390/e22091037
13. Hodicky, J., Hernandez, A.S.: Wargaming, automation, and military experimentation to quantitatively and qualitatively inform decision-making. In: Turnitsa, C., Blais, C., Tolk, A. (eds.) Simulation and Wargaming (2021). https://doi.org/10.1002/9781119604815.ch5
14. Global Firepower. https://www.globalfirepower.com/. Accessed 02 Aug 2022
15. JANES. https://www.janes.com/. Accessed 08 Aug 2022
16. WEKA. https://www.cs.waikato.ac.nz/ml/weka/. Accessed 08 Aug 2022

Modular Interface Framework for Advanced Soldier-Platform Interoperability

Israel Lopez-Toledo[1,2]([✉])(iD), Dylan Charter[1,2](iD), Raul Ortiz[3], Evan Schmitz[2], Charles Cheng[4], Dylan Pasley[1,2](iD), and Ahmet Soylemezoglu[1]

[1] Construction Engineering Research Lab, Champaign, IL 61822, USA
{Israel.J.LopezToledo,Dylan.T.Charter,Dylan.A.Pasley,
Ahmet.Soylemezoglu}@erdc.dren.mil
[2] University of Illinois, Champaign, IL 61801, USA
evanls3@illinois.edu
[3] University of Puerto Rico - Mayagüez, Mayagüez 00680, Puerto Rico
raul.ortiz11@upr.edu
[4] Northwestern University, Evanston, IL 60208, USA
charlescheng2024@u.northwestern.edu

Abstract. The U.S Military and other foreign Armed Forces have been slowly embracing the use of robotic systems in combat operations, enabling them to mitigate unnecessary risks for dismounted soldiers. As technologies continue to improve, semi-autonomous platforms can carry out complicated tasks and keep Warfighters out of harm's way. Nevertheless, no matter how good the technology is, it remains susceptible to failure or encountering situations that it does not know how to handle. This means that soldiers must be prepared to assist or take over the robotic systems at a moment's notice. To ensure that Combat Engineers can smoothly transition between active and supporting roles throughout the mission, robotic platforms must have robust user interfaces that adjust to the soldiers' needs. To address this gap, we introduce a framework that allows a user to take full control of a Robot Operating System (ROS) based platform utilizing interfaces such as wearable devices, Virtual Reality (VR) headsets, and traditional workstations. With this framework, users may gather situational information, execute autonomous routines or tele-operate a ROS-based platform from any device that has access to the robot's network. We present three user interfaces to demonstrate the use of our framework and discuss its impact to the role of Combat Engineers and robotic platforms in future operations. These user interfaces include a military tactical mobile application, a simulated workstation in virtual reality, and a smartwatch application.

Keywords: Autonomous Platforms · ROS · User Interfaces · Modular Platforms · Virtual Reality · Wearable Technology · Mobile Devices

J. Mazal et al. (Eds.): MESAS 2022, LNCS 13866, pp. 282–298, 2023.
https://doi.org/10.1007/978-3-031-31268-7_17

1   Introduction

This paper introduces the research, including the challenges and successes that were encountered while (1) developing a modular user interface (UI) framework that is software and hardware agnostic, and (2) exploring new technologies and techniques for graphical user interfaces (GUIs) that will improve soldier-platform interoperability. The three GUIs developed in this research include a virtual reality (VR) suite, a plugin for an already existing UI used in military applications known as the Android Team Awareness Kit (ATAK), and finally a wearable device.

1.1   The Problem Space

The limits and capabilities of robotic platforms are expanding as the technologies they depend on evolve at a rapid pace. Currently, it is common practice to design a platform to fit the needs of a particular task resulting in a mix of bespoke hardware and software solutions. With the ad-hoc nature, and speed in which platforms are developing, special consideration needs to be given to platform control, and robot-human interaction solutions. With these conditions in mind, a unique problem space presents itself as we introduce these complicated platforms into the dynamic operating environments of the Warfighter's mission. During any point in a mission, there are a number of unpredictable events, which could interrupt proper connection, and operation of a platform in the field. These unpredictable events highlight the Warfighter's need for easily digestible and highly flexible ways to interact with their semi-autonomous platforms. Additionally, unforeseeable circumstances could add to the scope of a mission. Therefore, the need to innovate platform-soldier interoperability stems from the unpredictable nature of the Warfighter's operating environment. A modular interface framework gives ground troops a flexible and robust solution to establish and maintain control of their platforms in a safe and secure manner.

1.2   Paper Outline

Section 2 provides an overview of the reasoning why the Combat Engineer needs semi-autonomous robotic equipment along with an overview of the hardware and software utilized. Section 3 describes the literary review that was done in order to determine the current state of the art technology in this area. Following, Sect. 4 goes into the in-depth review of the framework and the user interfaces. Finally, Sect. 5 details the final remarks and how this work can be improved upon in the future.

2   Project Background and Rational

Developing robotic platforms to aid in the use of combat operations is not a well-defined nor simple objective. Combat Engineers and soldiers are highly trained individuals that deal with making life-threatening decisions that must often be made instantaneously. The first step taken to approach this is to offer tele-operated robotic systems, where the solider is able to still perform these quick thinking actions from afar, while not being in danger. However, tele-operation has its own challenges including radio signal loss due to interference or jamming, lag in the system both from the sensors as well as the commands being sent to the robotic platform. With these challenges in mind, semi-autonomous operation is the next phase towards fully autonomous robotic systems. Semi-autonomous operations allows for the valuable knowledge of the Combat Engineer to be used to direct the pieces of equipment to perform desired tasks without putting them in danger. This also allows for better situational awareness as these robotic platforms are able to perform large area scans creating a near real-time semantically labelled 3D environment. In order for these robotic systems to be useful, the soldiers must have an easy and intuitive way to adapt this technology into their current workflow which motivated the research presented in this paper.

Robotics for Engineer Operations (REO) focuses on developing these robotic applications to help address these issues. After developing tele-operated Army engineering equipment, REO has been focusing on semi-autonomous site characterization vehicles that produce a near real-time semantically labelled 3D environment. This 3D environment is not only useful for situational awareness, but also provides information about the environment to be processed in the future by semi-autonomous construction equipment. The Combat Engineer commands the robot to perform certain actions such as navigate to the unknown area for reconnaissance or obtain soil information via a cone penetrometer. REO's mission space also requires research to develop Global Navigation Satellite System (GNSS) denied localization due to issues with signal being easily jammed or spoofed.

2.1 Requirements

One of the main requirements in the development of the framework and user interface for platform control is the ability for the system to be modular. The Robot Operating System (ROS) is an open-sourced message framework that is designed for modularity [6]. ROS is already commonly used in military applications, where the open-sourced framework has been developed closed-source and renamed ROS-M [4]. Developing in ROS also provides an abstraction layer such that the hardware, like radios and computers, is interchangeable as long as they provide the same communication protocol and architecture. For the system developed in this research, the standard internet protocol (IP) network is utilized such that any radio system whether that be a standard WIFI router or an encrypted software defined radio (SDR) is supported.

Given the large lead time required for new technology to be used in battlefield, it is crucial to develop the framework to be compatible with some of the technology already utilized in battle. Beyond this, the UI must be able to convey the information provided back from the robotic platform in a way that is easy to view the data collected quickly in near real-time without having to utilize valuable time to process the data. ROS can be operated in a distributed network such that the data could be processed on the soldier's side of the operation, however, given the mission space of REO, these robotic platforms process all of the data onboard. Finally, the solider must be able to easily interact with the robotic platforms in a quick manner with the ability to override the semi-autonomous features in case of emergency. In the warfighting scenario, human lives will not be put at stake to save the robotic piece of equipment, so safety implementations such as emergency stops and return to base functionalities are critical to ensure a successful and safe operation.

2.2 System Hardware

The three GUI's explored in this research will be described in more detail below, but they are all hosted in different types of devices, showcasing the framework's modularity. The virtual reality system utilizes an HTC Vive Pro running in Unity in a Windows 10 environment. A Samsung Galaxy tablet running the stock Android operating system is utilized for ATAK. The ATAK plugin is compatible with ATAK on any Android device, but the tablet was chosen for its large screen and ease of operation. The wearable device utilized in this research is the Samsung Galaxy Watch that utilizes the Tizen OS; however this development is compatible with any Tizen OS wearable device. Figure 1 provides an overview of the hardware utilized for the UI.

Fig. 1. System Hardware Utilized from left to right: HTC Vive Pro, Samsung Galaxy tablet, Samsung Galaxy Watch

The robotic platform being utilized in this research is a modified version of Clearpath's Warthog as seen in Fig. 2. The Clearpath Warthog is an amphibious four-wheeled robotic platform that is configurable to utilize four tracks in place of the wheels. Upon receiving from purchasing, the base system comes configured with an onboard computer running Ubuntu 18.04 headless with ROS Melodic. This onboard computer publishes information such as the battery voltage of the system and wheel odometry information. There are four onboard emergency stops located at each corner of the system, and one off-board emergency stop. By default, there is a standard pulse width modulation (PWM) remote controller to tele-operate the system. This platform was chosen for its size, the large amount of documentation that was available online for the system, and the ROS computer that is delivered factory installed. The system was modified to include sensors such as LiDAR, inertial measurement units (IMUs), and cameras in order to perform the semi-autonomous mapping and navigation. Given the use case of this effort, these platforms contain a series of high Central Processing Unit (CPU) core count computers that contain Graphic Processing Units (GPUs) in order to perform all of the data processing onboard the platform. This not only just allows the system to operate and perform mapping in near real-time, but also allows the system to be operational given loss of communication.

Fig. 2. Clearpath Warthog in wheeled and tracked configurations. [1]

2.3   System Software

As described above, a critical piece of software to be compatible with, from the robotic platform's side is ROS; however, the framework developed doesn't require ROS to be running on any of the UI devices. The only requirement is that a ROS server is running on one of the computers within the network. Typically this would be on the robotic platform. In the research detailed in this report, ROS Noetic, running on Ubuntu 20.04, was utilized. However, with some modification, this framework could be utilized on other versions of ROS and Linux distributions. ROS Noetic is the first version of ROS to standardize Python 3 so older versions would have to utilize this. Development of the user interfaces also requires the use of some tools and software. The virtual reality interface requires the Unity engine which is a common video game development platform. This engine was chosen for its ease of development and high compatibility with the HTC Vive headset. It also utilizes SteamVR which allows for VR support in Unity. The developed Android interface runs as a plugin on top of the Android Team Awareness Kit (ATAK) application. ATAK is an Android smartphone geospatial infrastructure and military situation awareness app. It allows for precision targeting, surrounding land formation intelligence, situational awareness, navigation, and data sharing [5]. The motivation for developing a plugin for ATAK arises from the fact that the app is already deployed in the military, and that eases the plugin integration into future operations. This plugin was developed in an Android Studio environment. The wearable device GUI was developed as a Tizen .NET application, in a Visual Studio environment.

3   State of the Art

The increasing interest in the areas of cloud computing and Internet-of-Things (IoT) has led researches to explore how to integrate robots into the Internet. Past work has focused mainly on the server side of the problem, particularly on exploring the best ways to expose robotic systems over the network (i.e. utilizing REST and SOAP web services). Although our research also looks into exposing a robotic system utilizing web services, it puts special attention into the client side as well. In this work we develop graphical user interfaces hosted on devices that are not commonly used in robotics, in order to explore their practicality and effect on user experience. In this section we will discuss some of the past works related to this research.

In [9], the author presents a novel approach for integrating Web services into ROS. The researcher develops both SOAP and REST Web service interfaces for exposing ROS resources to client applications. This work focuses on designing a complex software architecture utilizing the ROS-JAVA environment, on the other hand we go for a simpler setup in the ROS-Node.js environment, since it was convenient for supporting more ROS resources in future iterations. This work also pays no special attention to client GUIs in the system.

In [14], the authors propose a platform for mobile robotics that complies with the REST architectural style. In this work the authors utilize a mobile robot that is not ROS based and their client side is limited to Matlab and JAVA applications; this highly differs from our work which focuses in ROS platforms and accepts any client application.

In [12], the authors propose an application of laser-based autonomous robot navigation techniques to the problem of data center monitoring. In this work the authors rely on a remote cloud platform to run certain layers of their architecture, but this setup is not optimal for combat environments. This is why our proposed solution runs mostly onboard the robot, to ensure that difficult environment will not hinder the Combat Engineers' missions.

In [13], the authors propose an architecture to enable the development and deployment of companion robot applications. Their architecture is REST-based and consists of different layers, ranging from low-level services to communicate with hardware devices to high-level application components for interacting with end-users. In this setup clients are able to directly interact with low-level hardware components through RESTful interfaces. This architecture raises security concerns, since the low-level services could be exploited to harm or take over the robotic platform, thus it is not viable for our use cases.

In [7], the authors develop a virtual reality-based teleoperation interface for autonomous systems by bridging ROS and Unity. Utilizing their system, a user can take control and teleoperate a robotic ground vehicle through a virtual reality platform. This work focuses more on the mapping aspect of the robotic system and the interface lets the user control a simulated vehicle in a 3rd person view. Our research focuses on a virtual workstation that is equivalent to one in real-life, the benefit being that this workstation is customizable to maximize user efficiency and adjust to any robotic platform.

In [16], the authors present a human robot interaction (HRI) approach that allows a hands-free natural interaction with a mobile robot. The motion of the user's wrist is recognized by means of a smartwatch and translated into control inputs for the robot. This research explores the use of wearable technology as a practical means for HRI, but while they focus on a completely hands-free approach, we have developed a smartwatch application that requires users to actively interact with the device on their wrist.

In [8], the authors present a smartwatch application able to support operators in hybrid assembly lines, offering dedicated interfaces and putting the operator in the execution loop. This research explores the capabilities of smartwatches as user interfaces for robotics and makes a good case for these devices as tools for human-in-the-loop scenarios. The authors focus solely on industrial robotics, thus differing greatly from our work's use case and implementation.

4   Design and Results

The following sections present the system architecture developed in this work. This research was conducted in order to develop a modular user interface framework, along with GUI elements, that improve user experience and task completion with semi-autonomous robotic platforms. This section concludes with a discussion of the separate components that comprise our system. Using the processes outlined below, we were able to successfully establish a user interface framework that is able to expose a ROS-based semi-autonomous robotic platform, over the network, to any graphical user interface (i.e. a smartwatch application). The foundational platform that was established with these methods allows end-users to utilize the GUI that best fits the current task and permits easy transition between multiple GUIs during an operation, this ultimately improves user-platform cooperation and mission performance.

4.1   Architecture

An overview of the proposed architecture can be seen in Fig. 3. As shown in the figure, the system is comprised of three layers: the Robot Layer, the Service Layer, and the Client Layer. The general overview of the system is as follows; the Robot Layer hosts all the applications that manage the platform's semi-autonomous behavior and its low-level controllers. The Service layer hosts all the web services that expose the robotic platform to clients. The Client layer hosts all the graphical user interfaces that allow end-users to interact with the robotic platform.

For the purpose of this work, we have developed three GUIs: a smartwatch application, a virtual reality command station, and an android application plugin. By utilizing wearable technology, virtual reality and mobile devices, users can better adapt to different mission environments, roles and tasks. Although in this work the GUIs and technologies explored were the aforementioned, any desired GUI, hosted on any device, can be utilized with the system presented in this research.

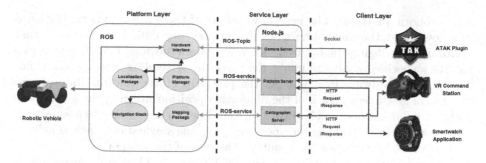

Fig. 3. System Architecture

4.2   System Back-End

This section will present an in-depth description of the server side of the system and the software setup of the robotic platform. As previously mentioned, the robotic platforms are developed utilizing ROS Noetic running on Ubuntu 20.04, but this framework could be applied to any ROS1 system running on any distribution of Linux. These platforms utilize state of the art encrypted network radios; however this system could be easily replicated over a standard internet protocol (IP) network.

Platform Layer. The robotic platform layer holds the components that manage the platform's hardware and semi-autonomy. This layer is comprised of five components: the hardware interface, the localization package, the navigation stack, the mapping package and the platform manager. All of these components are collections of scripts & libraries that operate within the ROS platform.

The hardware interface enables communication and data transfer between the hardware resources, such as sensors, actuators, and controllers, in the robotic platform and the rest of the system. This component takes advantage of the ROS middle-ware platform to provide an abstraction layer for the hardware resources and expose them to the rest of the system. The hardware resources are exposed as streams of data via ROS topics and ROS services; utilizing these ROS communication schemes, other components in the system can process sensory data and manipulate low-level hardware (i.e. motor controllers).

The localization package is a collection of non-linear state estimators for robots moving in 3D (or 2D) space. Each of the state estimators can fuse an arbitrary number of sensors (i.e. IMUs, odometers, GPS receivers, etc.) to track the 15 dimensional state of the robot [11]. This component is a customized version of the standard ROS robot-localization package developed in [11], and overall takes care of broadcasting the accurate position of the robotic platform to the rest of the system.

The navigation stack takes in information from odometry and sensor streams and outputs velocity commands. This component is a customized version of standard ROS navigation package [10], and handles the autonomous navigation of the robotic platform. The general workflow of the autonomous navigation is as follows; first the navigation stack gathers sensory data from the platform's environment utilizing the hardware interface's data outputs. It then generates a path to a specified goal, and moves the platform by sending velocity commands back to the hardware interface. As the platform moves towards its goal, the navigation stack keeps track of the platform's position utilizing the localization package and monitors the platform's surroundings to adjust the path as needed. Once the platform reaches the specified goal, the navigation stack concludes navigation and broadcasts the results to the rest of the system.

The mapping package takes in sensory data of the platform's surroundings and generates 2D & 3D maps [15]. This component processes and stores, in a database, relevant environment information tied to real-world positions. With the stored information, various type of maps can be generated containing useful information like RGB data, material classification, navigability, etc. These maps can be useful to end-users for mission planning and location scouting. Overall, this component generates 2D & 3D maps autonomously and in near real-time while the robotic platform roams an unknown area.

The platform manager monitors the robotic platform's status and controls its behavior. This component interacts with all of the other components discussed so far and exposes them to end-users via ROS services. Thus, through the platform manager it is possible to execute commands and gather sensor data or the robot's status information. To give an idea of how this component works, we will present the platform manager's battery monitor.

The battery monitor is a platform manager's feature that broadcasts the current robot battery information via a ROS-service and handles platform behavior as battery levels drop. In order to monitor battery levels, the platform manager subscribes to the battery voltage ROS-topic, that is published by the hardware interface. Once subscribed, the platform manager receives battery information continuously and makes it accessible for the rest of the system via a ROS-service. When battery voltage drops below optimal levels (battery operational levels are specified by the user), the platform manager begins emitting system warnings and attempts to return to base (a designated home coordinate, that is specified by the user), by sending a goal command to the navigation stack. Finally, if battery voltage drops to critical levels, the platform manager sends a shutdown command to the hardware interface, to safeguard the platform's batteries. This feature demonstrates how the platform manager makes use of other platform layer components to control the robot's behavior autonomously and exposes important information to the system by hosting ROS-services. The platform manager is also able to accept user input through ROS-services, to set system settings (i.e. the home coordinate) or execute commands (i.e. initiate a navigation command to a user specified goal).

Service Layer. The system service layer holds the servers and web services that expose the robotic platform, over the network, to clients outside the ROS environment. This layer is comprised of three components: the platform server, the camera server, and the cartographer server. All of these components are HTTP servers developed in the Node.js environment and are hosted in the robotic platform. A RESTful architecture was utilized to implement the web services.

The platform server holds the web service that allows clients to set robot system settings, execute certain commands and request sensory data or robot status information. This component interacts with the robotic platform using the previously discussed platform manager. To achieve this, the platform server utilizes the rosnodejs [2] library and interacts with the platform manager as a ROS-service client. The overall workflow of a client interaction with the robotic platform is as follows; first, the client sends out an HTTP request to the platform server with optional JSON data in the body of the request. The server receives the client's request and processes it, then it sends out a ROS-service client request to one of the platform manager's ROS-services. The platform manager processes the received ROS-service request, and responds to the platform server using a ROS-service response. Finally, the server returns an HTTP response to the client with JSON data attached, containing the information received from the platform manager. Table 1 includes some examples of the REST resources with their descriptions and HTTP actions. Figure 4 illustrates a client's interaction with the robotic platform through the platform server.

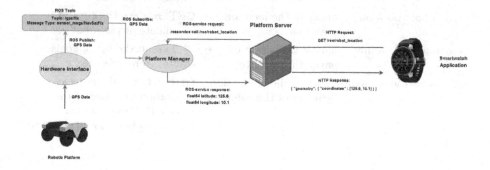

Fig. 4. Client Server Interaction

The camera server allows clients to stream camera feedback from the robotic platform. The overall workflow of a client streaming the robot's camera feedback is as follows; first, the server subscribes (utilizing the rosnodejs library) to the robotic platform's camera ROS-topic, which is hosted by the hardware interface. Once it receives the camera stream, as a raw binary data buffer, the server encodes the data buffer into base64 and continuously broadcasts it to a socket (utilizing the socket.io library). The client must then listen to the socket, to retrieve the encoded data buffer. Afterwards, it must decode the data buffer from base64 and convert the it to an appropriate image format that it can display to the end-user.

The cartographer server allows clients to request 2D maps of the area surrounding the robotic platform. These maps can contain an optional marker identifying the robotic platform's exact location. The mapping package, previously mentioned, takes care of generating the 2D maps and broadcasting them to the rest of the system. To generate these maps, the mapping package consumes apriori satellite imagery and fuses it with live sensor data [15]. The resulting maps are then pushed to a tile map server (Geoserver [3]), hosted on the robotic platform, as TIFF files. As an alternative, the maps are also accessible through a ROS-service as ROS images. These ROS map images display a smaller area around the vehicle compared to the ones in the tile map server. The cartographer server specifically allows access to the ROS map images, since the larger maps can be accessed directly through the tile map server's API. When a client requests a map to the cartographer server via HTTP request, the server creates a ROS-service client request and receives the map from the mapping package's ROS-service. The map is then sent to the client as a PNG image attached to the HTTP response.

Table 1. Examples of REST Resources

Resources	Description	HTTP Action
/reo/battery_level	manages the voltage of the robot	GET: retrieve the current voltage of the robot
/reo/robot_position	manages the location of the robot	GET: retrieve the current coordinate of the robot
/reo/navigate_route	handle the action of navigating a route	PUT: send the list of goals (route) to be executed
/reo/navigation_mode	manages the navigation behavior of the robor	GET: retrieve the current navigation behavior of the vehicle PUT: update the navigation behavior of the robot

4.3 System Front-End

This section will present an in-depth description of the Client Layer of the system, going over the three GUIs developed for this research. All of the GUIs presented in this work interact with the robotic platform by listening to a socket or making HTTP requests to the servers hosted in the robotic platform. This means that the devices that host the GUIs must be on the same network as the robotic platform.

ATAK Plugin. The plugin developed for the "Android Team Awareness Kit" android application, allows users to interact with a ROS-based robotic platform from any mobile device. This plugin takes advantage of ATAK's mission planning tools, such as route creation and tile map sever access, to improve user experience when operating the robotic platform. The main features that the developed ATAK plugin can perform are the following: change navigation mode, display map, execute route, return home, execute point of interest, monitor robot system status, and display platform's position. The change navigation mode feature allows users to set the navigation behavior for the robotic platform. The three navigation behaviors supported are: hold position (platform ignores any command to move), manual mode (platform only follows teleoperation commands), and autonomous mode (platform only follows navigation stack commands). The display map feature retrieves a user selected map, from the tile map server hosted on the robotic platform, and displays it on the main screen of the app. The execute route feature allows users to draw a route on the current map and have the robotic platform follow it; this route is in fact a list of goal positions that is sent to the robotic platform through the platform server and it is executed by the navigation stack. The return home feature allows users to specify the location of the home base on the current map and have the robotic platform return to it autonomously, when needed. The execute point of interest allows a user to set a particular goal on the current map and have the robotic platform navigate to it. The monitor robot system status feature displays important system information to the user, such as: current navigation mode, battery level, emergency stop status, etc. Finally, the display platform's position feature places a live marker on the current map, that always points to the robotic platform's current location. Figure 5 presents the ATAK plugin menus, this image shows the current map, the user drawn route (white line), the home position (blue square), the robot status (underneath vehicle information) and the change mode buttons (at the bottom of the screen). Figure 6 presents maps generated by mapping package and displayed on ATAK.

Fig. 5. REO Control ATAK plugin main menu (Color figure online)

Smartwatch Application. The smartwatch application allows users to monitor and interact with a ROS-based robotic platform from a wearable device. This application provides users with the convenience of quick access to the robotic platform from anywhere in the field. The main features that the smartwatch application can perform are the following: change navigation mode, find robot, leader-follower, secure user mode, display platform's position, and monitor robot system status. The change navigation mode feature allows users to set the navigation behavior for the robotic platform. The find robot feature displays the distance from the user to the robot's location, this allows users to track down a platform that is no longer in line of sight; this is similar to commercial services like Tiles and AirTags. The leader-follower feature periodically broadcasts the user's location (with a safety distance to ensure the platform does not get dangerously close to the user) to the robotic platform, and this location is used as a goal for the navigation stack resulting in the robotic platform autonomously following the user. The secure user mode feature periodically broadcasts the user's location to the robotic platform, and this location is presented as an obstacle to the navigation stack and results in the robotic platform avoiding the provided location and ensuring user safety. The display platform's position feature displays the current position of the vehicle on a satellite map; for this iteration of the feature, we utilized the Google Maps Tizen API. The monitor robot system status feature displays important system information to the user, such as: current navigation mode, battery level, emergency stop status, etc. Figure 7 presents some examples of the smartwatch app screens,

Fig. 6. ATAK Costmap (left), ATAK Classification (center), ATAK Moisture Map (right)

Fig. 7. (From left to right) The smartwatch UI menu, the robot system status, the platform's position on the map

VR Command Center. The virtual reality application allows users to monitor and interact with a ROS-based robotic platform from a VR headset. This application provides users with the opportunity to have an immersive virtual workstation that is fully customizable to adjust to the user's needs and robotic platforms' features. The main features that the VR application can perform are the following: change navigation mode, camera stream, VR teleoperation, monitor robot system status, indicator lights, and display platform's position. The change navigation mode feature allows users to set the navigation behavior for the robotic platform. The camera stream feature displays the live camera feedback from the robotic platform, utilizing the camera server. The VR teleoperation feature allows the user to manually operate the robotic platform utilizing the VR controllers or the arrow buttons seen in Fig. 8. The monitor robot system status feature displays important system information to the user, such as: current navigation mode, battery level, emergency stop status, etc. The indicator lights feature communicates to the user if there is an issue in the robotic platform. For example, if the indicator light associated with signal strength is green that means that the robot is connected to the network, if the light turns red then the robot has been disconnected. The display platform's position feature displays the current position of the vehicle on a map in a virtual tablet as seen in Fig. 9. This feature utilizes the cartographer server to gather the map, with the robot's marker, and display it to the user.

Fig. 8. Virtual Reality command center showcasing the operational room with the three live camera feedback (left) and a close up image of the front and right control center (right) (Color figure online)

Fig. 9. VR command center left side with the robot status, indicator lights, and teleop control (left). VR command center right side with the change mode buttons, and platform's position display (right)

4.4 Evaluation

To evaluate the proposed architecture, two field tests were performed. In these tests, soldiers were assigned a scouting drill mission, which they would then attempt to complete utilizing a robotic platform through the modular interface framework. The objective of these tests was to observe the robustness of the system and its usability for end-users. The tests were carried out in controlled environments and were not part of actual military deployments, but they did closely resemble combat scenarios. The experimentation described in the following sections were part of large scale US Army assessment events, and therefore we can only provide a general description of mission details and results.

Forest Mission. The first test involved a group of six combat engineers tasked with gathering intelligence along an off-road forest path. The trial went as follows: first, the engineers were trained on the use of ATAK, virtual workstation, and the robotic platform; afterwards the engineers planned out and executed a series of autonomous tasks on the robotic vehicle utilizing ATAK; finally, the engineers gathered data and scouted the target area utilizing the virtual workstation. Through this trial, it was observed that the modular interface framework had no noticeable lag in its operation; interactions with the robotic vehicle through the GUIs were immediate and the sensor feedback (LiDAR & Camera) was near real-time. The slight delays observed in the sensor feedback were due to radio bandwidth limitations outside of the scope of this project. There were also no connection or communication issues with the framework; the framework was able to smoothly handle two GUIs, that actively interacted with the robotic platform for long periods of time (approximately 4 h of continuous use). In terms of usability, the soldiers were able to complete their mission with just a few hours of training and no previous knowledge on the GUIs or the robotic platform. The soldiers' feedback was that the system was easy to utilize and made the operation smooth. The robotic vehicle was able to gather data from the forest trail autonomously, while the soldiers monitored and recorded the scouting information remotely over a kilometer away.

Desert Mission. The second test involved a group of four combat engineers tasked with scouting and mapping a large desert area. Similar to the previous test, the trial went as follows: first, the engineers were trained on the use of ATAK, virtual workstation, and the robotic platform; afterwards the engineers planned out and executed a series of autonomous tasks on the robotic vehicle utilizing ATAK; finally, the engineers gathered data and mapped the target area utilizing the virtual workstation. Performance wise, the system maintained a stable connection between GUIs and robotic platform, near real-time requests and responses between GUIs and robotic platform (again radio limitation being the cause of the lag), and there were no request/response errors identified. Regarding user experience, the soldiers were able to use the GUIs and robotic platform with just a few hours of training and no prior experience; their feedback was that they were satisfied with the system and observed high responsiveness that allowed them to easily complete their mission. These results confirmed what had been observed on the first test, highlighting the success and practicality of the developed GUIs and framework.

5   Conclusions and Future Works

In this work, we presented a system architecture with a modular interface framework that exposes a robotic platform over the network. The objective being, that any client device may interact with the robotic platform, thus, allowing users to utilize the graphical user interface that most benefits their current task. We explored GUIs in three different devices, to see their practicality in operations, their effect in user-platform cooperation and possible improvement in mission performances. The three GUIs being a smartwatch application, an ATAK plugin and a VR command station. The smartwatch application, which is not a common choice for robotic user interfaces, resulted in a useful tool for on the field human in the loop operations. In combat scenarios, warfighters may wear a smartwatch, to execute commands or monitor the robotic platforms. This wearable technology gives soldiers the freedom to move around the field and carry on with other objectives, while still being able to interact with the robotic platforms at a moments notice. The ATAK plugin had the advantage that it has already been deployed in the Army and thus, users are already familiar with it and need less training to operate robotic platforms with it. This GUI is especially useful for mission planning and situational awareness, since it takes advantage of ATAK's tools. The VR command station had the advantage that it acted as a regular workstation but it is completely customizable to the users needs; the immersion that the VR provides, combined with a convenient placement of buttons and screens may improve user performance. Even with this in mind, the technology is still the less practical of the three. Overall the presented system coupled with the GUIs, may improve soldier-platform interoperability, allowing soldiers to quickly adjust their role during missions as the work alongside robotic platforms. The system was tested out with two groups of soldiers, that with little training on the system, were able to plan, execute and complete missions with the semi-autonomous robotic platform through the developed GUIs. These tests highlighted the success and practicality of the proposed GUIs and framework. Future works should include expanding the current supported features, so that users may be able to achieve more objectives with the presented system and developed graphical user interfaces. Also, this research should be expanded into exploring multi-platform operation by a single user; what needs arise in those situations and are the current interfaces capable of providing a good user experience.

References

1. Clearpath.   https://clearpathrobotics.com/warthog-unmanned-ground-vehicle-robot. Accessed 08 Aug 2022
2. Rosnodejs (2016). http://wiki.ros.org/rosnodejs/overview. Accessed 19 June 2022
3. Geoserver (2022). https://geoserver.org/. Accessed 4 June 2022
4. ROS-M ROS military public website (2022). https://rosmilitary.org/. Accessed 21 Aug 2022
5. Tak product lines (2022). https://tak.gov/products. Accessed 13 July 2022
6. What is ROS (2022). https://ubuntu.com/robotics/what-is-ros. Accessed 15 July 2022
7. Codd-Downey, R., Forooshani, P.M., Speers, A., Wang, H., Jenkin, M.: From ROS to unity: leveraging robot and virtual environment middleware for immersive teleoperation. In: 2014 IEEE International Conference on Information and Automation (ICIA), pp. 932–936 (2014)
8. Gkournelos, C., Karagiannis, P., Kousi, N., Michalos, G., Koukas, S., Makris, S.: Application of wearable devices for supporting operators in human-robot cooperative assembly tasks. Procedia CIRP **76**, 177–182 (2018)
9. Koubaa, A.: Ros as a service: web services for robot operating system. J. Softw. Eng. Robot. **1**(2), 123–136 (2015)
10. Marder-Eppstein, E.: Navigation (2020). http://wiki.ros.org/navigation. Accessed 25 July 2022
11. Moore, T., Stouch, D.: A generalized extended Kalman filter implementation for the robot operating system. In: Menegatti, E., Michael, N., Berns, K., Yamaguchi, H. (eds.) Intelligent Autonomous Systems 13. AISC, vol. 302, pp. 335–348. Springer, Cham (2016). https://doi.org/10.1007/978-3-319-08338-4_25
12. Rosa, S., Russo, L.O., Bona, B.: Towards a ROS-based autonomous cloud robotics platform for data center monitoring. In: Proceedings of the 2014 IEEE Emerging Technology and Factory Automation (ETFA), pp. 1–8 (2014)
13. Safaripour, R., Khendek, F., Glitho, R., Belqasmi, F.: A restfull architecture for enabling rapid development and deployment of companion robot applications. In: 2014 International Conference on Computing, Networking and Communications (ICNC), pp. 971–976 (2014)
14. Souza, R., Pinho, F., Olivi, L., Cardozo, E.: A restful platform for networked robotics. In: 2013 10th International Conference on Ubiquitous Robots and Ambient Intelligence (URAI), pp. 423–428 (2013)
15. Toledo-Lopez, I., Pasley, D., Ortiz, R., Soylemezoglu, A.: Robust decision making via cooperative estimation: creating data saturated, autonomously generated, simulation environments in near real-time. In: Mazal, J., et al. (eds.) MESAS 2021. LNCS, vol. 13207, pp. 273–289. Springer, Cham (2022). https://doi.org/10.1007/978-3-030-98260-7_17
16. Villani, V., Sabattini, L., Riggio, G., Levratti, A., Secchi, C., Fantuzzi, C.: Interacting with a mobile robot with a natural infrastructure-less interface. IFAC-PapersOnLine **50**(1), 12753–12758 (2017)

Modelling the Impact of Space Situational Awareness Disruption on the European and Arctic Security Landscape

Antonio Carlo[1(✉)] and Nicolò Boschetti[2]

[1] TalTech - Tallinn University of Technology, Tallinn, Estonia
ancarl@taltech.ee
[2] Johns Hopkins University, Baltimore, MD 21201, USA

Abstract. More than half a century of space activities has resulted in the placement of thousands of space objects in the Earth's orbit. Understanding the questions of how, where, and who is moving in orbit is essential for the management of space infrastructure. Since the beginning of space missions, this task as been carried out by Space Situational Awareness (SSA) systems. SSA systems are made up of several subsystems, such as optical recognition instruments, radar and radio. In recent years, these terrestrial systems have also been joined by satellites with similar capabilities. Historically, these systems were maintained by the military. It was only recently that the private sector became a major actor in the field. Consultation, Command and Control (C3) allows for a strong collaboration of civil and military bodies that focus on information sharing and interoperability of the systems. SSA systems have proved critical in collisions between satellites and in preserving the structural stability of the International Space Station several times. The security of these systems hence has a strong impact on space and international security. The growing importance of the space sector and its progressive recognition as a critical infrastructure shows that a model and simulation of the scenario are essential for a centric defence. This paper will identify the areas that pose external threats focussing on the European and Arctic region. Following the threats' evaluation, their level of disruption will be considered, whether partial or total, permanent or temporary. This approach will enable the development of a European and Arctic scenario analysis of SSA disruption and evaluate the SSA security in the coming years. The scenario will take into consideration environmental, kinetic, electronic, and cyber sources of disruption.

Keywords: Outer Space · Space Situational Awareness · Cyber Security · Arctic · Space Traffic Management · Critical Infrastructures · Consultation Command and Control

1 Introduction

As planes could not fly safely without the support of control towers, beacons, and geolocation, any active spacecraft in space needs support from the ground. Every space asset

J. Mazal et al. (Eds.): MESAS 2022, LNCS 13866, pp. 299–311, 2023.
https://doi.org/10.1007/978-3-031-31268-7_18

operates in a highly hostile environment, increasingly populated by debris, decommissioned satellites, and spacecraft performing complex orbital manoeuvres. To minimise the chance that this wide variety of objects collide with each other and generate additional debris and human and economic losses, numerous networks of Space Situational Awareness are in operation. These systems are responsible for constantly monitoring objects in orbit, their behaviour, position, status, and possible interaction with environmental hazards. Space, however, is also a place of strategic confrontation between powers in which being able to operate incognito could bring significant advantages. For this reason, SSA networks could be as much a strategic target as other segments of the space sector.

This study applies this concept to the strategic and security situation of the Arctic and Northern Europe. Areas of the globe of high strategic interest both for the effects of climate change and for the growing political tension between NATO and Russian forces in the area following the Ukrainian crisis that began in February 2022. The primary outcome will be a study of the reasons that can lead an attacker to attempt to disable or influence an SSA system and an attack tree analysis of possible case studies. The analysis is based on an abstract architecture of SSA networks; however, based on real operating systems described below.

2   Approach

We combine data from several open-sources intelligence sources on military and commercial SSA infrastructure and juxtapose this data with the current European and Arctic Security landscape. The outcome is an attack tree analysis of two case studies for hostile operations against SSA networks operating in the area.

An attack tree consists of a technique employed to enumerate attack paths and highlight the vulnerabilities of a system. They were first proposed in 1999 by Schneier [1]. The structure is one of directed acyclic graphs, where the source node contains the primary attack goal. Offspring of the root node, named branches, contain sub-goals such that completing all sub-goals accomplishes the primary attack goal. Leaves of the attack tree comprise the actions necessary to achieve the respective sub-goal. If multiple actions are required to achieve a sub-goal, the two leaves are joined by a logical "AND", if either of multiple actions achieves a sub-goal, they are joined by a logical "OR".

Attack tree analysis has previously been conducted for space systems [2], but none has focused on Space Situational Awareness systems. Each SSA system or network segment presents different weaknesses that different hostile methods can exploit. The attack tree analysis presented in this paper is not comprehensive of the various possible hostile goals but intends to show the considerable number of nodes at risk. Furthermore, this analysis does not apply to a single SSA network, but the goals of the attacker are tailored to the strategic priorities of the European and Arctic region.

3   Space Situational Awareness Overview

The community lacks a single definition of Space Situational Awareness and for the purpose of this study is essential first to define it. SSA is a fundamental component of what is called Space Operations Assurance (SOA), the risk management process of space activities in orbit. Flanked by Space Environment Management (SEM) and Space Traffic Management (STM), it reduces the risk of on-orbit collision while at the same time monitoring the population of objects in orbit, being them debris or satellites [3]. For this paper, we will take as a better definition of SSA the one provided by the United States Air Force.

"SSA involves characterizing, as completely as possible, the space capabilities operating within the terrestrial and space environments. SSA information enables defensive and offensive counter-space operations and forms the foundation for all space activities. It includes space surveillance, detailed reconnaissance of specific space assets, collection and processing of intelligence data on space systems, and monitoring the space environment. It also involves the use of traditional intelligence sources to provide insight into adversary space and counter space operations. The components of SSA are intelligence, surveillance, reconnaissance, environmental monitoring and command and control. The tasks of SSA include find, fix, track, target, engage, and assess. Accomplishing these tasks ensures coherent battlespace awareness for planners, operators, and commanders" [4].

The four main functional capabilities of SSA are [4]:

Detect, Track, Identify (D/T/ID): Being able to search, identify and track space objects is fundamental to maintaining an updated knowledge of what and how is flying. Distinguish between operational or decommissioned spacecraft and space debris is crucial both for STM and strategic purposes. Therefore, it serves both the Defensive Counter-Space (DCS) and Offensive Counter-Space (OCS) missions.

Threat Warning and Assessment (TW&A): The space environment is hostile, with an vast variety of natural hazards and man-made threats. SSA systems must also detect in advance and assess what kind of risks the space asset will have to face. Combining D/T/ID data with, for example, solar activity forecasts or the analysis of third-party launches can make it possible to predict if a defunct spacecraft's orbit will decay faster or an asset is victim of an ASAT weapon [5].

Characterisation: This function deals with the identification and characterisation of the activities of space assets. It focuses both on friendly assets in order to help their control and enemy assets in order to assess eventual hostile operations. Ground, link and space segments are object of this function.

Data Integration and Exploitation (DI&E): As already mentioned an SSA system with the capabilities to perform D/T/ID and constantly monitor every object from LEO to GEO does not exist. For this reason is fundamental to fuse and integrate multi-source data to enable more precise decision-making processes. Sources can be international, commercial and open-source (Fig. 1).

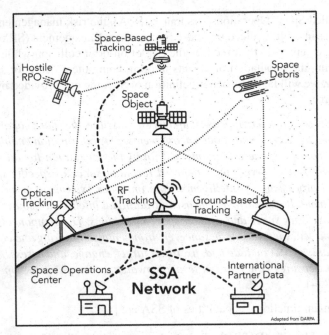

Fig. 1. Space Situation Awareness Network [6]

3.1 Main Non-private SSA Networks

USA

The United States Space Situational Awareness (SSA) network is a global system of sensors and other assets that detect, track, catalog, and identify artificial objects orbiting Earth. Various government agencies operate this network, including the United States Space Force, NASA, and the FAA. The SSA network includes a range of assets, such as ground-based radars and telescopes, satellite-based sensors, and other space-based assets, which are used to track objects in various orbits, including low Earth orbit (LEO), geostationary orbit (GEO), and beyond.

The SSA network maintains an up-to-date catalog of satellites and other objects in Earth orbit, known as the Space Object Catalog. This catalog tracks and monitors objects in space and provides data on their location, orbit, and other characteristics. The SSA network is primarily used to protect US and friendly space systems and promote data exchange with other organizations that are tracking space debris. In addition to providing space situational awareness, the SSA network is also used to support space traffic management efforts, including developing traffic rules and regulations, collision avoidance strategies, and communication and coordination protocols for space activities.

European Union/European Space Agency

Europe has two different SSAs providers, the European Union Satellite Centre (SatCen) in Madrid and the Space Situational Awareness Programme of ESA. These centres track objects in orbit that could disrupt other satellites or affect ground-based infrastructure. Moreover, they monitor the space environment, and space weather phenomena. The services are provided upon request to all EU Member States, the European Council, the European Commission, the European Union's External Action Service, public and private spacecraft owners and operators, and public authorities concerned with civil protection across the European Union. Up to today more "than 140 organisations are receiving these services and more than 290 European satellites are safeguarded from the risk of collision". The ESA SSA Programme has been founded €200M between the period 2009 and 2020 [7].

Russian Federation

Legacy of the advanced Soviet space programme, the Russian sensor network is the second in the world for capabilities and dimensions of the space object catalogue. The Russian Space Situational Awareness (SSA) network is a system of sensors and other assets operated by the Russian Aerospace Defense Forces. Named Система контроля космического пространства (СККП/SKKP) or System for the Control of the Outer Space, it is used to track and monitor objects in Earth orbit, including both active spacecraft and space debris. The SMS is designed to provide timely and accurate information on the location and orbit of objects in space, which is critical for ensuring the safety of spacecraft and crew during spaceflight operations and mitigating the risk of collisions between spacecraft and other objects in orbit.

The SKKP, similarly to its American counterpart, includes ground-based radars, optical, satellite-based sensors, and other space-based assets like RPO-capable satellites. These assets track objects in various orbits with also intelligence purposes.

In addition to its role in space situational awareness, the SKKP is also used to support space traffic management efforts, including developing traffic rules and regulations, creating collision avoidance strategies, and establishing communication and coordination protocols for space activities. SKKP is also used to support missile warning and other military applications and is a crucial component of Russia's national defense and security capabilities.

China

The Chinese network includes a similar composition of assets to American and Russian ones. The People's Liberation Army Strategic Support Force (PLASSF) manages China's space situational awareness (SSA) capabilities. They are designed to provide real-time knowledge of a space flight vehicle's location, the ability to track and predict its future location, and catalog all space objects. SSA also includes understanding a potential adversary's intent for their spacecraft. China's SSA system is expanding in scope and sophistication to accommodate its growing presence in space and address perceived challenges from other space-faring nations [9].

The PLASSF's SSA network includes a range of assets, such as ground-based radars and telescopes, comparable to the previously described networks. The PLASSF's space surveillance and control system include, for example, a tracking center in Xian, fixed land-based sites, at least one mobile system, and as many as seven Yuanwang tracking ships capable of operating throughout the Pacific, Atlantic, and Indian oceans. The PLASSF also operates foreign satellite ground stations. In the last years, China developed mobile tracking station that provides a fast and dynamic response in case of necessity [21]. Moreover, China agreed with third nations the temporary sovereignty of ground station sites.

4 The European and Arctic Security Landscape

Always a place of confrontation between superpowers, the Arctic is attracting more and more attention in the strategic and economic field due to the effects of climate change. The increase in the temperatures and the consequent ice withdrawal will open new marine routes and return to exploitable rich deposits of raw materials. However dramatic the effects of these environmental changes may be on the planet, this leads many international players to increase their regional investment [8]. These investments also involve the space sector in both the civil and military fields [9]. The remote stretches of the sea that will be crossed by more and more ships will need the most advanced GNSS services and possible communication to ensure the safety of crews and goods.

Moreover, the control of naval traffic and the defence of remote borders will require a wide use of space assets. Among the many peculiarities of this region, there is the fact that geostationary satellites, in areas north of 75° N, are too low above the horizon to make radio communication links possible. Communications with geostationary satellites are problematic as far south as the Arctic Circle, as the line-of-sight is easily blocked by terrain. This issue has led to the growth of projects that intend to use satellites in Low Earth orbit (LEO), Medium Earth orbit (MEO), or Highly Elliptical orbit (HEO) that can provide efficient and reliable communications in the polar regions. The Arctic is, therefore, on the one hand, a place of proliferation of highly strategic radio stations for both civil and military purposes, but also the prominent place of military exploitation of new broadband satellite connectivity systems such as Starlink and especially OneWeb [10].

This trend has both economic and strategic repercussions for the entire European region. The Arctic and Northern Europe are dotted with an increasing number of commercial radio stations of eminent dual-use nature that, in addition to receiving satellite information essential for the two regions in question, also provide services to the rest of the continent. Moreover, private and state satellite constellations in LEO, MEO, and high elliptical orbit heavily depend on the security of space infrastructure in these regions. Consequently, the entire ground segment up to end users also depends on the space segment's proper functioning [11].

The strategic and military organisations of the growing importance of special infra-structures in the Arctic and Northern Europe are mainly due to the environmental pecu-liarities of these areas. Although connected to the continent through undersea fiber optic cables, territories such as Greenland or the Svalbard Islands struggle to be equipped with reliable and efficient communication infrastructure for geographical and climatic reasons. Thus, NATO forces in the region are progressively switching to using the aforementioned satellite-based broadband services like OneWeb and Starlink [12].

5 Terminology: Critical Infrastructure

Currently there is no universally agreed definition of "critical infrastructures" (IC) since the protection needs and the characteristics of the individual infrastructures may vary according to their geographical location or national policies, or on the basis of the positions taken by the scientific literature. However, we can provide an all-encompassing definition of IC contained within Directive 2008/114/EU: a critical infrastructure is "an element, a system or part thereof located in the Member States which is essential for the maintenance of the vital functions of society, health, safety and economic and social welfare of citizens and whose damage or destruction would have a significant impact in a Member State due to the impossibility of maintaining these functions".

The definition of "critical infrastructures" (IC) can be considered dynamic and pris-matic as it is a concept in continuous evolution and takes into consideration a multiplic-ity of different scenarios and scientific bases. The focus on critical infrastructures has shifted from the debate regarding policies on public works and sensitive objectives, to a pre-eminent topic of national security and a guarantee on the quality of life of citizens or an essential service. Specifically, at first, those threats affecting the "efficiency" of the infrastructure were considered, then moving on to consider its "availability", thus arriving at the current panorama of physical, logical and organisational risks.

The definitions of critical infrastructures provided by the various governmental bod-ies, national or international, are different according to the needs or values attributed to each service or good provided by a given infrastructure. In particular, what is considered essential for a community in the broad sense is critical: this essentiality therefore makes any infrastructure vulnerable and exposed to threats.

Specifically, the criticality is based on the definition of the risk and the strategic direction to be pursued. The risk can be summarised in the formula

$$R = (T \cdot V \cdot I)$$

where:

- R is the risk, which expresses the combination of the consequences of an event associated with the possibility of occurrence;
- T expresses the threat, that is the potential cause of an unwanted accident, which can cause damage to a system or organisation;
- V expresses the vulnerability of an asset that can be exploited by one or more threats;
- I is the impact, or the damage that the event can generate.

The threats tend to be divided into two macro-areas: natural and anthropogenic. Natural threats can be predictable or unpredictable and relate to the land or the climate. Anthropogenic threats can be voluntary or involuntary and conventional (economic, cyber) or unconventional (NBCR). This subdivision is necessary to catalogue the various types of threats that today appear heterogeneous and multifaceted; however, not all threats are controllable. In this regard, we speak of the so-called black swan.

The space sector has become increasingly important due to its criticality in everyday activities. CI comprises the complex networks and systems that include industries, institutions, and distribution structures that, operating synergistically, produce a continuous flow of goods and services essential for the organisation, functionality, and economic stability of an industrialised country. The destruction or temporary unavailability of CI can have a debilitating impact on a nation's economy, society, and on its defence capabilities [13].

While the growth of satellite systems has made it possible for CI to be more interconnected, it has also resulted in CI systems being more interdependent. Since satellites play a critical role in monitoring CI to ensure security and resilience, the rapid development of satellite capabilities has validated the needed investment in their construction and placement in orbit. The continued investment into satellite capabilities has also pointed towards future possibilities of reducing the costs of CI connected to outer space [14].

6   The External Threat

The space sector has changed profoundly in recent decades. Not only are the technologies advanced, but above all, the number of objects in orbit and their importance for terrestrial activities have increased exponentially. Many satellites that fly amid an even greater number of debris impose the need to rely on exact control of the orbits to protect the space assets and ensure that the operations dependent on them are not interrupted [15]. These operations range from financial operations to geolocation for food delivery but also include vital search and rescue activities or support for military operations. If the NATO countries suddenly lose their SSA and STM capabilities while still keeping in touch with their satellites, they will not be able to know their position, and by which objects they will be approached. In this paper, an SSA system's disruption will be considered a counter-space weapon comparable, for probability of use and severity of consequences, with others such as ASAT or jamming.

6.1   A Subsection Sample

An opponent's reasons for getting a denial of service or intercepting and corrupting an SSA system's data can be multiple. Temporary blinding of NATO's or individual nations' SSA capacity operating in the two regions covered by this study can lead to strategic advantages both on land and in space. For example, in recent years, the growing interest of Russia, China and the United States in the advancement of conducting Rendezvous and Proximity Operations (RPO) demonstrates the importance of having precise control of objects in orbit, but also being able to manoeuvre their spacecraft in the most hidden way possible [16]. A satellite, in fact, to approach a target in orbit at a close distance must perfectly know the orbital parameters of the second. However, as demonstrated by the encounter, in January 2022, between the American satellite USA 270 and two Chinese satellites Shinjian-12, an efficient SSA can allow timely avoidance manoeuvres able to thwart RPO missions [17]. Moreover, as already described, since SSA systems are very expensive and complex, a space actor may have both an interest in disabling another SSA network in order to achieve strategic parity, is to acquire any strategic information otherwise impossible to obtain with its own means [18].

In summary, the main reasons for disabling or infiltrate an SSA system can be:

1. Covering domestic RPO activities;
2. Thwart opponent's RPO activities;
3. Reaching strategic parity with an opponent with higher SSA capabilities;
4. Cover the launch of strategic and classified space assets;
5. Inject false data to pass as debris, classified space assets;
6. Intercept classified data (for intelligence or black market);
7. Hinder STM capabilities as a counter-space weapon, thwarting collision avoidance.

Considering the peculiarities of the European and Arctic Region, we present two non-exhaustive use cases to show how an opponent could disable or infiltrate the SSAs operating in the area: temporary blinding orbit monitoring (denial of service) and data interception and corruption.

6.2   First Use Case: Temporary Blinding Orbit Monitoring

Preventing orbit monitoring can have serious strategic implications for the North European and Arctic region. First it can allow the deployment of satellites in polar or Molnya orbit without these being detected. Second, it can allow RPO activities on LEO and MEO satellites orbiting above the area covered by the victim system, facilitating, for example, eavesdropping of EO satellites operating in war areas such as the Ukrainian theater. Thirdly, it can prevent the detection of counter-space weapons against targets orbiting in polar and Molnya orbits or transiting above the region. Finally, it can be used as an indiscriminate counter-space weapon, making impossible the STM of satellite constellations such as those for broadband connectivity particularly strategic in the Arctic.

6.3   Second Use Case: Data Interception and Corruption

The interception of SSA data related to the European and Arctic region can serve multiple purposes (Fig. 2).

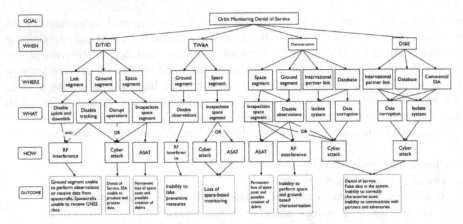

Fig. 2. Orbit Monitoring Denial of Service Tree

First, it can allow to know exactly which spatial assets orbit above areas of interest and what their orbits are. This, in addition to bridging an information gap, can mitigate the effects of EO operations or even apply countermeasures such as false targets or the use of ASAT weapons [19]. Secondly, as shown in the attack tree, being the ability to intercept this type of data closely linked to that of corrupting or modifying the victim's data with results similar to the first use case. In this case, any weaknesses could be exploited both to acquire data, but also to hide own space assets operating on targets located in the Arctic or in Europe. Third, the intercepted data in case it refers to strategic and classified assets could be resold on the black market at high prices or used for blackmail.

7 Discussion

The main outcome of this exercise is highlighting possible attack vectors and classes of risks to the SSA networks operating in the Arctic and European regions. Although not complete, the presented attack trees can clarify to the community the security situation of SSA systems and provide insight to the weaker or more difficult to monitor nodes of the system (Fig. 3).

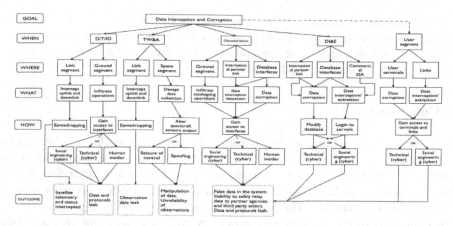

Fig. 3. Data Interception and Corruption Tree

This study contemplates the commercial providers of services SSA as a single joint of the network without investigating in detail its actual organisation in numerous nodes to they time singularly attackable or interceptable. Every single commercial provider has its own internal organisation, its own technical instrumentation and its own security practices and protocols.

The importance of Space Situational Awareness (SSA) systems requires that they are highly resilient and continuously active, as any disruption or downtime can have significant consequences. These systems provide crucial information about the location, orbit, and other characteristics of objects in space, including active spacecraft and space debris. This information is used to ensure the safety of spacecraft and crew during spaceflight operations, to mitigate the risk of collisions between spacecraft and other objects in orbit, and to support a wide range of other activities related to space situational awareness, space traffic management, and missile warning.

However, SSA systems are also vulnerable to cyber attacks, as hostile actors are constantly attempting to breach them to gain access to sensitive information or disrupt their operations. The cyber threat landscape is rapidly expanding and evolving, and SSA systems must be constantly updated and secured to protect against these threats.

To ensure the security and resilience of SSA systems, it is vital to follow international and national standards and best practices. This can include the establishment of Computer Emergency Response Teams (CERTs) and Computer Security Incident Response Teams (CSIRTs), which are responsible for responding to cyber emergencies and incidents. These teams should be coordinated by Security Operational Centres (SOCs), which serve as central hubs for collecting and analysing cyber threat intelligence [20].

To ensure a continues activity of the SSA infrastructure mitigation measures shall be considered and implemented. It is essential to clearly identify the necessary steps to resolve present and future issues as well as to define a mechanism to monitor threats and opportunities (e.g. Key Performance Objective); and segmentation and segregation of the systems.

In addition to these measures, strong national and international cooperation can also help to ensure the security of SSA systems. Cooperation can include sharing best practices through Information Sharing and Analysis Centres (ISACs), as well as the inclusion of SSA systems on the European and national lists of critical infrastructure. This ensures that they receive the appropriate level of protection and are prioritised in the event of a cyber incident or other threat.

8 Conclusion

Space Situational Awareness systems and networks can be targeted by malicious actors to gain strategic advantages in orbit or for intelligence purposes. The complexity of the networks and the wide variety of sensors that compose them makes the number of vital links exceptionally high, multiplying the weaknesses against external threats without increasing their redundancy. The community needs greater attention to the problem, both in the light of the international contingency and the constant increase of debris in orbit. In addition, the growth of the space sector requires more significant levels of resilience of support and control structures.

References

1. Schneier, B.: Attack trees. Dobb's J. **24**(12), 21–29 (1999)
2. Gregory, F., Viswanathan, A., and Santangelo, A.: Cubesat security attack tree analysis. In: 8th International Conference on Space Mission Challenges for Information Technology (SMC-IT). IEEE, (2021)
3. McKnight, D.: A practical perspective on space traffic management. J. Space Saf. Eng. **6**(2), 101–107 (2019)
4. U.S. Airforce: Counterspace Operations. Air Force Doctrine Publication **3**(14) (2018)
5. Carlo, A., Veazoglou, N.: ASAT weapons: enhancing NATO's operational capabilities in the emerging space dependent era. In: Mazal, J., Fagiolini, A., Vasik, P. (eds.) Modelling and Simulation for Autonomous Systems. MESAS 2019. Lecture Notes in Computer Science, vol. 11995, pp. 417–426. Springer, Cham (2020). https://doi.org/10.1007/978-3-030-43890-6_34
6. DARPA. https://www.darpa.mil/. Accessed 01 Aug 2022
7. European Union Satellite Entre: Space Situational Awareness (SSA). https://www.satcen.europa.eu/page/ssa. Accessed 01 Aug 2022
8. European Space Agency: SSA Programme Overview. https://www.esa.int/Space_Safety/SSA_Programme_overview. Accessed 01 Aug 2022
9. Stokes, A., et al.: China's Space and Counterspace Capabilities and Activities. US-China Economic and Security Review Commission (2020)
10. Harri, M.: The Geostrategic Arctic. Hard Security in the High North, FIIA Briefing Paper (2019)
11. Wickman, L.: Near-term space support for arctic operations. Center Space Policy Strategy Online **4** (2017)
12. Rainbow, J.: Hughes and Oneweb Get U.S. Air Force Contract for Arctic Broadband. SpaceNews. https://spacenews.com/oneweb-gets-u-s-air-force-contract-for-arctic-broadband/. Accessed 01 Aug 2022
13. Salmeri, A., Carlo, A.: Security-by-design approaches for critical infrastructure: mapping the landscape of cyber and space law. In: NATO Legal Gazette, N 42

14. Carlo, A., Casamassima, F.: Securing Outer Space through Cyber: Risks and Countermeasures. In: 72nd International Astronautical Congress, Dubai (2021)
15. Oltrogge, D.L., Alfano, S.: The technical challenges of better space situational awareness and space traffic management. J. Space Saf. Eng. 6(2), 72–79 (2019)
16. James, A., Garza, A., and May, C.: An Analysis of the Potential Misuse of Active Debris Removal, On-Orbit Servicing, and Rendezvous & Proximity Operations Technologies. United States: The George Washington University (2019)
17. Jones, A.: China's shijian-21 towed dead satellite to a high graveyard orbit," Space-News. https://spacenews.com/chinas-shijian-21-spacecraft-docked-with-and-towed-a-dead-satellite/. Accessed 01 Aug 2022
18. Pavur, J., Martinovic, I.: On detecting deception in space situational awareness. In: Asia Conference on Computer and Communications Security (2021)
19. Gregory, F., Boschetti, N.: A security risk taxonomy for commercial space missions. In: ASCEND (2021)
20. Carlo, A.: Cyber threats to space communications: space and cyberspace policies. In: Froehlich, A. (ed.) Outer Space and Cyber Space. SSP, vol. 33, pp. 55–66. Springer, Cham (2021). https://doi.org/10.1007/978-3-030-80023-9_4
21. China's ground segment, China Aerospace Studies Institute, https://www.airuniversity.af. edu/Portals/10/CASI/documents/Research/Space/2021-03-01%20Chinas%20Ground%20S egment.pdf?ver=z4ogY_MrxaDurwVt-R9J6w%3d%3d. Accessed 01 Dec 2022

Simulation: The Great Enabler?
Synthetic Data for Supercharging AI Military Systems

Christian Johann Liegl[1], Tobias Nickchen[1] (ID), Eva Strunz[1] (ID), Andreas Horn[1], Alexander Coppenrath[1] (ID), Ugur Uysal[2], Martin Ruß[3], and Florian Luft[1](✉) (ID)

[1] Atos Information Technology GmbH, Munich, Germany
{christian-johann.liegl,tobias.nickchen,eva.strunz,
alexander.coppenrath,florian.luft}@atos.net
[2] German Army Concepts and Capabilities Development Center,
Cologne, Germany
UgurUysal@bundeswehr.org
[3] Bundeswehr University Munich, Munich, Germany
martin.russ@unibw.de

Abstract. Autonomous systems (AxS) have successfully been employed in military tasks such as search and rescue, logistics, and reconnaissance. Whether it be on land, at sea, or in the air, diverse and representative training samples are indispensable for operationalising recent advances in artificial intelligence (AI). Applying deep learning to the task of armoured fighting vehicle (AFV) recognition, we examine the role synthetic data are capable of playing in training image classification and object detection models. To this end we implement a modular pipeline for the controlled generation of synthetic samples and their combination with real data with downstream building blocks for data augmentation and adversarial machine learning. This lets us conduct well-structured experiments (e.g., involving varying lighting conditions or adversarial perturbations) and develop hypotheses regarding the most beneficial composition of the training data set and the influence of individual pipeline building blocks on performance or robustness. In order to bridge the simulation-to-reality gap we use data augmentation techniques akin to domain randomisation. In particular, we fuse images with fractal pat-terns, which, in their structural complexity, resemble many forms of military camouflage. Anticipating adversarial attacks on our computer vision systems, we also train a set of more robust models by means of adversarial training, a well-studied defensive measure. Our experiments follow a rigorous evaluation protocol accounting for the multidimensional nature of both performance and robustness. We envision future applications of our thorough approach to training AxS beyond AFV recognition – in all dimensions of modern battlespace.

Keywords: Modelling & Simulation · AxS · AI · Deep Learning · Image Classification · Object Detection · AFVs · Land-Based Systems · Simulation-to-Reality-Gap · Data Augmentation · Fractals · Camouflage · Robustness · Adversarial Machine Learning

J. Mazal et al. (Eds.): MESAS 2022, LNCS 13866, pp. 312–325, 2023.
https://doi.org/10.1007/978-3-031-31268-7_19

1   Introduction

The battlefield of the future will see a substantial increase in the number of sensors, producing an abundance of information that soldiers, owing to cognitive overload, can no longer meaningfully interpreted. Therefore, sensor and effector data will have to be evaluated in an automated manner. While automation equips modern armed forces with fast and efficient decision-making, it essentially rests on the pillars of data-driven artificial intelligence (AI), also called machine learning (ML). The evaluation of sensor data by means of ML takes place at the beginning of the intelligent sensor-effector chain [17].

In civilian contexts, AI computer vision systems have outperformed human judgement on unclassified public benchmarks, mainly due to the availability of vast amounts of annotated high-quality training data [10]. In military contexts, training and test data are often scarce, which continues posing a significant challenge for the development of military AI systems, especially autonomous systems (AxS). Moreover, AxS are typically deployed in safety and security critical environments where it is imperative to prevent collateral damage, whilst preparing for the presence of hos-tile forces. Hence, military AI systems must be robust to both poor data quality and adversarial efforts aimed at degrading their performance.

In our work we study the task of armoured fighting vehicle (AFV) recognition, where computer vision systems are trained to distinguish between various types of infantry vehicles and main battle tanks. To tackle the fundamental problem of data scarcity, we rely on the use of synthetic training samples to supplement available real imagery [13]. In a suitable 3D environment, we generate images of combat vehicles from different angles and distances, while varying terrain types and sensor input quality (e.g. due to attempts at concealment). In order to bridge the simulation-to-reality gap we use data augmentation techniques akin to domain randomisation. In particular, we fuse images with fractal patterns, which, in their structural complexity, resemble many forms of military camouflage (see Fig. 1). We account for the presence of adversaries by employing adversarial training, a common defensive countermeasure.

In practical terms, we draw on two common computer vision approaches to solve AFV recognition, i.e., image classification and object detection. Image classification involves learning a mapping from input images to a fixed number of output classes. Object detection, by contrast, aims at both localising and classifying objects within a given image or video frame. The main strain of experiments is dedicated to AFV recognition of 10 individual builds (e.g., T-14, BMP-1Ksh, and T80U), with a second strain exploring recognition of vehicle types such as main battle tanks and infantry fighting vehicles.

Our main contribution is the systematic evaluation of the utility of synthetic data for training AI military systems according to a rigorous protocol. To this end we implement a modular pipeline for the controlled generation of synthetic samples and their combination with real data with downstream building blocks for data augmentation and adversarial machine learning. This lets us conduct well-structured experiments and develop hypotheses regarding the most bene-

Real Synthetic

Original

Augmented

Fig. 1. Data augmentation with fractals bridges the gap between the distributions of real (Source: Wikimedia, https://upload.wikimedia.org/wikipedia/commons/b/bf/4thTankBrigade_-_T-80U_-37.jpg, last accessed 2022/08/11) and synthetic images

ficial training setup and the influence of individual pipeline building blocks on performance or robustness. In particular, we explore four crucial aspects:

1. Supported by a host of literature (e.g. [7]), there is strong evidence that synthetic data can at least play a supporting role during training. Whether they alone are sufficient for building highly performant AI systems, will be investigated in a series of experiments.
2. We will examine how synthetic data can be fruitfully employed in the specialisation of AI modules for real-world military applications, when useful real data are scarce. The surveillance of critical main roads, for instance, relies only on a small number of practically relevant vehicle perspectives.
3. To our knowledge, the relationship between synthetic training imagery and robustness has not been explored in the adversarial machine learning literature. Our works makes a foray into a potentially novel area of re-search by tracing the impact of synthetic training data on the robustness of our computer vision models.
4. Last but not least, we will evaluate and measure by a series of tests whether our data augmentation downstream building block has been successful in closing the simulation-to-reality gap. This is necessary as synthetically generated data exhibit image statistics different to real data.

The method we establish is novel and, within a military context, unique.

Atos is studying this approach as a contractor in collaboration with the German Army Concepts and Capabilities Development Center, the Bundeswehr Verification Center, and the Universität der Bundeswehr München.

2   Related Work

2.1   Synthetic Data for ML

[7–9] study the impact on detection performance of various real and synthetic training and test datasets within the context of vehicle detection on aerial imagery, while conducting an in-depth analysis of influencing factors and parameters. To identify factors influencing the reality gap between real and synthetic image data and the detection performance of a synthetically trained vehicle detector, several image descriptor metrics are introduced in [9]. For the evaluation, dedicated UAV flights were conducted with telemetry data and a digital twin created within a virtual environment informing the training dataset [7]. The results showed the simulation-to-reality gap to comprise two components, i.e., the appearance gap and the content gap. While combining real with synthetic training data generally leads to a lower generalisation error of the detector, selectively augmenting general real-world benchmark training datasets with practically relevant synthetic images, provided a significantly better fit of the detector model to the prevailing deployment conditions. The Content Gap analysis performed in [8] with respect to real-flight parameters showed that vehicle model and position had the strongest strong influence on performance. In terms of corruption robustness, it was noted that the trained detector was susceptible to blur, contrast changes, overexposure, and impulse noise. As regards applications outside the military domain, autonomous driving and civilian drones are prominent use cases that have been shown to benefit from synthetic data. While the authors in [14] use a simulator to generate both training and test data for autonomous vehicles, [12] introduce a framework for the systematic composition of synthetic driving scenarios. Civilian drones trained on synthetic data, by contrast, have been successfully employed for disaster monitoring [1]. At a more general level, digital twins as a synthetic mirror-image of the physical world are discussed in [11] as well as [5].

Our Contribution. Approaching the generation of synthetic training data in a systematic manner, we propose a modular training pipeline and a rigorous evaluation protocol to det to assess their utility across various training setups.

2.2   Fractals and Data Augmentation

Fractals are patterns that repeat infinitely on different scales. Not only can they be naturally observed in, say, flowers and trees or in waves and clouds, but they also account for the characteristic roughness of a landscape via the fractal dimension, a statistical index of complexity [16]. Due to their ubiquitous presence in nature, fractals have inspired many types of military camouflage such as Flecktarn or digital patterns which aim at reducing visual signatures over a range of scales. In the field of machine learning, recent contributions extol the virtues of fractals for pre-training computer vision systems [6]: in particular, they show promise of equipping models with structural world knowledge, reducing the need to train them with large datasets such as ImageNet. Unlike [6], Hendrycks et al. [4] rely on fractals and similarly complex patterns for the purpose of data augmentation. Within the context of image classification, their approach has been shown to boost model performance across a range of safety measures, establishing a new state of the art.

Our Contribution. Our work follows [4], whilst extending their data augmentation method to the task of object detection. Due to the strong similarities between fractals and military camouflage, we introduce fractals-inspired ML to the military setting.

2.3 Safe and Secure AI

AI military systems should not only be safe in unfavourable conditions, but also be secure in the face of hostile interference. Unfavourable conditions commonly ex-press themselves in degradation of data quality that causes the distributions at training and inference time to differ. This phenomenon has been discussed in the corruption robustness literature. [3] group common corruptions and perturbations into four categories:

- Noise,
- Blur,
- Weather, and
- Digital.

Hostile interference, by contrast, requires malicious human agency. While at training an adversary may attempt to poison the training data set or introduce a secret backdoor to the model [15], an adversarial attack at inference will no longer be able to alter the model weights. Rather, it exploits the given parameter values in such a way that a minimally modified data point causes the most damage possible. Such data points are referred to as adversarial examples and have spawned a vibrant line of research. To mitigate the risks associated with adversarial examples, a common recourse is adversarial training, where a model is iteratively presented with adversarial examples to foster robust decision-making [2].

Our Contribution. We establish tests to measure the safe and secure functioning of our AFV recognition models. Within the context of image classification, we showcase the effects of adversarial training.

3 Method

3.1 Modular Training Pipeline

Our approach to solving AFV relies on a modular training pipeline that has building blocks for the generation of synthetic data, techniques for data augmentation, as well as adversarial machine learning. The modular design is key to specifying arbitrary training setups. Individual building blocks can at any given time be altered or updat-ed by the user without affecting the other parts of the pipeline.

Controlled Generation of Data. With the utility of synthetic data training taking centre stage in our work, we approach their generation in a systematic and controlled manner. In practical terms, we pursue four different strategies for producing a rich and diverse training dataset. For one, we stochastically vary vehicle properties, the geometric setup as well as scene characteristics. As object detectors should be able to distinguish between multiple objects in a given image, we also introduce random elements to the generation of images containing multiple vehicles. The following list provides greater detail regarding our method:

- **Vehicle Properties:** Modified Builds, Antennas, Camouflage, etc. and
- **Geometric Setup:** Positions, Size, Perspective, and
- **Scene Characteristics:** Geography, Scene Components, Lighting Conditions.
- **Object Detection Requirements:** Random number, and random combination of different types of, vehicle builds within an image.

As we have control over which vehicle is being rendered in a scene, there is no need to manually annotate the resulting images for the image classification task. However, to make the created samples suitable for the training of an object detector, we take additional steps to exploit the information hidden in our rendering engine. That is, we resort to colour coding the vehicles with stark colours not appearing naturally in our scene (e.g., pink). This allows us to calculate bounding boxes via min and max operations. By constructing appropriate filters, we are also able to exclude minuscule or irrelevant structures such as antennas or roof racks.

Fractal-Inspired Data Augmentation. In terms of data augmentation, we employ the PixMix [4] method for both image classification and object detection. PixMix fuses the samples of the training dataset with pictures exhibiting structural complexity such as fractals and feature visualisation of artificial neural networks (also referred to as the mixing pictures). More precisely, in an iterative procedure an image is fused with a mixing picture or a trans-formed version of itself. These transformations include standard augmentations such as the addition of, say Gaussian, noise or changes in colour and position (e.g., rotations). For the task of object detection, we discard transformations, however, that are not bounding box-preserving.

Adversarial Machine Learning. Showcasing our building block for adversarial machine learning, we perform adversarial training for image classification models. Practically, we introduce an additional term to our loss function, which is said to induce adversarial regularisation. Technically, this corresponds to an adversarial attack bound by the l_∞ norm, meaning each pixel may only be altered to a fixed extent. Hence, the generated adversarial examples are by and large inconspicuous to human observers. However, they cause maximum damage to the image classification model under attack. In our setup, the output is shifted to an arbitrary false class in what is known in the literature as an untargeted attack.

3.2 Evaluation Protocol

We gauge the impact of individual pipeline building blocks and, especially, the utility of synthetic training samples through a large number of systematically structured experiments. We measure performance, robustness, and the simulation-to-reality gap by appropriate test datasets. Practically, we apply mappings to our original test dataset that result in distribution shifts characteristic for corrupted or adversarial input, or artistic renditions of physical reality.

Performance. In our main strain of experiments, we aim to assess the utility of synthetic training samples by measuring performance, varying fundamental factors in the training of our AFV models. The fundamental factors we are considering are the basic training setup, the size of our training datasets, and the use of data augmentation. We measure the performance of our image classification models and our object detectors with the accuracy and the mAP, respectively.

Regarding basic training setups, we contrast two approaches:

a) the combination of real and synthetic data as to form single training dataset, and
b) the usage of synthetic samples for pre-training, with fine-tuning drawing on real imagery.

Note that training datasets comprising only real or synthetic samples are contained in a), as we may choose to combine, say, real images with an empty set of synthetic data, and vice versa. Both setups may be combined with the optional data augmentation module.

For both training setups, we vary the amount of both synthetic and real data in what amounts to two separate grid searches. While we expect that a larger amount of training data will almost always confer benefits in terms of (ultimately, vanishingly small) performance gains, we aim at using real images sparingly, as these may be scarce. For setup a), we note that we run independent lines of experiments when ei-ther only synthetic data or solely real images are comprised in the training dataset.

Ultimately, this gives rise to 8 distinct constellations for each AFV task. As the requirements for the training of object detectors may differ from image classification models, we shall duly report any such findings in the results section of our work. For each AFV task, we select the most promising models and pass them on to an evaluation of their robustness and potential for bridging the simulation-to reality gap.

A second strain of experiments is dedicated to sketching a solution to the practical use case of road surveillance. Observing that optical surveillance sensors are usually set up at a fixed place, we hypothesise that suppressing certain vehicle views in our synthetic training samples might result in an overall training distribution that more closely resembles the distribution of data at inference. Moreover, if an AFV recognition system is deployed as an alarm system at a strategically important border, it should red-flag the arrival of hostile vehicles long before processing their rear views. In a slight modification to our AFV recognition problem, we consider vehicle classes (e.g., main battle tank) rather than individual builds (e.g., T-14).

Robustness. Our evaluation protocol of robustness takes into account both corruption and adversarial robustness. In both cases we apply perturbations to the test dataset. An adversarial perturbation, unlike a perturbation arising from, say, inclement weather, is a worst-case perturbation.

To measure corruption robustness, we borrow 15 types of common corruptions[1] from ImageNet-C [3] and apply them to our test dataset (examples shown in Fig. 2), varying their severity across three levels (i.e., mild, intermediate, strong). These fall into four categories:

- **Noise:** Gaussian Noise, Impulse Noise, Shot Noise,
- **Blur:** Defocus Blur, Frosted Glass Blur, Motion Blur, Zoom Blur,
- **Weather:** Snow, Frost, Fog, and
- **Digital:** Brightness, Contrast, Elastic, Pixelate, JPEG

As a measure of corruption robustness, we compute the accuracy and the mAP score for each type of data quality degradation as well as for each severity level.

In an exemplary evaluation of adversarial robustness, we study the behaviour of image classification models under attack. The adversarial attack in question is bounded by $l_\infty \leq \varepsilon$. By choosing larger bounds an adversary is able produce stronger adversarial examples, potentially sacrificing their inconspicuousness for human observers. We test our models with respect to three different values for ε and benchmark them against an adversarially regularised version. The accuracy of a model under attack serves as a measure of its adversarial robustness.

Simulation-to-Reality Gap. The last part of our evaluation protocol concerns the simulation-to-reality gap. Since synthetic images exhibit textures different to real imagery, we are interested in measuring whether our models use cues based off shape rather than texture to arrive at their decisions. To this end we transform our test dataset into artistic renditions of the original images, drawing on the styles contained in the Stylized ImageNet source code [15]. For

---

[1] In this work, we use common perturbations synonymously with corruptions of data quality.

Fig. 2. Common and adversarial perturbations across three severity levels (Source: Wikimedia, https://commons.wikimedia.org/wiki/Category:T-14_tanks#/media/File: T-14_Armata_(27053434067).jpg, last accessed 2022/08/11)

three levels of severity, we randomly sample from the available styles, transferring them onto our test data (Fig. 3). We compute the accuracy for our best image classification models and the mAP for our most promising object detectors. If these performance measures remain roughly constant, we argue that it is safe to assume that the simulation-to-reality gap has been successfully closed.

4   Experimental Setup

The real imagery used throughout this work was partly provided by the *Bundeswehr Verification Center*, partly collected by Atos from open-source resources. The synthetic data were generated in Virtual Battlespace 4 (VBS4), a simulation environment for military training. We implemented our pipeline in Python 3.7 and utilised the following libraries:

Fig. 3. Randomly chosen styles across three severity levels

- Tensorflow 2.7,
- Keras 2.7, and
- Neural Structured Learning 1.3.

All experiments were conducted on a machine with the following specifications:

- **Processor:** AMD Ryzen 9 5900X 12-Core Processor, 3701 Mhz, 12 Cores, 24 Logical Processors,
- **Graphic card:** NVIDIA Geforce RTX3080 Ti, and
- **RAM:** 64gb.

5   Results and Discussion

The completion of our experiments alongside their thorough evaluation using our protocol helped us generate empirically founded hypotheses. While we were primarily interested in studying the utility of synthetic samples for training ML-driven AFV recognition systems, our approach was general enough to allow conclusions regarding other factors influencing training outcomes and model behaviour. Our hypotheses are actionable insights meant to spawn further research and development of AI military systems

Hypothesis 1: *synthetic training data successfully support training of AFV recognition models.*

We set out to compare different training setups. We varied the amount of both synthetic and real training data, optionally applying fractal-inspired data augmentation.

Within the image classification context, abundant availability of real imagery translated into the highest accuracy. When solely real training data were used, our augmentation method conferred no considerable advantages on the ultimate performance. However, the training with a purely synthetic dataset produced uncompetitive models, with PixMix providing some relief. When both real and synthetic training data were relied upon to supplement scarce real data, the models' accuracy received a significant boost. Pre-training with synthetic samples and fine-tuning with real images trumped the combination of both sources into a single training dataset (Table 1).

Table 1. Performance across image classification task (pre-training and fine-tuning setup shaded in light gray)

Number of real images	Number of synthetic samples	Accuracy, no augmentation	Accuracy, PixMix applied
50	0	0.84	0.84
100	0	0.93	0.93
250	0	0.96	0.95
500	0	0.96	0.97
1000	0	0.97	0.98
0	100	0.48	0.53
0	500	0.52	0.62
0	1000	0.56	0.65
0	2500	0.60	0.69
0	5000	0.62	0.71
50	2500	...	0.87
50	2500	...	0.91

In the object detection setting, synthetic data significantly increased performance when real training data were scarce. This applies to both training setups, where we relied on PixMix to bridge differences in distribution between real and synthetic images. We observed that object detectors trained on an abundance of real images could not by matched in terms of mAP, however. Table 2 offers a summary of our experiments with a small number of real training data. Unlike in the image classification task, merging real and synthetic images into a single training dataset produced the best performing model.

For both approaches to AFV recognition, we draw the conclusion that synthetic data provide significant benefits to the development of highly performant computer vision systems, especially when there is a short supply of real imagery.

Table 2. Performance across object detection task (pre-training and fine-tuning setup shaded in light gray)

Number of real images	Number of synthetic samples	mAP IOU50, no augmentation	mAP IOU50, PixMix applied
50	0	0.63	0.61
0	2500	0.26	0.47
50	2500	...	0.71
100	2500	...	0.75
250	2500	...	0.80
50	2500	...	0.71
100	2500	...	0.76
250	2500	...	0.81

Hypothesis 2: *synthetic training samples help models learn the distribution of real-world data.*

As a potential illustration of the benefits of synthetic training samples, we explored the automated monitoring of strategically critical roads. As not all vehicle perspectives are relevant for our use case, we hypothesised that a strict subset of vehicle views might more closely approximate the distribution of real-world data at inference. Our claim was corroborated for both the image classification and object detectors task. Corresponding models were trained on a practically relevant subset of vehicle perspectives (i.e., their side views), whereas the training of a control group of models made use of all perspectives. We conclude that synthetic training images increase model performance, as their controlled generation allows mimicking the distribution of data points at test time.

Hypothesis 3: *the use of adversarially trained models should follow tactical considerations.*

Following our evaluation protocol, we assessed the robustness of our AFV recognition systems. While we observed a drop in performance as the severity levels across all perturbations increased, any configuration involving PixMix proved remarkably robust. Synthetic data supplied additional boosts in mean robustness measures. As we compared our adversarially regularised image classification model with regularly trained models with respect to common corruptions, we noted vulnerabilities with respect to all categories except noise. While adversarial regularisation induced reliable model behaviour under adversarial attack, regular performance was somewhat sub-par. In the literature, this phenomenon has been described as the tradeoff between generalisation and robustness. Concludingly, we recommend the development of a large set of AFV recognition systems accounting for different tactical requirements, where the deployment of adversarially robust models should be conditional on the presence of adversarial attacks.

Hypothesis 4: *fractal-based data augmentation alleviates challenges to performance arising from training setups involving both real and synthetic images.*
In our ultimate series of experiments, we studied model behaviour when the domain of the test data was shifted by the application of artistic styles. This evaluation aspect allowed us to assess the decision bias of AFV recognition systems, with a shape, rather than texture, bias potentially proving beneficial, when training relied on both real and synthetic data. While the severity of the artistic rendition, as expected, unfavourably impacted decision-making, the introduction of fractal-based data augmentation, nonetheless, ensured satisfactory recognition performance. We conclude that a sensible approach to data augmentation equips image recognition models with sufficient versatility to cope with domain shifts at test time.

6   Conclusion

In our work we showed the merits of synthetic training samples for the training of deep learning based AFV recognition models. Not only do they supercharge performance in settings where real data are scarce, they also have great value for the specialisation of computer vision systems that, during deployment, encounter only a limited number of vehicle perspectives. Fractal-inspired data augmentation has proven to be boon to AI military systems: we have seen significant improvement across all measures of performance and robustness, with the simulation-to-reality gap significantly shrinking. As our adversarially trained models show greater vulnerability with respect to degradation of data quality, they should not be deployed uncritically. Rather, we recommend their tactical usage once adversarial attacks have been detected.

With our modular training pipeline and our rigorous evaluation protocol, we have laid the groundwork for future ablation studies involving, for example, novel approaches to data augmentation or adversarial machine learning. Although we were able to produce rich and diverse training samples using VBS, we suspect that more sophisticated game or rendering engines would deliver even better outcomes, owing to greater flexibility in manipulating scenes and vehicles. We, furthermore, strongly encourage the research of fractals for military purposes. A yet unexplored avenue to developing AI military systems could translate the camouflage patterns of potentially hostile forces as well as the unique characteristics of the deployment environment into a corresponding dataset of fractals for pre-training or data augmentation. In future work we aim to extend our evaluation protocol with regard to adversarial robustness, incorporating a greater number of adversarial attacks such as (printable) adversarial patches. Ultimately, we envision future applications of our method to problems beyond AFV recognition.

References

1. Żarski, M., Wójcik, B., Miszczak, J.A., Blachowski, B., Ostrowski, M.: Computer Vision based inspection on post-earthquake with UAV synthetic dataset. IEEE Access **10**, 108134–108144 (2022)
2. Bai, T., Luo, J., Zhao, J., Wen, B., Wang, Q.: Recent advances in adversarial training for adversarial robustness (2021)
3. Hendrycks, D., Dietterich, T.: Benchmarking neural network robustness to common corruptions and perturbations (2019)
4. Hendrycks, D., et al.: PixMix: Dreamlike Pictures Comprehensively Improve Safety Measures (2021)
5. Jones, D., Snider, C., Nassehi, A., Yon, J., Hicks, B.: Characterising the digital twin: a systematic literature review. CIRP J. Manuf. Sci. Technol. **29**, 36–52 (2020)
6. Kataoka, H., et al.: Pre-training without natural images. Int. J. Comput. Vision **130**(4), 990–1007 (2022). https://doi.org/10.1007/s11263-021-01555-8
7. Krump, M., Ruß, M., Stütz, P.: Deep learning algorithms for vehicle detection on UAV platforms: first investigations on the effects of synthetic training. In: Mazal, J., Fagiolini, A., Vasik, P. (eds.) MESAS 2019. LNCS, vol. 11995, pp. 50–70. Springer, Cham (2020). https://doi.org/10.1007/978-3-030-43890-6_5
8. Krump, M., Stütz, P.: UAV based vehicle detection on real and synthetic image pairs: performance differences and influence analysis of context and simulation parameters. In: Mazal, J., et al. (eds.) MESAS 2021. LNCS, vol. 13207, pp. 3–25. Springer, Cham (2022). https://doi.org/10.1007/978-3-030-98260-7_1
9. Krump, M., Stütz, P.: UAV based vehicle detection with synthetic training: identification of performance factors using image descriptors and machine learning. In: Mazal, J., Fagiolini, A., Vasik, P., Turi, M. (eds.) MESAS 2020. LNCS, vol. 12619, pp. 62–85. Springer, Cham (2021). https://doi.org/10.1007/978-3-030-70740-8_5
10. Lecun, Y., Bengio, Y., Hinton, G.: Deep learning. Nature **521**(7553), 436–444 (2015). https://doi.org/10.1038/nature14539
11. Liu, M., Fang, S., Dong, H., Xu, C.: Review of digital twin about concepts, technologies, and industrial applications. J. Manuf. Syst. **58**, 346–361 (2021)
12. Majumdar, R., Mathur, A., Pirron, M., Stegner, L., Zufferey, D.: PARACOSM: a test framework for autonomous driving simulations. In: Guerra, E., Stoelinga, M. (eds.) FASE 2021. LNCS, vol. 12649, pp. 172–195. Springer, Cham (2021). https://doi.org/10.1007/978-3-030-71500-7_9
13. Nickchen, T.: Deep learning for automating additive manufacturing process chains. Ph.D. thesis (2021)
14. Niranjan, D.R., VinayKarthik, B.C.: Deep learning based object detection model for autonomous driving research using carla simulator, pp. 1251–1258. IEEE (2021)
15. Schwarzschild, A., Goldblum, M., Gupta, A., Dickerson, J., Goldstein, T.: Just how toxic is data poisoning? A unified benchmark for backdoor and data poisoning attacks. In: International Conference on Machine Learning, pp. 9389–9398 (2021)
16. Theiler, J.: Estimating fractal dimension. J. Opt. Soc. Am. A **7**(6), 1055–1073 (1990). https://doi.org/10.1364/josaa.7.001055
17. Uysal, U.: Machine learning & simulation for military applications. Github (2020). https://github.com/UgurUysal86/MLS4MIL

Growing an Explanation of Health Inequities in Norfolk, VA with an Agent-Based Model

Virginia Zamponi[1]([✉]) [iD], Kevin O'Brien[2] [iD], Ross Gore[2] [iD],
and Christopher J. Lynch[2] [iD]

[1] Old Dominion University, Norfolk, VA 23529, USA
vzamponi@odu.edu
[2] Virginia Modeling Analysis and Simulation Center, Suffolk, VA 23435, USA

Abstract. In Norfolk, VA there are significant health disparities among residents. Several explanations exist for these disparities, however, none of these explanations have been formalized into an unambiguous model. In this paper we grow an explanation as to how repeated exposure to harmful environmental elements can create health disparities within Norfolk, VA despite all residents following the same daily schedule. The agents in our model accurately reflect the demographic characteristics of residents within each census tract of Norfolk, VA. Each agent has a home which reflects a residence in the area, and a place of work and place of leisure that represents an actual physical address in the city. All agents travel from home to work and to places of leisure. During their travel, agents are exposed to various levels of harmful environmental elements including bad air quality (also referred to as smog), and excessive noise. The extent to which an agent is exposed depends on the prevalence of the harmful environmental element where the agent is located at that timestep. Our results show for every demographic of agent represented in the model and across the census tracts in Norfolk, VA that one group is exposed to a statistically significant amount more harmful environmental elements than another group. Correlating the exposures of these groups with the variance in health outcomes in the area provides a path to explaining and remedying the health inequities in the area.

Keywords: Agent-Based Modeling · Environmental Exposures · Civilian Routes · Health Disparities · Simulated People · Generative Model

1 Introduction

Various mechanisms exist to collect human geographic data. These include surveys, sensor mechanisms, demographics, and spatial analysis. These data often inform fine-grained geographic interventions aimed at addressing health inequities and improving future health outcomes (i.e., reduced rate of asthma, obesity, heart attack and stroke). These interventions are typically measured in terms of a population's aggregate response to them. However, it is important to note that individuals make up a population and drive aggregate results. Furthermore, while a top-down approach can geographically pinpoint health inequities and identify other variables correlated with them, decision makers lack

© The Author(s), under exclusive license to Springer Nature Switzerland AG 2023
J. Mazal et al. (Eds.): MESAS 2022, LNCS 13866, pp. 326–338, 2023.
https://doi.org/10.1007/978-3-031-31268-7_20

the means to effectively operationalize this data to understand at the individual level how and why the inequities are manifested.

One manifestation of this problem is in Norfolk, VA [5, 6, 12, 19], as there are significant health disparities among residents within the area. Several explanations exist for these disparities and numerous interventions have been applied. While some interventions have experienced targeted success, the extreme health inequities in the area remain a systemic issue [23].

To formalize a hypothesis of the partial cause of these health inequities, a representative agent-based model of Norfolk was created. Our model can produce a 1:1 representation of the Norfolk area of Virginia, where each agent within it reflects an anonymized member of the population. Our model provides a platform to explicitly and unambiguously encode subject matter experts' hypothesis that the extreme health inequities in the area are, in part, caused by all individuals following a similar daily schedule; but that schedule requires certain geographic and demographic segments of the population to encounter repeated daily exposures to harmful environmental elements.

In what follows, we provide the necessary background material to understand the importance of addressing health inequities and why taking a geographic and demographic specific approach is paramount. Next, we provide an overview of the: (1) process for generating representative agents with Norfolk, VA, (2) agent-based model and (3) way environmental exposure data is overlaid on the model. Finally, we present our results, summarize the findings, and discuss directions of future work.

2 Background and Related Research

2.1 The Importance of Addressing Health Inequities

Health inequities are defined as significant gaps or differences in the overall rates of disease incidence, prevalence, morbidity, mortality, or survival within a population compared with the health status of the general population. The way health inequities are manifested and how they can be eliminated cannot be explained in a single theory. Furthermore, it is recognized that the causes of health disparities are complex and multifactorial, and stem from not only the healthcare sector but also the social determinants of health (i.e., the conditions in which people are born, grow, live, work, and age). Sustainable multi-academic-healthcare systems, as well as public and private partnerships, exemplify the importance of the collaborative engagement needed to accomplish this goal. To this end, the Hampton Roads Biomedical Research Consortium (HRBRC), has helped to sponsor this project, exploring one cause of the health inequities within the region.

2.2 Geographic Information Systems

The data mapping process has different definitions, each one tailored to fit with the discipline it is used in. In computational terms, data mapping can be defined as the process of creating data element mappings between different data models. Geographic Information Systems (GIS) are spatial data management systems that can integrate, store, adjust, analyze, and arrange geographically referenced information [8] from data. GIS were created to satisfy the advancing needs of data mapping and visualization in social science disciplines [8] and now possesses a myriad of applications within them [14] and has been found to be promising in both quantitative and qualitative research [20].

From pandemics to social theories, GIS have contributed to bridging the gap between researchers and administrators [2] and showing the importance of social demography in epidemiology [25]. For this project, GIS were used for multiple objectives, including locating and mapping the buildings into a simulated map, and generating census tract data for each of the people agents and each home, work, and leisure place in the city of Norfolk, VA.

2.3 Related Research

The importance of finding the possible environmental exposures and their effects on the population is not novel. During the completion of this experimental project research was conducted to find other projects, articles, or studies that would relate to the work being done. Although this kind of research is not recent, the use of GIS and agent-based modeling (ABM) for the detection of possible environmental exposures that the population is open to, is.

The articles that were discovered range from actual projects done on a community's current, or possible, environmental exposures – "The Built Environment And Health: Impacts Of Pedestrian-Friendly Designs On Air Pollution Exposure" [4] which discusses the possible unintended consequences of the popular, growing, idea of pedestrian-oriented community designs, due to the continuous inhalation of pollutants – to the recommendation of particular techniques for these purposes. For example, the article "A Dynamic Activity-Based Population Modelling Approach To Evaluate Exposure To Air Pollution: Methods And Application To A Dutch Urban Area" [1] which examines the application of activity-based models to establish dynamic exposure assessment to air pollution in a Dutch urban area. This methodology is applied to demonstrate that a dynamic population modeling approach is recommended over traditional methods, as it offers new and more sensitive ways to estimate exposures.

The use of methods that consider the movement people in real life make has also made a difference in the estimation of exactly how much people are being exposed to harmful environmental elements. The article "Beyond Air Pollution At Home: Assessment Of Personal Exposure To $PM_{2.5}$ Using Activity-Based Travel Demand Model And Low-Cost Air Sensor Network Data" [16] discusses the possible exposure measurement errors that can come from studies that solely rely on residential estimates of outdoor air, not considering the personal exposure that comes from human movement. Furthermore, the article (book chapter) "Modeling Human Exposure To Air Pollution" [15] reviews basic inhalation exposure patterns, which differ with the varying types of activities a person performs.

Some articles found had the same objective as the project being presented. The article "Agent-Based Modeling To Estimate Exposures To Urban Air Pollution From Transportation: Exposure Disparities And Impacts Of High-Resolution Data" [10] discusses a study done in the city of Tampa, Florida to develop an exposure modeling framework that integrates agent-based activities and travel simulations with air pollution modeling, while characterizing exposure inequalities for different types of air pollution. The article "Assessing Personal Exposure Using Agent Based Modelling Informed By Sensors Technology" [3] introduces the first approach at simulating human movement and interaction behavior using ABM for the urban city of Thessaloniki, Greece, to find personal exposure levels in its habitants. In addition, the article "A Model For Population Exposure To $PM_{2.5}$: Identification Of Determinants For High Population Exposure In Seoul" [9] discusses the development of a population exposure model for the purpose of predicting seasonal population exposure in Seoul, Korea, taking in consideration the different levels of air pollution that can be found in and out of buildings.

As this field of study will continue to grow, it is important that foundations are established to make the realization of project involving ABM for human exposures coincide and give the correct results. For this, different frameworks and software are being developed. The article "An Agent-Based Modeling Framework For Simulating Human Exposure To Environmental Stresses In Urban Areas" [26] describes an ABM framework that can dynamically simulate human exposure levels, along with their daily activities, in urban areas that are characterized by environmental stresses such as air pollution and heat stress. Furthermore, the paper "A Conceptual Framework For Modeling Aggregate And Cumulative Exposures To Chemicals" [21] provides a conceptual framework which separates and models the processes that determine uncertainty, inter- and intra-individual variability, as well as the processes that determine the relationships between the individuals and sources of exposure. Finally, the article "A GIS-Based Urban Simulation Model For Environmental Health Analysis" [7] introduces an urban simulation model for environmental health analysis: SIENA, a tool used to explore urban interactions and processes with regard to exposure assessments.

3   The Model

An agent-based model that can represent each resident of Norfolk, VA, was constructed. The goal of our model is to develop a formal, and unambiguous, theory of how individuals living in the same city and following the same schedule could be exposed inequitably to harmful environmental elements. Growing on this explanation will provide a platform to explore correlations between health inequities and environmental exposure inequities within Norfolk.

The initialization, execution, and analysis of our model results are shown in Fig. 1. The initialization consists of constructing geo-located agents who are assigned: (1) representative demographics of their geographic area, and (2) addresses reflecting a residence, place of work and place of leisure. Agents were also representing geo-located harmful environmental exposure data related to noise pollution, extremely hot temperatures, and poor air quality. Our model is built and executed to scale on the HASH.ai agent-based modeling platform [11]. The output is parsed and analyzed in the RStudio integrated development environment using the statistical programming language R [24]. In this section, we describe each of these pieces in more detail.

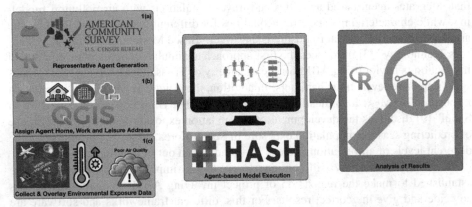

Fig. 1. Overview if the initialization, model execution, and results analysis process.

3.1 Initialization

Representative Agent Generation

Our representative agent generation process is a Monte Carlo algorithm for creating agents from a specified census tract based on aggregate demographics. The process uses an aggregated data table which specifies the number of agents within a census tract for every choice in each of our demographic categories. This data reflects the 2021 American Community Survey. These categories and choices are: 4 races, 12 age groups, 10 income levels, and 9 education levels.

For each census tract the Monte Carlo algorithm creates a distribution for each of the four categories. Each distribution reflects the number of individuals in each category from a given census tract. Then for each person in the census tract, the algorithm samples each distribution.

The result is a representative agent generation process where the aggregate demographics of the created population match the American Community Survey data for each census tract in Norfolk, VA.

Table 1 shows the demographics of five agents from the Norfolk population that were generated with the Monte Carlo algorithm. Specific labels for the race, income, education, and age demographics have been omitted.

Table 1. Sample of representative agents generated using Monte Carlo method for Norfolk, VA based on ACS data.

agent id	race	age group	income range	Education level	Census tract id
1	race 1	age 5	income 5	education 8	51710001100
10	race 4	age 2	income 4	education 8	51710006100
29	race 2	age 7	income 10	education 3	51710001100
35	race 3	age 11	income 7	education 9	51710003400
40	race 1	age 5	income 2	education 4	51710004100

Agent Assignment of Home, Work, and Leisure Addresses

Each agent that is generated is assigned a census tract within Norfolk, VA upon inception. After every agent in every census tract in Norfolk has been generated, each agent is assigned three addresses. One address reflects the agent's home, a second address reflects an agent's place of work, and a third address reflects a place in Norfolk where the agent goes to participate in leisure activities.

Each address that is assigned to an agent (home, work, or leisure) reflects an actual address in the city of Norfolk. These addresses were gathered using the Norfolk Open Data portal [18], and the open-source geographic information system software QGIS was used to ensure that the home address assigned to each agent is within the census tract assigned to the agent upon inception [22]. Table 2 shows an example of the mapping of physical address, latitude /longitude point, and census tract, while Table 3 shows the demographic characteristics, residence, place of work and leisure addresses for three example agents.

Table 2. Sample mapping of physical address, latitude, longitude, and census tract for assignment to an agent.

FULL_ADD	MUN	xcoord	ycoord	GEOID20	TRACT_DESCRIPTION
9600 Grove Avenue	NORF	−76.22637029	36.93750508	51710001100	Ocean View
1717 Cloncurry Road	NORF	−76.31492123	36.91104929	51710001200	Lochaven, Meadowbrook
3848 Abingdon Circle	NORF	−76.24485875	36.88973041	51710006000	Norview, Five Points

Table 3. Example mapping of agent demographics, home, work, and leisure addresses.

Agent Id	Race	Age Group	Income Range	Education Level	Census Tract Id	Home Address	Work Address	Leisure Address
1	race 1	age 5	income 5	education 8	51710001100	333 Forrest Avenue	206 Sterling Street	3421 Brest Avenue
5	race 3	age 7	income 10	education 1	51710000500	9233 Atwood Avenue	935 Washington Avenue	3348 Azalea Garden Road
20	race 2	age 1	income 5	education 2	51710001300	423 Timothy Avenue	5533 Levine Court	3332 Cromwell Drive

Harmful Environmental Exposure Data

Our model is also initialized with geo-located harmful environmental exposure data related to noise pollution, extremely hot temperatures, and poor air quality. Currently, this data is randomly generated from a uniform distribution with a weight minimum of 1 and maximum of 100. Each data value is mapped to a unique latitude/longitude point that covers the simulation landscape. The randomly generated data value reflects the total level of harmful environmental elements that an agent is exposed to if they pass within a set radius of 0.001 near the latitude/longitude point. A value of 100 reflects extremely harmful environmental elements, while a value of 1 reflects low-to-no harmful environmental elements.

Naturally, generating harmful environmental exposure data using a random uniform distribution will result in a model that is no longer grounded in reality. However, at this stage of our model's development, no valid source of environmental exposure data with at the latitude/longitude level of granularity could be identified. Addressing this issue in our model is an avenue of future work.

3.2 Agent-Based Model Implementation and Execution

Given the initialization data, our model can be specified and executed on the HASH.ai agent-based modeling platform, which is a scalable, open-source agent-based simulation web application with geospatial maps [11]. In this subsection we describe our model and its GIS capabilities.

GIS Capabilities

The HASH.ai modeling platform was chosen, in part, for its GIS capabilities. It provides an agent-based model landscape with native support for identifying city-level infrastructure at the level of latitude/longitude granularity. In addition, it provides built-in mechanisms to route agents between two locations' latitude/longitude along roadways, while minimizing travel time. This capability enhances the validity of our model and simplifies the implementation. We use this functionality to route the agents from home to work and places of leisure along realistic paths which minimize the agent's travel time. In the next section we describe how our model is specified to take advantage of HASH.ai's GIS capabilities.

Model Specification

During each timestep after the simulation has been executed, each agent follows the decision tree shown in Fig. 2. At every timestep, each agent will check if it has a route generated to a destination. If an agent does not have a route, it will check if is at its home, work, or leisure location. If the agent is at home, the agent's destination will change to their workplace. If the agent is at work, the destination will change to their leisure place. Finally, if the agent is at their place of leisure, the destination will change to their home. Once a destination has been set, HASH.ai will generate the shortest travel time route to the destination along Norfolk's roadways.

Next, an agent will make progress towards its destination along the set route. During its travel, if the agent is exposed to a harmful environmental exposure, their number of exposures tally will be increased by the exposure's weight.

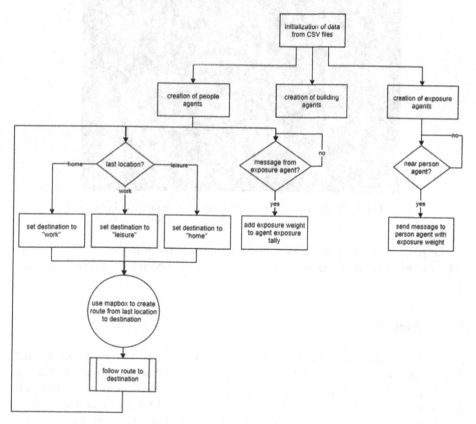

Fig. 2. Decision tree for agents in our model.

A screen capture of agents' movement in our model is shown in Fig. 3. The people agents are orange, the residential buildings are pink, the office buildings are blue, and the recreational buildings are yellow.

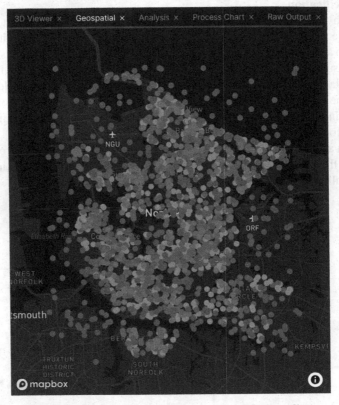

Fig. 3. Model view after 16 timesteps. (Color figure online)

For reproducibility, transparency, and replicability, the source code for our model and its input data are available at: https://core.hash.ai/@vzamponi/exposure-model-2 [27].

4 Evaluation

The goal is to give an explanation of how harmful environmental exposures can be distributed inequitably across different demographics and census tracts in a city despite all residents following the same schedule of actions. To ensure consistency of results, and measure our success in achieving this goal, our model was run at least 10 times and the results of the final run were analyzed. The analysis focused on showing visually the difference harmful environmental exposures that could exist for each demographic (race, age group, income level and education level) and census tract. In addition, for each demographic and census tract, the difference between the minimally exposed group and maximally exposed group was tested to check statistical significance. To do this, a paired t-test was applied to the 1–100 timesteps of average exposures for each demographic and census tract, and a probability value of 0.0001 was found. We review our findings and discuss the implications of our results in what follows.

4.1 Analysis

Each model run was executed for 100 timesteps. This number of timesteps was chosen as it enabled every agent to visit their home, place of work, and leisure place. For each timestep the extent to which each agent is exposed to harmful environment elements was tracked. Then for each demographic and census tract the average environmental exposure per group per time step was computed.

Given the use of uniformly random generated environmental data and its misrepresentation of the actual exposures in the city of Norfolk, the specific labels for the race, income, education, and age demographics were omitted. Figure 4 shows the distribution of average exposure by time step for the maximally and minimally exposed group for each of the four demographics. Figure 5 shows the distribution for the maximally and minimally exposed sample of census tracts within Norfolk, VA. In Figs. 4 and 5 the maximally exposed group is shown in red, and the minimally exposed group is shown in blue.

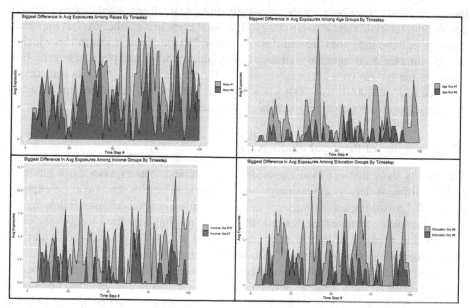

Fig. 4. Maximum and Minimum Exposures for each demographic (race, age group, income level and education level). (Color figure online)

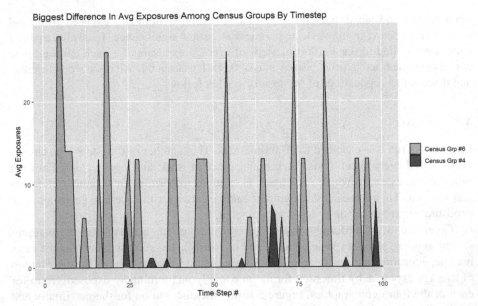

Fig. 5. Maximum and Minimum Exposures across a sample of census tracts in Norfolk, VA.

Figures 4 and 5 elucidate that extreme inequities in exposures to harmful environmental elements exists between the minimally and maximally exposed groups for every demographic variable and across a sample of census tracts in Norfolk, VA. It is important to note that these inequities are manifested in only 100 time steps in our model which is enough time for every agent to visit their home, place of work and place of leisure. Furthermore, each difference between the minimally and maximally group is statistically significant ($P < 0.0001$, $n = 100$) when a paired t-test is applied to the time series of average exposures for each demographic and census tract.

4.2 Discussion of Principal Findings

The results show that our model provides a formal and unambiguous explanation as to how different demographic groups and residents in census tracts can be exposed to harmful environmental elements at extremely different levels despite following the same schedule every time step. Specifically, agents residing in certain areas or traveling to work and or places of leisure along certain paths repeatedly get exposed to harmful environmental elements by simply following their daily routine.

Some readers may discount our results because we use a random uniform distribution to generate the environmental exposure data. However, this implementation decision is likely to dilute the extent to which health inequities are observed compared to using actual data. Related research has shown that the harmful environmental elements like noise pollution, extremely hot temperatures and poor air quality across a geographic area follows a bimodal distribution as opposed to a uniform one [13, 17].

This phenomenon occurs as the cause of each environmental element (noise pollution – construction; extreme hot temperatures – lack of tree canopy and poor air quality – industrial pollution) has a geographic center point, and around that center point the harmful environmental effect of the element dissipates. The result shows that, when bimodal data is used in the agents routinely traveling through specific areas of Norfolk, VA will accrue even more exposures resulting in more extreme inequities across demographics and census tracts.

5 Conclusion

In conclusion, we formalized an unambiguous explanation of how extreme inequities across demographic groups and census tracts in in Norfolk, VA could occur. Our explanation is produced by creating representative agent-based model of Norfolk. Our model can produce a 1:1 representation of the Norfolk area of Virginia where each agent within the model reflects an anonymized member of the population. Our model shows that despite all agents within the city following the same schedule, repetitive exposures to harmful environmental elements can be created across demographic groups and census tracts.

Next steps for the development of this exposure model will be to find – or obtain – new, real, data for the different exposure types, from the city of Norfolk. This step would allow the analysis on the elements of exposures that match real-life and will produce an accurate result for the question of health disparities, and how different minority groups are affected.

Acknowledgements. This work is funded by the Hampton Roads Biomedical Research Consortium (300675–010 IRAD).

References

1. Beckx C., Panis L.I., Arentze T., Janssens D., Torfs R., Broekx S., Wets G.: A dynamic activity-based population modelling approach to evaluate exposure to air pollution: Methods and application to a Dutch urban area. Environ. Impact Assess. Rev. **29**(3), 179–185 (2009). https://www.sciencedirect.com/science/article/pii/S019592550800139X
2. Benigeri, M.: Geographic information systems (GIS) in the health field: an opportunity to bridge the gap between researchers and administrators. Can. J. Public Health/Revue Canadienne de Sante'e Publique **98**, s74–s76 (2007)
3. Chapizanis, D., Karakitsios, S., Gotti, A., Sarigiannis, D.A.: Assessing personal exposure using Agent Based Modelling informed by sensors technology. Environ. Res. **192**, 110141 (2021). https://www.sciencedirect.com/science/article/pii/S0013935120310380
4. De Nazelle, A., Rodríguez, D.A., Crawford-Brown, D.: The built environment and health: Impacts of pedestrian-friendly designs on air pollution exposure. Sci. Total Environ. **407**(8), 2525–2535 (2009). https://www.sciencedirect.com/science/article/pii/S0048969709000205
5. Dixon, C., et al.: Addressing racism through case study design: promoting career development of health professionals. In: APHA 2017 Annual Meeting & Expo (Nov. 4–Nov. 8) (2017)
6. Durgampudi, P.: Social and behavioral determinants of health and health inequities. In: APHA 2017 Annual Meeting & Expo (Nov. 4–Nov. 8) (2017)

7. Fecht, D., Beale, L., Briggs, D.: A GIS-based urban simulation model for environmental health analysis. Environ. Model. Softw. **58**, 1–11 (2014). https://www.sciencedirect.com/science/article/pii/S1364815214000917

8. Fradelos, E.C., Papathanasiou, I.V., Mitsi, D., Tsaras, K., Kleisiaris, C.F., Kourkouta, L.: Health based geographic information systems (GIS) and their applications. Acta Informatica Medica **22**(6), 402–405 (2014). https://doi.org/10.5455/aim.2014.22.402-405

9. Guak, S., Lee, S., An, J., Lee, H., Lee, K.: A model for population exposure to PM2.5: identification of determinants for high population exposure in Seoul. Environ. Pollut. **285**, 117406 (2021). https://www.sciencedirect.com/science/article/pii/S026974912100988X

10. Gurram, S., Stuart, A.L., Pinjari, A.R.: Agent-based modeling to estimate exposures to urban air pollution from transportation: exposure disparities and impacts of high-resolution data. Comput. Environ. Urban Syst. **75**, 22–34 (2019). https://www.sciencedirect.com/science/article/pii/S019897151830156X

11. HASH.ai. https://hash.ai/. Accessed 08 Aug 2022

12. Hege, A., et al.: Barriers to food access, health, and wellbeing in rural areas: the community members' perspectives. In: APHA 2017 Annual Meeting & Expo (Nov. 4–Nov. 8) (2017)

13. Helbig, C., et al.: Wearable sensors for human environmental exposure in urban settings. Current Pollut. Rep. **7**(3), 417–433 (2021)

14. Introduction: Geographic Information Systems In The Social Sciences. Humboldt Journal of Social Relations, **41**, 4–5 (2019)

15. Klepeis, N.E.: Modeling Human Exposure to Air Pollution. Stanford University, Department of Statistics (2006). https://citeseerx.ist.psu.edu/viewdoc/download?doi=10.1.1.460.8304&rep=rep1&type=pdf

16. Lu, Y.: Beyond air pollution at home: assessment of personal exposure to PM2.5 using activity-based travel demand model and low-cost air sensor network data. Environ. Res. **201**, 111549 (2021). https://www.sciencedirect.com/science/article/pii/S0013935121008434

17. Mueller, N., et al.: Socioeconomic inequalities in urban and transport planning related exposures and mortality: a health impact assessment study for Bradford. UK. Environ. Int. **121**, 931–941 (2018)

18. Norfolk Open Data. https://data.norfolk.gov/. Accessed 20 July 2022

19. Pamplin, J., Bates, L.M.: Conceptualizing the measure of racism: a review of common proxies for racism used in public health studies. In: APHA 2017 Annual Meeting & Expo (Nov. 4–Nov. 8). (2017)

20. Pavlovskaya, M.: Theorizing with GIS: a tool for critical geographies? Environ. Plan. A: Econ. Space **38**(11), 2003–2020 (2006). https://doi.org/10.1068/a37326

21. Price, P., Chaisson, C.: A conceptual framework for modeling aggregate and cumulative exposures to chemicals. J. Expo Sci. Environ. Epidemiol. **15**, 473–481 (2005). https://doi.org/10.1038/sj.jea.7500425

22. QGIS Homepage, https://www.qgis.org/en/site/, last accessed 2022/07/25

23. Rosenthal, J., et al.: Design and baseline results of an immunization community intervention trial in Norfolk. Virginia. Pediatr. Ann. **27**(7), 418–423 (1998)

24. R Core Team. A language environment for statistical computing. R Foundation for Statistical Computing, Vienna, Austria (2022). https://www.R-project.org/. Accessed 05 Aug 2022

25. Trentini, F., et al.: Modeling the interplay between demography, social contact patterns, and SARS-CoV-2 transmission in the south west Shewa zone of Oromia region. Ethiopia. BMC Med. **19**(1), 89 (2021). https://doi.org/10.1186/s12916-021-01967-w

26. Yang, L.E., Hoffmann, P., Scheffran, J., Rühe, S., Fischereit, J., Gasser, I.: An agent-based modeling framework for simulating human exposure to environmental stresses in urban areas. Urban Sci. **2**, 36 (2018). https://doi.org/10.3390/urbansci2020036

27. Zamponi, V., O'Brien, K, Gore, R.: Exposure Model (2022). https://core.hash.ai/@vzamponi/exposure-model-2. Accessed 4 Aug 2022

Author Index

J. Mazal et al. (Eds.): MESAS 2022, LNCS 13866, pp. 339–340, 2023.
https://doi.org/10.1007/978-3-031-31268-7

Printed in the United States
by Baker & Taylor Publisher Services